A GIRL CALLED ADOLF

By David Fettes

© David Fettes. January 2012

A GIRL CALLED ADOLF

To Nicola

Who let me go

And who waited for me.

"Do not go where the path may lead, go instead where there is no path and leave a trail.

Ralph Waldo Emerson

A GIRL CALLED ADOLF

FOREWORD

This is a story about a journey of discovery, in equal measures physical, emotional and developmental. A tale of outrageous risks taken, and perceived boundaries of behaviour ignored. Above all it is a story of how love can transcend difficulty, separation and reunion, how it can be sustained into a timeless partnership and friendship.

We surprise ourselves when we discover the boundaries and rules others warn us of are no more than gossamer barriers, so easily breached if only we have the courage to take that leap of faith.

When pushing the limits, luck can often be an essential ingredient of survival. This is a story of repeated luck.

We are each influenced and changed by experiences. Some of those experiences can transmute the way we think, about ourselves and about the world about us. There is no doubt this story did that for me. The lessons I garnered from it formed me for the life that was left to me when the journey was over, and for what remains of my life today.

To the countless people who showered us in kindness and generosity I remain indebted, a debt I can only repay vicariously by doing the same myself. To some of the police and officials I met, I send my gratitude for letting me come home alive.

To anyone reading this tale, I urge you to believe much more is possible than you can begin to imagine.

You just have to be brave enough to try.

Dare to dream.

A GIRL CALLED ADOLF

Chapter 1

Vera Cruz - Mexico 1972

"A dreamer is one who can only find his way by moonlight, and his punishment is that he sees the dawn before the rest of the world."

Oscar Wilde

A weak glow from the street light shone through the barred window, high up on the wall of the dark and gloomy cell. I jumped up and caught the bars, pulling myself up to peer out onto a deserted, rubbish-strewn back street lit, by a solitary dim street lamp. Moths and insects fluttered about the light, bumping against the cracked plastic cover. There was no glass in the narrow window, and the warm breeze on my face brought with it the unpleasant odours of the detritus in the street. Vera Cruz was asleep, quiet apart from the muted voices of the policemen I could hear in the large open air courtyard onto which all the cells opened. A drunk was shouting obscenities from a neighbouring cell, a lone wolf howling hopelessly at the moon.

"People disappear in Central and South America you know. Are you sure you guys want to do this?"

These prophetic words, uttered by a friend a few months earlier when Sam and I were planning our odyssey through the Americas, came to mind as we stood in the semi dark of the cell. We were a mere five hours into our trip and already we had 'disappeared'. No one knew where we were - well, the police did but they hadn't seemed inclined to tell us where they were taking us when they dragged us from the bar in the square at one o'clock in the morning. I doubted they had Gazetted our detainment for the world and our relatives and friends to see. There wasn't going to be any cavalry riding over the hill to our rescue. We were on our own and that was a chilling thought.

Of course, we shouldn't have been on land at all. We should still have been on board the good ship M.V Gela where our Passports had been confiscated earlier that afternoon by the Immigration and Customs Officers who had come on board when our cargo ship docked after our Atlantic crossing from Le Havre in France. Looking for a bribe, they said we should have visas to enter Mexico. This was contrary to the advice of the Mexican Embassy in London where we had been told we should get them at our point of entry. The Immigration Officers left the ship saying they would come back on Monday to sort it all out, and that we should stay on board for the rest of the weekend.

How on earth could it all have gone wrong so soon? Being in trouble was a familiar state, and indeed an expectation before leaving England, but I had at the very least hoped for a few weeks or even months of fun, travel and adventure to tell my children and grandchildren about one day. At that moment it looked as though I was going to have trouble keeping their interest up for more than a couple of minutes as I regaled them with the details of a story covering an Atlantic crossing and five hours on Terra Mexicana. This trip could turn out to be a bit of a disappointment, a moment of underachievement, a nadir that would be hard to beat during whatever remained of my life. It occurred to me I might not even have that 'one day' to sit with my descendants at my feet, captivating them with my tales of foreign and intrepid adventures.

I found some consolation from the fact the cause of our predicament in this cockroach infested gaol had also been arrested. He was a young boy who had been selling cigars and his toothless older sister's favours to the customers of bars around a large square in Vera Cruz. He had either been put in a separate cell or released, because he was no longer with us. Perhaps that was for his own protection, but I rather imagined he had been released while the police puffed on the free cigars he handed out to them. We had no such charms with which to bribe the police. In any event, we were gringos with whom it seemed they wanted to have a friendly chat, perhaps one that involved some quite enthusiastic, indeed vigorous physical encouragement from them. They hadn't appeared too interested in building a cozy relationship with us when they brought us in. Moreover, they seemed remarkably keen to demonstrate the finer aspects of their guns which spent a lot of time in our faces. Instinct told me it wasn't quite the right moment to put the principles of Habeas Corpus on the agenda. Human rights had yet to be discovered in Mexico.

Our large cell was remarkable for being completely bare. Dank, damp, unlit and urine scented, there were no beds or chairs in it so Sam and I stood and leant against the cement walls awaiting our fate, aware that all our worldly goods remained on board the cargo ship that had brought us to Mexico, and she was due to sail in just a couple of days. I wondered at the forlorn humanity this intimidatingly harsh room had watched over, the horrors that had been perpetrated in it. Various possible outcomes for us crossed my mind, ranging from a shallow grave in some Mexican wood, through a common or garden beating to possible deportation. That we were in trouble with men who had never read the Queensbury Rules was not in doubt. Nor was the fact that there was nothing we could do about it. Escape was impossible so we could do little more than stand and await our fate.

Perhaps I should explain how we got to be in Mexico in the first place, how we had decided to give up our glittering desk bound careers on the road to corporate anonymity, choosing instead to set off for Australia. What was the original plan? It surely couldn't have been to end up in a back street Mexican gaol as soon as we landed and started our venture into the unknown. 'Here be dragons' could easily have been written on our map. Unfortunately we had found them and fiction had become fact in stark reality.

Many years later, when I was watching the only Premiership football match I have ever been to, I was reminded of my Mexican gaol moment as I watched a visiting team supporter being forcibly and quite violently ejected from the ground by the police, a few minutes before the game started. The match was in London and the visitors were from Birmingham. He had come a long way, only to see and experience nothing more than the business end of a couple of police truncheons and the discomfort of a police cell. I felt a strange sense of empathy with him, perhaps because of rather than despite the idiotic behaviour that culminated in his early bath.

So, let me go back to the beginning, where so many journeys start.

A GIRL CALLED ADOLF

CHAPTER 2

London and Surrey - 1971

"Faced with crisis, the man of character falls back on himself."

Charles de Gaulle

London in 1971 was a place of transition, not just from one decade to another but perhaps to a more troubled and unsettled time after the revolution of the young in the '60s, with their demands for freedom of expression, a voice in the management of a more peaceful and loving world world, a new expectation of free love and an end to the hated and reviled Vietnam War. The flowers of the Flower-power generation were wilting in the searing heat of the Northern Ireland troubles, where internment started with the dawn arrest of three hundred suspected IRA terrorists, to be held without trial. Within a day the IRA responded by killing twelve people. The relentless attrition of sectarian violence notched up a gear or two, fueled by bigoted and unfounded hatred of neighbours and people with exactly the same aspirations, hopes and dreams but who just happened to be of a different religious persuasion. The destructive acts carried out in the name of religion in the decades of the '60s and the '70s, and indeed at the time of the Crusades, were the same as those carried out now, in the twenty first century. The game has not changed, it is just that new teams have risen to the top of the Premiership of ignorant fundamentalism.

The new year opened with decimalisation of the UK currency a couple of days after US Vice-President Spiro Agnew hit three spectators with his first two shots at Bob Hope's Desert Classic golf match. My notes do not tell me whether the three spectators were Democrats, but I remember being impressed by the fact he managed to get two with one ball, demonstrating a certain economy of effort. Agnew was sworn in as Vice-President in 1969, President Nixon's choice eliciting the comment that the most frightening words in the American language were "Hey, Spiro, I'm not feeling too well". Good old Spiro went on to be indicted on tax fraud, extortion and bribery charges, a true politician to the end.

In England, Margaret Thatcher proposed snatching free milk from the mouths of schoolchildren, in some eyes becoming a modern day Herod with her casual slaughter of the innocents. History shows that an entire generation of children did not in fact develop rickets.

Little did we know at that time the power and strangling hold over the country that she would snatch back from the Unions in her later guise as Prime Minister, demonstrating an iron will forged in the searing furnace of the milk campaign, later acknowledged as a mere skirmish in the foothills of her combative career.

On the international stage, I wondered whether British politicians and closet Imperialists breathed a quiet sigh of relief when Idi Amin, who had been trained by the British Army, took control of Uganda in a military coup over the incumbent, President Milton Obote. Obote had been implicated in the smuggling of gold in partnership with Idi Amin and had responded to demands by Parliament for an investigation by suspending the constitution and declaring himself as President in an election where only one person voted, thus guaranteeing himself one hundred percent of the vote. Amin had repaid Obote's loyal protection in an '*Et tu, Brute*' act of overthrowing him.

In their celebration the British Government must have turned a blind eye to a British Officer's reported opinion that Amin was '*bone from the neck upwards and needs things explained to him in words of one letter*'. Idi Amin was of course completely bonkers, as many cannibals are. I imagine the politicians were initially influenced by how effective he had been in counter-insurgency operations in the bush, without quite realising his modus operandi of lining up men in front of their village with their forcefully extracted and exposed penises resting on a table pushed up against them, threatening to cut them off unless they gave him the information he wanted. I assume Amin felt these unfortunate men's emotional attachment to their sunbathing penises would outweigh any loyalty they might have to insurgents operating in the area. On calm and objective reflection, I would have found his reasoning quite persuasive, thus quickly avoiding the twin dangers of amputation by a deranged sadist and sunburn in the hot African day.

The authorities at Royal Ascot races ventured into equally contentious territory as they agreed to allow ladies to wear hot-pants, but only if 'the general effect is satisfactory'. Well, to me, satisfactory is a subjective issue. I came to the conclusion that opinion would be divided on gender lines, with the majority of male racegoers lasciviously muscling their way into the 'Aye' lobby when asked to vote on the subject. Rolls Royce went bankrupt, a corporate failure that somehow shook confidence in the very foundations of capitalism; Liechtenstein pushed the peanut of female emancipation back a couple of inches when the State's male population voted not to allow women the vote - I think they too would have joined the 'Aye's' at Royal Ascot; a vehicle was driven by American astronauts on the Moon for the first time - hence all driving is on the right up there; the world's first heart and lung transplant took place, a winner and loser making history together.

England's grip on the pop music world was still strong with some memorable hits that have stood the test of time, and some that have thankfully not. George Harrison sang about his 'Sweet Lord', and still does posthumously to this day. The Rolling Stones served up

'Brown Sugar' to be taken liberally with T. Rex's 'Hot Love' in the dying months of the year. Middle of the Road somehow fooled the record buying public to make 'Chirpy Chirpy Cheep Cheep' a hit, thankfully for a blessedly short time. Clive Dunn's paean to dementia was immortalised in the thick syrup of 'Granddad', which he sang on Top of the Pops in a rocking chair that much of the thinking public wished could be connected to an electrical socket and turned on, bringing that missing little sparkle to his faded eye.

Against this backdrop of what Harold Macmillan had once referred to as "Events, dear boy, events", with the 'hot-pants at Ascot' issue clearly being the most feverishly debated, I was enjoying a full and fun life in London, the hotbed of European youth's revolution with its groundbreaking music and fashion. My flatmate Sam was putting the finishing touches to his plans to drive a Land Rover east across Europe, Afghanistan, India and through Burma to end in Australia. The journey would follow the well trodden path of the early backpackers irresistibly responding to the siren calls of the sands of Bondi Beach, beautiful girls and sparingly clad suntanned bodies. Hopefully female ones. Sam had advertised for someone to accompany him on this venture. A number of would be adventurers turned up at our flat in Earls Court, their travel credentials carefully rehearsed and ready for Sam's scrutiny. From amongst these hopefuls he had selected an individual who became eagerness personified, a regular visitor for planning and beer drinking practice, one of the criteria Sam had put on his wish list for a travelling companion. As the weeks and months passed, their joint excitement increased inversely to the rate at which our beer supply shrank.

A week before their intended departure, after more than six months of planning and work, the putative globetrotter decided he was not going on the trip, for no particular reason that we could divine other than he had developed cold feet. I arrived at our flat the evening Sam got the good news to find him despondently drinking beer to drown his sorrows. It was clear from his dejected look that something fairly dramatic had happened that day, something more than a trifling issue such as being dumped by his most recent girlfriend.

"What's wrong with you?" I said, seeing his more than glum expression.

"He's pulled out" Sam replied, downing more beer.

I thought this seemed a sensible and inexpensive, if somewhat last minute Russian Roulette, form of contraception and told Sam so, thinking he was referring to a particularly sexually enthusiastic Canadian flatmate of ours.

"No. The trip's off" he said.

"Well, if you can wait just a minute while I finish my exams, I'll come with you" I said, without hesitation, deviation or repetition.

To this day, I have no idea where that offer or my spontaneous response to Sam's disappointment came from. Whilst I had no talents that justified any ambition, I fully intended being at the top of the corporate tree. All I had to do was find a tree I could climb. Up until that moment, galavanting around the world had not been part of the grand plan. I had a wonderful girlfriend, with whom I hadn't had too many intimate and inclusive conversations about pushing off for a year or more without her. I was quite happy with my life. I hadn't been particularly envious about Sam's proposed trip. But despite the inevitable upheaval, and without the faintest idea of the enormity of the romantic gamble I was proposing, I was immediately excited by the prospect of the adventure I was committing myself to. A step into the abyss to plumb the depths of the unknown. As a good friend said to me many years later when I started my own business, 'There's nothing quite like walking along a crumbling cliff edge to keep the adrenaline flowing'. I hadn't yet woken up to the need in me for adrenaline in my life. A much buoyed Sam came with me to our local pub to complete the formalities of our 'contract', a meeting that lasted until closing time.

And so the planning started all over again. Our first big decision was to change going east to going west. It seemed to us that going east along the clichéd path was becoming too easy, too well trodden and thus stereotypical of we supposed free spirits who were prepared to ditch the wisdom and safety of careers. This decision was made without a world atlas or map in front of us and thus without necessarily noticing there is quite a bit more water in the Atlantic than in the English Channel. As for getting to Australia from South America, we agreed to defer that part of the plan until we actually had to face the problem. Our first major hurdle was to work out how to get our vehicle across the Atlantic to somewhere in the Americas. Our Land Rover was affectionately called Adolf because of the letters on her number plate, ADF. We assumed we would have to ship Adolf to New York and then fly there to pick her up. The rest of the week was filled with drawing up lists of jobs for us each to do. Embassies had to be visited for visas. Letters were to be prepared for sponsorship if we could get it. Supplies needed to be listed, categorised and sourced. Inoculations and prophylactic medicines researched. Shipping companies had to be approached, maps bought and studied and spares for Adolf thought about.

It didn't occur to me during what remained of that busy week to tell my girlfriend about my decision. It never crossed my mind that it would be important to her. We were in the pub together on the Sunday following my spontaneous commitment to Sam when I remembered to slip it into the conversation with her. Not much bunting was hung out on the casual delivery of the news, and I don't remember the pop of champagne corks, which came as a bit of a shock to my Neanderthal mind. She was visibly quite upset, which on one level was gratifying, so I was glad to wrest a positive out of the moment. Seeing it from her side, I could understand that perhaps it was a bit of a shock. That said, we agreed these were things we needed to get out of our system before settling down, if that was what we were eventually going to do. With the overwhelming optimism of youth we decided that if we could survive the separation, we could survive anything together, and if not, it wasn't meant to be. On this platform of her selfless generosity I was able to focus on planning.

We agreed that I would stay in my job until our departure, whereas Sam, the considerably more mechanically minded of us, would leave his computer programming job at Thomas Cook in London and work at Dunsfold Land Rovers, a garage in Dunsfold village in Surrey that specialised in the maintenance of these versatile and robust vehicles. Brian Bashall and Frank Smith owned and ran this amazing garage, which to this day still operates in the village under the control of Brian's son, Philip. We have much to be grateful to Brian and Frank for, including their generosity of spirit and their willingly given and shared knowledge.

While Sam learnt everything there was to know about Land Rovers, we adapted Adolf for the rigours of the trip ahead of her. Aware that we would be in some very remote spots where fuel would be hard to come by, we installed two extra internal fuel tanks operating via two completely separate fuel systems that could both be secretly disconnected to confuse would-be thieves. These additional tanks gave us a total fuel capacity of over fifty gallons, more than doubling Adolf's range. The more delicate electrics such as the coil were moved from the engine compartment into the cabin to help with waterproofing. Since the vehicle was going to be our life support module for many months, our literal home, hotel, drawing room, office and bedroom without en-suite facilities, we built storage boxes on the floor in the back. These in turn supported a firm foam mattress that exactly filled the back to make a somewhat disconcertingly snug double bed. To ease the mind of the curious reader, we slept head to toe for the entire trip, neither considering the other attractive enough to wake up to face to face.

Adolf was a canvas topped, long wheel base Series II Land Rover that I think was previously owned by an Electricity Company. We fitted her out with a new hat - a navy blue canvas roof. My girlfriend got her sewing machine out and made us a mosquito net that hung in the roof and could be let down at night. During the day the sides of the net could be rolled up and tied off, leaving the back open and easily accessible. Special driving seats with full harness seat belts kindly donated by Britax were designed to keep us firmly in our seats on rough roads. We weren't to know then how useful they would become. We bought real sheepskins to go on the seats and replaced the middle seat with a large, lockable storage box with a padded top.

Along each side of the vehicle we bolted on fuel racks to carry six army jerry cans, with one more on each side on the front. These we clearly marked for their intended uses of spare fuel, engine oil and water. Lorry step-ups went onto the front wheel hubs to be used as crude winches if the need arose to pull us out of any quagmire we might find ourselves in. All purpose Army issue tyres were fitted to give all round grip and traction on difficult terrain. They were also designed to deal economically with tarmac roads, a generic hybrid compromise for the wide range of surfaces we anticipated we would find beneath our wheels. To finish Adolf off, and to emphasise our British heritage, we painted a Union Jack on the tail gate.

The extensive works on Adolf took a few months to complete. We both had day jobs so all our extra curricular tasks had to be done in our spare time. Most of the mechanical work was done by Sam while I mopped his brow like a theatre nurse and made him coffee. Our pleas for sponsorship produced very little other than the valuable and much appreciated seat belts and an offer from the Bank of London and South America (BOLSA) of help with our banking. They were I think somewhat misguided about the detail of the trip and the fact that we weren't often going to be in reach of banking facilities. Nevertheless we gratefully accepted their offer, which resulted in them inviting us to the leaving party of the British Army Expedition that was setting out to cross the Darién Gap between Panama and Colombia. BOLSA was one of the sponsors of the Expedition, donating a little more to the Army expedition than the use of a few fly-blown banking halls. The crossing had been done before by people on foot, but very few vehicles if any had done it the whole way. The Army intended taking two Range Rovers through, accompanied by a couple of Series II Land Rovers like Adolf. Range Rovers were very new to the world having been launched in the UK in June 1970. Innovative and lauded as better off road than Land Rovers, but with saloon car comfort, the idea of taking them through the Gap was exciting and challenging. The Expedition was being led by Major John Blashford-Snell who was known for having undertaken exploratory expeditions in his trade mark pith helmet, including the Nile Expedition of 1968.

The Darién Gap is made up of one hundred miles or so of impenetrable rain forest and swamps. Lying between Panama and Colombia, an interruption in the Pan-American Highway that runs the length of the western seaboard of the Americas, it is infested with insects and venomous snakes that make life unbearable. At times the forest and jungle is so dense that when it is cut, there is nowhere to put the felled vegetation. For those seeking tourist tips, you have to put the cut debris behind you, blocking your exit as you slowly hack your way forwards. Going south from Panama, the Expedition would first have to traverse mountainous rain forests before coming down to the Atrato River delta on the Colombian side. The Gap is a hostile region that few attempt to cross, but after the leaving party in London, Sam and I resolved to give it a go. Clearly this decision was fueled by the excellent BOLSA sponsored wine at the party since we had not thought about it before that evening. Furthermore, we had made absolutely no plans for such a trek, only vaguely being aware it could take us about three months on foot. We casually brushed aside the obvious detail that it would be extremely unpleasant, with a high risk of failure and disease or complete disappearance. We did not calculate how this would impact on our itinerary, but in fairness, at that time we intended being in the United States for at most a couple of months, leaving plenty of time in South America where our Carnet de Passage would be needed.

A Carnet is a bond that has to be put down in the country of origin and embarkation, to be forfeited if the vehicle to which it applies is not removed from any country demanding the Carnet. It is a form of tax designed to prevent anyone selling a vehicle without paying tax. Our Carnet had a lifespan of one year from its date of issue in the UK, which meant we had to be out of South America pretty much within one year of our departure from the UK. We knew that, whatever happened, Adolf could not be left in any South American country, to the extent that should she irreparably break down or be badly damaged, we would have to drag her to a point between Customs posts at country borders, to be left in No Man's Land. This would mean us leaving one country with a vehicle and entering the next on foot. The Carnet bond was for £3,000 which, in 1972, was double what most people earned in a year. A powerful incentive to stick to the rules.

Adolf's needs were paramount in all we did as she was clearly going to be our safety net. Supplying her with spares was a carefully considered operation. Spare dynamo; spare spark plugs; tools. The myriad of things a girl needs on a little adventure. Her handbag was full. For us there were some emergency food supplies, basic medicines that seemed mainly intended for targeting hangovers and a limited supply of clothes for both warm and cold temperatures. We restricted ourselves to the fundamentals of a stripped down life, free of want and only acknowledging need.

Through the early months of the year we contacted and visited all the Embassies of those countries we thought we might visit and pass through, potentially at least nineteen countries if we didn't make it to Venezuela and the Guyanas, which were somewhat out on a limb from our proposed route. Each country had its own entry restrictions and arrangements and wherever possible we obtained our entry visas in advance.

Our port of landing and means of crossing the Atlantic were resolved by the generosity and help of two brothers with whom both Sam and I played rugby. They and their family were in the shipping business and happened to own some cargo ships, as one does, one of which was scheduled to sail from Le Havre in France to Mexico and then on through the Gulf of Mexico to the USA. For the princely contribution of $50.00 each for our food for the two week crossing, the family said we could put Adolf on board in the hold and sail with her as the only two passengers. This was a minor miracle, simultaneously saving us money and affording us a convenient way to keep an eye on Adolf for the trip. And so, without too much paperwork, we were booked to meet up with the M.V Gela in Le Havre at the end of April. Weighing about 9,500 tons, 170 metres long and 20 metres wide, she was a small general cargo ship, easily able to accommodate Adolf.

The matter of our International Driving Licences had to be addressed. They were needed to supplement the UK driving licence, which in those days was a small red book Chairman Mao would have been proud of. The International Licence could be obtained from the Automobile Association's headquarters in Leicester Square. Armed with the relevant paperwork, application forms, our UK licences and two passport sized photographs of each of us, I approached the appropriate desk in the AA offices and introduced myself to the resident International Driving Licence expert. Balding and with a wispy moustache a pre-pubescent schoolboy would have been embarrassed by, he seemed to have perfected and honed indifference to a level of refinement unattainable by we mere mortals with an interest in service, courtesy or empathy. Methodically and slowly he scanned the paperwork, sucking on what can only have been ill-fitting dentures, scanned the photographs, scanned me, and then filled out the two licences, carefully sticking our photographs in the pre-marked squares like a child at kindergarten putting stickers in a book. Expecting to walk out with the documents, I held out my hand as he folded them over on the pre-marked lines where they needed to be folded, but was somewhat surprised when he snatched them away.

"I need you both to sign these licences before I can stamp them" he said, summoning the authority of a career that must have been burnished in some civil service office where attention to bureaucratic detail was paramount, irrespective of the consequences or cost.

Now this was just a bit of a problem and an inconvenience. An irritating hurdle since I was not coming back up to London and with a full schedule and little time left, was not sure when that could be possible.

"Have you got a pen?" I asked.

He handed me one and I held out my hand for the Licences, which he handed to me. At this stage I should point out that Sam and I weren't exactly twins. One fairly obvious difference was Sam had a beard and I did not. I was alone in front of Mr Licence. Sam was not sitting next to me. Sam was not in the room or the building. Sam wasn't even in London, he was under Adolf's bonnet in Dunsfold. With the Licences opened on the counter I signed both of them with our appropriate names. The bureaucrat watched me do this before I handed them back to him with his pen. I watched as he carefully, indeed lovingly, reopened them and solemnly stamped them before handing them back to me. I walked out of the offices clutching those valuable documents, expecting to be called back as realisation of what had just happened dawned on Mr Licence. I felt I had learned a valuable lesson. If you do things brazenly and openly enough in life, you can get away with almost anything. Perhaps that is how magicians keep us bemused and amused. The sleight of hand that tricks the eye by being so obvious that we see through or past it to what we expect to see. It was a lesson I carried throughout our trip, using it many times in some very remote places and sometimes at some very difficult and potentially dangerous moments.

And so the day of our departure approached. Before going there was one good-bye that had to be endured, the least welcome moment of the whole madcap scheme. My girlfriend had been given the opportunity to work a summer season in a brand new hotel in the north of Corfu in Greece and had accepted on the premise there was little to hold her attention or interest in England or London. Sited outside a tiny fishing village called Roda, the hotel was opening for its first season in a part of the island that had not been touched by tourism. Undeveloped and populated only by Greeks, it was an idyllic corner of true Greece. The hotel was operated by a well known UK travel company, and therefore catering for almost entirely English speaking guests. The management needed English staff to work alongside and for the local Greeks. We felt this was an ideal opportunity for her to have her own adventure, safe and a complete change from the routine of her life. Her departure date for Athens was before ours and so her day loomed large in my mind. Saying good-bye I realised I was taking the biggest gamble of my life, potentially a form of voluntary emotional hara-kiri. No one had coerced or forced me into this trip. I didn't have to go, and yet I was risking all to do it, including risking losing the one thing I valued above all else. But somehow we both felt it was the right thing to do at that time in our lives, to get these things out of our systems. Perhaps more accurately to get them out of mine. It being the right thing to do didn't make it any easier and the pain of that farewell, the emptiness it left, the fear of permanent loss I was to live with in the coming months, are as clear to me today as when I drove away from our emotional valediction.

Our own departure from Southampton was set for the 30th April, a Sunday. The sailing was late at night and after a big farewell lunch party we drove Adolf down to Southampton Docks. We met Frank and Brenda Smith from Dunsfold Land Rovers there with Sam's brother. They joined us for a quick final meal before we bade them farewell and headed off to Passport Control and Customs where some wide-eyed Customs Officers decided to search Adolf. Little did we know this was to be a training exercise for many searches to come. The Officers came to the conclusion we were not criminals and let us board the ferry. It sailed at about midnight as we lay down to sleep on some benches in the ship's nearly empty bar. The crossing to France must have been relatively smooth as I slept through most of the night, waking only once to find we were surrounded by passengers sitting at tables drinking beer. We were woken at 6.00 am by the smell of deep pans of grease being heated and bubbling to boil bacon for breakfast.

We disembarked at seven o'clock in the morning and were greeted by the humourless French Customs officers who decided to search Adolf and us. This was getting to be a bit familiar. The beginnings of a pattern was emerging where patience and a long suffering smile would prove to be useful tools of engagement with an officialdom we quickly realised held all the aces and had all the time in the world. Eventually getting bored of not finding drugs, contraband, weapons, IRA quality Semtex or any other prohibited items, they told us to repack and be on our way. We left the port and drove through Harfleur with a silent nod to Henry V and his dysentery afflicted army. Indeed, I am sure I got a whiff of the remains of that inconvenient little outbreak amongst those siege soldiers in the late summer of 1415 as they sat about the walls of the beleaguered port, which eventually succumbed. The French must have thought they were surrounded by an army of skunks. Not wishing to hang about to test our constitutions we moved on to seek out a suitable place to camp for the week we had to kill before the M.V. Gela's scheduled sailing date. By contriving to drive a complete and fruitless triangle through the hinterland we ended up back at Le Havre where a cup of coffee and the relaxing ambience of a French café gave us time to re-study the map.

The road to the Pont de Tancarville looked promising so we set off and about four miles outside Le Havre found a large quarry. Hidden from the road by a high bank, but close enough to it to be convenient, it seemed ideal. Pulling into the quarry through a narrow gap in the bank we realised this would be a perfect spot for a couple of days, and so set up camp, deciding to put up the small tent we had brought along for emergencies. In reality it was suitable for one and a half adults, or for an adult and a child. Perhaps it had been designed by Baden-Powell himself, accommodating him and like minded carefree campers who shared his proclivities.

Despite all the preparations over so many months, there were still jobs to do that we had not had time to complete. Numbering all the keys to the many padlocks on the vehicle was one of them. In the warm weather we did some mechanical jobs on the engine and then, late in the afternoon, opened and drank a bottle of champagne we had been given by my girlfriend's sister. Suitably mellowed we cooked supper on the open fire and went to bed, tired and eager to get going.

After a couple of days of camping and preparation, we broke camp and drove into Le Havre to meet the shipping agents for the M.V. Gela. An indifferent, almost somnambulant Monsieur Bohu had absolutely no idea what the Gela was up to or when she would sail, and what is more, he really didn't seem to care. Bucked up and encouraged no end by this excellent news and his general ennui, we took his advice and went to a cheap camp site on the hill overlooking the port where we proceeded to demolish two litres of wine through the length of a warm, sunny day. We thus started our vigil for our ship in an alcoholic haze. Our camp gave us an excellent view of the comings and goings of ships into and out of the port. Other campers included some Canadian couples killing time before boarding the S S France, one of the great luxury liners of the '70s. They were heading back to Canada after living in France for a few months. Having finished the wine we decided to walk back into the nearby village to stock up with some more. As we passed through the camp site we realised its offices were housed in an old German bunker that had survived the Second World War. It seemed appropriate somehow that the camp lavatories were situated next to it, a fitting monument and tribute by the French to their appreciation of the German Occupation. Sampling the re-supply of wine on our return ensured a sound night's sleep on the grass.

The next day two more visits to the shipping agents proved to be a bit more fruitful as a significantly more interested and better informed Monsieur Vallet cheerfully informed us that the M.V Gela was leaving for Le Havre from Antwerp that evening. We celebrated with coffee in the harbour at what was fast becoming a favourite cafe. We wandered around the old town, changed money at a bank and then went out to the end of the pier to watch the SS France set sail for her transatlantic crossing. She was a beautiful sight, no more than about one hundred and fifty metres away from us, sounding her deafening horns in farewell to the port and well wishers waving to loved ones on board. Elegant and stately, she slowly moved past us and then out into the open sea, radiating the allure of a long voyage on a transoceanic liner. Watching her serene passage out of the harbour, it was easy to understand the mystique and romance that had grown around the tragedy of the Titanic. A ship takes on a personality. Somehow ignoring the illogicality, we anthropomorphise, turning a cruise liner that is an inanimate object into a glamorous woman, one that exudes an air of mystery, of romance, of escape from the humdrum of life. We close our eyes and imagine ourselves cosseted by her, wooing us and letting us forget the day to day issues that suffuse our land-based lives.

Relaxing and reading in the camp later in the afternoon I became aware that I was being closely watched by a French woman in a caravan that was parked next to Adolf. We had learned from her the day before that she was in the campsite with her husband, who left early each morning and returned in the evening. I assumed he was going to work although it seemed a bit odd that they were living in a camp site. She spent most of her day sitting in a chair in front of a large window in the caravan. Through its glass she could survey the campsite's grounds and, more disturbingly, us. She was enormous, filling her clothes like an overstuffed, bursting sofa. Her low cut, cheap floral print dress showed the edge of a bra that seemed to contain two baby hippos. Every time I caught her eye she smiled with all the allure of a manatee in oestrous. When I say smile, I suppose leered salaciously would be a more accurate description of the grimace she obviously took to be irresistibly sexy. To me it hinted more of someone suffering from trapped wind. I didn't doubt her anabatic emissions would have all the charm and allure of a bear's breath after a long hibernation. Her libidinous intentions became clearer when she propped up a book in the window entitled *The Love Machine*. Sadly the mechanic of this particular French love machine had not oiled or maintained the engine. There were definite signs of decay, a sense that the machine was beyond its useful life. There was evidence of some past servicing, presumably by her unfussy husband, given the two young children running in and out of the caravan during the day. She was a truly terrifying sight and I resolved to keep Adolf between us and to lock the tent that night.

The M.V. Gela was delayed by fog on her journey down from Antwerp but finally, a day later than anticipated by the agents, we were able to drive down to the docks to greet her and to prepare to board. We had spent the night back at the quarry, mainly to avoid the love machine who showed disturbing signs of shifting up through the gears and asking for her engine to be revved. Driving down to the docks was an exciting, exhilarating moment. We were on our way. The agents helped us clear Customs and Immigration, this time too busy with the ship's cargo to bother searching us. We drove Adolf along the length of the dock and parked her next to the ship before boarding to meet Mr Simpson, the Captain. He confirmed we were to be the only passengers on board and showed us our cabin. It was small with two bunk beds and a wash basin and perfectly adequate for our needs. We were also to have exclusive use of the owner's room, a large drawing room with a desk, armchairs, sofas and a coffee table. Large windows down one side wall let in welcome light to brighten the room which was darkened by its wood paneled walls. As far as we were concerned we might as well have been first class passengers on the S S France. It was certainly a world away from a disused quarry on the outskirts of Le Havre, or from a small square of grass on a hill with the resistible promise of unbridled passion bubbling and festering in a chair mere feet away.

As it was lunchtime, we went down to the wardroom and joined the British officers for our first meal and to introduce ourselves. The atmosphere around the table was relaxed and casual with the Captain fully part of the banter whilst seeming to retain the respect of the others, which was comforting. No Captain Bligh here. The first mate was called Martin, a large, bearded and loud Scotsman. Brian the wireless operator sat next to me on my right and introduced himself, as did a young apprentice called Gordon who took a seat on my left. The officers were immediately welcoming, inclusive and accepting of us and we quickly felt at home as we answered their questions about our trip and our loose plans. We in turn listened to their conversations about the logistics of the next leg of their voyage.

Loading cargo was to take all day and so after lunch we amused ourselves by taking turns to explore the ship, whilst the other of us stayed with Adolf keeping an eye on her as she sat alone and expectant on the dock, the wallflower at the party waiting to be asked to dance. She was scheduled to be loaded onto the ship last, either late in the afternoon or in the early evening, so Sam decided to go to our cabin to sleep. Part of the ship's cargo was a consignment of Cognac which was being loaded into the aft hold. The bottles were packed in crates and I watched a few of the dockers working at the crates to open them to steal some of the bottles. The docker overseeing the loading shouted and stopped the crane above as he went up to the pilferers and told them to put the bottles back, which they did. No sooner had he climbed up the ladder to go back up on deck, they reopened the cases and took the bottles back, only to be spotted by the supervisor on the deck above who shouted at them to put them back again. They complied reluctantly, looking decidedly disgruntled at the outcome of this well rehearsed fandango. The hold consisted of two or three levels. When the cargo reached a certain height, heavy wooden planks were laid to create a new floor, sealing off the compartment below. Once the new floor was secure loading recommenced. I assumed this was an efficient and simple way of distributing the weight of the cargo, preventing too much pressure from bearing down on the goods at the bottom of each section.

Adolf was destined for the top floor and when she was lifted off the dock by a huge crane, it became clear she was going to be the only item of cargo in the cavernous top level. As I stood on the dock and watched our home lift off the dock and then suspended high in the air, I was suffused with a sense of protective paternalism. As the crane started to swing her over the side of the ship I raced up the gang plank in time to see her being lowered into the gaping black maw of the hold. Running down the stairs and then down the ladder into the hold I arrived as her wheels touched the floor, and just in time to see a large, heavily tattooed docker jump into Adolf's driving cab and start searching for things to steal. He looked like a bare knuckle fighter, one who owned a bulldog that chewed on his ears and face. It was clear someone had also tried to steal engine oil from the two jerry cans on the front of the vehicle as they had been opened. After a little discussion in an international dialect globally understood, the docker agreed to get out of Adolf empty handed. He nonchalantly marched off without any apparent sense of shame. This scene had been witnessed by his Cognac stealing colleagues who came over laughing, offering me a drink from the bottles they had stolen and which they were enthusiastically tucking into. They obviously had no intention of taking the bottles ashore, only the contents.

Having imbibed substantial amounts of Cognac, the dockers cheerfully set about chaining Adolf to the floor of the top hold. The roof of the hold must have been a good five metres above our heads, and with a beam of about twenty metres in the hold, Adolf looked small and forlorn in what now resembled a small aircraft hanger. Somewhat skeptical about the work standards and attention to detail of the Cognac infused dockers I checked the chains but instinct and years of practice had thankfully guided their drunken hands because Adolf was firmly chained to the floor. She wasn't going anywhere. As the top hatch closed I climbed the ladder out of the hold and emerged on deck under a night sky and in the full glare of the dock's lights.

Just after midnight, with two tugs in attendance nudging and pulling like pilot fish feeding on a large predator, the M.V. Gela slipped her ties with the shore and put herself at the mercy and in the control of what appeared to me to be an entirely drunk crew. I have no idea how we got away safely. One or two of the crew could hardly stand and were incapable of unhitching the mooring ropes from the huge steel bollards on the dockside. Others did so, but before being told to. But for the tugs holding the ship's nose to the dock we would surely have drifted out into the harbour. Thankfully Martin, the first mate, and the other officers were sober and once we were free we passed safely through a lock and into the channel leading out of the harbour. As we reached the open sea the pilot's small vessel came alongside and he climbed down, jumped across into it and waved us off. He seemed relieved to be getting off.

It was nearly three o'clock in the morning and it hit me that I had now passed the point of no return. We were on our way, finally, fully and irreversibly committed to whatever the months ahead threw at us. I think I felt like a parachutist leaping from a plane, pulling the cord and, looking up at the canopy as it opens, realising it is made of a collection of string vests. I was entering a phase of my life stripped bare of security, of certainty. It was unexpectedly exhilarating and liberating. We could make the rules, if we wanted any. We could decide our destiny, our course, our destinations. There was no clock, no diary, just empty roads ahead, unmade memories to come into being. I stared into the night ahead from the wing of the bridge, a strong sea breeze in my face, my heart in Athens but my mind in the Americas. I went to bed on the top bunk in our small cabin feeling a mixture of sadness, loss and gleeful anticipation.

One of the benefits of being the only passengers on board and not being on a protocol stiffened cruise ship was we had the run of the entire ship, from engine room to bridge. The M.V. Gela's officers were all British but the crew were Chinese, and it soon became clear that many of the crew didn't speak a word of English. We were apportioned part of the Captain's steward's time. His sole job for us seemed to be confined to bringing us tea in bed in the morning. Tang had a few words of English that were decipherable, and many that weren't, so conversations with him were always gratifyingly and mercifully short. Breakfast for the officers was served at eight o'clock in the morning and so Tang would bring us our cups of tea in our cabin at seven o'clock. If the sea was calm, he would silently hand them to us. If the sea was rough, he would put the plug in the sink and then place the full cups and saucers in the sink with the words,

'Ship, she lolling today".

It was then a race to get to the few drops of tea remaining in the saucers before they followed the rest of the contents of our cups into the sink. Since the M.V. Gela was a cargo ship and not a cruise liner, there were no stabilizers so flexible sea legs became de rigeur in heavy seas. Meals also became a challenge as the ship pitched and rolled and our plates grew legs and moved around the table in front of us. The Chinese waiter's solution was very simple and effective, and clearly often used. He would appear at the end of the table holding a jug of water. Without a break in conversation, the officers would all lift their plates off the pitching table, and the waiter would hurl the contents of the jug onto the table cloth. The officers would replace their plates on the soaking cloth and carry on eating, their plates now sticking firmly to the table.

I learned much about Chinese ingenuity on that two week voyage across the Atlantic. Martin the first mate recounted how, when the ship was in one port, he had seen some of the Chinese crew returning to the ship with about a dozen live ducks under their arms. A few days later at sea, he could hear the ducks below deck and, curious, went down to investigate. He found the ducks side by side in a row on a plank of wood, their webbed feet nailed to the plank. There was a long trough in front of them and newspaper behind them, food on the former and droppings on the latter. This simple if inhumane solution to the wandering, reluctant-to-be-cooked duck problem in the close confines of the crew's quarters speaks of a savagely creative mind and reminded me of the complete indifference to the well being of animals in some races. As a nation we are used to a far more sensitive approach to the care of animals, even those we intend to slaughter for our tables. Given the Chinese predilection for fresh cat meat, it was noticeable there was no cat on board. The officers told us there had in fact been a succession of cats on the ship but each had mysteriously disappeared. The last cat to go missing had been replaced by a small dog, which seemed to have a charmed life as it had survived more than a few months.

One of the Chinese crew stood out in particular, largely because he was about six foot two whereas all his compatriots struggled to get past five foot five. In the whole of our two week voyage I never saw him change his clothes. Each day he wore the same pair of ancient dungarees, a baseball cap and seemingly nothing else, no matter how cold it was. The front buttons of the dungarees were always undone revealing a large, naked chest, devoid of hair. Once blue, the dungarees now looked as though they and their owner had been in an explosion at a paint factory. They seemed to be splattered with every shade and hue of colour, as was his cap. He resembled a huge tube of Smarties or M&Ms. When I asked one of the officers about him he explained the over-developed Chinaman was the ship's painter. His job was to paint everything that didn't move, and some things that did which must have included his clothes. The officer said that on one occasion the man had been over the side of the ship in a bosun's chair when they had been in port somewhere and had somehow contrived to fall off the chair into the water. As he splashed around in the water waiting to be rescued, he still held the large paintbrush in his hand. Rather than let go of it he shoved it inside his dungarees, covering his chest in paint.

Two weeks at sea on a cruise ship are filled with daily activities. Shows, entertainment, and games are all laid on to keep the passengers amused and occupied. Dressing up for dinner, or down for the pool or sun decks gives a ship's fare paying community the opportunity to show off their wardrobes and fashion sense. On a working cargo ship, there is little for a passenger to do, and absolutely no need for displays of fashion. Sam and I kept ourselves occupied with jobs on the ship. We freed some rusted winches on the deck in the prow of the ship. We read books, wrote letters, checked on Adolf down in the hold and learned how the ship worked. The engine room deep in the ship was noisy and hot, the huge pistons pumping relentlessly. They were like giant oiled dustbins, rising and falling in a relentless rhythm, dispensing their immense power through the revolving prop shaft to the giant propellor pounding through the water behind and beneath us. On the bridge we learned about the navigation equipment as we watched the large screens showing the radar maps. It was strange to see other ships on the screen and to realise they too were out in this oceanic wilderness. Invisible to our eyes, the only evidence of them was those little blips of green under the sweeping line of the radar. We studied weather fronts ahead of us and could see when storms were building in the distance. Generally the ship seemed to sail herself and it was rare to find more than one person on the bridge. The officer on watch would walk amongst the illuminated displays and screens, and occasionally scan the horizon through binoculars.

A day or so out of harbour we were entertained to a boat and fire drill. I say entertained because it was hard to take seriously the chaotic shambles the Chinese turned it into. It was mayhem, with the Chinese crew all talking at once, shouting at each other in their native dialects as tempers frayed. A lifeboat was to be swung out over the side and I watched proceedings from the bridge with the third officer. By the time the lifeboat was finally over the side of the ship the Gela would have been on the ocean floor if it had been a real emergency. Three of the Chinese crew had been put in the lifeboat, perhaps to give a sense of realism, or as ballast. As they hung and swung precariously over the sea, eyes wide with fear and hands clutching onto the side of the lifeboat, their colleagues started to argue as to who was going to bring the boat back in. It was like watching small children fighting over a favourite toy. Since all the screaming and shouting was in Cantonese or Mandarin, we had no idea what they were saying but somehow through the cacophony a pecking order seemed to emerge, and one of the individuals on the deck eventually won the right to rescue the lifeboat with its ashen faced passengers.

As soon as the lifeboat had been safely stored back in its cradle, it was time for a fire drill, which was supposed to involve the firing of a fire cylinder. The third mate turned to me and said he thought most of the Chinese crew were high on drugs all the time. As he said this, the crew member delegated to set off the extinguisher somehow managed to release all the gas propellant from it. This would of course have only served to fan any real fire he was trying to extinguish. He was roundly abused by his countrymen as they all disappeared beneath deck, chattering in their strangely staccato language, seemingly delighted with the efficiency of their performance.

In the evenings the officers would regularly show films from the ship's library. Film shows always happened after the obligatory drink from the extremely cheap bar. There were only three films on board, and each was shown more than once during the crossing. The cheap drinks had the affect of making us all forget the details of the films we had already seen so, like goldfish rounding the corner of a circular bowl, it was as though we were seeing each for the first time. One of the films was the iconic *Catch 22*, the adaptation of Joseph

Heller's novel written about the Second World War. *The Violent People* didn't lie about its content, nor its intent. Its story was a continuous bloodbath of gratuitous savagery, mostly in Le Havre. I felt we might just have had a lucky escape and kept looking to see if the love machine in the campsite had any part in it. The officers loved it, which I found mildly disturbing. There was a dartboard in the bar and regular games were held. My ability to hit a dartboard in a pub remains limited to this day. In a bar whose floor moves the whole time, I was lucky to hit the wall around the board, let alone the board itself. More often than not I got the floor. Strangely any officers in the bar quickly learned to stand behind me when I stepped up to the mark.

    We sailed past the Azores at midnight about three days after leaving Le Havre, then headed out into the Atlantic's vast emptiness, the Gela's mighty engines ensuring we averaged about fifteen knots an hour. We saw porpoises, whales, Portuguese Man O'War jellyfish with their long tendrils trailing behind them in the azure water. At first I thought they were small, transparent plastic bags inflated with air as they bobbed about on the surface of the water. Dolphins played in our bow wave and close to our side, easily pacing us as we pushed through the water. Flying fish skimmed just above the water like small birds, gliding further than seemed feasibly possible. On one memorable evening on the bridge, I saw a distant green flash on the horizon as the sun dipped out of sight and its rays shone momentarily through the surface of the sea. As we moved west the daytime temperature rose, eventually reaching the low nineties Fahrenheit in the shade. We sailed through the

Bahamas within sight of land, and then passed Cuba. Our first port of call was to be Vera Cruz in Mexico as some of the cargo was destined for the Central American market. During the voyage the Captain had offered to take us on to the ship's next stop at New Orleans but on reflection we decided to stick to our original plan. After two weeks at sea we were restive and felt we had had enough of inactivity and decided we would prefer to get off in Mexico and then drive up to Matamoros and cross into the United States through the border at Brownsville.

Two weeks after leaving Le Havre, on Saturday 20th May, Mexico appeared on the horizon. I felt like a latter day Columbus and empathised with his crew's surely inevitable frisson of excitement at seeing solid land rather than the rim of a waterfall into the void off the edge of the world. Perhaps the only explorers now who can feel that same tension of the uncharted unknown are those travelling to the moon or into the depths of the ocean. They voyage into the truly unknown where the smallest slip or error, or a catastrophic system failure can mean being eternally marooned, far from home, loved ones and all that is familiar. I didn't quite feel in that exalted body of adventurers since I was pretty sure others had been across the Atlantic since Columbus' first foray in 1492. I did however feel excited at the sight of the new world in front of me. We went through the first reef in the early afternoon and, as we approached harbour, met our pilot. His boat came out to us and turned to run alongside, but his somewhat decrepit vessel could not keep up and so the officer on deck had to slow down to allow it to catch up. I leant over the side and watched the unfortunate pilot trying to get onto the lowered steps without falling into the water between the boats. Once on the bridge, he guided us into harbour where we moored. Landfall at last. Let the fun begin.

Little did I know just how much fun there was to be, nor how soon it was to begin.

The M.V. Gela in harbour.

Camping near Le Havre while waiting for the M.V. Gela to dock.

Adolf in the M.V. Gela's hold - mid Atlantic.

A GIRL CALLED ADOLF

CHAPTER 3

Vera Cruz - Mexico - 1972

"It is better to remain silent and be thought a fool than to open one's mouth and remove all doubt"

Abraham Lincoln

The M.V. Gela slowly manoeuvered into the harbour and was nudged to the dock by an asthmatic tug. The Chinese crew threw mooring ropes to the waiting Mexican dockers, all of whom bore a remarkable similarity to their French counterparts, albeit seemingly a bit more tanned but no less unpleasant. I watched proceedings from the flying bridge listening to the dual noise of the shouts from the dockers and the instructions being given calmly from the bridge. One particular docker caught my eye as he shouted and gesticulated instructions to those catching ropes and preparing the dockside for our cargo. Dark and swarthy like the rest, he was noticeable for having half one arm missing. Steve, the officer standing next to me also saw him and said,

"See that guy with half an arm missing. He got that way by being caught in the cabin of an American cargo ship here. He was stealing, filling his pockets. When they caught him they cut off the end of his arm."

I had no idea whether this story was apocryphal but looking at the tough motley group on the quay I didn't doubt they lived life to a different set of rules to the genteel folk of Surrey. Imagining the differences could not prepare me for the months to come where I learned that the rules are set by the man standing in front of you, by the man with the gun who's only code of honour is self first, and you don't matter. We had been given dire warnings about Mexico before leaving England, including the advice not to drive at night, something we were regularly to ignore with some near spectacular consequences. Seeing the one and a half armed docker, and feeling the heat of the Mexican day, it finally dawned on me how different was the world I was about to enter, how alien to anything I had experienced before this point in my life. Up until now the planning and conversations had not brought with them the reality of the situation we were throwing ourselves into. It had almost been a fantasy, a dream we had discussed and with which we were only tangentially connected. Now the sights, the smells and the heat all combined to turn on a light on this Damascene road I was walking. A light that so far had been no more than a dim bulb I had hidden away in some unvisited corner of my mind. I had no idea what we were going to do next, except that we were heading north up the coast to America. I wondered if a map would be useful and made a mental note to try and find one in Vera Cruz. We didn't know quite how up to date the maps we had were. The fact we only had one item and date on our itinerary, which was to be out of South America within a year, didn't seem to matter. What could be difficult about that?

By now we were moored, the ship's engines shut down with only the generators running to provide power. A small bus appeared alongside the ship and a large group of men in suits and uniforms got out of it.

"Customs and Immigration" Steve said. "They're here to clear the cargo and fill their cases. They'll want to see you and Sam too so you'd better go down".

I had no idea what he meant by 'fill their cases' but since the men below were hurrying up the gangplank I went down below to our cabin where I collected Sam and our travel documents and headed for the Captain's cabin. It was a reasonably good sized room for a small ship. The Captain's desk was at one end of it, facing its length, his chair pushed back against the wall. A couple of sofas, armchairs and a small coffee table were grouped together in front of the desk. Captain Simpson was seated at the desk with documents spread out on it and nodded a greeting without interrupting the task of sorting the papers. We sat on a couple of upright dining chairs at the far end of the room from the desk and as we did so there was a knock on the cabin door. Before the Captain could call out a welcoming answer, the door opened and the men I had seen getting out of the small bus on the quay entered in single file. They were led by a very short, stout man with an enormous moustache, a ransom strip of dense undergrowth between his mouth and his nose. He had a huge, ornate, pearl handled revolver hanging from a belt around his waist under his overhanging stomach. The gun bounced against his upper thigh as he walked in. Imperious and swollen with Napoleonic self importance, he stood in the middle of the room, legs apart, looking like an overinflated beach ball on two cocktail sticks. His dark suited or uniformed colleagues, their bulging stomachs hanging over belts, followed him in.

In addition to the suits or uniforms, an essential part of their badges of office seemed to be a moustache and greasy hair. Without waiting for an invitation, they all sat down in the available sofas and armchairs, sweating profusely. Each member of the delegation was carrying a large briefcase which they put on the floor at their feet. One officer was even shorter than the strutting leader, and could not reach the floor with his feet from his seat in the armchair he had requisitioned for himself. He perched on the cushion with his feet sticking out in front of him, like buffers on a train, and looked like a child in an oversized chair, an Alice in Wonderland character. I could see a large hole in the sole of each of his shoes. He had an enormous pitted nose which looked capable of overbalancing him and which his fat index finger constantly excavated. His mining exploits were eventually successful when he extracted his finger with a large glutinous lump wobbling on the end of it. He wiped it on the armchair where it nestled threateningly next to his leg like a pet gelatinous slug.

Our presence at the back of the room was ignored amid much smiling and talking amongst the officers and the Captain. Tang came through the door with impeccable, and clearly oft practiced timing. He was bearing a tray laden with bottles of beer, mugs of coffee and plates of biscuits, all of which quickly disappeared into twelve hairy and chubby hands, to be slurped over and chewed on with relish. The Mexicans descended on the tray of drinks and drank them all. They demolished the biscuits like starved locusts, and then all struggled to their feet and lined up next to the Captain's desk on which were stacked bottles of Cognac and cartons of cigarettes. They moved slowly forwards past the desk, like a line of graduating students getting their Degrees. Each had his briefcase open expectantly before him. The Captain placed a bottle and a carton into each of them. Clearly tax collecting in Mexico was of a highly personal nature. The little Emperor with the gun then went back to the desk, leant over it and signed the cargo release papers, without so much as looking at a single page. For this act of meticulous scrutiny and professionalism, his voracious briefcase received another bottle and carton. It was all done quite brazenly, without a scintilla of shame or embarrassment over what was obviously a recognised, if somewhat unofficial part of the Customs formalities.

"You will need to clear our two passengers for immigration" Captain Simpson said to the rotund leader. "They are disembarking here with their vehicle". He gestured towards us, still sitting quietly at the back of the room, so far still unnoticed.

The sweating officials turned towards us and I noticed the briefcases were each immediately unclipped and held ajar. We stepped forward and proffered our Passports and Carnet for inspection. The short leader of the group smiled an oleaginous smile and took them. He pulled himself up to stare haughtily up at us as we towered over him. He leafed through the pages of our documents, raising his eyebrows and sucking on a corner of his moustache, no doubt resampling lunch. He handed them to one of his colleagues and said to us,

"You 'ave no visas, no tourist cards".

He was absolutely right. Spot on. Clearly a bright chap and Brain of Mexico.

The open briefcase was given a little shake, which seemed to set the other eleven cases off in sympathy, each quivering their expectant and wholly unsubtle hints.

"We were told by the Mexican Embassy in London that we should get our visas at our port of entry," I replied. "They told us we didn't need any other papers."

"Is not right," he said. "You must 'ave visa and tourist card before come 'ere. You cannot enter Mexico without visa."

Suddenly the calm of the room was disrupted by all twelve officials talking at once, shouting at us, talking to each other, looking at the Captain, shaking the gaping briefcases in our direction, like a clutch of hungry chicks in a nest when a parent returns with a succulent caterpillar. We had absolutely no intention of paying any bribes to this motley crew of crooks and persisted in repeating that we knew we could get visas and tourist cards on landing and that the Embassy in London had refused to give them to us. When it became clear to them that we were not going to conjure a donation to the Immigration Department Ball from our wallets or drinks cabinet, our Passports disappeared into the leader's briefcase which was then firmly shut.

"You must stay on ship. Immigration will come on Monday. Take you to Immigration office. You stay here".

We argued this point with him and eventually he relented and said we could get off the ship but not go far into the town. He said he would keep our Passports so we could not leave Vera Cruz and go on into mainland Mexico.

We protested and demanded the return of our Passports but the clearly irritated men were not for persuading and trooped out of the room. It was a cardinal rule of ours that we should never let our Passports out of our sight. Seeing them disappear out of the door before we had set foot on New World soil was a bit dispiriting. Columbus didn't have to put up with this. In truth, as we had the option of staying on board and sailing on to New Orleans it did not really matter if they refused us entry. Having already decided to disembark in Mexico however, Vera Cruz was still our preferred choice as our point of entry into the Americas. It was clearly going to be a somewhat frustrating weekend on the ship. There is only so much dockside activity and cargo unloading one can watch in a day and still remain interested. By now the ship was infested with people trying to sell us sombreros, ponchos, post cards and other tourist tat. There seemed to be no control over who could come on board and so we made sure our cabin door was locked before going aft to keep an eye on Adolf in her hold, and to watch more plunder of the cargo.

As evening fell, the harbour quietened for what remained of the weekend and we joined the officers in the ship's bar for a quiet drink to celebrate our arrival. Since they were now off duty and preparing to head into the town for their evening's entertainment, drinks flowed freely. I had not particularly noticed how much we were all drinking but it vaguely occurred to me that things were getting out of hand when Martin dropped his glass eye in my hand for me to inspect. There was something surreal about being stared at by this disembodied, tear dampened eye. It glared unblinking at me, myopically judgmental and somehow displeased at what it saw. Given the amount we had drunk, to this day I am convinced Martin put it back in his head upside down. He looked very odd with one eye seemingly fixated on the ceiling. Gordon the apprentice, and Brian the wireless officer, joined us and the rum flowed.

At some point in the evening, someone suggested we should all go into the town to a few bars the crew knew well. This seemed an excellent idea so, forgetting the Immigration Officer's instructions banning us from going ashore and far into town, we set off, eager for an evening of fun and frivolity with the gentle folk of Vera

Cruz, little aware that no such people existed in this tough port, nor that some of the crew were looking for a little more than just a drink.

The officers led us to a couple of bars where we had a few drinks. Somehow Sam and I became separated from them and found ourselves in a large square in the town. The square was surrounded by two and three story buildings housing shops on the ground floor that were under colonnaded walkways. There seemed to be dozens of bars in amongst the shops, with hundreds of tables and chairs outside in the walkways. It was too hot to be sitting inside and the pavements, tables and colonnades were full of people enjoying a Saturday evening out. We selected a table occupied by a grey haired man.

"May we join you?" I said.

"Sure, please do" he replied in an American accent. With a neat goatee beard, trimmed moustache, and greying hair swept back from his forehead, he had a fragrant air about him. It occurred to me he was somewhat effeminate. It took about five seconds to work out he was gay, and another five to work out he was interested. In me. Not in Sam, just me. This was grossly unfair and I felt Sam's jealousy keenly. Lowering the timbre of my voice and buffing up my heterosexuality, I pulled up a chair and sat down. The American's name was Chris and he was holidaying by himself down in Mexico. It was quite clear what he was doing by himself in the middle of the night at the bar,. His clear objective was an outlet and receptacle for his unrequited passions.

As far as I was concerned, unrequited was the way they were going to stay.

The main square was busy with its full bars. Cars were cruising around, filled with young men leering at the girls walking under the colonnades, occasionally sounding their horns to catch the girls' attention. The girls ignored them, which fueled their frustration with the lure of the unobtainable. I could smell the testosterone in the air. The universal game of chase and catch, played out all over the world. I have watched pigeons in London engaged in the same ritual, but perhaps with more finesse. Bar customers were seated out in the warm night air with waiters moving swiftly and efficiently between them. The sound of Latin music was coming out of some of the open doors and windows. A soft yellow light shone from the street lamps, which were muted enough for me to be able to pick out stars in the black cloudless sky above. Street sellers were plying their trade, touting souvenirs similar to those we had seen and been offered on board during the afternoon. I was watching the people walking past, chatting to Chris the American and enjoying my drink when I felt a tug on my sleeve. A young boy was standing next to me.

"Hey, Meester, you want my seester?" he said.

"Uh, excuse me?" I said. His diction was stereotypical and cliched, straight from a Hollywood B Movie. At first I thought he must be joking.

"My seester meester, you want her?" The underage pimp waved his hand towards a young girl, not yet twenty, sitting at a table nearby. She smiled at me, if gurning can be described as smiling, revealing two teeth and a couple of hectares of blackened gums. I immediately assumed a fond kiss on her menu of services was probably often refused by any of her customers who still had their sight and thus no use of a guide dog. Perhaps our ship's half blind officer Martin would get caught out if she approached him from his left side, but head on, both eyes working, she was a gorilla. With her lank, greasy hair and unwashed appearance, she was a petri dish for every sexually transmitted disease known to man. I felt her marketing and business plan, and unique selling point of a guaranteed syphilitic outcome, were doomed to failure.

"Er, no thank you" I said, having another sip of my drink to calm the nerves. Chris looked relieved at the failure of this unwelcome challenge to his own aspirations. His hopes remained high.

My sleeve was tugged again.

"Meester, you want ceegar?" said the boy, pushing a small and dirty cardboard box of cigars towards me. I realised he carried more than just his sister as stock for his mobile business.

"No thank you, I don't smoke" I said.

"I'll have a cigar" said Sam.

The boy walked around to Sam's side of the table and held out the box containing the cigars.

"How much? Sam said.

"Ten pesos, one" said the boy.

"Ten pesos! I'll give you one peso" Sam said.

The boy had obviously been to RADA on some British Council scholarship. His eyes rolled, he clapped his hand to his face as though we had called his mother a prostitute, and squeezed a fake tear, fake because she probably was.

"Meester, one peso?! These good ceegars. Best. Eight pesos?"

They haggled back and forth and ultimately settled on a price for two cigars which Sam took from the boy's shopwindow and put in his shirt pocket. He offered a Mexican note and the boy handed Sam change and started to move off quickly, but not quickly enough. Sam grabbed his arm.

"Wrong change" he said. "You need to give me more." As he said this, Sam grabbed a handful of cigars from the boy's cardboard shop counter, holding them hostage.

Clearly this Mexican Artful Dodger and polymathic entrepreneur had a wider arsenal of tricks than pimping and tobacco sales up his sleeve. The detail of the conversation became lost in a cacophony of shouting from the boy, his sister and what seemed to be his extended family, none of whom had heard of an early night to bed. Sam and I held our ground, Sam still holding the boy's arm, and insisted that he had given the wrong change, our euphemism for stealing, and that he should cough up the rest like an honourable chap. At that early stage of our trip we were of course blissfully unaware that 'honour' did not feature in the Mexican lexicon or nature, and if perchance it did appear, it was only as an expression of weakness. As the shouting and yelling reached a crescendo, a group of policemen appeared, muscling their way into the crowd that now surrounded us. They too were shouting in Spanish, adding to the chaos. One of them spoke a little English and we tried to explain to him what had happened. He seemed unimpressed.

"You come to station" he said.

Our arms were grabbed by the police and we were marched to the pavement where a police car had drawn up. Sam was put in the car first and clearly decided to occupy the first seat he came to, leaving me no room to get in. With a gun in my face I leant over and immediately became aware that a pair of hands was moving quite firmly over my buttocks. Glancing over my shoulder I saw the effete and somewhat tumescent Chris smiling affectionately at me while he fondled my backside. His demeanour was that of someone who has 'pulled'.

"Er, Chris, this is not a good time" I said. He seemed to take this as me playing hard to get and started kneading me like someone testing melons in a market for ripeness.

I was unable to fend off his amorous advances as my arms were held by two policemen, my path forward into the car blocked by Sam. Undeterred Chris continued his general fumbling and fondling, which appeared to have entered a more urgent phase in his idea of foreplay. Feeling somewhere between a rock and a hard place, the latter now alarmingly apparent in Chris' jeans, and unwilling to fight on two fronts, I quickly jumped into the car, pushing Sam across the seat, no doubt frustrating the priapic American who was elbowed back by the police. I viewed his loss as my gain, preferring to take my chances with some rather hirsute and heavily muscled police than the gentler attentions of the love-struck Chris. The boy with the cigars was pushed in next to me, the door closed and two policemen got in the front. We drove off at speed into the dark, metaphorically and literally. The driver seemed to be a St Vitus's dance sufferer, jerking the car back and forth up the road like a yacht tacking into a marina. Perhaps he had seen the film '*Bullitt*' and fancied himself as a Steve McQueen facsimile. With the three of us crammed into the narrow back seat of the car, the cigar selling boy was squashed firmly up against the door. I pressed hard against him, pushing his shoulders up next to his ears. His squeaks of complaint were ignored by the two policemen in the front seats. It occurred to me he was probably having difficulty breathing as I tried to take some more cigars hostage from his now rather crumpled department store.

60

The police station was some distance from the square. It was a forbiddingly large, slab-sided building with barred windows high up on the wall. The car stopped, the doors were opened and we were frogmarched in through the large wooden doors that opened out onto the dark street. Walking through the doors we went through an archway into a large courtyard that was open to the sky. A few policemen were wandering about, crossing from one side to the other or standing in small groups chatting. One side of the courtyard was given over to what were clearly cells. Other doors were open, with dim lights shining out of them. I could see desks and chairs and assumed these were offices of some sort. Without any formalities or any necessity to record our arrival, we were taken to a cell and pushed in, the door clanging shut behind us. The boy with the mobile cigar shop was kept in the courtyard with the policemen and seemed worryingly familiar with them.

That is how we came to be in a back street Mexican gaol the night we landed in the country. It was not, and never had been, part of the plan. It was time to take stock, to assess the damage and make a plan as to how to escape our predicament. We were a few thousand miles from anything that was familiar. We had no Passports. We were in the town against Immigration's instructions to stay on board or in the dock area. No one knew where we were or what had happened to us. This didn't look or feel good and we felt it could be slightly tricky. I had inspected the barred window when I had pulled myself up and knew the bars were firmly cemented into the surrounding brickwork so there was no chance of getting out that way. Negotiation seemed to be the only option open to us and for that we had little to bring to the table other than some rather unseemly begging. We had absolutely no idea how long we were going to be detained and the police did not show much interest in enlightening us. There was little else to do but stand around and wait in the gloomy cell. Sitting on the damp floor was not an attractive option as we had no idea of the origin of the dampness, although the smell in the cell gave us a clue.

After about an hour the cell door opened and we were escorted back out into the courtyard. A phalanx of grumpy looking police faced us, one or two with suspiciously familiar looking cigars glowing in their hands. There was no sign of the cigar boy, who had clearly left the price of his freedom in the fingers of the smoking policemen. The English speaking one from the bar ominously gestured to us to follow him. Three or four of his colleagues fell in beside us as we were marched back across the square to the huge doors to the street. There was a police car outside with a back door open.

"You, in car" said the policeman, pointing at Sam.

Another of our cardinal rules was that we should not be separated in the event of any difficulties so, as Sam got in the car, I tried to follow him in. The gun in the face routine seemed to be a habit with the police. I was yanked out and pushed away from the car, the muzzle of the gun barrel leaving a mark in my chest. The door slammed, two policemen jumped in the front seats and the car drove off. The remaining policemen waved me off and turned back to the front doors, slamming them behind as they returned to the inner courtyard. I was alone in the street, alcohol fumes swirling around in my head and with the beginnings of an explanation to Sam's parents in my mind. Asking to go back into the police station to demand to know where Sam had been taken didn't seem to be the brightest plan and so I set off, wandering the dark back streets to try to get my bearings. Vera Cruz was hiding its charms well. I seemed to be in a poor part of the town, or at least poorer than the rest I had seen. Poor is a relative term, so areas of the town we in England would have looked on as impoverished were relatively affluent in comparison to the part of the town we had been taken to by the police.

By locating the general direction of the harbour I was able to work out where the square we had been arrested in was located and eventually found it. It was still alive with activity, bustling with nocturnal commerce. I had of course completely forgotten about Chris, the amorous American. From the moue he gave me as I walked up to the bar it was obvious he felt cuckolded by the rather masculine muscular police. After of-handedly greeting me, he returned his attention to the more compliant and faithful companion he had discovered after our departure, his arm draped over the back of his new love interest's chair. From their body language it was obvious their embryonic relationship was going to be consummated that night. With no clear plan in mind, and disinclined to go back to the ship until I had worked out how to find where Sam had been taken, I ordered another drink and settled down to chat to Chris and his new best friend. Alcohol clearly has an affect on the concept of time since I have no idea how long I was there or how many more drinks I had. It also has a significant impact on the concept of urgency as I sat pondering on a selection of useless solutions in my head. I do recollect the group around the table enlarging, conversation flowing with much laughter.

Suddenly, like a rabbit out of a hat, Sam was standing by our table, pulling back a chair and sitting down. A drink was hurried to him as he explained that he had been taken to another police station for questioning. He had the impression his answers were incomprehensible, which was hardly surprising given how much we had all drunk that evening, but he did have a clear recollection of needing to pee and asking if he could be shown to a toilet. The inquisitor had refused so Sam had stood up facing his desk and unzipped his trousers. As he reached for his peeing gadget the officer leapt around the table, grabbed him and pushed him out of the office and then into the street. Perhaps being loud, noisy, demanding and ultimately obnoxious was the way to deal with Mexican police, but hindsight taught me that was a high risk strategy. I somehow felt this was not the last time we would test this theory on this trip, and that perhaps we had been lucky that night.

As we enjoyed a few more drinks, Gordon and one-eyed Martin joined us and sat down at our table, ordering more drinks from the apprehensive looking waiter. They had heard about our little holiday in the police station from one of the crew who had been in the square at the time. They seemed to be pleased, if somewhat surprised, that we had been released so soon. Martin had somehow had a photograph of himself taken and developed during the evening, perhaps for some official papers he needed, and I thought how well it floated in the pool of alcohol on the table. I also thought how bored with proceedings his glass eye looked as it stared off centre, its interest caught by something in the corner of the room. It was about two thirty in the morning when we all decided to head back to the ship. We walked through the town to the harbour, arms around each other's shoulders, singing at the tops of our tuneless voices as we celebrated our escape. When we got to the ship, Martin realised he had left his important photograph at the bar, so he and I set off back to get it while Sam and Gordon both gave up the unequal struggle of staying upright and elected to go to bed. Although I was filled with good intentions to accompany Martin, by the end of the quay they had all dribbled away and I sat down on a huge iron mooring bollard embedded in the dockside. It was swathed in the mooring ropes of the M.V. Gela. Martin carried on and I sat watching the harbour lights dancing on the water, or perhaps my dancing eyes watched perfectly still lights on the calm water. Whichever it was, the outcome and affect were the same. I fell fast asleep sitting on the bollard and have no idea which branch of physics it was that kept me upright on it and prevented me from falling headfirst into the water. I only vaguely remember going to bed in my bunk, and stepping over Sam who was fast asleep on the floor outside our cabin.

Tang's cheerful "Ship, she not lolling today" in the morning as he put the cups of tea down with a clatter was not welcome. Groaning we struggled out of bed and went down to the dining room for breakfast. A number of the officers were already there looking a little second hand. Gordon was somewhat disgruntled as he had woken up face down on his bunk to find that someone had pushed something up his backside. It turned out Gordon had been found by Brian the wireless officer, naked and fast asleep on a chair with his face in the cabin's basin. Brian had heaved him onto his bunk, which is where he left him as he found his way to his own cabin. Martin, on getting back from the bar with his sodden photograph, saw Gordon naked and fast asleep on his front. He had felt it a good idea to take Gordon's temperature with his own toothbrush, bristles first. Distracted by something, he then forgot to remove it and left for his own bunk.

Not only did Gordon wake up to find a strange object up his bum, he also realised that there was a prostitute lying in his bed, patiently waiting for him to wake up. She offered him a special deal of 55 pesos for the rest of the night - £1.50 in 1970's money. It was a testament to his constitution that he accepted her offer, but he didn't seem to be able to remember whether he or she removed the toothbrush. I stared queasily at my unblinking fried egg lying on my plate as it nestled up against the bacon, and understood the rationale behind the legend of 'a girlfriend in every port' for merchant seamen, whilst taking some issue with their definition of 'girlfriend'. I also wondered whether Gordon's parents were fully aware of the range of subjects their son was going to be exposed to in his 'apprenticeship'. The hallucinogenic properties of Latin American alcohol, particularly of the home made variety which was so often to be found in the bars in poorer areas, was new to us.

Little did we know we would become reacquainted with similarly outrageous consequences.

"So, what happened to you two last night?" asked the Captain. He seemed unpleasantly healthy and refreshed from a good night's sleep.

"Well, there was a bit of local difficulty at a bar" I replied. "Some kid tried to rip us off and the police got involved." We proceeded to give him and the other officers around the table a rundown of our night on the town.

"Well, the first I knew of it", said Captain Simpson "was at two this morning when Steve came back and woke me to tell me you had been carted off but he had no idea where you were. I thought of sending out a search party but decided there was little point and that if you had not reappeared by Monday I would get in touch with the local Consul." I was relieved we had not been left to stew in the cell for the whole weekend.

Needless to say, in the cold light of a sober morning, we decided not to go back ashore until we had seen the Immigration authorities in the morning, and so spent the rest of the morning packing in the optimistic hope that we would get our visas. We went down into the closed hold to tend to Adolf and spent a couple of hours repacking her in preparation for unloading her the next day. She had survived the voyage intact and in perfect condition, her chains holding her down still tight. As we worked the sun climbed into the sky and the heat in the hold became intense, aggravating our already insufferable headaches. We went up to the bar and, again rather forgetting the instructions of the Immigration officers and our decision at breakfast to stay on board, we went ashore with Gordon, Martin and Steve and walked to the Hotel Vera Cruz which we heard had a swimming pool. We sat by it for the afternoon, sweating pure alcohol onto the sun beds, each swearing we would sign the pledge at the first opportunity, become monks and never visit another bar. I once worked with someone who had 'signed the pledge' as a teenager and for the first time I envied him his wisdom. The water in the pool cooled us at regular intervals as we sank gently into it.

Monday started with the clatter of teacups and saucers as Tang made his morning delivery. A bright Mexican sun shone through the open porthole, through which we could also hear the dock coming alive for the week's work ahead. We went to breakfast and then up on deck to see the hatch covers being lifted. We looked down on Adolf for the first time in daylight in over two weeks. She looked small and alone down in the shadows in the cavernous hold, but strangely reassuring. Our home on wheels. I stood looking at her and wondered if in 1969 the astronauts Neil Armstrong and Buzz Aldrin had gazed with similar endearment and trust on the Eagle, the Lunar landing module for their scheduled flight to the moon, as it sat parked in some hangar in Florida. Perhaps they too had wondered at the fragility of their proposed life support system, their temporary home. I was reassured that our chances of getting home were probably better than theirs had been. Gazing down on Adolf engendered a sense of affection for her. She contained everything we possessed and would need on the journey ahead of us, and in some ways came to define us.

The ship's agent came on board and told us Adolf was going to be unloaded and put on the quay, but we could not move her until we had clearance from Immigration and had our visas. He felt there was a good chance we would get them that morning. At about half past nine he took us to the Immigration offices where, without any fuss, arguments or bribes, our Passports were returned to us and thirty day visas were issued. Since we were going to go north to the border immediately the fact they would only grant us thirty days did not matter. We could argue for a longer stay if we needed the time when we came back south again, which we expected to be in a couple of months time.

Having got our Passports back, and with a sense of entitlement to be in Mexico officially at last, we headed back to the quay and the Gela where we collected the rest of our belongings from our cabin and said our farewells to the crew and Captain. The Gela had become remarkably familiar and comfortable over the two weeks we had been on her and it was sad to say goodbye. Over the following months I said goodbye a lot, and learned that for every goodbye there is a hello, a new face and a new relationship, and thus to look forward to the new and let the old lie in the past where I could do little about it. Travelling light emotionally unburdened my mind, leaving plenty of space for me to really miss those who mattered most. My mind turned to Greece, to a small village in the north of Corfu and a shimmering beach and I wondered if the whole caper would prove to be a gamble too far, one roll of the dice too many. Any relationship can have elasticity and tolerance, but in the end they all have limits. It was too late for changes of mind, the future would take care of itself. For now we needed to concentrate on getting Adolf safely out of the docks.

Sam and I went down onto the quay to watch the unloading. The dock cranes were lifting the cargo out of the ship's holds. Crates of cognac, huge steel tunnel sections and other unidentifiable packing cases. Suddenly Adolf emerged on the end of an extremely fragile looking wire, dangling far below the jib of a crane and high above the ship. Slowly she swung out above us, hovering precariously in the air before being lowered gently to the ground in front of us. We breathed a sigh of relief as her wheels settled on the quay and the webbing straps slung beneath and around her were released. We got in and turned the engine on. Faithfully she fired up immediately and we drove her to a safe spot against the warehouse wall where we could keep an eye on her until we were cleared by Customs.

We sat by Adolf for three hours before two uniformed Customs officers appeared at the end of the quay and ambled over to us. The pattern that had begun to appear with European Customs was repeated as the officers said they wanted to search us for drugs, adding weight to my growing belief that we were going to be a bit of a target on this trip. Adolf was sitting in full sunshine on the quay and with the sun at its zenith it felt as though we could roast a turkey in minutes inside her. We were told to open the built in wooden boxes on the floor in the back. They were packed with spares for Adolf, tools to service her. Also there were some clothes, toiletries, medicines and the general stuff of life for us. Each box had its own lid and all the boxes were locked down by three leaves from suspension springs. They were bent flat across the lids and locked to the floor at each end. It was impossible to get a fingernail under the springs once they had been flattened down and the only way to get into the boxes would be to take an axe to the lids. Anyone managing to saw through the locks would get the benefit of a spring in their face as it leapt back to its original curved shape. Once locked down, the whole of the back was covered in a foam mattress, four inches thick. This was our bed.

For two and a half hours the two officers went through every box and possession. Sweat poured off their faces as they took it in turns to sit inside the vehicle. We refused to allow them to be in it by themselves as we did not trust them not to steal, so they could only be inside one at a time as Sam and I took it in turns to be inside the sauna with them. Hunched in the back, I was watching one of the officers as he rummaged through our possessions and suddenly realised we had a potential problem as he picked up our medicine box. Since the officers' stated aim was to look for drugs, I wondered what he would make of the syringes and ampules of morphine we had in the box. I had completely forgotten about them until the box appeared in his hand. We had somehow managed to persuade someone to give us the morphine in the UK, to be used in dire necessity. I was not convinced I could explain this to a Customs officer who would either be looking for a large bribe, one commensurate with turning a blind eye to a controlled drug, or a significant bonus and promotion back at base for having busted a couple of drug runners.

It was time for the magician's sleight of hand. If it is outrageous enough the onlooker doesn't believe his eyes, or perhaps sees what he expects to see. As the officer turned the box over in his hands, I reached across and took it from him, signaling I would help him to open it. I took the lid off and reached in to pick up all the syringes and ampules whilst talking to him, looking him straight in the eye to hold his attention. Hiding the offending items in my right hand, I handed back the opened box for him to inspect. He rummaged through paracetamol sachets, water treatment tablets, potions for turning bowel contents to concrete and anti-malarial tablets, all padded out with bandages, scissors and the other details one would expect to find in a basic medical kit. Satisfied, he gave me back the box and turned his attention to the next item as I put the syringes and drugs back in. I secured the lid and put the box behind me out of sight. There was a large box of multi-vitamin tablets which he opened. He took one out and put it into his mouth, biting down on it to test its contents, still convinced he had a couple of drug cartel mules in his sights. The expression on his face convinced him he wished he hadn't done that since they were designed to be swallowed whole and un-chewed.

The next item he found was a box of a gross of condoms, given to us as a leaving present by one of our flatmates. A prodigiously copious copulator, the standard pack of three had proved to be woefully inadequate for

72

his enthusiasm for the sport and for his rate of consumption and somehow he had found a distributor who could supply them on a regimental scale, perhaps more usually to the Ministry of Defence for distribution to the troops. Mexico was then a very Catholic country in all senses of the word and it occurred to me the realisation by the officer of what the little sachets contained, or more accurately their prophylactic purpose, might cause us some problems. The officer insisted I open one of the sachets and when I did, it was obvious he had never seen one before as he asked for an explanation. I got him to get out of Adolf and I took him around to the front where I opened the bonnet and pointed at the spark plugs, explaining the objects were waterproof covers to be used if we went into rivers or deep water. He seemed satisfied with my explanation and we returned to the furnace in the back to continue the search.

Eventually they said we were cleared to go, somewhat dejectedly since neither the bribe nor promotion were going to happen. It took us about half an hour to repack all our scattered belongings that were basking on the quay, and in the middle of the afternoon we finally left the harbour and drove into the town. Needless to say, we didn't recognise a day-lit and sober Vera Cruz from the darkened drunken town we had been in a couple of evenings before. We turned north and headed out on the Carretera Federal 180, the main coastal road north. We were conscious that it was extremely dangerous to drive in Mexico at night, an often repeated instruction at the Mexican Embassy in London and in the Latin American traveler's bible, the South American Handbook. With the semi tropical sun dropping fast, we needed to get on and try to find somewhere to park up for the night.

 We drove on north through small villages and towns, through Tierra Colorado and Cardel. Near Santa Ana the road came down by the sea and we stopped and swam in the warm water, ignoring the protestations of some young boys who demanded we pay 10 pesos to use the beach. It seemed to have escaped their notice that the beach was about one hundred miles long and completely empty. I was beginning to realise that the national pastime in Mexico was squeezing a penny or two out of the unsuspecting, and the Mexicans would happily spend all day relentlessly pestering if they thought there was the slightest chance of success. I admired their optimism. The swim was a wonderful opportunity to wash off the dust of the road. As I floated in the waters of the Gulf of Mexico I felt a sense of liberation from the constraints of what had been a normal life, with its relentless cycle of work. That was now a past life, a different time. Life had become a blank sheet of paper and it was up to us what we wrote on it.

 It was getting dark and so we set off again, still heading north. The town and village names we passed through spoke of dignitaries and local barons. Important men with names like Emilio Carranza and Vega de Alatorre. Presumably the towns had been named after pillars of these communities, men now only known through their names and the memory of their deeds. I had visions of land owners riding their estates under large sombreros, bushy moustaches drooping in parenthesis either side of their mouths, owners of all they could see, imperious and haughty from that sense of ownership and entitlement some of the rich develop. We passed through a small unlit village called Nautla and in the dark mistakenly took the wrong road, heading we knew not where. We pulled off the track into some trees and settled down for the night, tired and hungry.

The early dawn revealed we were parked in an orange grove. We had driven quite deep into it to be invisible from the road. The dawn light filtered through the trees and the air was filled with bird calls as territories were marked. Looking carefully at the map in daylight we could work out where we were. After Nautla, the main road left the coast and headed inland to Tuxpan, but we could see a side road that cut the angle, the shorter side of a large triangle. We decided that taking it would save us a lot of mileage and time, with the added advantage of getting off the main roads and away from the lunatic Mexican drivers.

In the very short time we had been on the road we were beginning to understand all the warnings we had been given about the local driving. Unsighted overtaking was clearly an outward expression of Machismo Mexican Man and only the effeminate and effete didn't do it. The blinder the hill, the sharper the bend, the more masculine the driver proved himself to be as he swung out into the path of whatever unseen vehicle might be coming the other way. Russian roulette requires a gun with a largely empty chamber. Mexican roulette requires a car and a driver with a completely empty head and perhaps an empty tequila bottle rattling on the floor at his feet. There were a lot of empty heads and a lot of empty tequila bottles rattling away in Mexico in the early 1970's.

To avoid some of this mayhem we took the side road. It was marked on the map as a 'Carretera Grave', a bad road. We felt calling it a road was generous and bad an understatement, indicating a blind or very drunk cartographer had surveyed this particular section. Cutting through beautiful green forest it looked no more than some sort of logging track that huge vehicles had used, rutting the dirt and creating puddles like small ponds. The track was strewn with boulders and where it was not wet, the thick dust was thrown up and came into the vehicle in heavy clouds, swirling around our heads. Where the road was not rutted we were able to pick up some speed, ever watchful for seemingly bottomless holes in the path ahead.

On one of the clearer sections, we could see a large white cloud on the road ahead, spreading across the road and into the forest on either side. As we got to it and drove into it we realised it was a huge herd of butterflies. Countless millions of them. Orange and yellow wings fluttering, it was like driving in a blizzard, almost unsighting us. We realised we had driven into part of the great Monarch butterfly migration where the indomitable little insects move up and down between the northern and southern States of America in vast numbers with the changing seasons, some crossing over into Mexico. After driving through them for a few minutes we noticed Adolf was overheating so we stopped. Going around to the front to lift the bonnet to see what was wrong, the problem immediately became obvious. The wire grill covering the radiator was completely and thickly covered in butterflies, blocking any cooling air getting to the radiator. We scraped the dead butterflies off and carried on. We had to repeat the process a number more times before we eventually emerged from the other side of the swarm, many miles down the road.

By now the sun was quite high and the temperature soaring. Ahead in the road was a large black object. As we approached it, it became clear it was a dead cat, bloated in the heat. Clearly a cat in flatulent extremis.

"I wonder if it'll make a bang if we hit it?" I said.

"Let's give it a go" said Sam, who was driving.

Now, I have made one or two mistakes in my life, I will admit, but not many are quite as stupid as suggesting driving over a fully inflated and substantially dead Mexican cat lying prostrate in a dirt road in a forest, basking in the blazing sunshine. The bang was pretty spectacular, like an indoor firework going off. At first I felt vindicated. Unfortunately, whilst the bang was exceptional, so was the smell. We now had hot, deflated, decayed and largely liquid cat spread like a sticky toffee sauce around the inside of the wheel arch, all over Adolf's underside and in the engine compartment. It was over 30°C in the shade. Unfortunately neither we nor the cat were in the shade. Nothing in life prepares you for the smell of inside-out cat in the engine, simmering on the exhaust manifold and grilling under the engine block. The open latrines in a Calcutta slum are honey and nectar in comparison. An irritated skunk's ejaculating scent gland thrust under our noses as a pomander would have been a relief.

We soldiered on north, eyes watering copiously. It was becoming apparent to us that there were two types of road in Mexico. Fairly good tarmac or appalling dirt. The ones we had been on were also generally all straight for miles, like Roman roads. The dirt road we were following degenerated further, the ruts becoming canyons and the boulders mountains, all of which gave Adolf the opportunity to show us what she was capable of. Land Rovers really are the most amazing vehicles. Robust, strong and versatile, they inspire confidence and at times a sense of invincibility in the face of what to the rational mind are insurmountable obstacles. Having had 'Eau de Chat' dabbed behind her ears, Adolf hitched up her skirts and tackled the road with relish. Our full harness seat belts went on tightly to hold us into our seats as we bucked and heaved our way forwards towards the American border. The vehicle filled with thick dust which covered every surface and every object, our hair soon acquiring the texture of doormats.

Later in the day we swam in the warm sea again to wash the dust off. This time we found a completely deserted and beautifully sandy beach. It was an earthly idyll, palm trees rustling their stiff fronds in a breeze coming off the sea, tentative crabs pottering about and the sound of the waves lapping the shore. We passed through small villages, and at times came across isolated huts in the forest. There was obviously great poverty and many of the huts were made of cardboard and other detritus the people had managed to scavenge, with roofs made of banana leaves.

Night fell quickly and in our headlights we saw huge land crabs crossing the road in front of us. Because of the state of the road we were driving slowly enough to be able to avoid running over most of them. An occasional crunch indicated one that had not been fleet of claw enough to get out of the way. We were finding the dirt roads were a veritable safari of wildlife. All through the day we had driven past huge, dark tarantulas that were crossing, taking their lives in their eight hands. At one point we got out and put our bare feet in the dirt next to them to photograph them, our feet intended to give their relative size. Armadillos occasionally ambled out of the undergrowth to cross the road. Passing isolated huts or hamlets young boys would emerge holding large fat iguanas by the tail for our cooking pot. Most unwelcome of all were the mosquitos that descended on us in legions that night. We parked on a dirt track as they arrived, too late to shut them out of the mosquito net that we had dropped down from the roof. Slapping ourselves and spraying the vehicle with what seemed to be Agent Orange, we slept a hot, itchy, buzzing and uncomfortable night.

We set off at quarter past five in the morning, before the sun came over the horizon, hotly pursued by those mosquitos that had been at the back of the crowd queueing patiently in line for their turn to find a space on our bodies, and which therefore had not yet fed. Having not had the time or inclination to linger over breakfast, we stopped at a scruffy and very basic cafe by the road in a little village. It was mid morning and we ordered a coffee to go with the cheapest item on the menu, which appeared to be some sort of meat dish. Now there is fresh meat, mature meat, bad meat and, bringing up the rear, meat that needs shaving. Ours was particularly hirsute, sporting a fine down of fungal growth, like a teenager about to have his first shave.

The cafe owner plonked the dish on our table together with a plate of sliced tomatoes that was covered in dozens of feasting flies. The fungal fronds on the meat waved gently in the breeze like seaweed moving in the incoming tide. We found that by waving our hand low over the plate, the flies would take off in unison, allowing us to grab a fly-free tomato before the foraging hoard descended back onto their interrupted meal. I wondered if the contents of my plate smelt worse than Adolf, who was standing in solitary confinement and quarantine, banished to the dirt street outside the cafe. My brother was a jackaroo in the outback of Australia. On his station a fence rider had died out in the bush and not been found for a couple of weeks. At his funeral in the little local church his coffin was left outside because the smell from it was so bad. Adolf was in a similar state of exile.

By the time I had finished the meal it was quite clear I had eaten our cat's brother, which must have died a day before ours and thus had spent more time sunbathing. If this was the standard of catering we were going to encounter south of the US border, our alimentary systems were going to be tested to destruction. It was however a seminal meal. Faced with it in all its horrors, each plate a cess pit of unidentifiable mess, a Bacteria

Ragout, we took the decision that if we were going to develop any form of immunity to the culinary challenges ahead of us, we had to eat everything and anything. We included not purifying our drinking water in our resolve. The decision not to interfere with the water was a relief to me as the purifying tablets had a disgusting flavour, in my view outweighing any benefits they might bring.

As we worked our way through the meal we studied the map and decided to push for the American border in one long run, to cross some time that day. It was a long way, some of it on bad roads, but our new freedom allowed us to make arbitrary decisions without impacting on other lives, not a luxury many of us have back in the real world of work and play. We left the village with the heat building quickly and started the long drive to Matamoros. After a couple of hours on the road we came upon a mountain stream tumbling down a steep slope. It was an irresistible temptation in the heat of the day so we stopped, stripped off and washed and lay in it's cool, fresh waters, each probably ridding ourselves of five pounds of dust. A few yards down the road from the stream was a young boy selling fresh mangos from the shelter of a grass roofed makeshift hut. We bought some, carefully checking our change.

Refreshed by our al fresco bath, we pressed on and at Tampico came to a stretch of water separating the Vera Cruz District from the Tamaulipas District on the north shore. We could see Tampico on the other side but there was no bridge, only an oversized colander that the Mexicans had press ganged into acting as a ferry. Rusting, leaking, listing and overloaded, it took a leap of faith to drive Adolf slowly down onto it. The vessel sank further into the water when we drove onto its rotting deck. As we had to park on one side of it, there being no room anywhere else, the angle of its list increased. Just behind us there was enough room to fit a couple of wafer thin after dinner mints. The Mexican crew interpreted this as acres of opportunity, so we waited for a couple more vehicles, assorted bicycles and a dozen or so passengers to settle snugly into the space around us. As the motley crew cast off for the other shore, the ferry engines struggled against the stream which was pushing us out towards the Gulf to our east. The antediluvian vessel, possibly the blueprint for the Ark, valiantly refused to give in to whatever mechanical angina was afflicting it, and finally we docked on the Tampico side where we joined the manic rush for dry land. I noticed one or two passengers joining the vessel's captain in making signs of the cross on themselves in silent thanksgiving.

Relieved and perhaps just a little surprised to be alive and not playing submarines, we drove through an unremarkable Tampico and headed north yet again, determined to make the border that night, still over three hundred miles away at Matamoros. We continued to follow the coast road through Soto la Marina and San Fernando, finally reaching Matamoros at eight o'clock in the evening. Another fly-blown Mexican town intersected with dirt streets, there were lines of trucks in both directions, open bars and dimly lit streets patrolled by grubby looking prostitutes. Their murderous looking pimps lounged in doorways and on window sills, smoking cigarettes and watching their stock as it plied its trade. It was a facsimile of Vera Cruz, and perhaps of every Mexican town.

The only food of any significance we had eaten since we had left the M.V. Gela in Vera Cruz had been the small plate of slurry we had had that morning, so we pulled up outside one of the bars and went in to order a slightly more substantial meal. The capacity of our stomachs was still geared to the large meals we had eaten on the ship and it would be some time before they got used to our reduced food intake as we saved money by enforced dieting.

The bar was lit by a couple of naked low wattage bulbs hanging from the stained ceiling. They were yellowed from cigarette smoke and covered by flies surveying the tables below like vultures in a tree above a kill. Bare formica tables and hard, metal framed chairs filled the room. Down the length of one side was a filthy bar against which a few Mexican men leant, nursing their drinks. We sat down at an empty table and ordered our meal under the watchful and inquisitive gaze of the clientele. Enchiladas we would have crossed the road to avoid in London now tasted like fancies from an award winning delicatessen.

We ate our meal quickly, washing it down with glasses of murky water that looked as though it had been collected from the churned river in the wake of the ferry we had been on earlier. Settling the very cheap bill, we hopped back into Adolf and headed for the border post on the northern outskirts of the town. Perhaps because they may have been at the end of their shift, or just bone idle, the Mexican Customs and Immigration were distinctly disinterested in spending any time on ushering us through. We gratefully drove into the No Man's land between the border posts, leaving behind the darkened streets of Matamoros for the brightly lit US Border. We bumped up onto tarmac as we went over the half way point, our first hint that civilisation lay ahead.

America, the land of the free awaited us, arms out in fulsome welcome.

Or so we thought.

Adolf in the hold waiting to be unloaded - Vera Cruz, Mexico.

Adolf being unloaded at Vera Cruz, Mexico.

A GIRL CALLED ADOLF

CHAPTER 4

America - 1972

"I don't know who my grandfather was; I am much more concerned to know what his grandson will be."

Abraham Lincoln

    I'm not sure when America first came into my consciousness. Of course, we all knew it was there on the other side of all that water, that in some small way we had helped it win the last war, but it was a long way away across the Atlantic. I suppose for the youth of England its influence was felt more through its cinematographic and musical output. The history taught when we were at school focused on the Tudors or Europe, not on America.

    Charlie Chaplin and his contemporaries made us laugh. Errol Flynn flew through the air and the bedsheets. Scarlett swooned for the reluctant Ashley, and then good old Rhett appeared on the scene while Atlanta and Georgia burned. Hollywood glamour overtook the entertainment world and we saw America through its eyes, through its Prohibition and the violent turf wars of the mafiosi, where the contents of violin cases played a harsher tune than Stradivarius could ever conjure from the exquisite product of his craft.

Elvis Presley shook the establishment in the late 1950's through his music and oscillating pelvic contortions that an older generation interpreted as a vertical expression of a horizontal desire. His mesmerising music crossed racial barriers, challenging the legally sanctioned apartheid that existed at that time. Few people in Britain seemed to know about the segregation of the races in America, a dark chapter in its history. His explosion onto the music scene coincided with Rosa Parks' historic and unimaginable courage in refusing to give up her seat on a bus in Alabama in 1955. Perhaps by blending gospel and southern blues music that had previously only been heard in African American communities with rockabilly and rhythm and blues, Elvis laid the foundations of the platform Martin Luther King felt was firm enough for him to stand on and at a rally in Washington to declaim to a restive Nation, '*I have a Dream*'. I remember the power of those words, spoken in 1963, and I remember his assassination five years later.

I think my first conscious memories or realisation of America came at the time of the Cuban missile crisis when President Kennedy put down his latest daily paramour long enough to stand up to the nuclear sabre rattling of the Russians. The blustering, shoe banging President Khrushchev would have been amusing if he had not had the power to unleash Armageddon on the world. The man who said *"The more bombers, the less room for doves"* kept the world quaking in fear. President Kennedy's assassination brought America into sharp focus, transcending its film and musical culture so ingrained in our minds, uniting the world in a collective grief.

But what of the ordinary American? Is there such a thing as ordinary, or are we all each in our own way eccentric and unique, a few degrees off the normal? A rhetorical question of course, as indeed we are individuals, but there is a mean average and I had no idea how that related to Americans, no benchmark against which to measure one. Apart from an American school friend and his family, who were definitely not representative of an average, the only one I had ever met was in a Mexican port and seemed to have a permanent erection off which you could hang the Stars and Stripes. He was no doubt still in Vera Cruz taking his libido for a mincing walk past the bars, cruising before it became fashionable and respectable in its new guise on a ship in the Caribbean. Was he normal? For an American? If so, a couple of days to see the place would be more than enough for me.

I had no idea just how far the other side of heterosexual some of the Southern gentlemen we were to encounter were. The first five of them were waiting to greet us in the Customs office in Brownsville, the Texan Siamese twin of Matamoros, inseparably attached by the umbilicus of short road connecting the two towns. I had no concept of prejudice, of bigotry, of unreasoning hatred. In my naivety I had never heard of, let alone met, a hick, a redneck, a grit, a white sock. These definitions all distill down to the same thing, the embodiment of fundamentalist bigotry, three galaxies away from my eclectic, colour blind, egalitarian upbringing, both at home and in my schooling. Unknown to us as we happily approached the US border, hostile bigotry lay in wait for us in the form of the U S Customs and Immigration Department, or rather its representatives who were idling away the quiet night shift whilst guarding the portals to the Lone Star State on that late Spring night. I learned later that the name Texas was said to have been derived from an old language used in Oklahoma, and meant 'Friend'. That night it was a misnomer.

We arrived at the US Customs post in the dark at about nine o'clock. We first went to Immigration where we collected our visas, electing for six month permits. We returned to Adolf and drove on to the Customs section which was further towards the barrier blocking the road ahead. Because it was night the border crossing was quiet and there was only one other vehicle there, an American car whose occupants seemed to have popped over the border for a meal and were on their way home. They were obviously known to the Customs officers, with good old boy banter going on as we sat behind them awaiting our turn for some friendly banter of our own. The officers showed not the slightest indication that they were either aware we were waiting, or cared if we were, despite the fact we were only six feet behind the car in front. The cozy chat continued, and we sat and waited in the harsh glare of the border lights.

Finally the car ahead was waved through and we drove forward to take their place. The Customs officer approached us with a parade ground swagger. His head was shaved from the top of the ears down leaving a doily of closely grazed hair on the top of his skull, like a bowling green after a flock of hungry sheep have cropped the blades of grass to the soil. We got out of the vehicle, our faces wreathed in smiles of greeting, not quite mirroring his stony glare as he took in two dirty, unsanitary and unshaven travellers and their filthy and alien looking vehicle. As he got close to us he visibly blanched, beads of sweat breaking out instantly on his upper lip. Obviously he had never smelt dead cat before.

"Where you boys all from?" he said, unsmiling.

Something in us screamed this was not the time to be a smart arse, some instinct that told us that we were talking to the missing link, that bridge between a late model Neanderthal struggling to cope with upright ambulation and an upgraded and fully erect hominid. I resisted the temptation to point at Mexico and state the obvious, "From over there".

"From England" Sam replied.

"Where's that?" said the officer.

"Er, Europe." said Sam, a look of incredulity on his face. I stared up at the ceiling of the large, open sided

Customs shelter we were parked under, trying not to laugh.

"I thought you said England boy" replied the officer, his brow furrowed in displeasure. He gave the sense of someone who thought they were being messed with. The temptation had to be resisted.

"Well, yes, we do come from England," explained Sam "but it is sort of part of Europe. Like Texas is part of America."

"So how come y'all've come from Mexico when y'all say you're from this England?" he said. He was struggling. So was I as I continued to study the ceiling and look anywhere but at him, longing for a man sized handkerchief, a couple of socks and a shirt to stuff into my mouth. I was wondering if I could fit our mattress in as well and didn't dare catch Sam's eye.

"Well, our boat landed at Vera Cruz and then we drove up here" said Sam patiently. He avoided my eye.

"Boat?" said the officer. "Y'all mean you didn't drive here from this England?"

We were speechless. It was becoming hard to take this conversation seriously, and certainly not as seriously as the officer obviously took himself. We said nothing, and just stared.

"What y'all got in this truck?" the officer said, waving his arm at Adolf as she stood patiently in the harsh light.

We explained the bare details of our plans, to drive in America on a long road trip, to go south into Central America and then on to South America. We explained we had all our supplies and possessions with us in the vehicle.

"What d'y'all want all that water for?" he said, pointing at the jerry cans on the side of Adolf. We had painted the water cans white with large blue writing identifying their contents. The petrol and cans were blue, but also marked.

"For drinking" we said in unison.

"You being funny with me boy?" he said, clearly now convinced we were toying with him but not sure how.

He didn't wait for a reply but told us to pull Adolf over to one side next to some long trestle tables and to wait for him there. He disappeared into the Customs building and a short while later returned with four similarly gifted colleagues who turned out to be equally eloquent. One of the newcomers soon revealed himself to be in charge of this power-crazed quintet. He walked around Adolf looking at her and then turned to us.

"Empty it out" he said, pointing at the trestle tables. "Let's see what you boys got in here".

And so, we did. The Customs officers stood back and watched as we took out every item in the vehicle and laid it on the trestle tables, completely covering two of them. Because it was late at night, no one else seemed to be crossing the border from the Mexican side and clearly the officers had nothing better to do than indulge their curiosity and suspicions about us. They had the air of people who just knew they were going to find illicit goods, most probably of the hallucinogenic variety. We must have appeared as drug addicted hippies to them, good for nothing and needing to be taught a lesson. Their every fibre seemed to be itching for a confrontation.

Having taken all our possessions out and laid them on the tables, it was patently clear the officers did not want us involved in their search so we sat down on two chairs close to the tables and watched them. For four hours, the five of them went through every piece of clothing, feeling sewn seams and collars on shirts, through every box and container, flicking through the pages of books. And yet, they missed the morphine ampules and the syringes. America's most gifted hard at work. When they had finished with the vehicle's contents, they started to examine Adolf herself. They looked in the wheel arches and underneath her, blanching at the stench from Adolf's armpits. They tapped her steel chassis and generally kicked the tyres. I noticed one of them sweeping the dust off the floor of the passenger side and tasting it with a dampened finger, obviously testing for marijuana ash. I wondered if his constitution could cope with liquid cat, and if not whether we would still be at the border when he found out it couldn't. I wouldn't have wanted to be in between him and the lavatory when the jus of feline bacilli hit his intestines.

The aggressively unfriendly head of this merry little band lifted Adolf's bonnet and looked into the engine compartment.

"I think we should take the engine out" he said.

Sam and I looked at each other, aghast. We were going to be stuck at the border for a week if this bone head had his way, but common sense told us to sit tight and say nothing. A discussion broke out, each gorilla contributing to the discussion about a little bit of engine dismantling. It was quickly apparent the other four did not have the stomach for this and were more inclined to go in for a cup of coffee. Perhaps hitting that cat had been a good idea after all and their constitutions were wilting under the assault. Faced with their obdurate and sullen intransigence, the man in charge reluctantly turned to us.

"OK, y'all can go" he said.

To a man, they all turned on their heels and trooped back into the Customs offices, leaving us to repack Adolf. This took some time as every item had a place allocated to it in the vehicle, making things easier for us to find. It was long past one o'clock in the morning before we finished and were able to get in and drive up to the barrier. It was lifted for us and we drove into America. The day had started with a swarm of mosquitos and ended with a swarm of ignorance. We were exhausted.

About a quarter of a mile up the road was a Motel. We pulled into its car park, parked in a quiet corner that was empty of cars and settled down in Adolf for the night. Sleep came quickly.

We woke early as dawn broke and drove down to the road to get some petrol at a garage in Brownsville. We noticed the garage had free maps of the State and local area so we took one, grateful to the petrol company for their thoughtfulness to the traveller. This was a feature of all the garages we used throughout America. They offered free maps as marketing publicity by the petrol companies, which were conducting a continuous 'Gas War' as they competed aggressively with each other on price and services. Brownsville was a small town with a wide main street through the middle of it, lined by cars parked at an angle facing the shops. A cafe was open for the early birds and so we pulled in for a cup of coffee and took a pair of high stools at the counter, next to an enormous Texan who sat with his elbows on the bar, his large stetson pulled down over his eyes. I noticed his seat only supported about twenty percent of his capacious backside. The surplus, two waterfalls of buttocks, hung down all around it like flesh curtains. His stomach lay quietly and contentedly on his thighs like a lapdog. I picked up the menu and studied it carefully, as if I was studying Greek writing for the first time. A lot of the items on the menu were unrecognisable to us as meals, and certainly this was our first introduction to a short or long stack for breakfast. I asked the waitress what a short stack was and she explained it was six pancakes, piled one on top of each other to make the stack. I asked her what a long stack was and she told me twelve pancakes.

Twelve. For breakfast. The waitress pointed at the Texan's plate and said that was a long stack. It looked like a culinary Empire State building to me.

    The pancakes I was used to were delicate, gossamer thin affairs that came with fresh lemon juice and perhaps a light dusting of caster sugar. American pancakes were a different affair altogether. Smaller in diameter and much thicker, each one seemed to me to be a meal in itself. Six of them, one on top of the other with a monsoon of maple syrup poured over them, was a banquet. Twelve was going to need stepladders. I decided to try the short, and as I waited for them to arrive, studied my neighbour's methodology. It seemed the way to eat the mountain of pancakes was to pour the syrup on so they looked like a duck island in a pond of golden liquid, and then to cut down through them like wedges in a pie chart, as though cutting a cake. Every now and then my neighbour would pour more syrup on as the pancakes slowly soaked up the puddle they sat in. My wobbling short stack arrived and I manfully tackled it, taking my lead from the obese cowboy next to me. I was quickly aware I was unable to keep up with him in either the speed or quantity categories of breakfast consumption. Coffee arrived in a continuous stream, another departure from the English habit of selling you each cup anew.

    Full of breakfast and coffee, we left the cafe under the close scrutiny of its customers and set off in Adolf. Leaving Brownsville behind, the road took us through Harlingen, still heading north on Route 77, and then on out into the vast, flat, treeless expanse of Texas with its endless horizons. Not an ideal spot for agoraphobics.

There was only one main road with small roads leading off east and west through the vast fields, all seemingly at a uniform ninety degrees. Our first sight of America's sensible penchant for a grid system of road layout. Whilst resulting in a boring and uniformly featureless environment, the layout is logical and allows the visitor to know exactly where they are in a town or city. The Texan roads were completely straight, disappearing into the distance without a bend or deviation. The three hundred and sixty degree view was reminiscent to me of so many Hollywood films, where the landscape is featureless, the hero stands at the open door of his car at a dusty crossroad, an elbow on the roof whilst deciding which way to turn and the only sound the whistling wind as it blows dust devils and tumbleweed, like a boy kicking a can along the road.

Before leaving England we had fitted Adolf with a piece of antediluvian technology, a mechanical cruise control. It worked by moving a lever connected to the throttle cable along a half moon shaped and toothed bar, locking it in place at the desired point when the required speed had been achieved. There was no override, and putting a foot on the brake pedal had no effect other than warming up the brake drums. The only way of disengaging the control was to grab the handle and push it to the extreme left reducing the flow of fuel in the same way as taking your foot off the accelerator. In the twenty first century it would be illegal, and in truth it should have been then, but for those long, mind-numbing and empty straights of road it was a blessing. The leafy, tree-canopied lanes of Surrey were a different world and experience in every way.

We drove all morning, and as the heat built up, stopped to take off the windows and tops of the doors to get some air into the car. We engaged cruise control, sat sideways in our seats and hung our feet and legs out of the car, taking it in turn to steer without changing seats. It seemed very odd to me, in that heat, that every car we saw had all its windows closed. We British hadn't come across air conditioning in buildings, let alone cars, and at first we thought all Americans must be immune to the stifling heat. It finally dawned on us that perhaps they had this comfort thing worked out. We sweated on as we passed the very few daisy fresh Americans we saw that morning. Some time after mid-day we reached Corpus Christi, a large city on the Gulf coast that looked out onto Corpus Christi Bay. We crossed over onto Padre Island, part of a near 200 mile long spit that curved almost without interruption around the Gulf coast from Brownsville to Galveston. We drove out onto the Island and set up camp for the afternoon and night. For us setting up camp meant parking Adolf. The white sand, warm sea and glorious blue sky were irresistible and we spent the afternoon sunbathing and swimming on a largely empty beach.

Late in the afternoon, as the sun lost its heat and started to dip down onto the land, we collected some wood from the sand dunes and built a fire on which we were going to cook our supper. As the fire crackled into life, flames dancing in the evening glow of the fading sun, three people came up to us in that friendly way of all Americans and started to chat to us. John, Karin and Karin's cousin Brenda settled down with us in the sand

and we chatted for a couple of hours by the fire, cooking food on it that we shared with them. In turn they gave us a can of Dr Pepper's, which we had never heard of but enjoyed. They were from Gage in Oklahoma, where they were teachers, and were driving down to Mexico for a holiday. Sam and I were astounded when Brenda admitted she had only ever been on a train twice in her life, and both times that had been in Germany. Trains are so much a part of European travel, an integral part of our landscape, and we assumed the same would be the case in America. I held a romantic vision of hobos travelling the land, their legs dangling free out of the sliding doors of the freight carriages, hopping on and off whilst covering great distances across prairies and mountains to the comforting clatter of the wheels relentlessly turning on the tracks. My main exposure to trains during the months ahead was to be the rare haunting sound of a train horn at night as a freight train went through a town or came to a crossing where we were invariably held by a red light.

John, Karin and Brenda invited us back to the apartment they had rented for the night in Corpus Christi. Another surprise for us and our first introduction to the astounding hospitality of the many Americans we were to meet on our journey through their vast and enormously diverse country. We packed up and followed them into the outskirts of the city. The apartment was large and comfortable and had a spare bedroom they said we could use. They also invited us to use the shower. To this day I have no idea whether that was for their benefit or ours, but whichever it was, for me it was the epitome of luxury. The sheer pleasure of standing under a stream of hot water was indescribable. I was probably ankle deep in dust and dirt in the shower tray but that felt unimportant and the waste plug seemed able to cope with the top six inches of Mexico that was flowing down off me.

After my shower I joined the others as they watched the World Heavyweight Championship fight between Joe Frazier and Ron Stander. Frazier was at his most clinically brutal and the doctor stopped the bout after four rounds, sending the indomitable Stander to hospital to collect his prize of 32 stitches, his memento of the night. He was in truth facing insurmountable odds when he stepped into the ring to face an unbeaten World Champion with twenty four knock outs to his credit. Whilst he was comprehensively dismantled by Frazier, Stander's courage could not be questioned as he refused to go down, marching relentlessly forward into a blizzard of punches that would have felled an ox. He took it all with the courage of the fearless who at times need to be saved from themselves.

When the fight finished John suggested we go out for a pizza. He said they could show us some of the sights of Corpus Christi after we had eaten. We all fitted easily into their huge American car with its bench front seat. We used to have bench seats in older cars in England, and they were always known as passion wagons, there being no obstacles for amorous couples to have to vault over to get at each other. With the modern celebrity penchant for naming children after cities they were conceived in, I wonder if there are any people called Buick, Oldsmobile, Jeep or Hummer struggling to explain their history. I have met some who should have been christened Walmart. We cruised down a busy and wide street until we came to a pizza restaurant. Parking outside we entered the restaurant and squeezed into a booth. As a large pitcher of beer arrived on the table with the menus I remembered we had already eaten on the beach, but an extra meal seemed to be the American way so I didn't complain. Weight loss was not high on my agenda. Our pizzas demolished, we set off for the much vaunted sights, except there didn't seem to be too many, the highlight apparently being a three hundred and eighty five foot high, two mile long bridge over the Bay. I was glad to get back to the flat just after midnight to collapse into bed.

    The room that Sam and I had been allocated only had a double bed and so we continued our Adolf habit of sleeping head to toe, not waking up until after nine o'clock the next morning. We had a breakfast of what appeared to be styrofoam bread and fake jam and then set off as the others also left. They were going west and then south to Mexico whilst we heading towards Houston, two hundred and twenty miles away. It was slowly dawning on us how big America was and the great distances we were going to be travelling. We still had no clear plan of where we intended going in the country, except to follow Adolf's bonnet and see where she led us. Because we had set off late in the morning it became obvious we were not going to make Houston before nightfall. The only thing we really knew about the city was that it was the home of the Astrodome. It had been built in 1965 to attract Major League Baseball to Houston and was covered with a dome to provide shelter from the intense heat of the summers in the city. After it was built people started referring to it as the eighth wonder of the world. The apex of the huge dome was two hundred and eight feet above the playing surface. Uniquely for a covered indoor stadium, the field of play was initially grass, ignoring grass' need for sunlight for its natural photosynthetic processes. Eighteen stories high and covering nine and a half acres, it was an immense structure and we were interested in seeing it.

As we approached the city in the late afternoon, we studied the map and saw that we could easily get down to the sea. We thought we might be able to camp there and so we headed for Surfside Beach where we drove out onto the sand and along the beach until we came to a quiet spot in the shelter of some dunes. We parked and set up camp, collected wood and lit a fire on which to cook some fresh cobs of sweet corn we had bought earlier in the day at a road-side store. As the sun settled down to the sea and we sat by the fire eating we suddenly became aware we had visitors. Thick clouds of mosquitos descended on us for their supper. They were in our hair, our ears with their irritating drone and on every bit of bare skin. We eventually gave up the unequal fight and retreated to the relative shelter of the mosquito net in Adolf to read and write diaries by the light of a small lamp we ran off the vehicle battery. Occasionally we would slap one of the more resourceful mosquitos that had found a way in with us. It was a warm and quite humid night so we rolled up the seaward side canvas on Adolf in the hope that a sea breeze would cool us.

Since the beach was facing east, we expected to be woken early by the dawn sun, but our early morning alarm call came from a completely different sensory direction. The overwhelming smell of rotting fish permeated everything. There had been no sign of the stench the night before when we had arrived, nor while we were cooking and eating our simple meal, but now it was most definitely there, blending with the cat to sear the lining of our noses. Looking out to the dawn in the east through the netting, I realised the outside of the net was black with mosquitos, all eagerly holding on to the material and staring at the food counter inside, like refugees at a feeding station in a famine. This didn't seem a great place for a summer holiday.

We decided to run the gauntlet of the mosquitos and have an early morning swim, so ran down the beach and dived into the warm water, straight into a huge shoal of football sized jellyfish that bounced off our heads and shoulders. For some reason, neither of us was stung, but we didn't wallow in the water with them to find out if their intentions would remain benign. Tiring of the attentions of the local wild life, we headed inland towards the city, stopping for an early morning coffee at a cafe in the city centre. We assumed the police and locals might object to us building a fire to make our own breakfast by the roadside in suburban Houston.

I'm not really sure what I was anticipating from the Houston of 1972, at that time the fifth largest city in America, but small was not part of my expectations. The city seemed to be quite compact with an absence of the ubiquitous skyscrapers that I thought would be found in all the country's major cities. There was a lot of glass, on one building a golden colour reflecting the morning sun like burnished bronze. We found our way to the Astrodome to be told we would have to queue for at least two hours to get inside. We decided the outside view was going to be enough for us and that we would prefer to keep on going so left Houston to head for the Louisiana State boundary, dropping south back to the coast through Port Arthur. We crossed Sabine Lake on a toll causeway to arrive right down on Holly Beach, which smelt even worse than Surfside. We drove on the sand for about twenty miles, maturely resisting the temptation to drive over a dead porpoise that was lying at the water's edge. The memory of the dead cat moment was still clear in our minds, and the subject of our nightmares. I was becoming concerned reconstituted cat had hallucinogenic properties and adding overtones of rotting porpoise didn't seem a good plan. Crossing the estuary to Calcasieu by a small ferry, we decided to head inland. Louisiana was clearly a very wet State and given our nocturnal visitors the night before we felt it wise to try to find a dry area to camp for the night in the hope we might not be eaten alive again.

Looking at the map, Bell City appeared promising but when we got to it we found it was so small it didn't even have a bar. Calling it a City, was a complete overstatement. Lake Arthur further east, with its one bar, was a teeming metropolis in comparison so we decided to double its current clientele and stopped for a drink. We were parking Adolf outside the bar when a local sheriff approached us. He was an alarming sight. His eyeballs worked completely independently of each other, each moving around in its socket without reference to what it's twin was doing. I wondered if his mother had mated with a chameleon. Graves disease was probably the more likely cause, and his seemed to be an extreme case. Most of the time his irises seemed to inhabit the outer extremities of his eyes. It was impossible to work out which of us he was looking at, and moving left or right to catch one of his eyes only made him move his head to continue the confusion.

"Where you boys 'all from?" he said.

This sounded horribly familiar, a rather depressing déjà vu moment. It occurred to me to ask him if he had a brother who worked for Customs and Immigration in Brownsville but we were quickly learning that Americans did not seem to understand sarcasm. We explained the vision of our trip to him, at the end of which he asked to see our Passports. We extracted them from inside our denim shorts where they would permanently live for the duration of our journey, safely stashed in soft leather pouches that acted as money belts. We slept with them on and never let them out of our sight. We knew there were going to be few Consular facilities to issue replacements in many of the places we would be travelling through and for that reason they were probably the single most important items we had with us. He opened my Passport and stared at it, or rather pointed his nose at it while his eyes looked up and down the road.

"Y'all had your haircut" he said. It wasn't a question, merely a statement of the obvious.

I said nothing. He was absolutely right but I wasn't sure what he wanted me to say about it, apart from agree perhaps, but given his putative sibling's reaction to the slightest comment a few days earlier at the border, silence seemed to be the least contentious choice. He turned to Sam's Passport, seemed to think for a while and then handed the documents to us. Saying good-bye, he turned on his heel and walked away, narrowly missing emasculating himself on a red fire hydrant on the pavement with a deft side-step at the last moment. His gun bounced on his hip as he walked away and I shuddered to think of the collateral damage if he started using it. I assumed the safest person in such mayhem would be the one person he was shooting at. Relieved not to have to empty out Adolf for him, we went into the bar where a couple we chatted to gave us a couple of drinks they said they no longer wanted. We thought they probably did want them but felt sorry for us. We finished our drinks and had a hamburger each and then set off east once more, stopping for the night on a garage forecourt in a small place called Kaplan a few miles along the road.

The early morning news on the radio told us that the Duke of Windsor had died in Paris that day, the 28th May 1972. A tragic figure who changed the course of the United Kingdom, his self-imposed exile in France no doubt removed an irritating reminder of what might have been from the consciousness of the Establishment. I had never felt qualified to judge him and his decision to abdicate in favour of his grande amour, some would say his *amour fou*. Perhaps the divorcee from America felt she had scaled and reached the pinnacle of English society by capturing the Prince of Wales' eye and heart. As we pulled out onto the road I wondered whether those who said Wallis Simpson was a gold digging social mountaineer also felt she had received her just denouement with their banishment. She paid a heavy price for shaking the status quo to its foundations with an unprecedented constitutional crisis, the like of which was unimaginable in those straight laced times. Their critics' schadenfreude ignored the irrefutable fact that she had stood by the Duke throughout the remainder of his life, with all the rejection and loneliness that must have brought. She repaid his great sacrifice and exile, the inevitable result of his choice in 1936 of her over the Crown and his duty, with lifelong faithfulness and support. Perhaps the gold she dug for was him alone. No doubt he did some stupid things in his life, not least his apparent flirtation with Naziism and his fleeting fraternisation with Hitler, but perhaps history will be kinder to her in that her arrival in his life revealed a flawed character who stepped aside to make way for a more suitable and stable monarchic lineage, to the undeniable long term benefit of the country. I reflected on whether she had unwittingly done the United Kingdom and Commonwealth a favour. That judgement lies in the future and is not mine to pass. At that moment, as we drove east into the morning sun, an old woman sat in a window in Paris, alone with her thoughts as she mourned a lost husband, and perhaps reflected on a lost life and her supreme sacrifice in her prolonged exile.

Also in the news and on the radio as we drove were reports about the preparations for the Chess World Championship match between the reigning Champion, the Russian Boris Spassky, and the eccentric, unpredictable, American genius Bobby Fischer. It is easy to forget now, forty years later, how politically important this contest was becoming. At the time the Cold War was positively Arctic. The Cuban Missile crisis was still alive in our minds and memories. America and Russia had stood toe to nuclear toe in 1962, a mere ten years before. A fearful world held its collective breath as the young, articulate, glamorous but untested American President, John Kennedy, stood metaphorically eyeball to eyeball with the short, unattractive, shoe banging, politically hardened and ruthless Russian President, Nikita Khrushchev, Stalin's successor. Who would blink first the world asked itself, as did I one morning, aged twelve, whilst brushing my teeth, wondering if a nuclear war was about to break out.

I had been given a tiny insight into the character of the Russian President by my uncle. Whilst in the Royal Air Force he had been delegated to look after Khrushchev and the Russian Defence Minister Nikolai Bulganin on their official visit to England in 1956. My uncle told me he had arranged and attended a private dinner for the two Russians and that they 'ate like pigs'. Bulganin's support had helped Khrushchev win the Presidency of the USSR, but that counted for nothing when he was ruthlessly forced to resign by Khrushchev for his opposition to the President's reform programme. Khrushchev died in 1971 as we were completing our travel preparations, but his successor, the hairy caterpillar browed Leonid Brezhnev continued to keep the political fridge door wide open, ensuring a continuing and intense distrust between Russia and the West.

Against this backdrop, the Russian grip on the Chess world and its pride in its successive   hot-house groomed World Champions was intense. It was finally agreed the match should be held in the neutrality of Reykjavik in Iceland. The Russian Press saw the coming conflict as an opportunity for Russian world dominance to be endorsed. It was political symbolism. This was the metaphoric nuclear war some of the Russian hierarchy seemed to lust after. I was fascinated by it. Once more, the world was holding its breath but this time with the prospect that the only collateral damage would be hurt pride on the part of the loser, whichever nation that was. It had indeed assumed an importance of national proportions, with each Government vicariously preparing to accept the glory of the eventual victor as its own, the contest transcending the two protagonists in a private tournament into one man armies in a symbolic national confrontation. Would that all conflicts could be settled across a chess table. War bereaved widows and mothers might become a thing of the past. There was a David and Goliath sense to the contest. Fischer's extreme eccentricities alienated the Establishment and the American Government, and yet they were desperate for him to win, and in that self-confident American way, expectant of his victory as if it was their right. They just didn't want to be sullied by too close an association with their anarchic citizen. It was as though he was single handedly taking on the Kremlin and the massed ranks of the Red Army. His obduracy and brinkmanship were breathtaking, his demands outrageous. Perhaps if examined now in the better informed twenty first century he might be diagnosed to have Aspergers' traits but at the time he was just viewed as being extremely difficult, if not impossible to deal with. To his credit, he never wavered from this image, never bowing to any opinion other than his own.

In April 1972, as we were leaving England behind, The Hollies released their single *Long Cool Woman in a Black Dress,* originally just a track on the album *Distant Light.* I had heard the song once or twice before leaving, but it never achieved the same level of popularity in the United Kingdom as it did in America, where it became the number one or number two slot in the charts, depending on which chart you believed or followed. As we travelled through the iconic Deep South, relishing the Confederate names of Texas, Louisiana, Alabama, Florida and Georgia, the track was played repeatedly and with increasing frequency by all the local radio stations. Every time it came on, we would crank up the volume on Adolf's radio and drown ourselves in its irresistible rhythms and powerful underpinning beat. America loved it, and we felt proud to be British. Yet again our music had broken down American resistance to outside influences.

We had only been in the United States for a few days, but already we were discovering how geographically and politically introverted the average American was. They seemed to have no concept or understanding of the outside world, their international inquisitiveness being satisfied by news from their neighbouring States. The newspapers we had seen in bars and cafes we had visited carried no global or international news. It was strangely disquieting to hear a few die-hard Southerners talk of their belief that the Confederacy would rise again and the southern States could still achieve independence from the north. Clearly the advantages of slavery were high in minds that still mourned the end of segregation. Many of those same minds felt Martin Luther King got his just deserts. This last would not really have surprised me. An American schoolfriend of mine, Tucker MacKenzie, was in Memphis in 1968 on the day King was assassinated on the balcony of his hotel room. Tucker was leaving Memphis later that evening with some friends when their car was stopped by a police roadblock. All traffic out of the city was being examined in the search for the assassin. A Tennessee policeman came up to Tucker and his friends and, on looking in and seeing the occupants were all white, waved them through. Tucker asked them if they had found the killer yet and the policeman replied that he hoped not but if he came across him he would let him go through as he reckoned he'd done the States a favour. That is as shocking to me today as the day I was told it. The impact of bigotry is not diminished by time.

We woke early in our garage dormitory in Kaplan and set off for New Orleans, arriving at its outskirts at around midday. All we had read and heard about the city led us to imagine jazz and blues music and a free-wheeling hippy culture. We expected to find the remains of the flower power generation holding out against the end of their era, trying not to wilt in the heat of the changes sweeping through the world. Arlo Guthrie had recently released his successful song, *'The City of New Orleans'*. Whilst it was about a train and long distance travel, its very title and lyrics were evocative for me of our own journey, rolling past houses, farms and fields and being

"*.....gone five hundred miles when the day is done,*

"*... rockin' to the gentle beat
And the rhythm of the rails is all they dream".*

    We were very much looking forward to seeing the iconic city and had pulled in by the side of the road to study a map to work out how to get to the renowned areas such as the French Quarter and Jackson Square. A car drew up next to us and the driver rolled down his window and asked us if we were lost. When we said we were just studying the map to see how to get into the city and to the French Quarter he offered to lead us in. Gratefully we pulled out into the traffic behind him and, good as his word, he led us through the maze of streets directly to where we wanted to be. Whilst we would have found it, he saved us a lot of time with his simple act of kindness. With a wave of his hand out of his window, our Samaritan indicated we had arrived and then he pulled off to go to wherever he was going, leaving us to benefit from his act of altruism.

    New Orleans was everything we had expected, only more so. Jazz music from live bands blared out of full bars. One of the bands was playing as they walked up the street. The pavements were overhung by ornate balconies, under which men sat in rocking chairs smoking and drinking as they chatted and listened to the music. A huge African American, dressed like Jimi Hendrix and with a large ring through his nose, followed the band in the street gyrating to the rhythm of the music, lost in a world of his own, no doubt with the aid of some chemical infusion. The growth of the modern predilection for body piercing makes it a common-place sight nowadays, but in those unperforated times he seemed very avant-garde to us.

Jackson Square was filled with hippies, dressed in kaftans, shirts and trousers embroidered or printed with floral patterns. Many sat around smoking pot openly believing they were rebelling against conformity, whilst conforming to the stereotype of the new generation of liberated youth, both in their indolence and their manner of dress. The irony probably escaped them. The French Market near the Square was a long, low, open sided building filled with stalls and booths from which I think you could buy just about anything. The heady aroma of marijuana in it was intoxicating. We walked past a cemetery where all the bodies were interred above the ground. We were told this was because of the danger of flooding, to stop cadavers and skeletons floating around the area. It was thought bathing skeletons would be a little off-putting for visiting tourists, who would be expecting to find a slightly more vibrant and less supine community.

As the afternoon was moving to its autumn we decided it would be wise to leave the city for somewhere more isolated and therefore potentially safer to spend the night. We left New Orleans behind, taking with us fond memories of its extrovert eccentricity and its idiosyncrasy, which we somehow knew we might only see again in San Francisco. The city was a one-off, reveling in its uniqueness and non-conformity. We crossed Lake Pontchartrain and drove north to Slidell where we turned east once again, crossing the State boundary from Louisiana into Mississippi and then dropping down into Gulfport on the coast. We drove out to the end of a harbour wall and parked for an uneventful night. Dawn brought a clear blue sky and we set off into the rising sunshine to cover the one hundred and thirty or so miles to Pensacola in Florida, passing through Mobile in Alabama on the way.

The names of the States, cities and towns seemed so exotic to me, only encountered before in novels and films. So much history was wrapped up in them. The American Civil war that fought slavery and brought about the emancipation of the slaves. I imagined the beautiful daughters of wealthy plantation owners lying in shaded hammocks that swung gently under Spanish Moss hanging from trees. Southern gracious living was the epitome of refinement for the privileged wealthy landowners. There was a timelessness about these places, a sense that nothing had changed. For many nothing had.

In a small town outside Mobile we stopped and bought a large steak and a cabbage for our meal of the day, throwing them in the back of Adolf to be cooked up later. We salivated at the thought of our first decent meal for a week. Arriving in Pensacola we headed for the beach once more, passing through an extremely wealthy area with grand houses facing onto what appeared to be private beaches. We drove across the sand onto one of the beaches. The sand was quite soft and so we had to keep up sufficient speed to avoid sinking into it, weaving back and forth to keep the tyres moving and not building up a mound of sand in front of them. We parked Adolf in the lee of a large sand dune where we built a fire with driftwood we collected off the beach. The steak and cabbage cooked on Adolf's metal radiator grill suspended over the open flames were voted the best meal we had had in our lives. Of such little things the greatest pleasures in life are often derived, if only we could all see that through the mist of our pursuit of material wealth.

Our lunch over we washed our plates and the pan in the sea. The sand was startlingly white, the water so clear that when swimming in it we could see everything around with the clarity of a freshly filled swimming pool. Walking back to Adolf we spotted a couple by their vehicle on the beach. At first we thought the car had lowered suspension until we realised it had sunk into the sand. We wandered over to them to see if we could help. We had one hundred metres of tow rope in Adolf, in ten metre lengths that could be attached to each other with shackles sewn onto the ends of each length of rope.. We drove over to them, reversed Adolf to the front of their car and attached two lengths of rope together. Locking our differentials and engaging low box we slowly and gently pulled them out and took them back to where the sand was firmer where we left them dewy eyed with gratitude.

Unbeknown to us we had been watched in our rescue by five young Americans who came over to chat. They ended up spending the afternoon with us, sitting around our impromptu camp and fire as we all discussed the world we and they lived in, comparing notes. They gave us some of their beer and we reciprocated with our rum off the Gela. It nearly took their heads off which made me realise that perhaps we had had a bit more of it than was good for us, given that we didn't flinch when drinking it. Our new friends left us as evening fell. We decided that being parked on the beach near all the expensive properties was going to attract the attention of the police so we packed up, cleared away the remnants of the fire and headed into Pensacola where we parked in a car park for the night, falling asleep whilst being lulled by the sound of the Atlantic breakers on the Gulf shore nearby.

A new morning, a new stretch of road reaching out ahead of us to the horizon. Hugging the coast we stopped off at a tiny Grayton Beach where we swam in more crystal clear waters. We took the opportunity to clean out the sediment bowl in the air filter and as we did so a couple of young Americans came up to us to talk to us and find out where we were from. Once again the innate friendliness of Americans in rural America was evident. Kind, generous with their hospitality and ever welcoming, we were to be shown immense and unquestioning hospitality throughout our months in the States. These early encounters were bellwethers of many altruistic gestures we were to benefit from. When we had finished our minor service on Adolf's respiratory system, our two visitors invited us back to the house they and about twenty five others were renting for a few days. As one would expect with that many young staying in one large house, it was chaotic, noisy and fun. They were all curious about us and insisted we stay for lunch, a most welcome offer to two people on a budget enforced diet.

Tempting though it was to stay on to take part in their evening plans, we set off east again in the mid afternoon after another swim in the delicious Gulf waters. We headed for Panama City and from there, inland to Tallahassee, arriving late at night in Jacksonville on the east coast. Three hundred and sixty miles in the day, with some fun thrown in, and now it was time to turn north, but not before a hamburger in a little place called Baldwin just outside the city. Those first American hamburgers were something of a revelation to us, although we had come across them in a restaurant called The Hungry Years near our flat in London. Our main experience of hamburgers was limited to Wimpy burgers in England. With the texture and depth of the well trodden inner soles of a marathon runner's shoes, they were the UK's answer to billtong. Dumbbells for the jaw muscles. By comparison the thick, tasty American version was their nemesis and it is no wonder the brand eventually disappeared.

Driving through Jacksonville we arrived at the Atlantic Ocean at Neptune Beach some time after midnight and there we parked by the beach and settled down for the night. Deeply asleep we were woken in the early hours by the police and the flash of their blue lights. Wary and curious, it turned out they merely wanted to check us out, although we were fully expecting them to move us on, given our earlier experiences with the police. After chatting for a while, and no longer hovering their hands over their guns, they wished us a good night and pulled away into the darkness. I still found it odd to see guns being worn openly in the street. In England it never occurred to anyone that police would be armed. That was what the Army was for, and if the police needed to enforce their authority with a bit of persuasive physicality, bruised and dented skulls were the chosen method as truncheons rapped a rhythm on offending heads. In America you seemed to get a gun if you wore a uniform, no matter which organisation's uniform that might be. As the police drove off they left us to fend off the mosquitos which had popped in for supper. The mosquito net was conscripted into service once more.

In the light of day Neptune Beach was long and sandy and a reasonable place to do some housekeeping. We found a block of public Rest Rooms and decided to wash some clothes in it, but on going in realised we had walked into an incontinent and deranged chimpanzee's house. It was absolutely filthy and so, abandoning that idea we walked into the shopping area and bought some flip flops before finding a launderette which did a more than adequate job of coping with our dusty clothes. Sitting outside in a car parked against the curb was a very large woman dressed in a bath hat and dressing gown, a cigarette dangling from a pendulous lower lip like the inner tube of a truck tyre. She was not catwalk material and it was hard to work out whether she had absent mindedly left her house dressed like that, whether she wore bed clothes all day long or whether she had been thrown out of her house by an exasperated partner. We were discovering that America's eccentrics were more visible in their communities than we were used to in ours in England where the decline in numbers of village idiots was a welcome benefit from a more mobile and travelled population. Whilst the early hippies were eccentric to old England, they soon became accepted as being part of our society. Our true, embarrassing and perhaps mentally unstable eccentrics were hidden from view, in the shadows where they were probably still being fed on laudanum. This woman could have done with a couple of pints of the stuff. Avoiding catching her eye lest we get drawn into conversation with her, we made our way back to Adolf, packed our clean clothes and turned her nose north for all stops to New York. It was an exciting prospect to know we were on our way up to that famous city, most Europeans' vision of all that is American.

For me it held the prospect of our first letters, hopefully including at least one from Greece.

A GIRL CALLED ADOLF

CHAPTER 5

America - Going North - 1972

"He who is not courageous enough to take risks will accomplish nothing in life."

Muhammed Ali

Like all cities, Savannah at night was a blaze of light as we approached it at about ten thirty. About sixty miles before we arrived at the city we spotted a hitch hiker on the side of the road and stopped to give him a lift. Bill was on his way back to New York from Florida where he had spent three months working. Dropping him off in the city centre we turned towards the coast, reluctant to spend the night in the main metropolis. We eventually stopped on a beach on Tybee Island. There was a bar still open so we parked and walked over to it for a beer before settling down for the night.

Most bars, in fact most businesses, do everything in their power to attract customers but this place proved to be the exception to the rule. It was almost empty, a few seats at the bar occupied by morose looking men staring vacuously at a baseball match showing on the television high on the wall behind the bar. The barman polished glasses with a bored and desultory indifference. On a small dance floor two large, semi naked, very wrinkled and extraordinarily sweaty women were contorting their overweight bodies to the music playing on a juke box. They wore overloaded sequined bras with tidemarks of salt stains under the arms. Tasselled arrangements were attached to knickers, which appeared to have been made out of the sort of material used to control a bad case of varicose veins. As we entered the bar they sauntered over to us, wanting to know if we would like a drink with them, to dance with them, or perhaps lie underneath them. They were the bar's entertainment, the forerunners to Spearmint Rhino and its pole and lap dancers, there to teasingly titillate the red blooded males of Savannah. The bar should have been called Sweaty Elephant. It was no wonder the place was empty of any man of breeding age. On closer inspection it was clear the two women were well into their forties and the thought of them sitting on our laps, stopping the blood supply to our legs, was a thought too far. As for pole dancing, they would need a couple of scaffolding poles cemented into the floor as anything less would have bent. We gently declined their kind offer and ordered a beer, taking seats at the bar. The seedy joint hid its charms with commendable skill so we finished our drinks quickly and walked back to Adolf to settle in for the night.

Whilst we were busy repacking in the morning before setting off again, one or two people came up to ask where we were from and where we were going. One of them was a girl who returned with her mother bearing coffee and doughnuts. The girl's name was Joann and it turned out it was her twentieth birthday. When we had finished our coffees they invited us back to their house nearby for breakfast and a shower. The hours passed and we swam and sat on the beach with Joann and two of her friends who were from Tennessee and had never seen the sea before. Talking to them I began to question the value of an American education in the backwoods of Tennessee.

"What language do y'all speak in England?" one asked me.

"English, funnily enough" I replied, still not fully aware that sarcasm is an unknown quantity in America.

"So did y'all drive here?" she asked. Perhaps she was the Brownsville Customs officer's niece?

"No, we came over on a boat," I replied. "We landed in Mexico and have driven here from there."

"So, do y'all have banks in England? she asked.

I looked at Sam to see if he had a bone through his nose, fairly sure that I didn't.

"Yes" I replied, "Isn't the sea beautiful here."

I was keen to move the subject back to America where her knowledge might have been a bit more informed. I could see Joann was showing early signs of embarrassment and I did not want to return her kindnesses by taking advantage of such stunning ignorance of another culture. Joann's mother asked us about our plans and we said we wanted to get some work to build up money to see us through our months in South America, where we were pretty sure no work would be available. She said there was an island north of Savannah that was being developed with expensive properties, golf courses, a new marina and the infrastructure to support wealthy retired residents and well heeled holiday makers. She said the island, Hilton Head Island, was beautiful and unspoiled, almost completely undeveloped. She suggested we go there to see if we could get any construction work as she had heard they were hiring itinerant workers.

Late in the afternoon we went crabbing and caught about twenty, which we put in a bucket and carried back to the house where we had been invited to stay for Joann's birthday dinner. With a few of her friends around the laden table, we ate well and then went into Savannah late in the evening with Joann and a friend of hers. The two girls took us to a bar called Tom's Warehouse where a fantastic group were playing live music. There were no middle aged, loose skinned fat women offering to have a drink with us or snuggle up to us on the dance floor, drowning us in a tsunami of wobbling cellulite. The bar was full of young, taught fleshed vibrant people out to party and we listened to the music and chatted to all those wanting to talk to the English guys. I thought of the stark contrast of the depressives from the night before, probably still in the other bar staring sightlessly at the television.

In the morning, twenty four serendipitous hours after our first attempt to leave Savannah, we said our goodbyes to Joann, her mother and her friends and set off for Hilton Head Island, optimistic of the possibility of work. The Island was accessed by a causeway that crossed a smaller island before reaching Hilton Head itself. As we drove through the island it became clear that nearly all of it was completely undeveloped. Low lying and quite wet in parts, we passed through pine forests and past open marshland and untended fields. Egrets walked in low lying water and dotted the sky, their stark white standing out against the clear blue cloudless canopy. Alligators warmed themselves in the sun by lagoons over which brown pelicans drifted effortlessly, low to the water and in tune with the peaceful unhurried feel to the island. We seemed to have arrived in some sort of facsimile of Paradise.

There were road signs that directed us to Sea Pines Plantation which we had been told was the name of the main development being built. We followed the signs to a small shopping centre with a couple of cafes intermingled among the shops. Tables were occupied by people eating lunch in the sunshine. We drove through the shopping area and followed the road between the tall pines, passing large, single story shingle roofed houses set in the shade of the trees. We came upon one that was unfinished and a hive of activity with workmen and their trucks all around it. Stopping in its drive we walked in and asked a man, who appeared to be an electrician judging by the tools hanging in a belt around his waist, if there was anyone in charge.

"Hey, Jay," the man shouted, "A couple of guys here to see you." He gave us a friendly smile and walked on to his next task as a short man in his forties with long and curly strawberry blond hair came over to us.

"Hi," he said "How can I help you. I'm Jay."

Fifteen minutes later we were unofficial employees of Graves Construction Co, seconded to help Jay who was an interior designer and who was contracted to fit out most of the luxury homes being built in and around the Sea Pines Plantation area. We agreed a rate of $2.00 an hour in cash, that we could work whatever hours we liked and would answer to Jay, who would be our boss for as long as we stayed and worked He agreed that could be as long as we wanted.

Even now it is difficult to comprehend the forces of luck and chance that combined to lead us to pick on the one middle aged, open minded, free-wheeling hippy in South Carolina who would be crazy enough to take on two nomads to do the jobs no one else wanted to do, whatever they may be. So often life throws a chain of loosely linked opportunities and moments of sheer coincidence at us all. It only takes us to miss one link in the chain to change the outcome and an opportunity or danger we never knew existed passes us by unseen. Our chain started with a young girl walking up to us on a beach in Savannah, thirty five miles away, and ended with us picking that particular road through the pine trees and finding a man with a free spirit to happen to be there at that moment. A confluence of chance encounters and opportunities that merged in a delta of luck. I will never know what would have been if we had stopped for a coffee en route, if Joann had walked by in Savannah and not stopped to talk to us or if we had not stayed the day and sat on the beach with her and her mother. Our story would have been very different, and as it turned out, poorer in so many ways.

Jay turned to a tall good looking man of about his age and called him over.

"Baker, I want you to meet these two British guys. I've just taken them on to help me. This is Baker, boys, my cousin."

Baker shook our hands with a welcoming smile. He was the Public Relations manager of Graves Construction and he suggested we park Adolf at the house he was having built for himself near Harbour Town, the island's new marina.

"You can be our first house guests" he said.

He got in his car and we followed him to a half built property tucked into the trees. It was no more than a

127

building site, a wooden framed skeleton surrounded by scaffolding, piles of bricks and plywood sheets. I was amazed at how basic the construction seemed with its wooden frames and large wooden panels for walls. The scaffolding surrounding the two story property, one of the very few that height we were to see on the island, was also made out of wood. I was surprised to see wooden scaffolding in this most advanced of industrial countries, when we were used to metal scaffolding at home. Little differences seem to define nations and combine to give each its own unique culture and character.

Baker left us to settle in, which entailed parking Adolf out of the way and sorting out a few things in her to make room for an indefinite stay. Our plan was to work hard for a couple of weeks and then move on. After a while, Baker returned with his wife, Pat, and their four wonderful children. The family all seemed to have been gifted with the beautiful gene and we were to get to know them well during our stay on the island, regularly taking the kids swimming in the sea, treating them to ice creams and generally using them as an excuse to stay young as their slightly eccentric babysitters.

The family invited us back to the house they were renting while theirs was being built and then Baker took us into the Marina at Harbour Town. A large faux lighthouse dominated the harbour. Beneath it were a few shops and on the first floor a bar called the Quarterdeck. The marina was pristine and extremely smart. Filled with very expensive yachts and large boats, it exuded wealth and privilege. By large I mean boats big enough to have lifts in them and staffed by a large number of crew who seemed to spend most of their time when in the marina polishing and washing their respective boats. No doubt they were there to tend to the owners' every whim. It suddenly dawned on us we had landed in a millionaire's playground and retreat, a hideaway from the great unwashed plebeians, somewhere we would be an anomaly with our scruffy mobile home. I fully expected to find a restaurant or boat called the Marie Antoinette.

Under the Quarterdeck were shower rooms and a sauna for the use of the yachtsmen and boat crews. We were told to help ourselves to the facilities. As far as we were concerned we had landed in a five star hotel with en suite facilities, all of it free. At first that also seemed to include the drinks in the bar and later many of our meals. We were rarely allowed to buy a drink, but were bought hundreds which we manfully consumed, much to our livers' objections. I cannot remember how many meals we were given in various expensive homes by the friendliest and most welcoming people we had ever met. We were overwhelmed by the kindness and hospitality we were shown. Everyone on the island seemed to know about us and they would all, young and old, insist on coming up to us and chatting. They waved to us as we drove past them in Adolf or worked on the new houses being finished off by the construction crews.

Our working days were long and at times either extremely boring, or very physical. Our main jobs started after the workmen and decorators had finished and moved out of the newly built houses. Our primary task was to clean out any signs that the workmen had been there. Spots of paint on window panes were to be scraped off with razor blades. Paint and bits of cement and plaster had to be scraped off cool marble floors that each seemed to be an acre in size. Baths, sinks and lavatory pans all had to be scraped clean. Sometimes, after a particularly riotous and late night in the Quarterdeck, or at a night club and bar called The Marsh Tacky, we would take it in turns to sleep in one of the baths in the house we were working on that day.

A Marsh Tacky is a sturdy pony that was commonly found in South Carolina, thought to have been introduced by Spanish settlers in the 1500's. They were used for riding, pulling and general work and were once prolific but now there are very few left. Our Marsh Tacky was tucked away in dark woods in a desolate and deserted part of the island. It was a large, single story building and like all the properties on the Sea Pines Plantation, it had been made out of wood to blend in with its surroundings. It was spacious inside, simply furnished, with a long bar down one wall and tables and chairs for drinkers and diners. A small dance floor was regularly occupied by the energetic young who were its predominant clientele.

As well as cleaning out the houses ready for the new owners to take possession, we also did any construction work that required nothing more than muscle power, and certainly no skill. We drove huge trucks that by rights probably demanded the American version of Heavy Goods Vehicle licences we did not possess. Moving tons of bricks or breeze blocks took off the surface of our hands but kept us exercised. I spent one afternoon unloading heavy plasterboard sheets whose weight lengthened my arms by a couple of inches. We did anything that kept us working and earning money. Our working days were regularly twelve or thirteen hours long. We would usually start at dawn, the first onto the site, and finish long after the local workmen had gone home, all the while earning money. It would then be off to Harbour Town for a shower and up to the Quarterdeck. Weekends often followed the same pattern. Because many of the people we met were renting houses for their summer holidays, their evenings were not constrained by the need for a sensible bedtime routine in preparation for a day's work. Consequently many of our evenings moved from the Quarterdeck bar to parties that went on until the early hours of the morning. Everyone seemed to love our English accents and wanted to hear them. Beds were offered for the night, and on more than one occasion Sam found his occupied.

When we were not working we were invited onto yachts to sail and enjoy the beautiful waters around the island. Sailing always seemed to require significant amounts of alcohol to fuel the crews, which would sometimes result in impromptu water skiing parties behind a yacht under full sail. A seat cushion tied to a rope and thrown out of the back of a yacht under full sail is a small target to aim for when diving off the stern to catch it. Once I was holding on and being dragged through the water at six or seven knots, the next trick was to keep my mouth shut to avoid a complete alimentary flush with sea water, a sort of early version of the '90's fad for upper colonic irrigation. I have never felt so cleaned out or thoroughly sluiced since, and remember praying no one on board chose that moment to empty the on board toilet. Being dragged through a shoal of the same football sized jellyfish as we had encountered on the Gulf coast was an interesting quandary. As the huge creatures bounced off me the dilemma was whether to hold on and hope there was some end to the herd and the nightmare, or to let go and swim amongst them whilst trying to dodge them until rescued.

One yacht we regularly sailed on was owned by Ted Hunter from Asheville in North Carolina. Ted was a good friend of a family we were introduced to shortly after we arrived in Harbour Town. Friends of Baker and his family, Larry and Ellen Ford and their three young sons also lived in Asheville. Larry was a stockbroker and Ellen ran her own successful Realtors business. They became firm and caring lifelong friends who took us under their wing and provided us with a home from home in Asheville, with a limitless generosity of spirit for which I have remained grateful to this day.

Sam was an experienced sailor and one weekend helped Ted by crewing for him as he moved his yacht further up the coast. I worked for the weekend and then a few days later helped the Ford family at the end of their holiday by driving one of their two cars back to Asheville, some three hundred miles away. The plan was I would hitch hike back after a week in Asheville, which was a town up in the Blue Ridge mountains of North Carolina. Surrounded by beautiful scenery and tree clad hills, valleys and mountains, it was a quiet, sleepy mid-sized town, a far cry from the urban jungle of the big cities. Larry and Ellen took the opportunity for some peace and quiet by driving home in Larry's E Type Jaguar while I was delegated to take the three boys and two of their friends. There was a garnish of the eccentric family dog just to top off the joy of the experience. We were crammed into the huge Oldsmobile station wagon and the look of glee on Larry and Ellen's faces, like those of lifers escaping from Robben Island, should have warned me.

Larry Junior, Brent and Peter, variously aged thirteen, eleven and six were every parent's worst nightmare, and I loved them all. Giving Larry and Ellen six or seven hours of peace and quiet was the least I could do in return for their many kindnesses to us. I had regularly babysat the boys during their holiday in Hilton Head and, like Baker's children, taken them swimming and for ice cream outings. I knew them well and could guess at what the long journey held for me. Just keeping them in the car and preventing them from climbing out of the windows, whether we were moving or not, was in itself a challenge requiring parenting skills notable for their absence in my minuscule arsenal of talents. Larry Junior's shoulder was still healing from the affects of a coming together on his bike with a car's wing mirror. That did not seem to slow him down or dampen his enthusiasm for trouble, despite the one hundred and ten stitches he proudly told me had been needed to repair the damage.

Being one of three boys myself, I suddenly had an awful realisation on that journey of what my parents must have been through as my brothers and I grew up. I had a guilt ridden understanding that the stories my mother recounted of our own antics were not figments of her imagination but the retelling of her own living nightmares. Sometimes there is justice in life and perhaps that car journey was my mother's moment for it as I received a taste of my own medicine. I wonder how often she had wished she'd had three daughters. The journey was made more interesting by Henry the dog, a character of equal scale to the three boys. In his quiet moments, Henry liked to sleep with his head on someone's foot, and this included when he was in the car. He clambered over the seats and down into the footwell at my feet where he settled down for a nice long snooze, his chin on the top of my foot on the accelerator. Henry was like no other dog I had ever known, a canine aberrant in the form of a feisty Maltese Terrier. He had no water bowl in the house as he preferred to take his drinking water from the toilet. He loved to watch television. The family would put a chair in front of the it when they were watching anything and he would jump up and settle down with his nose four inches from the screen, following things and people around as they moved about. It did make watching anything rather trying as his head tended to block out the middle of the screen.

One afternoon at the Ford's house in Asheville I heard a frightening howling in the garden where I was doing some work clearing undergrowth. It was the day after Larry Junior and two of his friends had blown up a neighbour's letterbox with a home made bomb, and I had been sworn to secrecy to protect them. Rushing around the house I saw Larry Junior running about with his hand clutched to his eye and a pretty young girl his age rushing after him. Grabbing him and calming him down to try to get some sense out of him, I discovered he had persuaded the girl to give him one of her contact lenses, which he had put in his eye. When it disappeared up to the top of his eyeball under his eyelid, he panicked, as did the girl. Being the only adult on the premises this gave me the opportunity to try out my ophthalmic skills to remove it. Tricky to do when the patient is hopping about like a frog in a blender. Finally extracting the lens I handed it back to the girl and she and Larry headed off to find some other disaster to create.

Brent, the middle son, had a ladder of scars up both his shins which he told me Larry Junior had given him. Brent had been swimming in a lake behind a motorboat and was about to climb aboard at the back when Larry engaged the idling outboard motor. The spinning propellor had rattled its way up Brent's legs, but fortunately not through them. A few more inches and there is no telling what would have happened to Brent's ability to father children later in life. Accident prone did not begin to describe these semi house-trained boys, but they never once provided me with a dull moment. Peter was the youngest and extremely bright. He had a mass of curly blond hair and looked like a bonsai version of Art Garfunkel, exuding a beguiling innocence that he used to devastating effect. An accomplished poker player at the age of six, on numerous occasions I saw him take money off adults who had been lulled into an ennui of complacency as he dealt the cards. When they handed over their losses it was too late for them to realise they had been duped by a higher intellect. I made a mental note to become his agent when he was old enough to sign a binding contract.

It was now nearing the end of June and the news was full of the Sterling crisis that was raging in Britain. My interest in it was centred on whether we should change our British currency into US Dollars. Some of our money was sealed in plastic bags and hidden under a metal plate screwed to the floor on the passenger side of Adolf. The rate we were getting when we wanted to change was in a narrow range of about $2.62 to $2.64 to the pound, but immense pressure on Sterling was causing the rate to drop. Larry was a stock broker with Merrill Lynch in Asheville and he regularly updated me on what was happening. The rate had dropped to $2.58 and if there was a complete collapse in Sterling it could have a bit of an effect on our micro-economy, independent of the issues the British macro-economy was facing. The instability in the currency was a link in a crisis chain going back to 1967 when Harold Wilson's Government had devalued Sterling by over 14%, instantly dropping the exchange rate from $2.80 to $2.40. I remembered watching that sleight of hand specialist Wilson appearing on television and telling a sceptical public that the fifty pence in our pockets would be worth the same. Perhaps he meant the coin itself would not get any smaller, the sort of obfuscation he was capable of, a truth hiding a lie, like any political party's election manifesto.

As in 1967, the instability in Sterling was causing a crisis in other world currencies and 1972 was highlighting the death throes of the Bretton Woods international monetary system. Named after the town in New Hampshire where the agreements were signed in 1944, the Bretton Woods system was designed to provide a basis for exchanging one currency for another and led to the development of the International Monetary Fund as well as being the precursor of the World Bank. The central theme of the agreements was that the signatory countries would fix their exchange rates by linking their currencies to the US dollar. To assuage uncertainty in foreign Governments and markets, the US agreed to link the US dollar to gold at a rate of one dollar equalling thirty five ounces of gold. Crucially, the other signatories agreed to keep their currencies within one percent of this fixed rate.

In 1971, a year earlier than our little currency dilemma in Asheville, President Nixon had cut the link between the dollar and gold. In March 1972, the European Governments took their first steps towards a common European currency with the introduction of the 'snake' by which they hoped to control fluctuations amongst their own currencies to within relatively narrow margins. The net result of this was that Sterling was pushed up to around $2.65 to the pound, the rate we had been getting since we came into the States.

Against this backdrop the United Kingdom's trade balance had fallen back into deficit prompting the Chancellor, Anthony Barber, to produce an expansionary Budget in March. However, serious and continuous labour disputes combined with significant price and wage inflation threatened Britain's competitive trading position, all of which led through to a pessimistic attitude to Sterling, bringing it under severe under pressure to the extent there was huge selling of the currency on the 15th June when I was on the island preparing for the trip to North Carolina. By the 20th June, the rate had dropped to

$2.56 and showed no inclination to do anything other than go into free fall, with the cost to central banks of supporting Sterling rising to £2.65 billion in seven days. On 23rd June Sterling was floated in the middle of the currency storm, let free to drift on the uncertain seas of world exchange rates. Whilst no doubt European Finance Ministers were having sleepless nights, our interest was more selfish. We were pondering the decision whether to move what little Sterling we had into US dollars before the rate dropped through the floor. In the end, we changed a significant proportion and switched to the dollar as our base currency, a helpful move given its universal acceptance in Central and South America.

As Europe struggled to control its financial turmoil, a storm of a different nature pushed its first tiny shoots into America's consciousness. Little did any of us know on the 17th June 1972 the size of the tree that would grow from the acorn that lay hidden within the first news of a break in at the Democratic National Committee Headquarters at the Watergate office complex in Washington D.C. Nor was there any inkling as to how huge the problem would become for the Nixon Administration, and ultimately for the President himself, culminating in his resignation just over two years later in 1974. The obfuscation from the Administration about the issue in its early days of discovery was widespread and intense, and it was difficult to make any sense of it all. The Nation and the Press were intrigued.

With news reports covering the growing scandal, Larry, Ellen and I set off to go back to Hilton Head on the day Sterling floated off on its own little raft. For me it was the end of a hectic week of trying to control the three boys, driving Larry to and from work in his E Type Jaguar each day whilst having free use of it during the day, working in the Ford's garden and generally being kept busy. Larry arranged for a local newspaper in Asheville to write an article on me and our journey. I was interviewed by a young and pretty journalist at their offices and was then photographed leaning over the bonnet of Larry's E-Type. Fortunately the photographer was in front of me because it must have been a pretty unedifying sight from behind, given that an E-Type's bonnet is at knee level. At the end of the week Larry and Ellen had spontaneously decided to have a weekend break from their earthly hell in the form of their sons, and agreed to drive back down to Hilton Head for a couple of days. They had no qualms about saying farewell to the boys since they were leaving them to the tender care of the capable and no nonsense Betty.

Betty was a big girl and I loved her. In her fifties with numerous children and a dusting of grandchildren, she was an African American straight out of central casting. As broad as she was tall, she shuffled majestically about the house in carpet slippers that the Tom and Jerry cartoonists must have drawn inspiration from for their maid. She never appeared to do much and yet all the chores were done, the house spotless and meals always cooked and ready. She introduced me to the delights of Southern Fried Chicken, which was delicious. Betty ruled the three boys with an easy and casual authority, and they respected her. She was the only person I knew who could control them, and who they feared. One morning Larry Junior was lying on a sofa

Betty wanted to clean and tidy. She told him to move and he ignored her, his eyes fixed on the television. Betty didn't believe in second chances. No three strikes and out for Betty. To her such libertarian leniency was anathema and for the faint hearted. She walked over to the indolent and insolent Larry and picked him up by one ankle. Dangling the yelling boy upside down in the air she carried and dragged him out of the room and dumped him unceremoniously on his head on the floor by the back door. The sofa was soon pristine and ready for inspection. Arriving for work each morning, her antennae would quickly tell her if any of the boys were still in bed. If they were and refused to get up, not an irregular occurrence in their antipathy to authority and to schooling, the simple expedient of turning the mattress over onto the floor soon got an oversleeping boy down to breakfast. There was no arguing with someone who looked as though she could flip a parked car onto its roof with one hand.

Reaching the Island at about three in the morning we fell asleep on Ted Hunter's boat, The Princess. I woke early to a beautiful South Carolina day and went for a walk in the woods near the marina. After a mid morning brunch we cast off for a day of sailing in Calibogue Sound under the clear blue sky. After we returned I went to Harbour Town and met up with Sam who handed me a few letters that had been forwarded from the mailing address in New York we had given to anyone who had expressed an interest in writing to us. We had been on the road for eight weeks and it was wonderful to have that first contact. As a means of communication, it is hard to beat letters. There are so many ways of enjoying them. Sometimes sheer uncontrollable enthusiasm means a rushed tearing open of the envelope, pulling out the letter and racing through the words. More delicious in its suspended anticipation is the epistolary courtship. The slow wooing, putting the unopened letter to one side or better still, in a pocket next to the heart. Taking it out every now and again to look at it and feel it, turning it over, examining the stamp all add to the mouthwatering anticipation. Holding it, knowing it was held by the writer, somehow connects the recipient to the essence of the writer's being. Finally the right moment arrives, a quiet corner alone in the dappled shade under a tree, or sitting in the cool air as the dawn sky breaks with the light of a new day filled with hope and optimism. The envelope is carefully slit open and the precious words withdrawn and read slowly, with breaks to think and watch the sky brighten with the pastel colours of the early hours, or to let the sunlight dance on an upturned face, sometimes with a gentle tear a lone pearl on the cheek.

At the end of the weekend of sailing, eating and drinking, Larry, Ellen and Ted left to return to Asheville and we got on with the task of earning money. Our irregular accounting and timesheet reconciliation, usually done when we were down to our last few cents, offered us the opportunity to perplex and confuse Jay when it came to the calculation of what we were owed.

"OK boys, how many hours yesterday?"

"We worked from seven to seven so twelve hours, and we worked lunch so thirteen in all."

"But seven to seven is twelve hours" he would reply.

"Yes, but we worked lunch so adding that in is thirteen."

The same conversation was had a number of times and each time we would leave him scratching his head to try to work out the logic of our maths and how we could manufacture twenty five hours out of the more usual twenty four. His skills lay in design and creativity, but not creativity with numbers. To his eternal credit he cheerfully paid us in full at all times, and honoured his verbal agreement when we first met him and he took us on. For our part, we repaid him by driving him around when he was high on marijuana and not safe behind a steering wheel, and by doing jobs and errands for him, such as his shopping, for which we never charged him.

As we worked and played, we seemed to become something of a fixture in Harbour Town, always slightly eccentric oddities. The local paper interviewed and photographed us and people came up to us in the bar, always insisting on buying us a drink. It came to the point I felt our livers must be being overwhelmed by the onslaught and overtime they were being put through. Sam continued to attract the attention of an endless stream of tanned and pretty girls. Often I would work weekends by myself as he was entertained by them, and regularly I would sleep alone in Adolf or on someone's sofa or floor, with no idea where he was.

On one such night I had fallen asleep in the back of Adolf, exhausted, when I was woken bathed in light and with the noise of men's voices shouting at me. Getting out I was caught in the full glare of searchlights on three police cars. The six police were all from the same gene pool as the Customs officials and other police we had met. Aggressive and irritable they wanted to know what I was doing parked in front of Baker's half built house. They wanted to know where my driving papers were and, once they realised I was not an American, my Passport. A couple of them had their hands on their guns and kept them there so I made sure my hands were visible at all times, held away from my side and from the pockets in my shorts. Eventually they seemed satisfied that I was not a criminal and told me to move the vehicle and go somewhere else, without too much guidance as to where I should go at that time of night where I wouldn't be harassed by them again. It transpired there were three escaped prisoners on the Island and I had been caught up in the search for them.

One weekend morning Sam had disappeared. He stayed out the night before as usual, but this time did not turn up for work as he normally did. I spent some time looking for him in our regular haunts but without success and so went to work shifting plasterboard and bricks. We met up again in the evening when he told me he had been to Savannah to spend some time with Joann, the catalyst for our time on the Island. How on earth did that happen I asked myself? How did I miss the signals, the chemistry between them? My romantic experiences were the antithesis of Sam's in that it seemed the coven that Chris, the ageing gay in Vera Cruz belonged to was centred on Hilton Head Island. Many of these polygamous promiscuous men bombarded me with their unsolicited attention. I felt like a fencer parrying thrusts, an uncomfortably graphic image. One asked me if I would go around to his house and mow his lawns in an 'etchings' sort of way. Fortunately he baulked at my request of $4 per hour, turning his attention back to the more usual and used receptacle for his amorous emissions, an effete limp salad of a man balanced delicately against the bar in buttock hugging jeans. Looking at my clothes I wondered if my unrequited suitor looked on me as his potential 'bit of rough'. Fortunately for me I was befriended by a number of girls in Harbour Town who lived and worked there. They proved to be an invaluable and much appreciated firewall against the interest of a number of oestrogen infused men mincing about the Island.

In what spare time we had from work we made full use of the Island's beautiful, long, sandy and completely deserted beaches, often covered in hundreds of horseshoe crabs. Strange prehistoric looking creatures, they crawled about on the sand in seemingly aimless wanderings, often coming out in the late afternoon. As our time on the Island passed, more and more work became available as the extremely expensive properties were completed. We started working fourteen hour days seven days a week and the money seemed to roll in. I spent the whole of one memorable day unloading and carrying bags of cement, the dust of which covered my clothes. The heat was intense and my jeans became soaked with sweat, to the point I looked as though I had been in a shower whilst wearing them. That was when the mixture of sweat and cement chose to dry hard in the furnace of the sun, making crossing my legs a challenge, let alone getting the Pompeii like jeans off for a shower under the Quarterdeck. No matter the length of our working day, every evening started in the Quarterdeck Bar in Harbour Town and often went on into the early hours of the morning at some party. At the end of one particularly riotous evening I drove by myself to a deserted beach at the end of Turtle Lane and swam in a phosphorous lit sea until about four in the morning. Refreshed I then lay on the sand and slept until dawn when a cooling breeze and the early morning light woke me to the sound of the waves.

Many of the people we met on the Island were there to holiday and had no sword of Damocles by way of an early morning alarm hanging over them. We burned the candle at both ends and warmed it gently in the middle. We woke in strange places, like the floor of the laundromat, on unfamiliar sofas and carpets, in corridors and on yachts. The use of drugs was almost universal, though generally restricted to marijuana, but we refused all offers to sample them or join in. In only one case did I come across someone using harder varieties. No one could understand why Sam and I did not touch it. Neither of us had ever used any form of drugs, soft or hard, but even so, we had an agreement that neither would experiment with them or try them on the trip. There was too much at stake and we had too much to lose to be caught with the stuff, even if we were tempted which was highly unlikely. In those days it was common for those who played a lot of sport, which we both did, to eschew soft drugs, leaving that to the non-jocks to play with.

Things are different now and an industry has developed to prevent sportsmen and women from cheating or or even using them recreationally. The first indications of cheating came in the east European Communist teams. The Russians produced the Press sisters, Tamara Press being an Amazonian who could casually lob a shot put distances that were the envy of some of the male athletes. Interestingly, when the clamour of suspicion became sufficiently loud, the complainers too vociferous to be ignored, the sisters retired into oblivion, refusing to take gender tests or any of the primitive drug tests that were available then. Tamara Press' constant five o'clock shadow on her chin and jowls was becoming hard to explain. I particularly remembered her for her densely sylvan armpits.

On the 11th July, after a continuous stream of nightly parties to say goodbye to us, we finally said our farewells to the many friends we had made, to so many people who had shown us kindness and generosity in amazing quantity. We poured our exhausted bodies and minds into Adolf and left Hilton Head. Our intention of staying two weeks had turned into six weeks of hard work and fun, some dollars in our pockets, bruised and abused livers and many memories and friends. Now it was time to get back on the road and head for New York, but not before paying a visit to Asheville on our way to see the Ford family who had asked us to stop by on our way north. We wondered if Larry and Ellen were in need of babysitters, having exhausted the meagre supply in Asheville that were prepared to take on the boys. We decided to stay on the back roads and wended our way north through such places as Coosawatchie and Bamberg, ending up for the night parked in some woods a couple of miles south of Swansea.

The morning brought news on the radio of the first game in the World Chess Championship in Iceland. The reports about the negotiations for the event, made tortuous by Bobby Fischer's brinkmanship and unreasonable behaviour, had continued throughout our time in the States. The first game was finally scheduled to be played on the 11th July. Boris Spassky dutifully turned up on time and took his seat. The match arbiter started the clock, Spassky made his first move and sat back, staring at the empty seat opposite him. Fischer, who had missed the opening ceremony on the 1st July and had not arrived in Iceland until the 4th July, was nowhere to be seen. Seven minutes later he entered the hall, shook Spassky's hand and sat down. Fischer lost the game, perhaps distracting himself by leaving the board at one point for half an hour to protest about the presence of a television camera. His eccentricities were seemingly running amuck and had become irrational. He knew the cameras would be there as it was the television coverage that was financing the Competition. Knowing the income it would generate he had demanded a bigger purse for turning up.

Asheville was one hundred and seventy miles north and we reached it in the middle of the afternoon to spend three days with the Ford family before heading north again to Washington D.C. On our way we stopped off in a small town called Enfield some three hundred and twenty miles east of Asheville and spent the night with one of the barmen we had met on Hilton Head.

Neighbours heard the family had visitors from England and came around to the house with food they had cooked. They never asked to be included, only wanting to hand over the welcome gift for the exotic visitors, to say hello and then to leave. Wonderful Southern hospitality from which I particularly remember a delicious blueberry pie. On our way to Enfield we used an Interstate Highway rather than our usual choice of the back roads. Drivers in passing cars hooted and waved at us, one man turning one hundred and eighty degrees in his seat to look at us out of his back window, his right hand semaphoring an enthusiastic greeting. Fortunately his car seemed to know where the road was.

The news programmes told us Fischer had now lost the second game in the Championship, possibly because once again he commenced the game by not being there when the clock was started. He was instead still arguing about the television cameras. It was agreed they would be removed and Fischer said he would play the game if the clock was reset to zero. The match arbiter refused to reset it and Fischer refused to play so forfeited the game. Two nil to Spassky. The Kremlin was beginning to polish the silver and put the vodka on ice. The White House cancelled the champagne order, grateful for having bought it on a Sale or Return basis. Perhaps they envied the Russians their gulags in Siberia, wishing they could send the increasingly embarrassing and troublesome Fischer to one to cool his heels for a while.

Virginia was exactly as I imagined it to be. We drove gently through beautiful countryside and down avenues of trees that ran between verdant rolling fields.

Expensive and pampered looking horses were contained by perfect white post and rail fencing. Gates opened onto long drives that led up to immaculate stud farms and stables and the next generation of potential race winners frolicked in the paddocks next to their mothers, free of the pressures and gamblers' expectations that would soon enough weigh on them. We were eager to get to Washington as we had a lot of work to get through there. Our experience with the Immigration fiasco in Mexico decided us on getting as many visas and entry permits as possible for the Central and South American countries so we planned on visiting all the relevant Embassies in Washington. Looking at the map and the Embassy addresses we realised the task was going to involve a lot of legwork. Reaching the city late in the afternoon we parked and had a beer as we studied a city map we laid out on on Adolf's front wing, trying to decide where to spend the night. Washington was a dangerous place to be in, more so at night, but we needed to be near the centre to reduce the effort of going round to all the Embassies on our list. As we sat contemplating and discussing our options, the driver of a passing car shouted "Rule Britannia" as he passed, waving to us out of the window. We waved back. A short while later he returned and parked in front of us, getting out and joining us. We gave him a beer and he told us he was English, a Yorkshireman called Peter, but living and working in Washington.

After chatting for about half an hour he suggested we stay with him and his American fiancé in her flat, saying it would be much safer for us. Peter said he had been driving down a street in the City a couple of weeks earlier when he had seen a man tear out of a building and sprint up the street. A few moments later another man ran out of the same building and emptied a hand gun up the street after him. He missed both his target and any stray pedestrians, shrugged his shoulders, turned and walked away, putting the gun in his pocket. Apart from some dodging out of the way of the flying bullets, no one seemed to pay much attention to the noisy interruption to their day. This seemed a good enough reason to get off the streets so, not stopping to consider what Peter's fiancé might think about having two travel worn strangers to stay, we gratefully accepted the kind offer.

The apartment was about five miles outside the City and for the next two days we hitched a ride into Washington with Peter each morning and then spent the day going around the Embassies. Before starting on the visas we needed, we went into a cheap shop to buy some flip flops, our existing ones having been completely worn out on the Island. Most of the time Sam and I split up to hasten the process since some of the Embassies did not seem to need both Passports to issue the visas. Passing the British Embassy I popped in and asked for a glass of water, which they gave me, presumably on the basis I had been a taxpayer in England. We calculated we each must have walked about fifteen miles every day as the Embassies were not all situated in one district. Some had to be visited twice, the first time to fill in the forms, the second to collect the visa. The weather was hot and it was extremely humid so miles of walking the hot plates that were the pavements was exhausting, but satisfying once we had accomplished the task in hand.

The Costa Rican Embassy needed to keep our Passports for twenty four hours to complete their paperwork, so this gave us a day in which to be tourists and see the sights. We visited all the usual suspects, the Memorials, monuments and Institutions. The Smithsonian Museum was fascinating and we wandered around its capacious interior for a couple of absorbing hours. I was particularly interested to see its collection of used spacecraft and artifacts from the space race and marveled at how small the interior of a space capsule was, and how scorched their backsides from their re-entry through the atmosphere. There was a huge queue to get into the White House so we confined ourselves to looking at it through the railings across the manicured lawns that stretched down to us from its bowed front. Sitting by the water looking at the Jefferson Memorial on the other side of the Tidal Basin, we chatted to some Americans who were also visiting the City. They gave us some of their sandwiches for lunch, an act of kindness we really appreciated. To save money we were only eating a meal every two or three days, the rest of the time living off milk into which we would whip a raw egg. Peter and his fiance had kindly upped our intake by providing us with an evening meal, but lunch was not generally on our menu of daily activities as we tramped the streets of the city. When on the road up through the Southern States we would pick cobs of corn growing in fields by the road. In the evening we would make a fire and boil a pot of water in which we cooked the day's harvest for our meal of the day. We had both lost a great deal of weight in the three months since we had left England so an unexpected sandwich at lunch was a banquet.

Fully armed with those visas we had managed to obtain in Washington, we said our goodbyes to our hosts and set off for New York in searing heat, our clothes soaking up the humidity. We felt a snorkel and flippers would have been more appropriate clothing. Fifty miles short of the City we parked for the night in a rubbish tip, an unlikely place we felt for night prowlers to be looking for likely victims. During the night Sam developed severe sinusitis which, by collaborating with a significant toothache, put him in a lot of pain. We drove over the Outerbridge onto Staten Island and then across the island to the Verrazano-Narrows Bridge. We had never experienced a bridge like the Verrazano-Narrows, with its six lanes of traffic streaming across the water over two hundred feet beneath us. We were of course at that moment blissfully unaware that there were another six lanes beneath us, nor that at that stage it was the longest suspension bridge in the world, a status it held until 1981 when the Humber Bridge in England took on the mantle. As the gateway to New York Harbour, cruise ships and container ships must be designed to be able to pass beneath it. In particular the Queen Mary 2 was designed with flatter funnel tops, but that still only gives her thirteen feet clearance at high tide. We later learned that such is the length of the bridge, the tops of the towers at each end are just over one and a half inches further apart than the bases to account for the curvature of the earth's surface,.

As we approached New York and crossed over to Brooklyn, we were shocked at the appalling state of the roads. We had not realised the City was bankrupt, and the heavily pitted roads were the first clue to its dire financial state. Its fiscal problems probably started during the Mayorship of Robert Wagner in the period 1961-65. The profligate Mr Wagner increased municipal expenditure to curry and maintain political support, a form of political blatant gerrymandering still exercised unashamedly by politicians to this day, particularly by those of a socialist persuasion who seem to have no understanding of the relationship between expenditure and income, nor the dependence of one on the other, relying instead on their belief in the limitless capacity of the taxpayers' pockets to finance the feckless in society. The City began running budget deficits in this period as the powerful public employee unions began calling strikes. Riots in ghettos in Harlem fuelled the unrest as rental control slowed the growth in property taxes. While overall taxes increased they did not do so nearly as fast as the irresponsible expenditure. Wagner's successor, John Lindsay, came to the position in 1965 and carried on with the same policies whereby increased borrowing paid for city services. In 1969 extremely generous contracts were granted to answer the public employee unions' aggressive demands, and to avoid more labour unrest. All of this combined with optimistic and creative forecasting, particularly in relation to city revenues. The culmination of this crass irresponsibility was that in 1972 the City was two years away from its near default in 1974, and hence there was no money for basic services such as road maintenance. We dodged huge and completely unexpected potholes as we drove towards Manhattan, which glimmered in the sunshine in the distance, giving us our first real view of a skyscraper city. It immediately put me in mind of an overcrowded asparagus bed whose occupants were straining to outdo each other to reach the light.

Reaching Brooklyn we made our way to Brooklyn Heights where we had arranged to stay with an ex-girlfriend of Sam's and her husband. Liz and Fletcher had a large and comfortable two bedroom apartment in a classic Brooklyn Brownstone, with steep steps from the pavement up to the front door of the building which was situated in a rather affluent area. Sam's toothache had got worse and so Liz immediately took him to her dentist while I opened and read letters from Greece. The private opening ceremony was one of those heart stopping moments when one wonders whether the envelope contains the 'Dear John' moment, with painful words of farewell, thanks, loss and little comfort. The fact there was more than one letter, and that I had received a couple in Hilton Head, should have been a clue that I should neither despair nor give up hope. How many letters does it take to say good-bye and to tell you that you are out of the picture? Logic takes a back seat when the collateral damage of separation is self doubt and uncertainty. After reading and re-reading every reassuring word, I picked up the phone and called Tucker MacKenzie, my American school friend living with his wife Jeanne in the Bronx. He worked in Manhattan, and I arranged to meet him that afternoon and to go home with him for the night. Sam and Liz returned with the news he had an abscess that meant at least one tooth had to come out, a $300 service on his dentures. Fortunately the dentist had agreed a $200 discount. I didn't like to ask whether that was because he was going to do the job without anaesthetic and at the local abattoir, thinking Sam would find out soon enough.

We took Adolf from her spot outside the apartment and put her in a lock up garage that charged $4.50 for each twenty four hours. I then ventured into the New York subway system and made my way to meet Tucker. The subway was an alien world to me. Graffiti adorned trains ran to a schedule that had fast non-stoppers to such places as Harlem where we were told the safe world ended, and stoppers that took in all the stations a visitor might need. Emerging near 34th Street and Fifth Avenue, I looked up to get my first view of the iconic Empire State Building. It was a surreal moment to stand before this world famous building that to me so epitomised the soaring aspirations of New Yorkers and their vibrant city, in the land where anything was possible for those who dreamed large.

I watched passing New Yorkers whose effervescent ebullience and zest for life encapsulated what it meant to live there. All we had heard about New York spoke of an energetic, restless town that never slept. Seeing and standing in its vitality filled streets, in the rushing stream of its hurrying, feisty inhabitants, led me to wonder whether a City gets its reputation from its architecture or its population. How much influence does the architecture have on its people. No matter which way one looks at it, I don't think you could call Bognor vibrant. New York, London, Paris yes, but Bognor? I think not. Was George V's purported death bed comment 'Bugger Bognor' a reference to its people or to its design led ambience, whatever that may be? It was a chicken and egg thought and I remained undecided as to which had the greater influence. Either way, it was immediately clear that New York had a dynamism. Some osmotic process infused energy into those who lived there or visited, exuding an infectious vivacity that inspired the visitor to explore its secrets and wares.

Tucker and I caught the subway to the Bronx and walked together to his apartment where I met the delightful Jeanne for the first time. It was a wonderful evening filled with reminiscences, interesting conversation and watching a sweating Tucker escape the humidity by hugging the air-conditioning unit. The following morning Tucker and I reversed our journey. Instead of going on to Brooklyn, I decided to spend some time walking the streets so I emerged from the subway downtown to be greeted by a misty morning. The top third of the Empire State Building was in the clouds. I walked up and down some of the avenues, and laterally between them on the cross streets. People rushed by on their way to work, and later to meetings, and I relished the time I had to stroll at my pace, enjoying the moment. The avenues seemed like canyons to me, the light in them subdued by the low cloud.

When I returned later to the apartment in Brooklyn I discovered a plan had been hatched the previous evening for us all to go up to the family cottage in New Hampshire for the weekend. Travelling over long periods first detaches you from the calendar and then from the days of the week, each day seamlessly merging into the next. With no diary or appointments to worry about, no schedule other than the rhythms of the sun and stars, days of the week become irrelevant. I had no idea the weekend loomed but was delighted to leave the hot, dirty and humid city behind and head for the crispness of the countryside.

We left that evening and six hours later at around midnight arrived at a modern house two hundred yards from the shore of Squam Lake, overlooking Bennett Cove and five miles from a small village called Holderness. Squam Lake is just north west of Lake Winnipesaukee, the largest lake in New Hampshire and where we were told by Liz and Fletcher the first boy's summer camp in America had been sited. It had been built on Church Island, one of the lake's over two hundred and fifty islands. In 1981 the film On Golden Pond would be filmed on Squam Lake but in July 1972 we felt we had the whole lake to ourselves, such was our feeling of isolation there.

I woke early in the morning and stood out on a raised deck built out at the front of the house. The dawn light came slowly into the eastern sky, bringing with its soft hues my first sight of the lake below the house and the pine forested slopes of the hills around us. The dawn chorus of birds marking their territories with song was the only sound and I lifted my face into the cool breeze and smelt the clean air, so much the antithesis to the effluent laden air in New York. My bare feet on the wooden deck felt the damp dew and I splayed my toes out to feel the wetness of the wood beneath them. I leaned my hands on the rail and watched the horizon turn from deep red, through gold to pastel blue. Suddenly the sun itself flashed its first diamond sparkle through the trees and over the hills on the other side of the lake. At first a pinprick of yellow light in the pine trees, it got larger as the burning orb lifted into the sky and freed itself from its tether to the pine trees. The house slowly woke and between breakfast and lunch a slow procession of family members arrived from the city to join in the weekend break in the country. Finally ten in number, we spent the next two days rowing a racing scull on the lake, towing a floating platform out into the lake and diving from it to swim in the cold water. We climbed the hills through the pine forests, taking in views from the mountain tops. We ate simple food, played chess, drank beer and indulged in eclectic conversations. On Sunday evening most of the family left to go back home for the start of the week but Sam, Liz and I stayed on with Liz's brother David.

On Tuesday morning we paddled over to Church Island to enjoy its peace and sense of calm, charging our batteries for the long drive back to New York that afternoon. On the journey south to the city Liz rang Fletcher to tell him when he could expect us. He told her that Sam's girlfriend in England, Heather, had phoned to say she had arrived in the States and was in Florence, Massachusetts. She had mentioned in a letter that she might come over and the knowledge that she had actually done so lifted Sam's deflated spirits. His tooth and sinus problems had persisted and we had agreed we would have to get them fixed when we got back to New York. We arrived back at the apartment in time for Sam to be able to call Heather and to make arrangements for us to go and pick her up. She was going to travel to the west coast with us and then fly back east from San Francisco or Los Angeles as she was going to do some work in New York.

Shortly after the others had gone to bed I settled down on my own bed, which was the carpet in the drawing room. My bedding was a towel from the bathroom wrapped around me.

In the morning Liz took Sam to the doctor who confirmed he had inflamed polyps and there was little he could do for two weeks until the inflammation died down. We decided there was little point in staying around wasting time waiting for him to get better as he could be doing that as we travelled. We agreed we would leave New York on Monday and spend the time before we left seeing the sights. Where to start, with so many choices? The Staten Island Ferry; the Harbour Tour; Greenwich Village where I spotted a vagrant in a trash bin on the sidewalk sleeping off a lunchtime excess of either alcohol or some chemical additive in his bloodstream; Central Park, still safe enough to stroll in; Tiffany's to stand gazing at the diamond in its case under the watchful gaze of the security men who were a little unimpressed by our tattered shorts and shirts. The Empire State Building soared above us as we went into it to catch the lift to the observation deck. Looking south I had a view of Lower Manhattan with the silhouette of the twin towers of the World Trade Centre which were newly completed. Little did I know then that some twenty nine years later I would watch their collapse in my office in London, nor that the next time I would stand on that spot, the view would be painfully poignant in the absence of those iconic towers, in one of which a school contemporary of mine died as it collapsed.

For the weekend we met Tucker and Jeanne MacKenzie at Penn Street Station and headed south to a small place called Little Silver on the Shrewsbury River, which is more of a large estuary or lake. Tucker's parents lived there quietly, partially to provide a haven of peace for Tucker's father, also called Tucker, whose job carried immense responsibility, often at international Governmental level. The family had a habit of naming the first born son after his father so my contemporary Tucker was the third iteration in the MacKenzie dynasty. Tucker the third told me with a grin that he and his father shared the honour of both being under the scrutiny of the FBI at the same time. He was under surveillance because of his anti-Vietnam war activities, and his father was under their protection because, as Vice President of US Steel, his trade dealings with the Russians at Kremlin level had brought him to the unwelcome attention of anti-communist activists. Ultimately Tucker the third was to hop over the Canadian border to skip the Draft, so great were his objections to the Vietnam.

    I had already met one or two Vietnam war veterans on our trip north and to a man they were all possessed of scrambled brains and emotions. Many were cut adrift from any post war support by an uncaring nation that was questioning the war but not questioning the lack of choice given the sons of America sent out to fight someone else's war. They had been drafted and sent over to confront an unbeatable and indomitable foe. America's belief in its invincibility and omnipotent power, fuelled by endless dollars, foundered on the rocks of the North Vietnamese fighters' indifference to suffering and hardship. At times the enemy became a colleague. I was told 'fragging' was a popular method of retribution against those officers who ruled with hard discipline, where a disgruntled grunt would roll an unpinned hand grenade under an officer's camp bed at night while he slept in it in his tent, blissfully unaware his sleep that night was to be infinite.

I had come to know Tucker's parents when I was at school. They were as welcoming in their home in Little Silver as they had been in their smart apartment in Knightsbridge, where they had regularly allowed groups of us to sleep all over it on the many times large numbers of us had stayed there. We often turned their beautiful and classy apartment into something resembling a field hospital at the Somme. After a cup of tea and a wonderful welcome, Mrs MacKenzie told Sam and me we should take our clothes off so that she could wash them for us. We were in the bedroom we were to share for the night and she stood in front of us with her arms on her hips. We hesitated, waiting for her to leave, I with a sense of dread as I remembered this forthright woman's lack of respect for convention.

"OK boys, I don't have all day, what are you waiting for"?

Sam was nonplussed and looked at me beseechingly for a lead in extricating him from his vision of a bad nightmare.

"Er, for you to go out" I replied, taking control as I was the one who knew her.

"Don't be ridiculous" she said. "Take it all off. I've been married for over forty years. If I see anything new I'll shoot it off."

In the face of this homespun logic, bashfulness really has no place, so off came the clothes and she threw trousers and shirts at us to put on, clothes that seemed to have been rejected by a charity shop as unfit for sale even by them. We quickly put them on and rejoined the family for the start of a wonderfully relaxed weekend of conversation and laughter. We spent time on the water in the family motorboat, had glasses of champagne before breakfast and lunch to celebrate Jeanne's birthday, watched American football on television and also the Rolling Stones film, *Gimme Shelter*. The film recorded the band's tour of the States in 1969 which ended in the debacle at Altamonte. The concert in California was free. The bands scheduled to play in support of the Stones included Crosby, Stills Nash and Young, Santana, and Jefferson Airplane. Because the stage on which all the bands were to play was low to the ground, a Chapter of the Hells Angels were asked to provide security. When Mick Jagger was punched by a concert goer it was a portent of what was to come. The inevitable violence resulted in a death amongst the fans. Meredith Hunter, high on drugs and crazed to distraction, pulled a gun after being punched by a Hells Angel, and was stabbed by another member of the notorious bike gang. It was surreal to sit in the comfort of a TV room in Little Silver and to watch grainy black and white images of the event three years before, one that shocked the Stones and influenced rock tour security thereafter.

With the weekend over we caught the early train back to New York, a bag full of clean clothes and spare shorts under our arm. We were wearing our new trousers which, in my case had something of a Regency stripe and were the sort of trousers only the stupid, brave or unsighted would wear. I looked like a deckchair on Brighton beach. We bade Tucker and Jeanne a fond farewell when we arrived back at Penn Street and made our way back to Brooklyn Heights. From there, Liz drove us out to friends of hers in White Plains where we had left Adolf for a well earned rest when on our way up to Lake Squam. We knew Adolf would be secure there rather than leaving her at risk in the $4.50 a day lock up we had used when we first arrived in the City.

An unexpected by product of travelling for me was incurable itchy feet. I found I was always keen to be on the move, to be looking for the next moment, incident or adventure, the next scene, town or mountain, the next people to meet or check point to negotiate. What was over that hill ahead? The unknown brings with it a frisson of excitement, that essential ingredient that turns an ordinary life into a fun and interesting one. I had enjoyed New York. It was everything anyone said about it, and more. A maelstrom that scrambled the mind and senses and left the exhausted visitor crying for more. And yet I had had enough and was glad to be on the road again, turning slowly west with California in our sights.

But first, we had to find Heather.

Posing for the Press at Harbour Town aftar a day's work on Hilton Head Island.

A GIRL CALLED ADOLF

CHAPTER 6

America - Going West - 1972

"Life is either a great adventure, or nothing."

"It's wonderful to climb the liquid mountains of the sky"

Helen Keller

Heather was in Florence. Where the hell was Florence? Certainly not in Italy unless she had used Alitalia by mistake. Looking at the map we worked out it was about one hundred and forty miles north of us in White Plains. Sam had spoken to Heather and been given vague directions so we fired up Adolf once more, said a fond farewell to Liz and Fletcher and headed for Massachusetts. We managed to find where she was staying without too much difficulty and I stood back to watch the affectionate greeting Sam and Heather gave each other, my thoughts and envy focused on a sunny beach in Greece from where there was a tug on my heart. After a coffee and sandwich with Heather's host, the three of us climbed aboard Adolf and set off for Niagara. The front seat arrangements were unconventional. Series II Land Rovers had three seats and we had removed and replaced the middle seat with a locked wooden box specifically made to fill the space. We had put a covered padded cushion on the lid and used the box to keep items we might need on a day to day basis, including maps and papers that were too big to keep in the slim leather wallets we wore permanently beneath our trousers or shorts. Our Passports lived in the wallets at all times. The padded top of the box was a comfortable place for us to rest our elbows when on the move. It now became Heather's seat for the next three weeks and I would be surprised if the poor girl did not have to see an osteopath when she arrived back in the UK.

It was the last day of July and we had been on the road for three months, not keeping to any schedule, unworried about having to hurry anywhere in particular. For the first time since leaving France we had a timeline to meet, which was to get Heather to Los Angeles or San Francisco in about three weeks. She was scheduled to do two weeks work on the east coast and would have to catch a flight back from one of the west coast cities. As we left Florence with her perched on her middle seat, we still did not feel any particular time pressure but were aware we had to keep up the pace and keep going as there was a long way to go. I hadn't thought to ask Heather what level of comfort and accommodation she expected whilst with us, what dietary requirements she had or anticipated, nor quantities she was used to. In retrospect, perhaps I should have asked her if she liked corn on the cob, poached from the fields we passed. It had become our staple and usually solitary daily diet as we took advantage of the height of the growing season.

We left Florence late in the afternoon and soon came upon a long and steep hill that dropped down before us into a valley before climbing the other side. The road ahead was completely straight and the temptation to see what Adolf could really do with her skirts hitched up and with the help of a slope and following wind was too great to resist. I accelerated as we went over the brow of the hill and when I felt the engine had got Adolf up to her maximum speed, I put the gears in neutral and let gravity take over, leaving the engine to idle. We discovered that a fully laden Land Rover can reach ninety miles an hour under the right conditions, and probably has the stopping distance of an oil tanker. I vaguely remembered one of the M V Gela's officers telling me that was about twenty miles. Lady Luck rode with us yet again and I did not have to test the inevitably useless brakes to intervene in such an act of lunacy.

As it fell dark later that evening we pulled over onto a piece of wasteland by the side of the road, lit a fire and cooked some corn for supper. Heather was thrilled with the freshness of the corn and the al fresco restaurant with its camp fire under the stars. Having donated my bed-space to Heather, reassuringly free of the slightest hint of jealousy at not having to share it with Sam, I could not be bothered to put up our small tent and so just rigged up the fly sheet to try to keep any dew off me. I blew up the air mattress we carried for these eventualities and settled down to sleep. The night was absolutely freezing and the air mattress had flatulence and so seeped wind all night. I had to re-inflate it three times as the combination of the hard ground and freezing temperatures woke me. I only slept for a couple of hours through the night, eventually giving up. I got up and nudged the fire awake with some more wood I foraged. I sat huddled next to it, squeezing warmth out of it like the last traces of the contents of an old mangled toothpaste tube, wondering why the first day of August should bring such Arctic conditions. Because we had been in permanent heat for three months the cold was particularly difficult to bear, particularly as it had arrived so suddenly, giving no time for us to acclimatise.

    With over three hundred miles to go to Niagara Falls we drove all day, finally stopping in a field to make camp about sixteen miles from the Falls. During the afternoon a ferocious thunderstorm broke out and spat its venom at us for an hour or so, such that any wood we could find in the field was too wet to make a fire with. Three young boys with motorbikes came into the field to find out who we were and what we were doing. They sat and chatted with us for a couple of hours during which I persuaded them to let me have a go on one of their motorbikes. It was exhilarating to drive around the fields, with the wind in my face, not a care in the world, not a clue how to ride a motorbike but going flat out anyway since the throttle seemed to be the one part I could control. The boys and their bikes headed off and we started a fruitless fight with swarms of mosquitos and flies before retreating from the onslaught into our respective bedrooms. The vengeful hordes were still there in the morning and the flies in particular seemed especially keen to see the Falls with us since a couple of million of them joined us in Adolf for the ride. They certainly weren't with us for the cuisine as we had nothing to eat that didn't need cooking.

To our relief and surprise we sailed through the Canadian border quickly, the Customs officials not being remotely interested in us. I wondered if they were habituated to shabby individuals arriving at the border, who perhaps they assumed were generally hippy Draft dodgers escaping the States and Vietnam. People like us were probably too unhygienic to examine in anything other than a cursory way. We were grateful to be part of the great unwashed and unclean if it meant not being searched, accepted back our stamped Passports and set off without a backwards glance. From the border post we headed for the Falls, parked Adolf in a large public car park that was already filling up with tourists' vehicles and headed across to stand by the very edge of the flowing water, feet away from where it cascaded over the lip of the Falls. The power of the rushing water as it smoothly and relentlessly streamed past was breathtaking. I stood for a long time, mesmerised, just staring into its emerald green depth, humbled and overawed by the energy in this natural phenomenon. There was a tall observation tower by the Falls with lifts running up the outside and we rode up for a view that became less spectacular as we ascended into a thin mist. We could see enough to know the shape of the Falls and to see their full width. The curved front of the cascade stretched out before us and we could see what looked like toy boats approaching the base to soak the passengers, all of whom had paid good money for a freezing drenching.

After a couple of hours we came to the conclusion there was only so much rushing water we could look at in the company of so many tourists and so we set off for Toronto, about one hundred miles away around the western end of Lake Ontario. It was still cold and we soon entered another huge storm. Rain lashed the struggling windscreen wipers and the darkened world was lit by huge flashes of lightening. Frozen and damp, we decided to push the boat out for Heather and to let her know we knew how to show a girl a good time, to spoil her. We drove into a camp site some thirty miles south west of Toronto where, for the outrageous sum of $3.50, we were allocated a parking space and as much time in the hot showers as we wanted. I have no idea how much water the other two used but I believe after I had finished Lake Ontario had dropped by a couple of inches. We celebrated with a surprise supper of corn on the cob, cooking so much of it we had enough left over for breakfast. I was sure I noticed a slight glare of animosity from Heather as she tossed the increasingly familiar hot cob from hand to hand. I put it down to her being tired and excited after her shower. She was slowly realising we only ate every other day and was finally moved to comment that she would benefit from the diet but might need to buy a belt to hold up her jeans and shorts.

Finishing the cold corn at breakfast we set off for Toronto. On the way we came up behind a group of cyclists racing along the road, noses an inch above their front tyres, backsides high in the air. I was in the driving seat and slowly pulled Adolf level with the cyclist at the back of the group, a particularly eager looking chap. I moved Adolf over close to him and, leaning out of the open window, fondled his backside with my right hand, filling an idle moment with a prank I thought might be a bit of fun. From the expression on his face it was clear he was the one person in the group without a sense of humour. Unfortunately for him, there was little he could do about it. Braking was not an option as he was being propelled along by my hand on his bulging and pulsating buttocks. Instead he peddled faster to get ahead but his legs were no match for Adolf. Like a cheetah hunting, she picked up the pace and easily kept level with him. He could only cycle in a straight line with no chance for him to swerve to escape, with Adolf on his left and the curb on this right. Perhaps he invested in a Penny Farthing for his future cycling outings to lift his backside above window level. I wonder today whether now and again, in those quieter moments we all get when alone, his mind drifts back to that moment and whether he shudders or smiles. Heather seemed to be of the opinion I had been away from a woman for too long.

We left the traumatised cyclist behind peddling feverishly to catch his companions ahead of him. They were blissfully unaware of the abuse meted out to his arse but no doubt he was about to tell them. We drove on into Toronto where we came upon a fairground that looked as though it could be fun, and a nice way to show Heather even more of a good time. There was a queue at the pay-booth to get into its car park so we put Adolf's off road skills to good use and drove over the high pavement, around the booth and straight into the lot. We parked and went to see what the fair offered in the way of attractions but decided that it was too expensive to get in and so instead remounted the pavement and headed down town. Toronto seemed very modern with interesting buildings where architects had been able to use their imagination. Their brief must have had space and modernity in mind. The City Hall was housed in one half of two crescent shaped buildings with a large plaza and low lying domed building in front of them. Slightly turned away from fully facing each other, they were like two huge hands cupping an enormous mushroom between them. The buildings were completed in 1965 and had become something of a landmark in the city. Whilst still very cold, the sun shone for us as we walked amongst the buildings for a while. The whole area was clean and cared for.

Having seen enough, we headed north for a town called Sunderland where I was hoping to catch up with an Australian friend who was working there. As it turned out he had left a month before so we had no reason to stay but carried on north, camping by the Muskoka River for the night. On the way we passed Lake Simcoe and drove through some of the most beautiful scenery imaginable, filled with lakes and pine forests, all bisected by valleys with tumbling, tinkling streams and wider rivers. The Huron Indians had lyrically called Lake Simcoe *Beautiful Water,* or *Ouentironk* in their language. In a breathtaking piece of reverse nepotism, the Lieutenant Governor of Upper Canada decided it would benefit from being named after his father. History has never revealed to me quite why Simcoe Senior warranted a piece of water being named after him. Perhaps the

Governor was creating a monument to his father's wisdom in having collaborated with his equally adoring and indulgent mother one serendipitous night to conceive him.

I climbed into my little tent down by the river as the temperature plummeted further. Once again I spent a great deal of the night frozen cold. I became strangely glad of the opportunity to get some exercise by yet again having to re-inflate my slowly leaking air mattress five times in the night as it gave up the unequal struggle of remaining firm and repeatedly succumbed to flaccid airbed impotence. I emerged at dawn to see a low mist coming off the river that ran silently by us. I lit a fire and when Sam and Heather woke up we heated up some oxtail soup for breakfast in a forlorn attempt to warm up. Sweaters were donned for the first time since we had left England and we decided to drive on through the day, heading north and then west over the top of Lake Huron. By eight o'clock in the evening we reached Echo Lake, about fifteen miles east of Sault Ste Marie on the US border. Being far north it was still light and Sam and I had decided we needed to service Adolf given the mileage we and she had done. We searched the area around Echo Lake, a beautiful and peaceful place with pine trees down to the water, but could find nothing suitably secluded and flat enough to park up for the day or two it was going to take to do the work. A lot of our equipment was going to have to come out of Adolf and we didn't want to be interrupted or have to break camp before we were finished.

Because it was so cold we decided to drive back south into the States and then on right through the night to start the search for a suitable spot the next day. We stopped in a quarry where we built a fire and cooked supper. There was a tractor there which we tried and failed to start, which was disappointing as we were looking forward to the fun of driving it around. Finishing our meal we headed for the border and the night. Once again we were surprised to get through the border without an argument or a search. Heather settled down to sleep on the mattress in the back and Sam and I then took turns to drive, heading west with the Northern Lights playing their extravagant display all night on our right shoulders. Swirling greens and pale reds washed through and around the sky in a show that can never be equalled by man, despite his ingenuity. When I first saw the lights in the heavens, they were ahead of us and it took a few seconds for me to register what I was looking at. We gazed at them in awe and with a wonder at nature's ability to choreograph breathtaking entertainment that leaves the onlooker bedazzled. It remains one of the most wonderful sights I have ever seen. Otherworldly.

In the middle of the night Sam and I stopped and boiled some water in a water heater we had bought, deciding a couple of cups of coffee would be the chemical stimulant we would need to get us through the night. Heather slept on, perhaps lulled into a deep sleep by the movement of the vehicle. Having decided to drive on, we looked at the map to select the best way forward. The logical option may have been to drop due south on fast roads and Interstate Highways east of Lake Michigan but we continued with our wish to avoid the big highways where possible and instead decided to stay north of the lake and to head for Minneapolis and St Paul. Some time before dawn we crossed into Wisconsin and at about seven o'clock came to Rhinelander, a small town with a main street and little else. We pulled into a petrol station for some fuel and asked the attendant if he knew of anywhere we could camp. He said there was a small lake with a dam about six miles away and gave us directions as to how to get there. It proved to be ideal, with flat dry earth and grass running gently down to the water. Stands of trees and bushes ringed a small beach and were the perfect cover we wanted to hide us from inquisitive eyes. Sam and Heather drove back into town to buy some food while I set up camp. I gathered dry firewood and lit a large fire in a circle of stones. When Sam and Heather returned I discovered Heather had decided that another corn on the cob was a corn on the cob too far and a change was needed. I steeled myself for some cold turkey in culinary rehab as I tried to kick the habit of the little yellow chaps.

Turning south and leaving Canada had been a conscious decision, driven by the need for some warmth. The sun shone on us we busied ourselves around the camp and rested after the long night's drive, reaping the benefit of our choice to head for where the sun might be as the temperature rose. We packed our sweaters away as Sam started the process of servicing Adolf and I played matron and head theatre nurse, handing him tools and parts. Supper was a banquet of hamburger cooked on the mesh radiator grill taken off the front of Adolf and suspended over the open fire. Heather was particularly impressed by the entomological garnish of dead flies and assorted insects that transferred from the grill to her hamburger. For the next two days we serviced Adolf, dodged rain showers that delayed us as we huddled together in the tent, fought off plagues of mosquitoes in the evenings, and cooked exotic new foods like eggs that Heather had found in the darker recesses of the small supermarket in the town. Finally Sam declared the engine service complete and turned the key to start the engine. Nuclear explosions from the engine and the exhaust indicated Adolf thought otherwise and had either contracted terminal flatulence or was in need of a little more servicing.

    I left Sam scratching his head and hitched into the town to buy a bit more food. We had run out as we had been camped by the lake longer than we had expected due to the rain and now Adolf's reluctance to co-operate. When I got back Sam was still scratching his head and Heather was beginning to wonder about Los Angeles and her diary. The eureka moment came when Sam realised he had put the spark plug leads back in the wrong order causing chaos amongst the cylinders which were now jostling for first place in the firing order, like competing Russian peasants in a bread queue. With the engine now running smoothly, Heather stopped frowning and we were able to finish the service by attending to the brakes and oil levels. As we did we acquired an audience of small boys. News of our arrival had reached the local hamlets around. Two of them were the sons of a State Patrol Officer and once the service was complete we gave them an off road ride around the lake in Adolf, which they loved. They left us and an hour or so later returned with their mother who had made us a bowl of spaghetti bolognese, yet another example of typical rural hospitality and generosity in America. We didn't just have lunch that day, we banqueted.

It was as we were eating the spaghetti that Heather noticed her signet ring was missing. As we were looking for it in the grass around the camp a boy called Peanut came up and asked us what we were doing. We explained our search and his face lit up as he told us his grandfather had a metal detector. Excitedly he ran off to get him, returning about twenty minutes later with a kindly looking, grey haired man with a warm smile. Without him and his detector we would never have found the beer bottle tops and ring pulls from beer cans buried in the soil around us. I began to wonder if we had been camping in that secret place where members of Alcoholics Anonymous (Failed) gather to commiserate with each other. When Peanut's grandfather finally found Heather's signet ring, it was buried in the mud down by the water's edge. It must have slipped off her finger when she was washing her hands, or washing plates after one of our meals. Yet again, I was amazed at the combination of chances that came together to influence an outcome. What was the likelihood that young Peanut would happen to come upon us in the middle of our fruitless search? That he would turn out to have a grandfather with a metal detector who happened to live nearby and who was at home at that time and would have the kindness and patience to systematically search for a tiny metal object?

Heather didn't seem to waste too much time wondering about this tenuous web of serendipity. She was just grateful to have her ring back and Peanut's grandfather seemed delighted with his reward of a kiss on the cheek from a pretty young girl. He and Peanut bade us farewell and walked off together, the grandfather's arm affectionately hanging over Peanut's shoulder, his young arm around the old man's waist. We could hear them chatting happily about the success of their mission of recovery and my mind memorised the epitome of what it must be to be the perfect grandfather, an aspiration for me to carry into my later life. For our part, we were left to deal with an officious and extremely obnoxious warden who had appeared in the middle of the great search, demanding to know why we were camping there. It was nearly dark as the evening was closing in and he told us we had to leave in the morning, taking Sam's name and address in case he wanted to get hold of us to come back and clean up any mess we may have left behind. I wonder at what point in the ensuing hours it occurred to him, as he studied his notebook, that writing to us in England to get us to come back and clear up any mess bordered on the imbecilic.

When he left we ate a blueberry pie that had been delivered to us by a couple of other children who had obviously reported to their mother that three starving castaways were beached on the lakeshore. Their report prompted her to start baking the pie for us, and it was delicious. We were just preparing for an honourable retreat to bed to escape from the evening raid by the mosquitos when Peanut returned to invite us to have breakfast with his family in the morning. Naturally Heather accepted on our behalf as she eyed the quaking clutch of corn on the cob, huddled in the pot like missionaries in a cannibal camp awaiting their hot bath over the fire in the morning.

Waking to our usual alarm call of the dawn chorus, we washed and bathed in the lake and walked over to Peanut's house, following his directions on how to get there, as if the scent of crisping bacon was not a sufficiently clear trail for us to follow. Peanut proudly introduced his exotic find to his attractive and smiling mother, Polly. She greeted us as she busied herself with cooking breakfast. The mother of six children, five of whom were the shyest people I had ever met, she was alone with them in the week as her husband worked away from home in Milwaukee. Looking at the six children around the table, silently tucking into their cereal and scrambled eggs, it dawned on me what her husband's weekend hobby must be. It certainly wasn't gardening. Polly gave us an enormous breakfast after which we said our grateful goodbyes and returned to our camp to clear up, mindful of that authoritative letter awaiting us in England if we didn't. With just ten days to get to Los Angeles we set off and drove uneventfully all day, stopping for the night in a field, which attracted the attention of two farmers who appeared within five minutes of our arrival to enquire what we were doing there. Once they realised we were harmless and unlikely to pollute their land they said we could stay the night. Strangely they didn't threaten us with a letter.

Two more days of driving west brought us to the barren Badlands in South Dakota, an extraordinary geological sight of harsh desolation with its sharp pinnacles of worn rock dividing deep ravines, interspersed with great prairies across which thousands of buffalo once roamed. We were told the American Indians learned to stampede the buffalo so the huge beasts ran off the edge of cliffs to their death on the rocks below. It was obviously an easier way of hunting them and no doubt tenderised the meat in the process as the unfortunate animals jumped in their terror and landed on the valley floor below. The Lakota Indians were eventually elbowed out of their own lands by European settlers and the soldiers who accompanied the intruders to protect them. After the massacre at Wounded Knee in 1890, the remaining Indians were forced into reservations, their way of life destroyed and replaced by alcohol, an alien drink to them but one that ruined many lives. I was saddened to see a number of listless Indians sitting on the porches of small wooden houses, dressed in full Indian clothes, some of the men with feathered head dresses. They were objects of curiosity for voyeuristic tourists to gape at and photograph. That such proud people with a history embedded in the very soil of their land should be reduced to this zoo-like existence of hopelessness was for me a stain on the soul of those who trumpeted the benefits of the land of the free. Those early evictees and successive generations paid a terrible price for having the temerity to live where mineral and vegetive wealth lay, victims of the invader's greed. In 1980 the Supreme Court confirmed that the wresting of the Black Hills from the Indians was illegal and awarded them significant compensation, which the proud and non-materialistic Indians have refused to accept or take, rather demanding the return of the land to its rightful owners. There is no adequate compensation for extinction.

Crossing the vast Missouri River we came to Mount Rushmore and gazed up at the extraordinary carvings in the cliff face above us. Presidents Washington, Jefferson, Roosevelt and Lincoln stared sightlessly into the distance, frozen in time. Work on the sculptures started in 1927 and the whole enterprise was fourteen years in the making. Four hundred and fifty thousand tons of rock was extracted, no doubt populating many a rockery in gardens around the country. My lack of artistic talent struggled to comprehend how the project could have been conceived, let alone achieved, and how the artists had managed to portray the Presidents' faces so accurately and on such a scale. I read one of the information boards giving facts and statistics and noted that the Presidents' mountain top noses were twenty feet long and was encouraged to note that people like me could rise to such positions of power and fame.

From Mount Rushmore we drove on into the beautiful, pine covered slopes of the Black Hills. Granite outcrops and mountain meadows with dancing wild flowers broke the dark face of the crowded forests that had prompted the Lakota Indians to name the area as they had, a name that lasts to this day. We eventually stopped to build a fire in a clearing by the road to cook Heather a surprise supper of plundered corn on the cob. Setting off again into the night we saw a huge storm brewing in the sky ahead as we crossed into Wyoming. We stopped at a garage for some fuel late in the night and as we filled up we chatted to some locals, one of whom had just caught a rattlesnake which he proudly showed us. I had never seen a rattlesnake before and so was not too familiar with their normal demeanour, but even I could work out this one was mildly irritated and obviously just a little short tempered as it waved and shook its pointed arse full of marbles at us. As we left the garage I suggested to the man that he might struggle to house-train it and make it the family pet.

After nineteen hours on the road that day we were looking forward to a few hours sleep and came to a rest area by the side of the road. With the threat of the storm now gone, and being tired, I dispensed with the tent and lay out on the ground under the stars and immediately fell asleep, dreaming of Yellowstone, the next significant point of interest on our travels, rattling tails and huge rock noses, visions in the cliffs I passed as I walked in the light surf along a golden Greek beach with a girl's soft hand in mine.

With a long way still to go to get to Yellowstone, dawn found us on the road again, driving across the flat plains and into the spectacular Bighorn Mountains. We reached an elevation of 8,950 feet as we passed through Granite Pass. The temperatures had soared and our thermometer indicated 96°F so we stopped at a tumbling mountain stream and bathed in its freezing waters before descending into the vast rolling prairies of the mid-west. We stopped in Cody where Heather insisted on buying us coffee and apple pie in a cafe in the town. She was becoming concerned she was taking on something of a corn on the cob, canary hue and that her ribs were showing, such was her weight loss from lack of food. The cafe was full of a cosmopolitan crowd of people who, from snatched conversations we could overhear, were all also on their way to Yellowstone. Luxuriating in the unfamiliar sensation of full stomachs we set off from Cody and eventually stopped in a camp site by a beautiful lake in the shadow of mountains, about forty miles short of the park.

Another dawn start got us ahead of the sleeping occupants of the camp site and we climbed up to the East Gate into the Park where we were let in without charge as a reward for being British. Sometimes it pays to be on the same side as the Americans in a War and listen to them tell you how they won it for you. The East Gate was at an altitude of 6,951 feet and from there we climbed straight up to the Sylvan Pass at 8,541feet. I had no preconceived ideas about Yellowstone, except perhaps that we might see bears, so had no idea how mountainous it was, nor how wonderful and naturally beautiful. From a high vantage point about twenty miles past Sylvan Pass we were able to gaze down on Yellowstone Lake, which lay quietly about five hundred feet beneath us. It languished in its solitude, glistening in the sun with a pine tree clad ring of steep mountainside enclosing its one hundred and thirty nine square mile area. The scenery was spectacular as we drove on down to Pelican Creek, crossing it via a fishermen festooned Fishing Bridge, bristling with expectant fishing rods. From the Bridge we drove on to Hayden Valley which was a large green plain of marsh and marsh grasses.

As we arrived in the valley we spotted a huge moose at the bottom of a slope by the side of the road, one that I felt just needed a little visit and a photograph for its family. Taking my flip flops off I clambered down the steep slope and was soon up to my calves in thick, gelatinous mud. The moose was a morose creature whose mother can have been the only creature to find him attractive, particularly as he seemed to carry his testicles under his chin, which was puzzling as he had another pair, aft facing in the usual site. A scrotal sized bag was swinging in the breeze from beneath his lower jaw. I wondered if moose had a spare set, as Adolf had spare tyres, or perhaps they were under his chin to lift them clear of brambles. I realised I had much to learn about moose anatomy. As I approached him, in full view of a gathering crowd of tourists at the top of the slope, he turned a baleful eye on me, methodically masticating the grass in his mouth. He seemed to be weighing his options, one of which was obviously a bit of charging at me for some vigorous trampling. I got to within about six feet of him, which is when I found out just how enormous a male moose is. We eyed each other for a while before I took my photograph and turned for the climb back up to the road, now covered in mud. The onlookers seemed to feel cheated that the moose had not engaged arms, like a front row of tricoteuses denied their moment by a guillotine's blade failing to fall. Somewhat selfishly I felt he had made the right choice.

The Grand Canyon of Yellowstone has been formed by the Yellowstone River which enters the Park from the north and exits from the south. It is an artist's palette with the most amazing colours in its steep sides, particularly in the area of its two sets of waterfalls, perceptively called Upper and Lower Falls. We gazed along the Canyon's length from Artist Point and then from Inspiration Point, both aptly named for the creative eyes that would gaze down and wonder how to recreate the colours on canvas, to me an almost impossible task. How can we ever do real justice to nature's magnificence when she really decides to put on a show? Leaving Inspiration Point we came upon a camper van that seemed to have stalled on the steep road leading up from it, the incline being too severe for the driver to get started on. We stopped and asked the driver if he would like some help. His wife and young children looked at us beseechingly, so we took that as an affirmative. Reversing Adolf down to the front of the camper, we hitched some tow rope to it, engaged low box and slowly pulled the vehicle to the top of the hill where it had the strength to carry on on the level ground under its own steam. The extremely grateful driver insisted on giving us $5, which Heather quickly requisitioned in her new capacity as Catering Manager.

Once we knew the man could restart his mobile home, filled with a now relieved family, we set off and almost immediately came upon a couple of black bears that were foraging by the roadside. We stopped and one ambled over to us, stood up and leant one arm on the jerry cans next to me, like a customer at a bar about to order a beer. That was the moment I learnt about bear breath. As scents that plumb the depths of atrocious, and with exploded inside out Mexican cat as a benchmark, bear breath goes the extra mile. A scent measurement scale that put Parisian perfume at one, skunk essence at eight and putrid Mexican cat at ten would rate bear breath at about one hundred and twenty. I sat perfectly still with the bear's face inches from mine as it sniffed at me through the open window. I was grateful it wasn't a grizzly bear as I would have been staring at its navel. It eventually seemed to get bored of this, dropped down and ambled off. I noticed there were no flies around its face so clearly even those remarkably unfussy insects could not take the vapours.

At Mammoth Springs we came upon three bald Chinese men who were visiting the Park with a tour guide. They had taken their clothes off and were posing in front of the springs in rather unpleasant looking G strings. The modern fashionista would probably call them stone age thongs. The reluctant, fully clothed tour guide was being made to take photographs of them with their cameras, their genitalia thankfully bagged up and out of view in little sacks hanging from their waists on thin ties. Whenever I see Hare Krishna devotees walking up and down Oxford Street in London chanting their beliefs, two fingers of one hand in little pouches, I am reminded of the three Chinese and their rather inelegant underwear. Leaving the little bathing party, we walked around the Springs absorbed by the spectacular array of colours. The water and mud bubbled, boiled, plopped and steamed about us and the smell of sulphur was at times almost overpowering. Returning to Adolf we came upon the Chinese trio once more. Clearly the heat of the springs was too much for clothing and so the prototype thongs had been discarded and the little men were sitting naked in the hot water. One of them was washing his colleagues' backs, soaping enthusiastically, perhaps a bit disturbingly affectionately. I assumed their testicles, freed from the constraints of their little cod pieces, were bouncing around in the bubbling water, like boiled eggs in a pan on a stove. Given the temperature of the water and its toxicity, I don't suppose any of them has ever been able to father children. The guide was busy slitting his throat.

Old Faithful dutifully ejaculated on cue, after which we went to buy ice creams but, to Heather's cheek-reddening embarrassment, were ejected for not wearing shirts. Heather dipped into the catering budget and brought the ice creams out to us. We left the Park through the South Gate and headed for the majestic Grand Teton Mountains where we found an old river bed in which to stop for the night. We sat by our camp fire to marvel at the range and wonder of the sights we had seen that day, a visual overload of colours, scale and vistas. They say Yellowstone may explode one day in a cataclysmic eruption. After what we had seen that day, I believe that would be the only thing to have bettered our experience, albeit how fleeting that sensational moment would be.

The next morning we washed and bathed in the nearby river that still flowed down the valley in its new course, and then had a leisurely breakfast. It was a Sunday and Salt Lake City was our next port of call. We needed to cash a traveller's cheque so there was no point in getting there until the following morning when the banks would be open. We chatted to an American couple who were wandering up and down the dry part of the river bed where we were camped. They were hunting for rocks, as one does. In retrospect, perhaps the man was Gary Dahl, the Californian who came up with the idea of the 'Pet Rock' and became a millionaire in 1975 when he marketed them as the ideal pet, easy to house train and to teach to 'Sit' and 'Stay'. Perhaps the failure of the pets to

'Walk to heel' was why the craze only lasted about six months and he subsequently received a few lawsuits from slightly unbalanced pet owners when they realised their pets were deaf. We left them to their foraging for suitable breeding stock for their Pet Rock zoo at about mid-day. As we had plenty of time for the drive to Salt Lake City Sam and I decided to take a somewhat off-road route to get away from civilisation, and for the sheer fun of putting Adolf through her paces. Heather happened to see the map opened out on Adolf's bonnet. Seeing our fingers tracing the thin line of the track we had spotted, she suggested it looked a bit rough and probably too difficult, so we took on her consternation and concern. Taking the rough track with me at the wheel, Sam and I were eager for some intrepid Adolf moments, the last of which we had had on some of the Mexican back roads. Heather was eager for an airport's departure lounge. Before disappearing off into the wilds we filled up with fuel and topped up the water in the drinking water jerry cans.

The small side road gave way to a reasonable dirt road which we followed for a few miles, tracking the shore of Bear Lake to a small village called Laketown, after which the rather smart gravel road disappeared to be replaced by its poor cousin, the mud track that followed a stream we had seen on the map. The dirt road had thrown up huge amounts of dust which, yet again, filled Adolf and lay on us like a shroud. A storm broke over us, the deluge turning the dust in the road to mud, solving the problem of Adolf looking like sepulchral ghost, and clearing the windscreen so I could see where the path was ahead of us. The track in the bottom of the narrow valley crossed the rocky stream seven times and so did we, giving Heather heart palpitations as we waded the deep water. The track began to narrow alarmingly so that bushes were scraping along each side of the vehicle. We were now driving along the steep bank with Adolf at a seemingly perilous angle as she slipped sideways towards the water. Heather had lost her jonquil hue and was now looking a more Arctic white as she clutched the roof bars to stop herself falling out of the vehicle. After about five miles, the track completely disappeared into an uncrossable, wide and deep pit, where the track had been washed away by the stream, so Sam and I reluctantly had to concede defeat and retrace our steps. Going back entailed reversing for quite a while as it was impossible to turn round, given our tilted angle and the vegetation and foliage pressing against us. With seven more river crossings with which to entertain Heather we finally made it back to Laketown.

Giving Heather the casting vote for a change, or in this case the only vote, we agreed we should stick to tarmac for the rest of the day, coming to stop by the road for the night an hour or so away from Salt Lake City. Sitting in the dark around the camp fire, eating our first meal for two days, a beef risotto we had brought with us in a packet from England, we were suddenly entertained to a huge eruption and firework display from the fire as three of the four batteries Sam had thrown into it exploded. Everything we had ever learned from watching the Red Arrows Aerobatic team was instantly put to good effect as we sprinted in all directions from our home made firing squad. I assumed the Red Arrows pilots don't have to do their displays whilst holding plates of beef risotto. Recovering a bit of composure we returned and rummaged in the burning fire for the fourth of the quartet but could not find it and consequently I lay on the ground in the open air by the fire for the rest of the night fully expecting to be shot.

The fourth battery remained tantalisingly inert, to be unearthed in the morning when I sifted through the embers before Sam and Heather got up. I took it down to the stream and immersed it in the cold water as I washed before breakfast. Salt Lake City later that morning was remarkable only for the size of the Mormon Temple in the centre of the city. Standing in the middle of a ten acre square, it seemed to take up all of it, shining white in the sunlight, a monument to the tithes from the faithful spirit-children of God that must have funded its construction. Over two hundred feet high, the building was started in 1853 but not finished until 1892 nearly forty years later. Unbelieving heathens like us were still not welcome inside. The earlier drive into the city centre was through filthy, smog-choked streets, the foul fumes emanating from the all pervasive industrial sites on the outskirts. There seemed to be little to hold our interest and we left after cashing our traveller's cheque and buying some provisions. On the way out we decided to visit the Bingham Canyon Copper Mine, the deepest open mine in the world. Another huge storm broke out as we arrived but even through the driving rain we were overawed by the mine's vastness. Two and a half miles wide and three quarters of a mile deep, it accommodated machinery and vehicles built to its scale. One of the earth carriers passed us, laden to its one hundred and twenty ton capacity. With tyres at least a foot taller than Adolf, she could have fitted on the monster truck's bonnet as an emblem. The Bingham Canyon Spirit of Ecstasy.

The western horizon was clear of clouds and rain and beckoned, so we left the mine and the deluge behind and headed for the Great Salt Flats. The final stretch of the road before getting to the Bonneville Salt Flats was straight for thirty six miles, without the slightest hint of a deviation. We stopped and walked out onto the salt, stooping to taste it. It was salty. The sun beat down on both us and the Flats. The harsh white reflection was painful on our eyes and we squinted as we looked across the completely featureless, almost snow white landscape, a mirage shimmering in the middle distance. Crossing into Nevada we left the salt plains behind, almost immediately replacing them with a vast flat scrub desert with mountain ranges always in view in the distance, left and right of us. Looking at the map we could see this desert was huge and would take more than the rest of the day to cross. For my night under the stars in the desert, I slung a hammock between two conveniently placed trees, climbed in and was rocked all night by a strong, warm wind blowing across the open desert. In the morning we drove on, stopping in Cold Springs to wash under a hose we saw attached to a tap near a garage. We crossed the Californian border at South Lake Tahoe and kept driving west towards Sacramento, once more stopping by the road for the night, this time in a stand of tall pine trees.

We were quite high in the mountains and with a completely clear night the temperature crashed. In a fruitless attempt to warm ourselves, a job the camp fire was failing in, we each had a glass of rum from a bottle left over from Hilton Head. I climbed into my sleeping bag on the ground to get warm, staring up into the huge sky that stretched horizon to horizon above me. Billions of stars shone and sparkled in the blackness of the cloudless night. As I lay there transfixed by the vastness of space, I seemed to be sucked further up into it as the stars took on a three dimensional illusion, breeding and multiplying, my sight traveling through and between them, ever deeper into limitless space. It was a surreal, almost out of body sensation which, whilst brief and transitory, vividly stays with me to this day. The hallucinatory sensation was branded into my memory, with neuronal paths and synaptic bridges that perhaps only dementia will destroy. Only occasionally under similarly vast black skies, untainted by Man's polluting light, have I been able to recreate that experience, and I always long to do so. Perhaps it would happen more often if I drank rum before sleeping under the stars.

The freezing air woke me early and I got up and relit the fire, sitting by it while I waited for Sam and Heather to wake. Shared body warmth was clearly a more effective soporific than a solitary frost encrusted sleeping bag on the ground. When they got up we made coffee and consulted our diaries. It was a bit of a surprise when it dawned on us we had two days in which to get Heather to San Francisco for her flight back to the East Coast. While Heather panicked, in the true spirit of our disdain for a timetable, breakfast for Sam and me was a leisurely affair before we were on the road again. I was at the wheel as we came into the outskirts of Sacramento where we came upon men painting white lines on the freeway. The freshly painted lines had been marked off with large and bright plastic cones set at carefully spaced and equal intervals on the right side of the road. Bored with the drive I decided to play a game of Cone Skittles and started to weave Adolf left and right, knocking over each successive cone with the front right edge of her bumper. Each cone made a satisfying thud as it was hit, tipping over and off the freshly painted white line it was jealously guarding. This was a great jape that we were completely unaware was allowing our front right wheel to drive over the wet paint in the fresh lines on the road. Sam looked back and suggested I look in the rear view mirror at the wonderful new weaving line now painted all over the road next to the straight one. Irate workman were screaming obscenities, shaking their fists and running around. One or two jumped into vehicles and set off after us. The posse was in hot pursuit, the chase was on. It was the Wild West, the exhilaration of being hunted creating a frisson of tension and a burning desire to escape, to win the race. We were the Pony Express to the road worker's Apache Indians, fully expecting our saddle to be pierced by flying arrows. A bright orange truck flashed past us with the driver speaking into a radio, waving his other arm at us, clearly indicating he wanted us to stop behind him as he crossed in front of us and pulled over. This did not seem a good time to stop for a cozy chat to cement international relationships, nor a time to tell him it was dangerous to have both hands off the steering wheel. It was more a time for right foot to the floor so I pulled out and overtook him as he slowed. We carried on as he climbed out of the vehicle, still on his radio and clearly calling for reinforcements. Probably the police we surmised. Unfortunately, the slalom line was now dead straight, a Hansel and Gretel trail leading those following straight to wherever we were going.

Sam was watching our rear and said the man had jumped back into his truck and was setting off after us again, following our tracks. On an objective level, it was amazing to us just how much paint a tyre could carry in its tread and how long it could keep painting the road. Someone really should patent the idea. On a subjective level we wished the bloody thing would empty itself so we could disappear and escape the avenging hordes. I could see our pursuer close behind in the rear view mirror, still on his radio in a conversation he carried on just behind us for the next ten miles. We came to an exit and he pulled off onto it, leaving us to continue. We assumed there would now probably be a road block ahead, but within a short distance another exit came up so I took that, dropping down off the freeway. We drove into a shopping mall's large car park, hid Adolf in the throng of vehicles and went for a walk for twenty minutes, hoping any waiting police would get bored and move on. As we got back to Adolf to drive away to escape the city, an elderly man came up in his pick-up and parked next to us. He got out and asked us if we wanted any melons. His truck was laden with them. Saying yes I asked him how much they were but he refused any money and gave us two ripe, huge honeydew melons. He told me he had cancer of the mouth and he grew melons to give away to the poor. Every now and then in life we come upon philanthropic altruism, or where someone can see above and through their own problems and focus on those of others they mistakenly believe to be worse off than them. He was a lovely man who in two minutes taught me a lifelong lesson. That's a special gift.

Our run in with 'paint man' and Adolf's highly distinctive appearance influenced our decision to leave Sacramento and keep on moving. We had little time to spare for a stay in another police cell, given that Heather's pilot was unlikely to be sympathetic to a request to delay take off in the morning. About forty miles from San Francisco we pulled into a camp site for a luxury stop that would allow Heather to freshen up in hot running showers rather than cold running streams. We decided we would have an early night and then leave very early to drive through San Francisco before it woke up, allowing us to see it in the dawn before going to the airport to drop Heather off at departures. Sam and Heather took the decision seriously and went to bed at seven o'clock but as I was not tired I went down to the Sacramento River running serenely by the camp and sat on a rock to wait for the sunset.

As I sat taking in the stillness and quiet, a family arrived at the water's edge, led by a gargantuan mother and an equally cellulite encased father carrying a clutch of fishing rods in a red, mottled and pudgy fist. Their three children followed behind, grumbling their irritation at being dragged away from the television as they clambered over the stones and boulders on the sloping riverbank. Mother hovered her huge buttocks over a terrified, trembling rock and settled down on it like a hippo smothering a baby. The oldest of the trio of children, a boy aged about sixteen, cast his line in the water, caught something resembling a shopping trolley and threw the rod down on the ground, stomping off to sulk. His sister, a rather plump bonsai version of her mother, was fishing a little down stream and also caught an immovable object, which could easily have been the opposite bank. Despite it being obvious that whatever she had attached to the end of her line was not going anywhere, she decided to pull it in. She heaved and strained on the rod, which bent double in agony. When this achieved nothing, she glanced over her shoulder and on seeing no one in the family was paying her any attention, she dropped the rod and grabbed the line with her hands, leaning back with her considerable weight until it eventually gave up the unequal struggle and snapped, dumping her on her backside, crushing a few square metres of insects sheltering in the grassy bank she had moved back to.

Mother continued to sit on the rock like an obese ostrich incubating an egg. The poor rock seemed to be oozing beads of sweat, like a damp sponge having the final drops of fluid squeezed out of it. The youngest child, a boy of about twelve, appeared to catch something big. Instead of reeling it in, his novel fishing style was to run up the river bank flat out dragging the fishing rod and his line behind him, towing his hapless catch through the water. His father's fishing line followed him as that was what he had caught. The bovine mother chewed methodically on her cud as she surveyed the chaos by the river, the rock beneath her now visibly bleeding as the life was crushed out of it. This impromptu entertainment filled a couple of hours for me, the sunset passing by unnoticed. As the bickering quintet left I retreated to the campsite to lie down for some sleep.

We left the campsite at one o'clock in the morning and drove into San Francisco. It was empty so we had an unimpeded trip around it as dawn came up. The Golden Gate Bridge was shrouded in an early morning mist as we headed down to Fisherman's Wharf where people were preparing for the day's arrival of tourists and shoppers. We drove to the Transamerica Pyramid, the eight hundred and fifty foot spear in the centre of the city. I had been interested in seeing it as one of our flatmates in London had been involved in insuring it at Lloyds of London when it was being built. He had explained to us the intricacies of the construction that allow the building to shake and sway in an earthquake. In 1972 it was still the tallest skyscraper in the west of the country and seemed to me to be ahead of its time with a timeless modernity. We climbed up and down the steep streets of the city, following the cable pulled street cars. In Chinatown we seemed to be a tourist attraction in our own right as the early birds on their way to work stopped and stared at Adolf, who was looking well travelled.

Heading out to the airport we were stopped by a police car containing two extremely aggressive policemen. They carefully examined my Passport and driving licence, scratching their shaved heads as they puzzled over whether the licence was appropriate for America. They were also interested in my drinking habits, unaware that we had empty beer cans rolling around at our feet inside Adolf, something of an offence under the strict driving laws of California. Finally satisfied I was not drunk and that we were harmless they relaxed, took off their rude badge and let us go, allowing us to reach the airport where we parked by a chain fence at the edge of the runway. We had quite a bit of time to kill before we had to drop Heather off so settled down for a quick sleep. I lay in the gravel strip by the side of the road and dozed off to the subtle lullaby of a nearby Jumbo's four engines revving up for take off.

It was sad to say goodbye to Heather. After having her with us for nearly three weeks we had grown used to her company, her cheerful acceptance of our eccentricities and desire to do things differently, her uncomplaining acceptance of the discomfort of our mode of travel and her restricted diet. She disappeared into the cavernous airport clutching her ticket and rucksack, hurrying to catch her plane. I do not know whether she was sad or glad to go. It must have been a relief for her to settle herself back into the luxury of a comfortable airline seat. Comfortable is a relative term and I use it in relation to the discomfort of being seated on a padded wooden box in a hard sprung Land Rover. As Heather merged with the gloom in the terminal building, our waving arms dropped and we pulled into the traffic to head south.

Mexico beckoned, but first there was Los Angeles to discover, a city that would change Sam's life and define his future.

A GIRL CALLED ADOLF

CHAPTER 7

Los Angeles to Mexico - 1972

"Your present circumstances don't determine where you can go. They merely determine where you start"
Nido Qubein

"Believe you can and you are halfway there"
Theodore Roosevelt

As Heather soared up into the blue Californian sky, we headed south on Route 1, hugging the beautiful coastal road. The Pacific breakers rolled onshore in their relentless rhythm. They were bathed in the sunshine as they crashed on the cliffs and rocks beneath us, throwing up rainbowed spray to be caught and dispersed in tiny droplets by the breeze. At Monterey we headed inland, driving through an arid landscape that was beautiful in its starkness. Near Templeton we visited a couple of vineyards, or wineries as many called themselves. At the second, Rotta Winery, we met and chatted to Mr Rotta the owner, asking if he had any work. He said he would employ us as grape pickers when it was time to start the harvest but it was too early and we should come back in a couple of weeks. We continued south, still mostly sticking to the small back roads that allowed us to see the real America. You cannot see or absorb the soul of a country from Freeways that whisk the traveller past a country's culture and heart, only allowing a fleeting view of fast moving landscapes. We passed cotton fields, our first view of the plant. Seeing the fields prompted us to stop and pick some to examine it in its raw state. In Lake Hughes we filled up with fuel whilst being harangued by a drunk woman swigging beer from a can. Her short, tight skirt hung under her bare belly, which hung down like a dimpled pelmet. With a damp cigarette hanging limply from her lower lip, she was trailer trash personified. Further down the road we came upon vineyards that were advertising wine tastings so we pulled into a couple and tasted, feasting on the little bits of cheese and bread they offered to accompany the wine. As we neared the sprawling suburbs of Los Angeles we succumbed to the inevitable and moved off the side roads we habituated out of choice and onto Route 5, the freeway heading south to the city.

It was early evening, a huge blood red sun was hanging low in the sky to our right and Lobo was singing on the radio. The line 'We motored stately into big L.A.' was particularly apt as we rolled down the freeways into the heart of the city. *Me and You and a Dog Named Boo* was a huge hit, Lobo's first single, selling over a million copies. It might have been written about us and even now some of its lyrics take my mind straight back to being on the road;

> "The bright red Georgia clay
> And how it stuck to the tyres
> Travellin' and living off the land
> Driving through the wheat fields of St Paul
> That old car's buggin' us to go
> Another tank of gas
> And back on the road again."

Whilst Lobo also sang about 'settlin' down', doing that was far from our minds and, like his old car, Adolf certainly did keep 'buggin' us to go', to get away. Truckers in the States seemed to hold a special and romantic place in the hearts of the American people. Perhaps this came from the journeys made by the early settlers who moved out into the unknown vastness of the west, like us under canvas but with real horsepower, always moving on and writing themselves into the history of the new emergent Nation. There were bumper stickers and posters everywhere saying 'Keep on Trucking". Americans were fascinated by the concept of being on the move, and many we met on our journey through the country referred to this when talking to us. The road trip story of the film *Easy Rider;* free spirited hobos jumping freight trains; the traveller always on the move. All somehow reached into the soul of Americans, appealing to their sense of exploration, imprinting their genes with a need for adventure, even if only vicariously through people like us where they could believe they were on the trip with us without subjecting themselves to any of the risks. Their celebration of adventurers on the move sat strangely with their introversion given that so many seemed to us to be unaware of a world existing outside their shores, or indeed outside their State or County. International news in the newspapers referred to what was happening in the surrounding or neighbouring States so we had been unable to find any world news, or that relating to Britain, which now seemed another planet to us, so detached had we become from it.

Our destination in Los Angeles was the suburb of Upland, east of L.A., where we were to meet up with Jim and Karen Rosser, family friends of my girlfriend. Burbank, Pasadena and Pomona all slid past us as we drove the seemingly endless Freeways running through the sprawling conurbation that was Los Angeles, almost a State in its own right. I had never seen a road network like it with its hundreds of miles of multi-lane freeways. Inevitably driving them was boring and so a bit of fun was needed to lighten the day. It was a hot afternoon so we had taken the tops off the doors and had rolled up the back screen to allow a draught of cooling air to circulate around us. Following and passing drivers were honking their horns at us, waving in that wonderfully friendly American way. Sam put on the uncontrollable cruise control while I put my bare feet out of the passenger window in the sun. I leant my right elbow on the padded storage box between us, so recently Heather's seat, and held the bottom of the steering wheel with my right hand, out of sight of any following drivers. Sam then climbed into the back on our bed and sat at the back waving at following cars, who could quite clearly see there was no one driving Adolf as she bumbled along the road at a steady fifty miles per hour, the driver's seat and steering wheel strangely deserted. Faces turned white at this Marie Celeste moment, and drivers rapidly overtook us to get out of harms way, getting a cheery wave from me as I lounged in the passenger seat, still with my feet hanging out over the open top of the door. In a long life filled with insane moments, I think this particular jape is up there with the best of them. Another of our nine lives was cashed in at the bank of fun that day.

We finally arrived at Jim and Karen's address at about eight o'clock in the evening and they came home about an hour later. In the hour we spent waiting for them we went to a nearby shopping mall and bought a Mickey Mouse wristwatch each at a J C Penney store. Mickey's arms moved slowly around the dial to semaphore the time, and at half past six to protect his genitals, like a footballer facing a free kick or a straying husband his irate wife. We assumed a Marilyn Monroe watch, whose legs moved, had proved something of a failure. It was the 18th August and we had been on the road for nearly four months. We experienced the ecstatic joy of being greeted by letters waiting for us at Jim and Karen's apartment and spent part of our days in the city reading them and replying to them. We also spent the time visiting places of interest around Los Angeles and buying equipment for Adolf to see us through the South

American leg of the trip. We pulled in to the Beverly Hills Hotel for a comfort break but on seeing the concierge's expression at the state of Adolf parked under the canopy outside the hotel's front door we felt it wise to move on and find somewhere less salubrious to relieve ourselves and to cruise Sunset Strip in West Hollywood. In the late 1950's and early 1960's a television programme called 77 Sunset Strip was pretty much required viewing for our generation, so it was fascinating for us to drive up and down its familiarity.

Old Baldy in the San Gabriel Mountains was an opportunity to get some exercise and clean air to clear out the Los Angeles smog as we scrambled and walked over its bare slopes. The Ontario Motor Speedway gave us the opportunity to see cars being driven faster than seemed possible. A slightly more matronly and sedate Adolf had a service in the car park outside Jim and Karen's apartment. Jim contacted a local newspaper, the Pomona Bulletin, which sent a very pretty young reporter to interview us for a feature in the paper. Sam and I still felt it would be a good idea to get some work for a month to replenish our stockpile of cash and so decided to make the long drive back to the Rotta Winery. Leaving at two o'clock in the morning we got to the vineyard by eleven o'clock. The kindly Mr Rotta said the grapes were still not quite ready for picking. This gave us the opportunity to kill a bit of time exploring more of California and so we drove on, heading for Death Valley, parking for the night overlooking Lake Isabella at the southern end of the Sequoia National Park.

We arrived in Death Valley the next day, driving along the Panamint Valley. Turning off the tarmac road we took a dirt track up to Mahogany Flats. Our altimeter indicated we were 8,133 feet above sea level. From the Flats we had the most wonderful view down into Death Valley. The variety of colours and landscapes in the Valley were astounding, as was the size of it. We realised we would be spending a few days in this fascinating place to unearth some of its secrets, hidden away off the beaten path. On the way back down we stopped to walk amongst old disused charcoal kilns. There were ten of them in all, shaped like beehives and about thirty feet in diameter. Disused for decades, some still had remnants of charcoal in them. Our information showed there was a ghost town in the Valley, Harrisburg, so we took Adolf off road into the trackless desert near where we thought it might be and after some tacking through the arid landscape, came upon it. In 1908 it was a tent city, and all that was left of it were some old mine workings.

About ten miles away we came upon Skidoo, another ghost town of mines, but with no houses. It was every Hollywood cowboy film cliché, with tumbleweed rolling through the deserted workings. Stopping and walking around, the only sound was the creak of rusty hinges as doors swung slowly in the wind. It was eerie to think of those tough men who had endured the harshness of the Valley in search of mineral wealth. The view down into the Valley was yet again breathtaking, with mist hanging in valleys on some slopes. From Skidoo we went to Emigrant Junction and then down into Stove Pipe Wells, the temperature rising by 20°F as we came down, an indication of the extremes of the Valley. Talking to one or two locals in a small store we were told there was not much open in the Valley as it was the off season and many of the roads had been washed away by recent storms. We drove on to Furnace Creek, an oasis and little village in the middle of the Valley, and at the store there bought a loaf of bread. The storekeeper noticed our English accents and gave us a bottle of wine as a gift and told us of a free rest area tucked away behind all the buildings where he said we could park and use the built in bar-b-que's for our cooking. For the next seven days the picnic table next to Adolf became my bed under the open sky, the car park and rest area our camp site and base.

We got up early in the cool of the day and decided to look for Marble Canyon, despite there being no roads due to the recent bad weather. We first went to the Ranger Station and told them where we were going, assuring them we had plenty of water and supplies but telling them that if we had not reported back in two days to look for a plume of smoke as we would burn a tyre as a signal. They seemed perfectly happy with this arrangement so we set off, asking for some directions. Memorising the vague and seemingly conflicting details we were given, we set off across the desert. What trail there was soon disappeared and we were now on what looked like an old river bed. The hills around had numerous canyons that opened out on the valley floor. For an hour or so we drove back and forth on abominable and at times seemingly impossible terrain. It was an interesting lesson and exercise in disorientation, and relying on and trusting a compass and the angle of the sun to bring logic to our searching. Once in the desert, everything looks the same. Each canyon and hill is a twin of another and it is easy to understand how those with no sense of direction or logic can become completely lost. We eventually found what looked like the trail again and followed it up Cottonwood Canyon before branching off onto the Marble Canyon track.

The heat beat down on us as the sun rose high. The walls of the canyon closed in on us, the latent heat in the high rock walls and sandy floor turning the place into an oven. The canyon got narrower, casting us into the shade, until eventually we slowed to creep forward through the gap that was left. There was literally no more than an inch on either side of Adolf and her jerry cans. Any narrower and we would have had to take the cans and their racks off to get through. As we came out of this tiny gap the canyon widened again and we found the canyon filled by a huge rock fall that lay like a dam across it, blocking our path. We got up and clambered up and over the fall, from the high top of which we could look back down into the canyon where Adolf basked alone in the sunshine. The silence, isolation and desolation were absolute and we felt as though we were the only people alive, in a true wilderness, surrounded by every conceivable shade of red, yellow and gold in the walls. We walked around the floor of the canyon for an hour or so, feeling the heat radiating off the sheer rock faces and then decided to leave the utter peace and silence and return to Furnace Creek. All that was left to do was renegotiate the narrowness of the closed in walls, suffer the appalling terrain on the return journey and find the right canyon to take. Since our tyre tracks were the only ones in the sand and gravel there was a fairly obvious clue for us to follow.

On our way back we came upon four young Americans in a Land Rover. They were completely lost. They had also somehow contrived to get themselves stuck on some rocks so we pulled them off and led them back to Cottonwood Canyon and then to the Valley floor. We felt if we tried explaining how to get to Marble Canyon they might never be seen again, so inept were their driving and navigational skills. Their almost inevitable desiccation in the dry desert was not something we particularly wanted on our conscience.

For the next six days we explored the Valley, sometimes just driving into the deserted canyons, again telling the Rangers where we were going and the direction in which to search for us if we were not back in two days. We put a pair of ladies tights over the air filter to try to keep some of the dust out of it. Nylon tights may seem a strange item to carry in a Land Rover's toolkit, but when my girlfriend donated them to us in England we just knew they might be useful one day. Adolf was completely white at the back, the plastic back screen in the canvas top completely obliterated by a thick layer of dust. We visited the usual suspects such as the eccentricity of Scotty's Castle and the colourful sunrise at Zabriskie Point. Scotty's Castle, a two story folly of a mansion in the desert, was actually built by the wealthy Albert Johnson in 1922. He was persuaded to do so by Death Valley Scotty who was looking for investors in his Death Valley gold mine. Walter E Scott was, above all else, a con man who tricked a succession of wealthy men into backing his gold mining schemes, all of which were complete scams.

Zabriskie Point was of interest not only for the astonishing colours that appear at dawn as the early morning sun falls on the rocks, but also because of the film of the same name that came out in 1970. Some of its scenes were shot in Death Valley and at the Point. I drove by myself to the Harmony Borax works and on to Mustard Canyon, seemingly carved out of yellow mud by some long ago river. I had the most wonderful sensation of solitude, of being completely alone in the stillness, many rough miles from anyone. Utter isolation is something few people experience. Life as we know it is stripped away, the material trappings we feel so essential reduced to the inconsequentially unimportant, replaced by a feeling of a primitive, primordial existence that leaves a sense of being at the complete whim of the elements. If we are cast out into the wilderness, all that we thought was indispensable is reduced to the trivial. Food and shelter possess our every thought, our every moment as we return to a life that is focussed on the simple act of survival.

Standing perfectly still and silent at the Devil's Golf Course, we could hear the salt creak and crack as it expanded in the intense heat. Ubehebe Crater was a seven hundred foot hole half a mile wide in the desolate landscape, surrounded by the ash thrown out by its original explosions. The Keane Wonder Mine, dug in the early 1900's and then abandoned, was a testament to the strength and resilience of those early settlers and prospectors. The list of wonders in Death Valley seemed to have no end for us as we busied ourselves visiting as many as we could. Those visitors with more sense either came into the Valley for a day, or rested in the heat of the day. It was in those siesta hours that we found ourselves having the points of interest to ourselves. Where that was not possible, we went off road where others would never follow.

One morning I worked in the store at Furnace Creek where the proprietor Al wanted some help stacking beer cans and other goods. He also arranged for me to do some furniture removal, all of which brought in some useful dollars. Next to the rest area where we parked Adolf at night a small stream flowed gently so we built a dam across it to form a pool we could sit in to cool down. After a couple of days workmen came along and dismantled it so we rebuilt it that night, reforming our pool like beavers in a creek. We heard news on the radio that Prince William of Gloucester was killed in an air crash at Halfpenny Green near Wolverhampton, the locals convinced he turned his plane away from the village moments before it came down to avoid and protect the people in the village. It is said the current second in line to the throne is named in his memory.

The 1st September came and passed whilst we were in the Valley, marking four months since we had left England. It was also the day Boris Spassky conceded defeat to Bobby Fischer. He did so in a telephone call to the game arbiter before the resumption of the twenty first game in the World Chess Championship. At first Fischer refused to accept the resignation over the telephone, insisting Spassky should come in and sign his score card as was the convention, but he did then agree to take on the mantle of World Champion, winning by 12.**5 to 8.5** and becoming the first American World Champion since 1888. Perhaps he won the mind game that chess is, the Championship naturally following as the additional scalp. America ecstatically accepted this further proof of their dominance of the world as empirical evidence of it being the greatest country on earth. Washington resurrected the champagne order. Fischer's subsequent life, disappearance and mental implosion is well documented but his genius remained and shone through his eccentricity, perhaps the very genesis of his aberrant sociopathy and inability to conform to normal social behaviour. Little is known of the Championship arbiter's state of mind at the end of the tournament, but I'm sure post traumatic stress syndrome became a factor in his life for a while.

In the midst of all this exploration into the untrammeled wilderness of the Valley we met and chatted to many other visitors who also used the camp site at Furnace Creek as their base. Most visitors would only stay for part of a day, defeated by the incredible heat and harshness of the environment, supposedly the hottest place on earth. An intrepid few stayed longer and we enjoyed drunken evenings with them in the Furnace Creek bar and camp site. Returning one afternoon from some desolation sited adventure we heard a commotion at one end of the camp site and went over to investigate. A French girl, visiting the Valley with her English boyfriend and her parrot, was in a state of panic because her parrot, Zigmund, had escaped and was sitting obdurately in a tree. He turned his back on us and defecated his defiance. It didn't seem to be the right moment to ask what interest a parrot would have in being dragged from Los Angeles to Death Valley. Whilst the collection of headless chickens ran about, panicking noisily and getting nowhere, Sam and I quietly unravelled a hose attached to a stand pipe, turned it on and directed a powerful stream of water at the stubborn Ziggie, who was sitting on a branch arrogantly sticking up a middle claw, still baring his feathered arse at everyone below. Parrots don't do getting wet very well, and when soaked and lying on their back on the ground, definitely don't do flying. We picked up the outraged but incapacitated bird and handed him to Dorine, the French girl, Sam's future wife.

    I don't know if that was the moment Sam and Dorine fell in love, or a night later under the stars on the last green of the Furnace Creek golf course, but fall in love they did, unbeknown at that time to Dorine's boyfriend, Stewart, who generously offered us shelter at his flat in Hermosa Beach west of Los Angeles. I am pretty sure the golf course's green keeper knew someone had fallen in love when he saw the state of his lovingly tended green in the morning. Those in our small group with jobs and lives to get on with had to leave and Sam and I decided to go too, feeling we had done the Valley justice in the week we had devoted to discovering its mysteries. We all headed for Las Vegas in a loose and impromptu convoy. The sinful city was the next stop on everyone else's schedule and we agreed to follow as it was somewhere we thought would be interesting to see. Dorine and Stewart were traveling in Dorine's open top Volkswagen Beetle and Sam seemed to accompany her quite a few times on the journey, demoting Stewart to being my passenger in Adolf. Stewart seemed graciously accepting of his new companion and we chatted about his and Dorine's work as radiologists in a hospital in Los Angeles. One member of our convoy was touring on a motorbike and ran out of fuel so, with my arm out of Adolf's window, I held his hand and towed him next to us for a few miles until we found a petrol station.

On a dirt road we took as a short cut we came upon a car stuck in the sand so Sam and I pulled it out using some of the tow ropes we carried. We were wrapping the tow rope up to put it away when a large station wagon came hurtling towards us, completely out of control. The driver managed to put two wheels into deep sand by the dirt road, which threw the car into a huge skid. It turned sideways and slid straight towards Adolf as Sam and I leapt for our lives. The car came to a stop so close to Adolf's front you could hardly fit a cigarette paper between the two vehicles. The driver didn't stop to discuss his little faux pas, instead slamming the car into reverse, pulling back and then heading off again, rear wheels spinning in the dirt, spraying us with gravel and sand whilst presumably peering through the windscreen in an alcoholic haze. Another life used by each of us.

The Las Vegas of 1972 was a small version of what now exists, but to Sam and me it still seemed a mad place, where anything was possible. We all parked in a free car park and I agreed to look after the vehicles while the others went off to gamble for an hour. To this day I have not the slightest interest in gambling and was happy to sit in the warm sunshine and write letters. Three hours later a clearly inebriated Dorine came back and took me to the casino they had found, Mr Sy's. On entering the casino each person was being given a book of vouchers for a free beer, a free gambling chip, a free hamburger and one or two other incentives the management were prepared to hand out to entice punters. One of the party had found where these were stored in a back yard and had filled everyone's pockets with the beer vouchers, discarding the rest. Many vouchers later we were finally asked to leave the casino as it was quite clear to the disgruntled management that the ratio of gambling to drinking was somewhat imbalanced. We somehow found ourselves outside a huge casino called Circus Circus, in front of which was a large fountain. When I got in the water I discovered it was waist deep.

Circus Circus was enormous and there seemed to be a few acres of slot machines on the ground floor, standing in serried rows like soldiers on a parade ground awaiting inspection. Some machines had styrofoam cups placed on their handles, reserved by obsessive players whose hands were stained by the silver dollars they were putting in the machines. Like automatons, they mindlessly walked up and down their reserved row feeding each machine and pulling its arm, not looking to see the result of the spinning wheels before moving to the next one in line. High above this slot machine farm was a mezzanine gallery with shops and fairground style booths, running around the whole building. From the roof acrobatic apparatus was hanging expectantly. A cyclist was riding across an impossibly thin wire, upside down. We watched his fly on a ceiling trick from the mezzanine gallery while standing at a rope barrier next to a trampoline that was right on the edge, overlooking the hall far below. Clearly part of the circus act, it was an irresistible toy and so I climbed over the barrier, hopped on and started some uncoordinated bouncing. The higher I went the more of the floor below I could see. To the gamblers looking up far beneath me I must have looked like clothes in a tumble dryer as I waved a greeting or tried a few somersaults at the zenith of my leaps. Like Romans at the Coliseum willing the lions to take yet another Christian morsel, a small crowd had gathered at the rope barrier by the trampoline, perhaps waiting for the inevitable moment when I disappeared over the edge, to be impaled on the raised arm of a priapic slot machine below. The more likely inevitable moment of the arrival of irate officialdom came before the parachute-less flight over the edge. A uniformed guard forced his way to the front of the gathered onlookers and shouted and gesticulated at me to get off. He didn't look at all happy. In fact he seemed rather unreasonably tetchy so it seemed a good idea to comply. I clambered off the trampoline and climbed over the rope barrier.

"What the hell do you think you're doing?" he yelled at me.

I thought it was perfectly obvious what I was doing since it hadn't exactly been a private moment, so I helpfully explained this to him. His mood darkened as he escorted me through the little audience. I suddenly realised he had disappeared so I wandered off in search of the others. I eventually found Stewart in the throng of people. Coincidentally, but perhaps unsurprisingly, he was also looking for me, mainly to tell me the police were after me. It seemed an opportune moment to hide so I went into the lavatories and lurked in there until it slowly dawned on me I would prefer to be arrested for trampoline trespass than for cottaging with intent. Even in my inebriated state I could work out that five minutes of inspecting my fingernails and whistling quietly to myself in a public lavatory was likely to put heterosexual visitors off their micturations. More worrying it was likely to excite interest from any gay visitors so I left, making my way through the crowd on the mezzanine floor. As I moved towards the staircase to the ground floor, a meaty hand the size of a soup plate plonked down on my shoulder and turned me round. I found I was looking up into the cavernous and hirsute nostrils of a large policeman, whose parents' chromosomal cocktail had produced a doppelgänger of Boris Karloff's as Frankenstein's monstrous creation. Thankfully, this version had no neck bolts. This model clearly didn't need to be connected to the National Grid to get started in the morning, an improvement on the earlier prototype. The conversation was brief.

"You on the trampoline boy?"

"Er, no, not me officer?"

"Turn round boy" he said, not waiting for me to comply, instead turning me with that large hand that continued to hold my shoulder like a lettuce leaf. For a moment I thought I was back in the lavatory, regretting the attractive whistling.

"It was you boy. You come with me."

Whilst conversation was obviously not a strong point for him, his message was quite clear as he marched me through the crowd, displaying his arrest proudly to the press of onlookers around us, like a sportsman showing the victor ludorum to the adoring crowds. It seemed the evidence he was looking for was to be found in the torn pockets on the back of my worn denim shorts, the giveaway clue identifying the culprit. He took me to the police room where everyone seemed to be wearing a large gun on their hip, the ubiquitous choice of jewelry for American officialdom. I was soon being interrogated and asked to show my Passport for identification. Realising this was not a time to be a smart arse, I politely answered their questions and took on the chin the lecture I was given about the dangers of 'messing with the equipment'. They obviously came to the conclusion they had a harmless imbecile in their custody and so finally said I could go. Thanking them with some contrived contrition, I merged with the crowds outside and headed for the main exit, meeting the others on the way. I was rather touched by the fact my friends had been looking for me rather than heading out of town and leaving me to my fate. It seemed an appropriate time to leave Las Vegas before our stay was involuntarily extended. Returning to Mr Sy's we collected our vehicles and headed off for the Grand Canyon, some two hundred and seventy miles away. Our plan was to see the Canyon and then go on to Lake Havasu to pay our respects to London Bridge. The fact not one of us was fit to be behind a steering wheel somehow escaped our attention.

The Canyon was almost too big to take in and we concluded we would need days there, or to fly over it, which we could not afford, to really appreciate its grandeur. The colours in the Canyon walls were almost every shade of red, orange or gold, a giant version of the canyons we had seen in Yellowstone and Death Valley. Standing on the rim I could feel the anabatic breeze on my face as I gazed down into the abyss, overwhelmed by a sense of awe at its majesty and sheer scale. At the other end of the spectrum of sights, London Bridge at Lake Havasu was a complete anomaly, particularly as it was in a desert and an artificial river had been built to go under it. It had been dismantled stone by stone, each one marked with a unique number enabling it to be rebuilt in exactly the same form at the end of its journey to America. We drove across it both ways, each time driving on the left hand side. This caused a bit of havoc with the traffic, but we felt it was still our bridge and should have been left in London. Slightly illogical in that I had never once driven across it when it spanned the Thames so could not really claim any prior attachment to it. Someone told us that the American consortium that bought it thought they were buying Tower Bridge. How I wish that story to be true, but I cannot quite believe it is.

The night before we arrived at Lake Havasu we had parked for the night in a Rest Area and built a fire to cook our supper. *Kal Kan Stew for Dogs* and half a fresh cabbage had the significant advantage of being very cheap. I had not spent many hours in my life dwelling on the conundrum of where all the tubes and other stuff that gets pulled out of animals at abattoirs goes but now realise they all go to nourish the canine population of the world. And jolly well they all appear on it. Tracheal tube tagine is interesting in that the main constituent takes on the properties of one of those children's toys, a flexible metal or plastic spiral that can walk down stairs like a somersaulting caterpillar. Veins and arteries were more pliant and flexible, if somewhat rubbery, squeaking between the teeth when chewed. Better to let them slip down whole I felt. The combination was absolutely disgusting but when we realised how little the meal cost us we decided that by buying it we could move to one meal a day rather to one every other day. Our diet for the foreseeable future was set, whilst promising each other that if we started sniffing each other's backside, or licking our genitals, we would switch back to a slightly more conventional menu. I wonder how Heater would have taken to our new diet if she had still been with us. With hysteria I imagine.

Leaving the Grand Canyon, our radio began to pick up broadcasts of a massacre at the Olympic Games in Munich. The day before, in the early hours of the 5th September, eight Black September Arab terrorists, or guerrillas as they were called in those days, had broken into the Olympic Village and then into the building housing the Israeli contingent. They killed two of the weight lifting team and took ten hostages, one of whom sprinted off, dodging bullets as he ran to safety. For the next twenty four hours we listened to the news reports as the disaster unfolded and ended at an airport with the nine hostages being killed by the terrorists, most of whom also died in a firefight with the police. Three were captured but within two months had been released by the German authorities when two more Black September members hijacked a plane and threatened to blow it up. Sometimes Governments do succumb to threats and, despite protesting otherwise, always do negotiate, eventually. The disaster overshadowed the Games, taking some of the lustre off Mark Spitz's unprecedented seven gold medals with seven world records in the swimming pool, the seventh mere hours before the terrorist attack.

Skirting south of Joshua Tree National Park we headed east back towards Los Angeles. In Indio we stopped at a vineyard to try to get work and were advised to try in Etiwanda, about ten miles from Upland. After a couple of rejections on the basis we had no Social Security numbers and shouldn't be trying to work anyway, we finally met someone at a vineyard who told us to follow a truck that was just pulling out. This we did for a couple of miles, finally following it down dirt tracks into the heart of many hundreds of acres of vines. The truck stopped and a Mexican jumped down from the driver's cab, gave us a hooked knife and a box each, pointed at the Mexicans bent over the vines in the field and told us we were hired, 20 cents per box. He said we would be given Social Security numbers and that if we heard a shout from the man standing on the roof of the cab of a large truck we should run for it as it would be a warning of a raid by Immigration officers, or Border Patrol as they were called locally.

For the next five days we picked grapes in the blazing sun, bent double over the low lying bushes, slashing at the stalks of bunches of grapes with the knives and dropping the ripe fruit in the large box at our feet. We regularly missed the stalks and caught our left hands instead, which were soon lacerated with cuts. Once the box was filled we ran to the truck and up a plank resting against it, tipping our grapes into the huge back that presumably carried rubble and rubbish in the off season.

We collected a small metal token that went safely into our pockets on the way down the plank before returning to molest and pillage another vine. The vines were of two varieties, one producing small white grapes and the other large, fat, juicy red ones. One morning we were told to pick the small white grapes but because of their diminutive size it seemed to take forever to fill each box, which slowed our productivity. Since our rate of pay had been reduced to 15 cents a box, this was going to impact on our pay so we started to fill the first two thirds of our boxes quickly with the large red grapes and then topped off with a layer of white ones to hide them. This halved the time it took to fill a box and our productivity soared but our duplicity was eventually discovered and they asked us to stick to the rules. To this day I have always recommended friends should avoid the 1972 Californian whites since they may not find it was a vintage year.

Our home for our stay was by a standpipe and hose in the yard of a farm in the middle of the fields. It was luxury compared to the facilities of one of the Mexican wet backs who lived in his car next to us. Each evening we would stand in the open under the hose and shower off the dirt of the day before attacking the dog food and cabbage supper cooked on our open fire. We had tried the stew without the cabbage but the taste was appalling and it was clear the cabbage was needed to run interference, masking the flavour so we could actually swallow it. Kal Kan Stew for Dogs was selling for 31 cents a can, which we thought was pretty good value until we came upon a new brand in the animal food section of the supermarket. *Horsemeat Balls* at 29 cents a can was a steal. Without a hint of guilt at the dive in Kal Kan's profits we switched allegiance and turned to the result of what must have been a mass castration of the American horse population. It was hard to believe but Horsemeat Balls tasted even worse than Kal Kan Stew, a nadir in flavour even a cabbage could not mask, and after a couple of days we returned to the fold like prodigal sons. Kal Kan reinstated their cancelled dividend and the price of their stock soared on the markets.

    At dawn each morning the truck would arrive where we were parked and we would jump in with all the Mexicans and head off to whichever field we were going to work in that day. One morning we were told the Border Patrol had picked up and deported one of the Mexicans, taking him down to the border at Tijuana. Later we could see the Immigration Officers and the Border Patrol cars, their blue lights flashing, racing about in the lanes around the fields that were full of Mexicans running in all directions. The Border Patrol had a large caged truck half full of the wetbacks they had caught and clearly intended staying until they had a full load to warrant the journey to the Mexican border. As our Mexican colleagues ran around the fields like headless chickens in full view of the watching Patrols, Sam and I dropped to our knees out of sight, crawled for a long way through the vines and then got up and sauntered off when out of sight. We went back to Adolf until the heat died down, returning to work a couple of hours later. The Mexicans who had escaped and also returned to work gleefully called us 'The Big Time,' saying the Immigration officers would be taking us to the airport rather than the Mexican border if they caught us.

This one comment got us thinking and we eventually came to the conclusion that 15 cents a box was not worth the risk of being put on a plane, so we spoke to John, the gangmaster, and said we had better go but did he know of any other work. As it happened, he owned a restaurant called the Toad in the Hole at the L A County Fair in Los Angeles, a three week event that was about to start. He said he was looking for a couple of busboys and we could start straight away. He said he would meet us at the restaurant the next day so we drove to it, arriving in the evening and parking behind it for the night. For me the prospect of working at a restaurant had the attraction of meaning we could probably give up the dog food diet. I was getting a bit concerned that I had been finding the farm dog at the vineyard rather attractive. I was only slightly reassured by the fact it was a bitch.

The L A County Fair was held alongside a horse racetrack. The oval track had large concrete stands overlooking the course. I assumed all the runners in the Gelding Cup had generously, if somewhat involuntarily, donated to our recent meals. In the grounds next to the stands were permanent shops and restaurants. For the duration of the fair they were joined by a village of small square tents that housed traders selling T Shirts, art, curios, clothes and tourist tat. At one end of the large site was a huge fairground with some fiendishly unpleasant looking rides, all designed with food regurgitation in mind, mechanical emetics to purge riders of their fast food diets. There were also the usual assortment of attractions where people could attempt to win stuffed toys and unattractive objects by shooting dented targets with inaccurate air rifles, or by throwing small rings over large objects designed to prevent winners. The prizes looked as though they dated from the 1800's so stock replacement was obviously not a problem to the stallholders.

The Toad in the Hole was a glorified cafe. It was rectangular with a horseshoe shaped central serving area surrounded by low pedestal stools fixed to the floor. Tables and chairs were positioned around the walls. The kitchens, stores and dishwashing area were all at the back of the restaurant and there was a large serving hatch through which the cooks could pass plates of the completed orders and take new ones from the waitresses. The morning after our arrival we were taken to a large car park and caravan site where the Fair's workers could park. We were allocated a slot by a man who seemed to be in overall control of the parking area, with the only instruction being not to come back to the site drunk.

As it turned out his instructions were superfluous as getting drunk was not an option. For the next three weeks we generally worked seven days a week and up to fifteen hours a day. Whilst our colleagues worked a shift pattern, Sam and I did only one shift a day that ran from opening to closing. For us every hour worked represented extra dollars for our travel fund in South America where no work would be available to us. On the few quieter days mid-week we managed shorter hours where we had time to rest and write letters or wander around the fairground. When the restaurant was busy there was no time to think, rest or eat. There was only ever time to clear the tables into large boxes and rush the dirty dishes and cutlery to the kitchen where Sonny, the huge African American dishwasher would grab them and push them through the production line dishwasher. Sonny was forty five years old and huge, a Paul Robeson lookalike with a deep brown voice that rumbled up from his boots, burbling and bubbling like a V8 engine. He was six foot five inches and weighed two hundred and eighty pounds. He had fourteen children and was already a grandfather. Sonny had lived hard and became a good friend in our short time with him. I think he felt a certain empathy with us as, being busboys, we were ranked equal with him in the restaurant staff pecking order. At the bottom of the pond of catering life although our colleagues never treated us as low life, showing us only kindness and friendship.

Some mornings we would crack open over seven hundred eggs for the largest scrambled egg breakfast I had ever seen. As the eggs cooked we fried half a dozen pigs to make small mountains of crispy bacon side orders. As catering Dalits, we were never in line for any tips customers left but all the waitresses shared any they received with us, which was kind and touching. They also took our trousers and clothes home with them and washed them for us. Our bottom of the catering gene pool status was outweighed by our exotic origins and our odyssey, and the girls loved to mother us. The restaurant's clientele represented a cross-section of America, old and young, large and small, the largest of whom I saw was a woman who came in and settled on two of the fixed stools at the horseshoe counter. Like a gargantuan hen settling on a clutch of cowering eggs, she lowered a buttock on each stool, leaving the lumpy unsupported section of her backside hanging down between the stools like a large bag of oranges. In those days it didn't seem possible for a backside to be that wide, but now of course it has almost become the norm in so many overfed developed countries. The cooks were a mixture of pony-tailed, weed-smoking hippy, old-timers and itinerant self-taught caterers. The head chef was a painter by trade and one of the others had just been breaking horses for a couple of months, but was more usually a stone mason. There was a third busboy, a Mexican we had worked with in the grape fields. He had been picked up by the Border Patrol in one of their raids on the fields and taken to the border to be deported. He was back in Los Angeles twenty four hours later when John, the restaurant owner, went down to collect him. For the next three weeks he did as little as possible in the restaurant, which made us question his value and wonder at why John continued to hire him.

When the fairground was in full swing the restaurant was almost overwhelmed with customers who came in relentless streams through the door, queuing outside for tables to come clear. In these hectic periods Sam and I would be rushed off our feet keeping up with all the jobs on our list of tasks. Collecting the dirt dishes and cutlery from the restaurant to take back for Sonny to wash was a priority since no clean plates meant no meals. The waitresses would put the dirty plates, knives, forks, spoons and glasses in large aluminium boxes that could be stacked on top of each other. In quieter moments we would carry these out one by one and empty the contents through the hatch to the washing area. When the service became manic, we started to pile the boxes on top of each other and carry them out in increasingly higher tottering towers to the terrified glances of the waitresses. At our zenith we got to five trays each, our heavy minarets filled to the brim and reaching above our heads like skyscrapers. In between the busy times we helped the cooks with food preparation, making campaniles of toast and fetching supplies from the store room. The chefs would come and go on their shifts, sometimes drunk throughout their time on duty. The customers never seemed to notice so the food must have been acceptable, although we noticed the most popular item on the menu, Chicken Fried Steak which we breadcrumbed at the back of the kitchen, came out of boxes labeled Beef patties. We were either cooking feathered cattle or chickens with horns. Either way, whatever cooking process was being used disguised the true origins of the restaurant's signature dish, a startling similarity to the current range of horsemeat contaminated ready meals that have fooled so many for so long.

In the lull between the lunchtime rush and the evening onslaught, we would clean the restaurant and take out new cutlery to restock the boxes in which it was kept for the waitresses. The cooks would stand at the back door and smoke and we sometimes got a chance to chat to them. One with a blond pony tail talked eloquently about the bigotry he faced in some of the southern States when he was travelling around on his motorbike looking for work. On one occasion he had been run off the road into a ditch by a pick-up full of good old country boys. The more egalitarian northerners had various names for these hicks. Rednecks referred to their suntanned necks obtained from days hoeing the fields. Sometimes they were called white socks after their chosen colour of foot covering, or Grits because of their liking for the thick, white, maize-based porridge often eaten with eggs and bacon at breakfast, usually with a large nob of butter melting on it.

One evening, having finished work at eleven o'clock and having only had a half hour break the whole day, we were walking back to Adolf to sleep when we passed an elderly T Shirt seller who was closing down his tent for the night. We stopped to chat to him and he told us his tent had been burgled a couple of nights before. He said he was looking for someone to sleep in it at night to guard it, for which he would pay a total of $25 for the next ten nights. The money seemed attractive and so I said I would do it, going to Adolf to get my sleeping bag and returning to settle in. The owner bade me good night and as he was leaving handed me a hammer, saying he was sure I wouldn't need it but I should have it "Just in case". I put it next to my large sheath knife on the counter, lay my sleeping bag on top, stripped off and hopped up to lie down for my night's sleep.

Like all the tents hired by traders at the Fair, this one was about twelve feet square with the wooden counter across the open the front, but now up against the canvas that the owner dropped down to close off the tent for the night. Lying on top of my sleeping bag because of the heat in the tent, the front of the tent was inches away so when the gun outside went off my right ear received the full benefit of the explosion. I assumed it was a gun although it might have been a firework, a detail I never discovered. I sat up and gripped the hammer in my hand behind my back as the front of the tent was lifted. A shaved black head appeared, level with my feet. It was a young man and he was looking to his right, away from me and obviously unaware I was there until he turned his head and saw me. His eyes opened like the headlights of a car, huge and white in the gloom. He jumped involuntarily, startled to see me so close to him. I gathered my dignity, a difficult task given I was stark naked, and said,

"Can I help you?"

The intruder quickly recovered his composure, presumably one of the skills learned by habitual burglars.

"What you doing here honky?" he said.

"I'm guarding this place so I suggest you get out or you'll get the benefit of this" I replied, bringing the hammer around from behind me and holding it in front of his face. He seemed unimpressed.

"Hey guys" he called over his shoulder, presumably to fellow burglars outside the tent, "there's a honky in here says he's gonna hit me with a hammer." There was much laughter outside, not the scampering away of terrified feet I was hoping for.

The intruder ducked and disappeared as the tent front dropped back to the floor. I could hear whispering outside.

"Honky, we're gonna get you". I recognised the intruder's voice, which was quickly followed by another huge explosion. "We gonna burn you out" he drawled, to the accompaniment of laughing voices. There was clearly a flock of them, which didn't make the odds look too good.

I decided I might be more intimidating if I had some clothes on and so pulled on my trousers and ducked down behind the counter out of any line of fire should they start shooting. I pulled the sleeping bag down onto the floor and sat on it and waited, the hammer in my lap. After a short while the front of the tent lifted again and someone started crawling through but stopped as soon as he saw me, hammer at the ready. He shot back out like a warthog retreating into its burrow. I hadn't been in the tent for an hour yet and was beginning to realise the criminal class of Los Angeles was entirely nocturnal. Five minutes later the back of the tent was being assaulted by another intruder, but he failed to get the edge of the tent off the ground. Perhaps it was him a couple of minutes later who did manage to get in under the front. I said nothing as I watched him crawl into the gloomy interior. When he stood up he jumped in fright when he saw me in front of him, by now completely at one with my trusty hammer that was swinging in my hand. This time it was a Mexican and when I stepped towards him and told him to get out, he dropped to his knees and bolted under the canvas.

All went quiet and eventually I lay back on the floor and thought about sleep. Not surprisingly given the amount of adrenaline rushing through my veins, it eluded me. I lay listening to the sounds of the night in the fairground outside. Just after one o'clock in the morning the front corner of the tent began to lift again. I assumed my Praetorian Guard stance once more, somewhat apt I felt since the Praetorian Guards were chosen by Roman Generals from the ranks to protect their tents. I waited for the inevitable intrusion when a torch lit up my face and blinded me. It was a policeman who had escorted the owner to the tent as he wanted an address book he had left there. He told me he had asked the policeman to come with him as he was concerned I might hit him with the hammer. I wasn't convinced by his lame explanation for the need to be accompanied, feeling there were wider issues at play, perhaps including checking I was still there earning my salary.

The owner and his attack dog policeman turned out to be my last intruders but the combination of the need to be alert and the hot, stuffy tent made sleep difficult, so at dawn I rolled up my sleeping bag and walked over to the caravan park for a shower and then went to the restaurant to start work. I had been there alone for about half an hour and was putting some rubbish out at the back when I was approached by an elderly and very shifty looking African American man, his cap pushed slightly back on his head revealing grey hair.

"Are you the guy who came out of that tent over there with the sleeping bag?" he asked, pointing to where I had spent the night.

I was immediately suspicious and wary. This did not feel like a pleasant human being.

"Yes" I replied, "why do you ask?"

"Was it you who threatened my nephew?" He was becoming increasingly nervy, looking over his shoulder as he spoke.

"If it was your nephew who stuck his head in the tent where it shouldn't have been, then yes, it was me and you can tell him from me that if he does it again tonight he'll get more of the same."

I asked the man why he was asking all these questions but he became very evasive, avoiding eye contact and ultimately turning and walking away, glancing at me once over his shoulder. I went in and started chatting to Sonny who had just arrived for work, telling him about my disturbed night and about the conversation I had just had. He rolled his eyes in their yellowish rheumy pools and said, with disconcerting authority, that in his opinion and experience they would return that night as a gang.

"They gonna come back and give you a whupping boy," was his summation of what the coming night held in store for me.

When Sam came in to work later we chatted about the whole affair and came to the conclusion the risks were too great to contemplate for a mere $25. In the afternoon, after the lunchtime rush, I snatched a half hour and went to see the T Shirt man to tell him I would not be guarding his tent again, given what had happened. His response was enlightening.

"I'm glad you told me that," he said. "Before coming to the Fair I got an anonymous call and was told if I opened here it would be the last thing I would ever open".

Whilst thinking *'the last thing I would ever open'* perhaps warranted slightly heavier artillery than a hammer, I accepted $2.50 for my sleepless night and went back to work. For the rest of the Fair I noticed an armed uniformed Silverback guarding the tent each night, a somewhat more proportionate response to the threat he was patently under.

At its peak over 160,000 visitors a day came to the Fair. After some of our double shift days we would walk back to the caravan park by detouring through the fairground, which would be in full swing, carrying on after the restaurants and tented town closed up for the night. Occasionally we would go on rides when everyone had gone home, with just the ride operators looking to have some fun with fellow workers. We took a couple of girls who were also working at the Fair on some rides that terrified them and which should only ever be taken on an empty stomach. The *'Bounce in Orbit'* ride was particularly unpleasant and whilst I survived it, Sam was not too well in a corner after getting off it. The two girls looked as though a couple of paramedics would come in useful. One night we saw a cage on a ride being opened after it came to rest. The *'Turbo'* was the fiendishly unpleasant product of a sadistically creative mind. There were two teenage occupants, clearly a brother and an older sister from the sister's language. She was a little unhappy, in a completely unhinged sort of way. She seemed a trifle upset about his having been comprehensively sick all over her. The younger brother made it clear he felt she was being a little unreasonable and over-dramatic. I was impressed and startled by both the sheer quantity as well as texture of what he had managed to produce, and so was she but for slightly different reasons given that he had somehow contrived to get a good coating over her hair. Her waiting boyfriend seemed to lose that air of sexual anticipation young lovers exude as she ran to him for comfort. No bromide was ever as effective or as instant in its affect, and comforting hugs were in short supply as he held her off at arm's length. Love was definitely unconsummated that night.

October arrived and on the 3rd we finished work. We were handed cheques totaling $420.50, payable to a couple of Mexican men we had never met. We exchanged them for cash with John the restaurant owner. He clearly had a system that the Social Security and Internal Revenue had not yet fathomed. The caravan park wanted $40.00 for our stay but we felt disinclined to pay so we left the fairground through an underground service tunnel and disappeared into Greater Los Angeles, arriving at Hermosa Beach that afternoon to stay with Stewart. There were a number of tasks to be completed before we left the States for Mexico and the south. Having been born outside the UK I needed a visa to enter Argentina, which I got from their Embassy in the city at a time when a British Passport guaranteed a smile of welcome at any border. Sam and Stewart serviced Adolf, and Sam and Dorine cavorted while Stewart worked and I found inventive ways to avoid playing gooseberry. One weekend, Sam and I drove up the road and around the corner where Sam jumped out of Adolf and into Dorine's VW Beetle. They took off for an illicit tryst and I headed for the hills by myself with three days to fill. I contacted John, our employer at the Toad and spent the time with him, his wife Joan and their attractive nineteen year old, well developed daughter Jill.

    The family lived with an enormous Alsatian dog called Shadow just over one hundred miles away in Hemet, and kindly included me in their lives for a couple of days. They seemed to accept me, even when one night I stayed up late chatting to Jill. When she went to bed, I continued to watch a movie on the television. Going to bed much later, the house completely dark, I had to walk down a pitch black corridor past Jill's bedroom, feeling the walls as I went. Just after passing her door I heard a faint noise just in front of me, a deep rumbling that suddenly exploded into an ear shattering barking and snarling as Shadow erupted in fury. No one had told me he slept outside John and Joan's bedroom door at the end of the corridor, just past my allotted bedroom. How do you explain to parents what you are doing in the middle of the night breathing heavily outside their daughter's bedroom? No matter the innocence of your mission, it doesn't look good, but they kindly never mentioned it the next day, and no mention was made of the need to visit a jewelry store to peruse engagement rings to uphold their daughter's honour.

    Back in Los Angeles, I spent one night working at Dorine's hospital as a porter, helping her by fetching sleeping patients through the night for X-Rays that could not be fitted in during the day. Wraith like I would appear next to the bed of a usually elderly patient who had generally been sedated for the night. Half asleep, they complained and moaned about being disturbed, all of them reluctant to leave their beds. The routine seemed to be the same for all of them, irrespective of their gender. A shake of the shoulder was followed by swinging them upright on the side of the bed. I put slippers on their feet and then heaved them into the wheelchair I was armed with. Whilst doing this I also tried to hide their naked bums as their rear opening night gowns fell forward. One aged woman was quite large and had an intravenous drip that I had to take with her. This meant pushing the chair with one hand whilst holding it aloft with the other. As we trundled down the wide, deserted and endless corridors, the wheelchair kept veering to one side so eventually I leant over, tapped her on the shoulder and asked her to hold her bottle of potion for me, an unconventional solution to my steering problem. She groaned and I felt bad.

    In the early hours a very young boy was brought in from the Emergency department for a skull X-Ray. He had been hit by a car and the doctors wanted to know if he had a fractured skull. Unfortunately he was alert, extremely distressed and uncooperative and refusing to stay on the X-Ray table. I was handed two folded towels which I was instructed to put either side of his head as he was pushed flat back onto the table. I had to sit at the head of the table and squeeze hard to hold his head perfectly still under the machinery above, independently of his thrashing and writhing young body. To this day I wonder if I changed the shape of his head forever, making hat choices difficult for him. There seemed to be a complete disregard for the patient, merely a focus on getting the job done. Could they not have sedated the boy. Could they have sedated the elderly patients I was sent to collect, and perhaps warned them I would be coming for them. Instead I was greeted with the overwhelming enthusiasm an executioner must get when arriving at the cell door for the condemned man's last short stroll.

In the early hours I was called to Intensive Care to help X-Ray a man dying from lung cancer. To do this we had to use a mobile X-Ray machine. It was like a large ice cream or hot dog vendor's wagon and quite heavy. I pushed it down corridors and in and out of lifts until I got to the Intensive Care Unit where I met Dorine. The Unit had about ten beds in it, each curtained off with side curtains but open at the front. Machines glowed and flickered in the dimmed lights and calm nurses moved quietly around between the beds and their central station. Our man was in a corner unit where all the lights were on. A doctor and a couple of nurses were beside his bed. I pushed the X-Ray machine in and then, gently manoeuvring my arms under him, helped to lift him off the bed for Dorine to slide the X-Ray plates under his back. I could feel his spine and ribs through his emaciated back. Four decades later I can still hear his cries of pain as I lifted him and can see the large transparent tubes coming out of holes in the side of his chest and leading down into bottles on the floor. Life strangling fluid flowed out of them from his chest cavity. As he fought for every breath I could hear and see the aerated liquid bubbling up and down the tube, and I thought of my father as he too died in the same way, every breath a gasping battle, only ever one finally unattainable gasp away from the end. I still wonder at the need to inflict such discomfort on a man with hours to live, the need for imagery that stated the obvious. He was dying and a nice portrait shot wasn't going to tell anyone anything. Dorine said it was so the hospital could bill for more services and I tried hard to believe this was not true. True compassion for a fellow human is a powerful emotion, and I was overwhelmed by its full force in those moments by that poor man's bed.

One evening when Sam and Dorine were out together I went by myself to see the film '*The Godfather*', the big hit of the time. It has stood the test of time and is as watchable today as it was then, perhaps thanks to the superlative cast. It was dark when I came out and I was walking down the street when ahead of me I spotted three young thugs swaggering towards me. Three abreast across the pavement, arms swinging across their bodies in that universal semaphore of testosterone fueled aggression, anyone approaching them would have to step out into the street to get past them. I carried on walking towards them until they were about twenty feet from me when they stopped as one, blocking the pavement and thus my path. Unexpectedly for them I carried on walking straight at them. At the last minute they had to part or let me barge straight into the one in the middle of the trio.

I walked through the gap and they turned and fell in step next to and either side of me. They seemed spaced out on some chemical stimulant and started talking to me. Being more interested in their physical presence and the signals they were giving out, I was not really listening and said nothing, but eventually realised they were spouting religious ramblings at me, evidently concerned I did not have sufficient quantities of the Lord in my life. I continued walking in silence and then suddenly stepped sideways to the right of the one on my right so I was now on the outside of the group and that little bit less vulnerable. They continued to walk and talk with me for three or four minutes until I stopped in my tracks and suggested we part company. It turned out that they were indeed harmless but I did point out that what they had done wasn't exactly bright. I told them the Lord was not a great deal of help in A & E, and look where he ended up that Easter all those years ago. As I walked on alone in the dark I thought how fragile life is, and how its course hangs on incidents, coincidences and chance meetings, the unexpected moments that change the plans we have made for ourselves to replace them with the reality of life. A few days later I went to see Stanley Kubrick's '*A Clockwork Orange,*' having recently read the book and this time was on the alert for marauding droogs as I walked the twenty minutes back in the dark by myself.

On the 16th October, five and a half months after leaving the UK, we set off for Mexicali, the border crossing we decided to use to go back into Mexico. I had loved my time in the United States, met wonderfully kind and generous people, troubled Vietnam War veterans my age, hippies, the poorest and the rich, a panoply of characters. We had made lifelong friends. We had had a few adventures and a huge amount of fun, and had come out alive and unscathed. We had seen unimaginable beauty in the landscapes and been amazed at the sheer diversity of the country, both in its people and its geography. Despite that, I was very happy to be leaving and starting the rougher, wilder part of our trip, where uncertainty and isolation were to become the norm, where living on our wits and dealing with hardship would test us and leave us everlasting memories.

I found America to be the most extraordinary and wonderful mix of cultures, topography, attitudes. Prejudice was alive and well and flourishing in many parts, particularly the deep south where I met many who felt the Confederacy would rise again and that black people should be kept in their rightful place, that being under the heel of the bigoted white. Not that they felt themselves to be bigots, just naturally superior by the quirk of their colour.

America's apotheosis of liberalism was in California, and of conservatism in the south where rednecks and true grits roamed the roads to harass and shoot at anyone who did not conform to their stereotype of the all American boy or girl. Americans were universally friendly and welcoming to us, and at times that had been overwhelming when so far from home. And yet, at times there seemed to be a shallowness to the welcomes, a feeling that we were viewed as somewhat alien and soon to be forgotten in the real world they lived in, the great America. Perhaps their friendships were more transient, but more likely it was we who were transient and they who realised the connection with us would inevitably be brief and therefore not worth investing deeply in.

I was surprised at the country's isolation from the world, its lack of knowledge and even interest in other cultures, other political systems, other countries. And yet the anomaly was and remains that it was America that led the way to exploration of space, which with the oceanic depths is that ultimate wilderness. So, a country of contrasts, of inconsistency, of conflicting views and ways. A wonderful place, but not where I would want to live out the rest of my life.

Time to go south into the darkness. Here be dragons. To the edge of the world we knew and understood. What lay over its edge?

An exhilarating thought.

Posing for the Press again - Upland, Los Angeles.

Death Valley - driving up to Mahogany Flats.

Death Valley - driving to Marble Canyon.

A GIRL CALLED ADOLF

CHAPTER 8

Mexico - 1972

> "I learned that courage was not the absence of fear, but the triumph over it. The brave man is not he who does not feel afraid, but he who conquers that fear."
>
> Nelson Mandela

We crossed into Mexico at the Calexico - Mexicali border at six o'clock on the evening of the 16th October 1972. Cracklin' Rosie by Neil Diamond at number four in the hit parade was playing on the radio to remind me of my girlfriend in Greece. We were aware we were hearing the last of intelligible if not quite intelligent radio and wondered how far south it would be before we lost signal from America. It seemed a bit theatrical and over dramatic to think of ourselves in the same category as astronauts going behind the moon and entering a dark, silent and detached world. But in truth, as far as our families and friends were concerned, that was what was about to happen. The communication options available in the early '70s meant to all intents and purposes we were disappearing off the face of the earth, and in fact had done so as soon as we left Le Havre except that we assumed mail going back home from the States would travel there faster than from Central or South America. Not for us email or mobile phones in those Dark Ages. Clues of our existence would be contained in our letters home, if they ever arrived. If they did get back, they would be weeks or even months old.

The border crossing was quick and clinical and I had a true sense of leaving civilisation as we bumped down off the tarmac of America onto the dust and dirt of the road through Mexicali. The town was a chaotic maelstrom of traffic and people walking in the streets, all of us enveloped in a fine dust thrown up off the road by the vehicles and the shuffling feet of the pedestrians. Street lighting was almost non existent and making our way through the dark streets it was more by luck than design that we found the road to San Luis Rio Colorado. We were driving south east, parallel to the border as we had to get around the entrance to Baja California, that epiglottic peninsular that hangs next to mainland Mexico, an impotently flaccid appendage. After driving through San Luis we pulled into an extremely dingy truck stop for the night. We had been on the road for about ten hours, with three hundred and forty miles under our belts, and did not wish to continue chancing our arm or riding our luck on the dark Mexican desert roads. There was a very grubby cafe at the stop and fortuitously, given we had a flat tyre, a tyre repair business housed in a shack whose leaning wooden walls defied gravity by refusing to fall down.

The truckers' dawn chorus of powerful diesel engines being started and revved woke us to a quickly warming morning. A pack of flea ridden and mangy dogs wandered around the dusty yard in a desultory meaningless meandering, their ennui symbolic of a place where nothing ever happened. When the tyre repair business opened we negotiated a fee of $1 for fixing our tyre, a bargain compared to the $3.50 we had been quoted and refused to pay in California. Once it was repaired we were on the road again, passing through a Customs and Immigration stop at Sonoyta where we got our tourist papers for Adolf. There was a free zone near the border in which car papers were not needed. It was left free to encourage US tourism into Mexico. We were driving through an expansive desert, the Mexican Sahara, which was populated by iconic cacti standing like candelabra, arms stretched to the sky. Rocky outcrops supported sparse scrub and anorexic bushes that somehow eked an existence from the parched ground. Dropping south we drove through Caborca and were a few miles past the town in the barren desert when we smelt cooking engine smells as the ignition light came on. Adolf seemed to be running some sort of temperature so we pulled off onto the sand by the road and opened her chest cavity. Sure enough, the dynamo seemed to be having its own little bonfire as smoke poured out of it. It was very much an ex-dynamo so we pulled further off the road down a narrow track, parked under the shade of some trees and retrieved the spare dynamo from the depths of our stores under our mattress. It did not take long to attach it to the battery to test it, and even less time for it to let us know it too was not feeling too well. For an hour we fiddled with it, got shocks from it, refitted it and still its obduracy left us immobilised and stranded. The only option open was for one of us to hitch a ride back to Caborca to find someone who could repair both defunct dynamos but it was now dusk and too late so we settled down for the night, during which three consecutive storms raged about us. At times the rain was so heavy it came through Adolf's canvas roof in a fine mist.

The morning brought yet another clear sky and the promise of another hot day ahead. As Sam was the mechanic of the two of us it fell to him to head back to Caborca with the dynamos while I stayed in the desert to guard Adolf. We were in luck in that he got a lift in the first truck to come along as I settled down against one of the trees with a book, prepared for a long wait as I had no idea when he might return. There was only one road in this part of the desert, running from Caborca to Santa Ana where it branched north and south. Trucks were the main users of the road, but infrequently, so when one came along I tended to glance up, as one might to a flickering television high in the corner of a bar, the eye being caught by a movement. Hearing a truck coming I spotted its dust down the road as it came in my direction on its way to Caborca. As it neared at great speed I noticed there was a second truck behind, a petrol tanker, that seemed to be following very close to the lead truck. It was only as they passed that I could see the petrol tanker was actually pushing the front truck along the road. The front one must have broken down and the driver had obviously negotiated a helping bumper to the nearest town. He also clearly failed to appreciate or care that his helper was a potential cataclysmic explosion on wheels. It must have been a relief to the lead driver that he had a nice clear view of the road ahead but I could only imagine at what was in the mind of the petrol tanker driver, whose horizon was the end of his bonnet.

Mind you, it would be hypocritical of me to take issue with these Siamese twins of the road since we too regularly used very similar fuel saving driving techniques as we tailgated huge trucks, driving a couple of feet from their rear bumpers. By driving in the near vacuum they created behind them, we could lift our right foot off the accelerator, almost idling the engine as we were sucked down the road, using virtually no petrol. Whichever of us was driving when we did this, the one task we had was to stare unblinking at the truck's brake lights. If they glowed red, ours needed to as well, immediately. Whilst I have yet to see this energy saving driving method in any official driver's manual, it certainly took the monotony out of some of our long distance stretches, with the added advantage we managed to get fuel consumption records that the Land Rover designers could only ever have dreamed of and salivated over. In the cold light of day I can see these moments competed with the cruise control fun of the Los Angeles Freeways as acts of sheer lunacy, empirical evidence of youth's belief in its indestructibility, and perhaps immortality.

As I waited for Sam to return, a small truck with three Mexicans on board came down the track and parked in the trees near me. The driver strolled over and asked me if I had a match to light his spliff, which was sticking up vertically out of the end of an empty matchbox. He lit up, smoking it through the other end of the matchbox. He cheerfully offered me a puff which I politely refused with a smile. He wandered back to his friends and lit their little rolls of oblivion with another of our matches. For the next hour or so they puffed away, ran around as they got higher and eventually drove off, crashing gears and getting stuck in the sand, all the while with glazed eyes and happy grins. It made me wonder how many of the Mexican truck and car drivers we were to encounter in the miles ahead would be in a similar state. From what we had seen of Mexican driving so far, I assumed all of them.

Sam returned later in the day with the spare dynamo, which was i fact working perfectly. Apparently we would have found this out if we had attached the negative cable to both terminals. We fitted it to the engine, returned to Caborca to pay for and collect the now repaired one and then drove on to spend the night under a bridge about twenty miles north of Guaymas on the coast. Guaymas was the town where the film '*Catch 22*' was shot in 1970. Joseph Heller's satirical book remains funny, witty, complex and dark to this day. At that time it was perhaps inevitably juxtaposed with the war in Vietnam, the doomed conflict that had cost too many young American lives had become openly unpopular in America and with the youth of Europe, which I find anomalous with our then young generation's penchant for wearing T shirts emblazoned with Che Guevara's handsome face. His peace loving adoring supporters must have been ignorant of his brutality and ruthlessly violent suppression of opposition or those who openly interfered with his revolutionary zeal.

The Vietnam war turned the public away from war related arts. It was irrelevant that Heller's story was set in the Mediterranean in World War II. Vietnam was so alive in the public consciousness it ensured the film was never the great success it deserved to be. The book's syncopated timelines bemused many and were perhaps too confusing for the big screen so were ignored by the film makers, who replaced them with an orderly chronology. The film's failure to achieve widespread popularity was perhaps exacerbated by the contemporaneous release of the other war film of the seventies, the better known, less complex and openly sardonic '*Mash*', which spawned the popular television series. Catch 22 remained a cult film, a black comedy unappreciated by critics and a war weary public. I loved both it and the book.

On the road again early the next morning we were stopped by a policeman in Guaymas who told us we had been speeding in a school zone. He pulled out his well thumbed book of traffic tickets but we told him we had no money for a fine so could we instead do five days on bread and water. This evoked a huge grin from him and a wave of the hand to go on as he returned to his vehicle chuckling to himself. At last, a policeman with a sense of humour, so unlike our experiences of them in the States. He waved a cheery hand at us as he pulled out and drove off, shaking his head and smiling to himself. Later that morning, whilst taking on fuel in a garage, we started chatting to an American couple. They were medical students from Colorado and had with them a South African hitchhiker. They were going to take a swim in the sea at Las Bocas so we went with them, down dirt desert roads that led to the sea. We parked under the trees by the white sandy beach and there enjoyed the warm waters of the Gulf of California, and the slightly warmer faecal lumps floating around in it from the collective and busy rectums of the nearby village. Sewage management had not reached Las Bocas. Drying off in the hot sun on the beach, we agreed to meet our fellow travellers in a small town called La Cruz about two hundred and fifty miles further south. Since their huge American 'Bronco' vehicle could go considerably faster than us, they set off and we bumbled after them, driving all day and into the night, arriving at the town at about ten o'clock in the evening after a day of uneventful driving, or as uneventful as driving in Mexico can be. I had come to the conclusion the country had no mental asylums, all the would be occupants being housed instead in cars and trucks and let loose on the roads.

Night had fallen as we approached a town called Culiacan just north of La Cruz when I suddenly spotted in our headlights a large tractor shuffling along the road ahead, no lights and half on and half off the road. The tractor's right hand tyres were in the dirt and throwing up a dust cloud obscuring the large vehicle. It was a miracle we didn't drive straight into it, and an even bigger miracle if the driver got home alive that night, given the huge trucks using the same road. After passing the tractor we nearly ran into a twitching cow lying in the road, somewhat prostrated by the large tyre marks across it, no doubt left by whatever vehicle had hit it. From its struggles we could see it was still alive but mortally wounded and for a moment we contemplated stopping to put it out of its misery, not the last time we would have this discussion in the coming months. We decided to keep going since owners of animals that have been hit in those southern parts tend to be a little upset and more than likely to want to have a little discussion of the machete sort. Again we were reminded of the oft repeated and wise advice not to drive on Mexican roads after dark. We drove around La Cruz and a number of the dirt roads in the bush and desert near the town, and then down to the beach about five miles away, but could find no sign of the Bronco. We assumed the others had not made it and so continued on south, running out of petrol about ten miles down the road, conveniently next to a spot by the road where we could pull off out of the path of following traffic and safely spend the night.

In the morning we filled one of the tanks from our spare fuel supplies in the jerry cans, but then had some difficulty in starting Adolf, perhaps because of an air lock in the fuel lines. We stopped some passing Mexicans to get them to push us. A lifelong addiction to enchiladas, quesadillas, cheap beer, cigarettes and marijuana is not a training regime I would advise if you are going to push start a fully laden Land Rover. Whilst closed chest defibrillators were invented in the early 1950's, I doubt they had become commonplace ten miles south of La Cruz but looking at the gasping Mexicans in our rear view mirrors as we drove away when the engine fired, they would have been useful that morning. Our cheery waves were a poor substitute as resuscitators for the men, now bent double in the middle of the road, hands on their knees and shoulders hunched as they gasped for breath.

About half an hour down the road the big white Bronco caught up with us. The three occupants had sensibly decided to stop driving as dusk fell the evening before. They were very concerned about driving after dark, and so had pulled into a camp site at Culiacan for the night, missing all the fun with the invisible tractor and prostrated cow. The American couple were heading off inland and so we took Lester, the South African hitcher, and drove on to Mazatlan on the coast, crossing the Tropic of Cancer on the way. Now we were in the tropics the landscape and vegetation had changed, desert and scrub giving way to green jungle in which we passed occasional clearings of banana trees and patches of maize. Large swarms of locusts carpeted the roads and filled the air and we regularly passed large tarantulas crossing the road, Mexican versions of our tyre dodging hedgehogs. The tarantulas were huge and at one point we stopped and got out to photograph one next to our bare feet to give some sense of proportion to these enormous arachnids. Patient vultures lurked expectantly in trees, waiting for something to die. Armadillos ventured onto the roads, hoping not to.

In those far off days, Mazatlan was a lovely sandy beach with a small town attached to it, a place where flocks of migrating hippies from America and Canada came down to over-winter, smoke dope and surf the beautiful sea. They were all over the place, their migration having started as the fall started further north. The sun blazed on the white sands and two small, deep green islands shimmered in the water just offshore, each wearing a necklace of sand where their steep slopes met the blue sea. I could quite understand the hippy community decamping to such an idyllic spot, but not their leaving it. If, like Lester our South African passenger, you meandered through life without the hint of ambition or motivation, I am not sure why you would want to leave a temporal depiction of Paradise. We swam and bodysurfed in the warm water and then went and sat in a cafe on the beach, burying our toes in the sand as we ordered a banquet of toast and coffee, our first meal since leaving America. Since crossing the border we had spent a total of about $1.00 between us on a daily taco each, bought from roadside food shacks. For some time now we had been having difficulty keeping our shorts from falling down to our ankles because of the weight we had lost. A White-nosed Coati, a raccoon-like animal with a long almost prehensile nose and banded tail, wandered amongst the tables hunting for bits of food. Occasionally it would jump up onto one to lick at crumbs. It was regularly kicked at by the Mexican staff and customers when it came near them but resolutely continued its hunt for scraps to eat. On one table it was on it knocked over the condiments as it was grabbed by the tail by a waiter, whose courage completely disappeared when it finally lost its willingness to accept abuse and turned on him. My sympathies were with the Coati as the man ran onto the beach to escape its justifiable wrath.

Chatting to other travellers in the cafe we heard of a three day fiesta taking place further south in Ciudad

Guzmán, about three hundred and seventy miles away, and decided it would be fun to see it. In the short time we had been on the beach, Lester had met some people who he had hitched a lift with a couple of weeks before, and had also osmotically absorbed the indolence of beach life, and so decided to stay in Mazatlan where we were sure he would enter the same form of warm climate hibernation that kept so many of the others there from doing anything with their lives. Despite having driven over five hundred miles the day before, we still had a long way to go to British Honduras and so we said our farewells and headed off, driving through Tepic on our way down to Guadalajara. Late in the afternoon, as dusk was about to fall, we were stopped by a couple of American girls in a Volkswagen Beetle who were frightened of driving in the dark and of camping by themselves. They asked if they could follow us and spend the night with us. We piloted them down the road until we came to a small quarry a couple of miles further on where we pulled in and helped them put up their tent. We built a camp fire and watched them eat their evening meal as we savoured a coffee each and the memory of our toast by the beach. A large electrical storm in the pitch black night in the distance gave us a son et lumiere show to marvel at. A red ant biting my foot gave me a throbbing night to marvel at. I was amazed that something so small could cause so much pain. During the first part of the night it slowly spread upwards to involve my leg. After a couple of hours the pain passed and I slept, dreaming of elephantiasis sufferers I had seen as a young boy in India.

In the morning the two girls thanked us for their protection and set off as we too left, driving an uneventful day as we skirted Guadalajara, arriving in Ciudad Guzmán at about five thirty in the evening with the fiesta in full swing. There was a fairground with some rides, market stalls and carts and stalls selling food, all to a backdrop of blaring music being played through large speakers set on high poles. We wandered amongst the revellers enjoying the festive atmosphere, attracting quite a bit of attention in our torn and scruffy shorts, and then headed back north out of the town, our aim being to head cross country to get onto Route 15 which headed east on the southern shores of Lake Chapata. At about nine o'clock we pulled off the road into a field for a good night' sleep, tired after a long day on the road. Little did we know.

Our heterosexually induced head to toe sleeping arrangement meant I always slept with my head at the back of Adolf, on the driver's side with my feet pointing at the steering wheel. On hot nights we would roll up the canvas back to allow a breeze in to cool us and to caress my face, and that is what we did that night. Settling down for the night and lying on my back, I looked up out of the open back at the panoply of beautiful stars in the ink black sky above. They were all still there when I woke at about two o'clock, vaguely aware of having been woken by a sound. Opening my eyes and looking up, I could see the night was now lit by a full moon, and in its bright light I could also see the twin barrels of a shotgun hovering and moving a couple of inches above my nose. Very slowly I sat up and turned. The gun was now pointing directly at my face, inches from it. It's owner was resting one foot on one of Adolf's rear grab handles with his elbow resting on his knee as he supported the gun. I could see his finger on the trigger. About ten feet to the side I could see a dozing horse, its head hung low. I gently shook the fast asleep Sam's leg, feeling empathy with the astronauts on the damaged Apollo 13 as I absorbed the implications of our own 'Houston, we have a problem' moment. The man was a scruffy looking individual, short and with a mass of matted hair swirling around his head. A thick moustache under his broken nose sheltered his mouth as he chewed on something.

"¿Qué estás haciendo aquí?" "What are you doing here?" he said.

"Estamos durmiendo" - "We are sleeping" I replied.

"¿Porqué?" "Why?"

It was two o'clock in the morning. It was the middle of nowhere, no discos, no bars. What else would I be doing? But, common sense prevailed and it was very apparent this was another of those times not to be a smart arse. We started talking to him quietly and calmly, all the while staring into the barrels of his shotgun, and fairly quickly understood he was telling us we were on Federal land, whatever that was. He said he was a Federal officer. This seemed unlikely given his torn and dirty clothes. The breeze in our faces wafted his scent over us, a delicate blend of brewery and cow shed. As he was talking to us I spotted the dozing horse lift its tail. It farted with enthusiasm, a molto forte blast in the wind section. Our interloper obviously had no idea the horse was there as he jumped and leapt back from Adolf. He swung the gun round on the startled animal, now closer to death and its destiny in a faux beef burger than it knew. As he turned, he also lurched and staggered, and we realised he was completely drunk. Calming down after his flatulent fright, he turned back to us, obviously finding it difficult to stand up, his gun waving all over the place like a conductor's baton as he was now unsupported by Adolf. We asked him where he lived. He indicated his hut was up the hill and suggested we should join him up there for a drink, before the police arrived and arrested us for being on their land. He said we could help him milk his cows. We agreed with him and said we would drive up and meet him up there. This seemed to please him and he started to trudge across the field to the dirt road. We drove after him across to the road and up the hill, passing a truck that had also parked up for the night. When we reached near the top we turned and thundered down the hill again, passing the drunk as he clambered up the side of the truck to wake its unsuspecting and sleeping driver. We didn't hang about to see if the driver got shot but instead decided we might as well now carry on driving through the night since we very definitely wide awake after what we concluded had been a bit of a close shave given the man's state of inebriation. Mexico City was our next objective, some four hundred miles away, on roads that were not all made for speed, but we decided to do the drive in one, taking turns to sleep in the back as we went, something we regularly did on long distance stretches.

Reaching Mexico City just after mid-day we drove through the affluent western districts with their well ordered residential streets, lined with large houses. Parking in a car park in the centre of the city, we went for a walk, looking for markets where we might buy some robust sandals to replace our destroyed footwear. A Tourist Policeman asked us if we wanted help and introduced us to a guide, insisting we would not have to pay, the most un-Mexican thing. The friendly guide took us to a couple of markets but we felt the sandals were costing more than we wanted to pay so we turned our attention to eating. It was five days since we had crossed the border and we had not eaten one proper meal, surviving on very small snacks when we could find them. Our normal diet was a breakfast of toothpaste and malarial tablets, then a light luncheon of a taco the size of a small cigar, rounding off the day with a little nightcap of coffee and toothpaste. We were absolutely famished and set off to search for a restaurant listed in the South American Handbook as a cheap place to eat, ideal for mendicants such as us. Sadly it was closed so we found something significantly more down market and ordered eight tacos each, a gourmand moment that gave us a glimpse of what Paradise might be like.

Finishing our meal we returned to Adolf and joined the swirling vortex of traffic and pedestrians as we negotiated our way through the maze of streets to leave the city. We stopped in a beautiful square with shady trees and got out to sit and enjoy it, but it started to rain so decided to move on. For some reason Mexico City reminded me of Turin. Perhaps I was influenced by the driving. The maniacal gleam in drivers' eyes as they fought for position in the traffic, refusing to give way to anyone lest their machismo be questioned was compelling and infectious as we too became assertive in our traffic management. To the average saloon driver who cared about the appearance of his car Adolf must have appeared to be a vehicular prize fighter with her imposing steel bumper at the front, and care worn dirty exterior showing a self confidant disregard for appearance or the collection of bruises on her. We found paths opened before us like the Red Sea before Moses as we pushed Adolf's mangled nose into gaps in the traffic. We exited the east of the city, a complete contrast to the affluent western suburbs. The eastern areas were very poor, the roads filled vehicles and humanity, with overcrowded buses focussed on dodging surrounding cars, all hooting at each other, the drivers gesticulating and shouting out of windows. In amongst the traffic, people crossed the road or tried to sell their wares to drivers and passengers. Newspapers, snacks, drinks and trinkets were all on offer through vehicle windows as the traders wandered around in the entangled vehicles.

Leaving Mexico City behind we continued driving until dusk. Somewhat tired after the long day that had followed our shortened night's sleep, we looked for somewhere to stop for the night and spotted a track leading off the road and running around the side of a thickly forested hill. We took it and after a while pulled in by it in the dark, collapsing in bed until the dawn and the chorus of early morning birdsong woke us. Climbing out of Adolf in the cool dawn air, we were presented with the most beautiful view of the snow capped twin peaks of Popocatépetl and Iztaccihuatl, glowing a pale pink in the early morning sun that brushed their peaks, slowly brightening as the light moved gently down their slumbering flanks. A mist filled valley lay sleepily below us, nestled under its duvet of cloud. The second and third highest peaks in Mexico respectively, the sheer unexpectedness of seeing them there took our breath away. Sam and I stood side by side in complete silence, gazing at their almost indescribable beauty, somehow realising that words were unnecessary. Any we could find to say would have been inadequate and completely superfluous, an intrusion into a moment of utter tranquility that could only detract from what was already a perfect moment. For me it seemed as though we were the only people in the world, isolated in the forest with only the dawn chorus of the birds to signify anything else existed. Instinctively I knew that until the day I died there would be only one other person who understood how I felt at that moment, overwhelmed by the majesty of the scene, the power of the forces that had created it and the ancient civilisations that had also no doubt looked on in wonder and awe. I am also now aware that those of us who prefer to travel alone and unencumbered by companions are denied shared moments of wonder and awe and somehow that diminishes the value and joy of the experience. Perhaps it is a fundamental and primitive part of the human spirit to share experiences and so we are not programmed for a solitary life.

The Aztec mythical history of the two mountains is a powerful story of unrequited love and loss. Iztaccihuatl was the daughter of an Emperor. She fell in love with Popocatépetl, one of his warriors. On realising this the Emperor sent Popocatépetl to war with the promise that on his return he could have Iztaccihuatl as his wife. While Popocatépetl was away fighting, the Emperor told his daughter her suitor had been killed. Unable to bear her loss, she died of a broken heart. Popocatépetl returned and took her body and buried her near Tenochtitlan, the capital of the Aztec Empire. He kneeled by the grave and the gods covered him and the grave in snow, then turning them into mountains. Iztaccihuatl, with its four peaks representing a head, chest knees and feet, is often called *White Woman* because the mountain looks like a reclining woman. The mourning Popocatépetl crouched close to her, raging at his loss, in his anger hurling fire and ash on the surrounding countryside as an active volcano. Like so many myths, I found this one both romantic and tragic, emphasising the beauty of love.

    The boundary line between the States of Mexico and Puebla runs north and south directly through the two mountains and we had crossed into Puebla in the early evening before stopping for the night. Reluctantly turning our back on the immortalised lovers we downed our breakfast of malarial tablets and drove south east to the city of Puebla, the State capital. The city is laid out in an ordered grid system and lies in the Cuetlaxcoapan valley. The layout is in a classic Spanish format that is centered on the zócalo or main square where we pulled over to the pavement and parked. We sat in the early morning sunshine as we waited for a bank and the Post Office to open. We needed to cash a traveller's cheque as we were low on cash. The square was filled with green lawns with benches under the trees overlooking them. Piped music was playing softly from speakers in the branches and I gazed up at them, wondering if some of those same branches had been used as gallows for the public hangings that used to take place in the square. In fact the gallows had stood where the fountain is now sited but perhaps on busy days some of the branches were pressed into service. The bullfights that also once took place in the square had been moved to a permanent dedicated arena elsewhere in the town. The whole square was dominated by the country's tallest cathedral, whose first stone was laid in 1536, although the building was not finally completed until 1768. I had come to realise the Mexicans did not like to be rushed, never quite getting to grips with the sense of urgency implicit in the concept of mañana.

While we waited and wrote our diaries, I watched a young girl sitting on a nearby bench. She was being pestered by a newspaper seller who seemed to be in a state of musth. He reminded me of an over sexed male town pigeon in London that lands next to a disinterested female and then struts and postures in front of her, puffing up his little chest and repeatedly dipping his head as he unashamedly begs for sex. The young girl told the persistent paper seller to go away and leave her alone but she was perhaps being too subtle for him to understand with his testosterone befuddled mind. As the female pigeons in London so often do, she eventually stood up and walked away to sit elsewhere in the square, leaving him bemused at the rejection and looking around the square for another target. As he did so, a man rode past on his donkey, gallantly allowing his wife to walk behind him. She was as loaded with bags as the donkey was with his corpulent carcass. They were narrowly missed by an out of control bicycle with four Mexicans on it, which made me wonder how many they might have fitted onto a tandem.

When one of the banks opened its doors we went over and spent the next hour and a half watching Mexican banking bureaucracy as the £10.00 travellers cheque we presented was held up to the light, taken from desk to desk, felt, sniffed, tasted and compared to a specimen cheque, all to the cacophony of a heated discussion about it. Finally the staff somewhat reluctantly agreed to empty the bank's coffers and handed us our cash which, in our usual way, we split between us and then further divided between our various pockets and shoes before leaving the bank. Our subterfuge and division of spoils was lest we were asked for a contribution to some criminal charitable cause once out on the streets again. We knew people leaving banks were often watched and targeted for a little involuntary endowment, with the logical assumption they might well have made a cash withdrawal. After climbing one of the cathedral's twin towers for an elevated view of the town and surrounding countryside, we drove east out of Puebla, heading towards Vera Cruz, our point of landing on the east coast in Mexico and about two hundred miles away.

Since leaving the west coast and crossing the country we had driven through a wide range of topography and vegetation. Vertiginous mountain climbs on narrow dirt roads, often cloaked with pine forests; large flat plains of grassland interspersed with fields and smallholdings; thick, impenetrable and humid jungle which came alive at night with a deafening chorus of tumescent and fecund frogs calling out to each other, making sleep difficult to achieve because of the dissonance about us. Now we came down onto the coastal plain and skirted around Vera Cruz, stopping for the night next to a beach at Alvarado. During the day we had stopped and picked oranges from laden trees, lifted a couple of pumpkins and later harvested a few ears of corn from a field. We had also spotted a turkey wandering around the dirt road we were on so, as Sam slowly reversed up the road I climbed out of the back and tried to entice the large bird to me. This was a week or more's food for us and too good an opportunity to miss. I was so engrossed in trying to catch the brainless bird that I was unaware I was being watched by its owner until she called out to me. The turkey lived to fight another day and we carried on our way, our meat larder empty. We pulled off the road for the night as the light failed but it was too late to start hunting for wood and building a fire. In any event we were fighting off the marauding and ravenous mosquito hordes, so we quickly ate a couple of oranges and went to bed hungry.

Still hungry when we woke up at dawn, we set off along the coast until our hunger pangs became somewhat unpleasant. We pulled over and gathered some wood for a fire. A couple of ears of corn bumped and nudged each other in the boiling water over the flames until we judged them to be ready. They looked enticing, particularly since the individual kernels of corn were huge, three or four times the size one normally finds. This should have been our first clue that they would be inedible. As our teeth sank into them and we tore off the first mouthful we realised they had been grown for cattle fodder. Chewing them was like biting into a roll of lumpy lavatory paper. We turned our attention to the pumpkins but they were like bricks so we put out our fire, packed our little kitchen and set off, stopping at a filthy roadside café in San

Andrés Tuxtla for a meal. The cheapest item on the menu was Sopa de Mondongo at five pesos, so we ordered a couple of those, oblivious of the fact that mondongo is tripe. I have never been able to eat tripe. I have never even been able to be in the same room as the stuff. Just the smell of it makes me retch, an involuntary reaction over which I have no control. When the soup arrived with a small flourish of pride from the cafe owner, I gazed down into it as the steam from it hit my nostrils and immediately stood up and walked out with the small piece of bread that came with the soup, leaving Sam to demolish both bowls. Given I had been eating dog food without flinching in California, the fact I couldn't stomach the soup or its contents says much about my aversion to tripe.

Reaching Coatzacoalcos we joined a long queue of cars and trucks waiting to catch a rudimentary ferry that was taking vehicles across the town's eponymous river. Walking down to the river at the front of the long line of vehicles we could see there were two ferries, each capable of taking about twenty five cars. In the usual Mexican way, the ferrymen were trying hard to fit about fifty vehicles on each. Drivers were being yelled at and abused as tempers frayed and the art of chaos was elevated to new heights. We chatted to an American couple in the vehicle in front of us. They too were on their way to the British Honduran border and they told us they had heard the bridge over the river upstream had been taken out of action when it had been hit by a ship, which by all accounts was now wedged under it. It was clear we had a long wait so we made some coffee with our over worked immersion heater, also making coffee for the Americans. They in turn produced a packet of biscuits and offered them to us. I fell on the packet like an Assyrian wolf descending on the vulnerable fold of Jerusalem.

After three hours it was our turn to be squeezed onto the ferry, last on and just behind the two Americans, with Adolf's broad bum hanging over the water at the back. Our boarding the good ship Bottom Feeder was in itself a matter for substantial discussion by the Mexican crew and the passengers, all irritated by the three hour wait we had had to get on the vessel. Some of the crew were determined we should be included in the sailing whilst passengers seemed concerned that Adolf on the cargo manifest was an Adolf too far, the straw that was going to break the ferry's back and sink us all in the fast flowing current of brown water. We sat for five minutes with our front wheels on the ferry and our back wheels on the land as the crew shouted and gesticulated at the drivers of the cars ahead of us to inch forward to allow all four of our wheels to fit on.

Finally safely, if only just on board, the crew cast off and the ferry moved out into the stream, valiantly fighting the strong current that was trying to push her downstream. The wheezing vessel struggled across to the other bank where we all disembarked in disbelief we had made it to safety, empathising with the survivors of the Titanic and how they must have felt when they finally made landfall. Looking at the map we could see we were close to the coast and so decided to bathe in the sea at Allende. On arriving we discovered there was an oil refinery there and the sea was an oil slick thanks to the refinery's uncontrolled dumping of effluent, so we contented ourselves with a shower using the water from one of Adolf's jerry cans, each taking it in turns to stand up on her wheel arch to pour water on the other from a height. A crude but effective al fresco power shower we often used in areas where water was plentiful. Where it was scarce we husbanded and rationed our water with care. Refreshed we drove on to a town called Villahermosa where we parked next to a shack for the night.

Dawn brought another cup of coffee in the cooler air that soothes the burnished land before the sun breaks over the horizon. Getting on the road again before the world got out of bed we headed south towards Chetumal and the border. About two hundred and fifty miles before Chetumal we turned off the road and headed for Palenque, the site of Mayan ruins we had read about that lay about thirty miles off the main road south. The Mayan culture and civilisation was, and remains, fascinating, and appears to have originated in about 2600 BC in the Yucatan Peninsular, where Palenque is sited. Over centuries the Mayans spread their influence through southern Mexico, Belize and Guatemala, reaching the zenith of their powers around 250 AD. From about 200 AD until the civilisation's decline in about 900 AD, the Mayans lived in contiguous kingdoms that traded with each other through corridors they cleared through swamps and jungles. They developed astronomy, a complex calendar and the ability to write in hieroglyphics.

Mayan lives were guided by a religion that lay at the heart of their culture. Highly ritualised, their beliefs centred on the influence the cosmos and their gods had on their daily existence. Skilled architects, potters, weavers, engineers and farmers, they built underground reservoirs to store rainwater where water was scarce. Their elaborate temples and buildings were constructed without the aid of metal tools, much as was the case with the Incas. Palenque is in fact the name of a village and the chronology of which was named first, the village or the site of the Mayan temples, is lost in the mists of time. In about 900 AD those Mayans living in the southern regions abandoned their cities, for reasons that have never been known. They were finally integrated into the Toltec culture in about 1200 AD, thriving within that until the Spanish arrived in the sixteenth century with that mistaken and arrogant belief of all conquerors that they were exporting and imposing a better way, a better society, a better civilisation. It is still happening today with the misguided conviction that western democracy is the only way and is craved by the unwashed savages in the world who don't yet have it.

The ruins at Palenque were rediscovered hiding under a thick forest duvet in 1773 and lie in the long shadow of the Tumbalá mountains. The site is on a shelf that looks down on the flood plains of the Usumacinta River north of the site, plains that run to the Gulf of Mexico. The flood plain is fertile and would have been an ideal area for the provision of food for the inhabitants of the area. The river itself would have been an invaluable passageway for trade with other areas, a fluvial motorway. The ruins lie about five miles into the jungle past the eponymous village. We arrived and payed our 5 peso entrance fee to the gatekeeper, realising when we got into the deserted ruins we were the only people there. We could see the site was still in the very early stages of being pulled out from under its vegetive bedclothes for the world to see. Only a small number of the buildings had been uncovered. The central square of the complex lay in front of the main pyramid, the Temple of Inscriptions, and that area had been cleared but the thick, impenetrable jungle still remained close around so the full extent of the ruins was hidden to us.

    The Temple was large and imposing, rising almost vertically in front of us. It consisted of eight terraces that formed a massive plinth on which sat the temple itself. Running up the centre of the terraces was a steep stairway bisecting the front of the structure. Standing at its foot in the quiet and damp air of the early morning, the atmosphere was eerie, like the set of an old fashioned black and white horror movie. I expected swirls of mist to appear and envelope us as monkeys hooted and called in the trees about us. Butterflies flapped by in their jerkily aimless meanderings. It was easy to imagine the fear and awe the place must have imposed on the mass of lower ordered Mayan Indians as they gathered in the square for whatever ceremonies they were made to attend, including human sacrifice. There is no doubt the Mayans sacrificed people but their reasons for doing so are not clear. Those down in the square looking up at the priests on the top of the Temple preparing to lob one of their number off for the short vertical flight down must have counted their blessings they were spectators of man's early attempts at flight rather than playing the central role in the ritual.

We climbed the vertiginous sixty-nine steps to the top of the pyramid and from there were able to look out over the jungle as we were now above the tree line. The grass square beneath us and in front of the pyramid seemed to have shrunk to the size of a postage stamp. The steps up were so steep that from the top it was like looking over the edge of a cliff face. It dawned on us that getting down safely without falling and reenacting the sacrificial rituals of old was not going to be easy. Each step was narrow, hardly a human foot length deep before the next one above. It was this construction that allowed the building to have its steep sides. Turning our backs on the descent problem, we moved into the temple at the top. It had five doorways, the piers separating them each having carvings on their outer surfaces. Inside the temple was divided into two large chambers with vaulted roofs. The structures at Palenque were a fine example of the inventiveness of the Mayans. Their buildings were designed to reduce the stress on load bearing walls, allowing the builders to construct their buildings with multiple doorways and piers, letting in light.

In 1948 four stone plugs in the floor of the temple were examined and it was discovered there was a passageway down into the bowels of the temple that ultimately reached a door behind which was a room containing a sarcophagus, eighty feet below the summit. Within it lay the remains of Hanab Pacal, the king who had built the temple. He died before its completion and his successor, Chan Bahlum, fulfilled that wish.

Archeologists had also discovered a duct inside the tomb that ran up next to the interior staircase to the temple above. I had heard about similar ducts in Egyptian pyramids, with the same theory that they were there to allow the sun to shine down to the tomb's resident, or to allow a passage for the spirit to pass to the stars or to the next world above.

Despite searching, we could not find the way down into the heart of the pyramid where there had also been discovered a carved tablet that we had read about. The tablet was a large slab of rock that had been shaped into a rectangular, flat surfaced canvas, a stela onto which the Mayans had carved a figure of a man. What excited our interest was this man appeared to be an early astronaut. The photograph of the carving we had seen showed him sitting in a backwards reclining seat, much as the astronauts we followed on television and in the press were positioned for lift off in their capsule as they popped up from Cape Kennedy to the moon for lunch. The carved man appeared to be wearing some form of space suit and helmet, but perversely, no shoes. The legs of his seat spat flames and as he lay back, he stared up into the stars carved at the top of the stone above him. Were the Mayans prescient? Had they an inkling of rocket propulsion? Had they been 'visited' and seen their more advanced guests return to their home in the vastness of space, as some now believe? I have no idea, but I do know there are some things in our lives we know will never be answered and that we shall never fully understand.

Reading about the Mayans, their culture and the rocket man, emphasised for me the intelligence of civilisations that have preceded ours. The Egyptians with the mathematical and geometrical complexity and precision of their pyramids, achieved whilst we Britons were running around in animal skins as partially house-trained savages. The Incas with their cities in the sky that we were yet to see and marvel at. The creators of Stonehenge. Like the Mayans, all with an extraordinary knowledge, and an understanding of astronomy. An ability to build vast structures that defy logic given their size and proportions, and all done without modern equipment, and in the Mayan and Incas' case, without any tools. Sitting at the top of the temple looking out over the thick jungle and distant plains, I reflected on the thought that as mankind acquires knowledge and skills, he also sheds it as successive generations fail to hand on the talents and knowledge they have. Perhaps it isn't a failure to hand on knowledge by an older generation, but more a refusal by a younger generation to accept old technology, to continue to embrace the old ways in tandem with the new. Why learn the art of mental arithmetic when we can use a calculator? Why thatch a house's roof when we can cover it with tiles? In twenty first century parlance, why follow and read a map when we can use a satellite navigation system? We slough off and discard old skins as we acquire new ones. New technologies allow us to build and do faster, but not necessarily always better. What happens when the new technology fails us? We have none of the now lost knowledge and skills of preceding generations and cultures to fall back on, our initiative and instincts somehow suppressed. Perhaps our reliance on advanced technology leaves us as much exposed as advantaged.

Since there was no way down into the depths of the pyramid we gingerly descended the outer steps on our backsides and wandered around the other buildings that had been exposed by the excavations and clearing work that had been carried out. The Mayans' architecture fascinated us for an hour and a half as we wandered alone through the ruins. We entered many of the old buildings. Dark and dank, they smelt musty, and of the monkeys that clearly sheltered in them. There was a small museum but it was closed and there was no one to ask whether it would open, so we left, picking two ripe, yellow grapefruit off a tree in the forest as we did. To this day I think the one I ate later that day remains the most delicious piece of fruit I have ever eaten, a juice-laden explosion of flavour, putting in the shade the oranges and bananas we had been living on for the previous few days. We had been picking wild fruit as we drove through the countryside, our sole diet with some interesting collateral consequences.

We made our way back through the dense jungle to the main road and turned for the border again, driving all day through the centre of the Yucatan Peninsular, crossing its jungles, mountains and plains, finally reaching the border at Chetumal just after sunset. We realised we had not sampled tequila whilst in Mexico, which seemed a bit of a shame, so we headed for the largest hotel in the sleepy town, the Las Cocas, and found its fly filled bar. It was empty and the barmaid was fast asleep on a shelf under a table so we woke her and placed our order. The two large drinks arrived together with their entourage of salt and quarters of fresh lime on a small plate. Not having tried tequila before we were not sure of the proper etiquette that goes with drinking it, the order of play and rules of engagement, so the barmaid explained we should dip a wedge of lime in the salt, squeeze it, lick it and then take a sip of the drink. It was potent and disgusting and to me, up there with sipping kerosene, but to the Mexican population no doubt it was nectar of the gods, and a certain path to oblivion. Sam and I manfully struggled through our drinks, having paid a few pesos for them, and when we had finished them ordered two Cuba Libras to try to kill the awful taste in our mouths.

Feeling quite refreshed in an alcohol infused, fail the breathalyser sort of way, we left the bar to pick up Adolf and drove around until we found a dingy looking cafe that appeared cheap enough for our dining budget. The pure alcohol of the tequila seemed to have made us even hungrier than we habitually were. A single weak and naked bulb hung from the centre of the ceiling, throwing a yellow light around the cafe. I noticed the bulb was covered in grease on which flies were dining, reassuring me we would not be the only customers that evening. If the place was good enough for the flies, it was certainly going to be good enough for us given our usual diet. We took a table by the wall and ordered eggs, somewhat uncertain about what form they would appear in. The cook, hidden somewhere in the back recesses of the joint and no doubt working with a cigarette dangling between his lips, was clearly feeling quite creative that evening as he conjured up a half way house between an omelette and scrambled eggs. Perhaps he was just feeling indecisive. The few other customers in the cafe largely ignored us as they too tucked into unidentifiable mounds of brown stuff on their plates.

Finishing our very welcome feast we drove the streets again looking for somewhere to sleep for the night, eventually settling for a spot in the road near the hotel where we had sampled the well hidden charms of tequila. Sleep came quickly, so perhaps there were beneficial side affects to Mexico's favourite tipple. Its hallucinatory qualities resulted in strange dreams of playing basketball with bouncing giant limes and oranges, and phone calls to Greece on banana telephones. Our vegan diet was obviously influencing my subconscious thoughts.

The murmurs of the town and its people waking up in the morning acted as our alarm call. As we connected up our immersion heater to the battery to make our customary morning coffee, we turned on the radio and were surprised to find we able to pick up the BBC World Service via Radio Belize, transmitted from British Honduras. British Honduras was a British colony and yet to achieve its full independence. Its eastern coastline was lusted after by Guatemala, which claimed it as its own. Decades of sabre rattling by the Guatemalans, with threats of invasion and the subsequent subjugation of the British Honduran population meant the British Government kept a military presence in the country to deter any military incursions and to reassure the colony. We were aware of this military detachment and had decided we would try to find the camp for a brief connection with home.

Finishing our coffees we walked to the local market to buy a dozen eggs for our next few meals. The ubiquitous market was huge and was in a warehouse sized building, all under one roof. The decrepit structure was old and rusting and although it was still quite early in the morning, it was bustling with people. Vendors were shouting their prices as the customers haggled with them. The air was hot and humid and walking around in the crowds thronging the narrow paths between the many stalls we could see people could probably buy anything they needed for the house or larder. In the meat area of the market we came across a couple of stalls that sold fresh chicken with the callous ease of those indifferent to animal welfare. The reason the chicken was fresh was the poor creatures were alive when ordered and dead when handed over by the despatch department. Live chickens were in circular bunches on the ground, their feet tied together at the centre of each circle as they lay like large floral arrangements on the dirt floor. This prevented them from getting up and walking around, or more sensibly heading for the exit and freedom. They lay squawking, flapping and complaining in amongst the guts and feathers of their departed brethren. We watched as one of them was prepared for a customer. After a brief discussion, the chosen victim was pointed out and selected. Its attempts to hide under one of its companions were in vain. The stall holder grabbed it by its feet, cut the string holding it to the group, wrung its neck and plunged the whole bird briefly into a large tub of boiling water sitting over a fire. Its feathers were stripped, its guts extracted and the warm carcass wrapped in paper and handed over to the customer. The whole process took less than three minutes and the stall holder was happy to pose for us as we photographed him at his work. The remaining chickens stared at us beseechingly as they lay in death circle.

Leaving the market we picked up Adolf and set off for the border crossing on the edge of the town, driving out of Mexico for what we thought would be the last time to head south into the other countries of Central America. Thankfully the Mexican border officials gave us no problems and we passed through the barrier and pulled up at its twin on the British Honduran side.

Trouble was a mere Passport stamp away.

A GIRL CALLED ADOLF

CHAPTER 9

Central America - 1972

"To travel is to discover that everyone is wrong about other countries."

Aldous Huxley

Belize, the capital of British Honduras, was about one hundred miles from the border. We had no problems with the officials when we crossed over and were quickly granted seven day visas. We assumed our British Passports eased our passage in the far flung colony. The officials at the border told us we would have to report to the police in the city to buy vehicle insurance and to have Adolf inspected. The road ahead was in bad condition and progress along it through the dense jungle was slow.

At times the road was so narrow the dense vegetation on either side of us almost brushed Adolf's flanks. The heat was intense under the clear blues sky, the humidity high. We sweated as we drove, thankful for our sheepskins on our seats as they helped the sweat wick away.

Passing a small collection of huts, we came across a man throwing stones at a large venomous snake from a safe but completely impracticable distance. The snake seemed undeterred by the incoming missiles, determined to gain entry into or under his house. The man gesticulated for us to stop. After a brief discussion we agreed to help him and shortly afterwards a deceased snake was returned to the jungle to trouble him no more. Afterwards I felt guilty about the snake and my part in its death. I am not given to killing animals and the snake had its rightful place in the eco-system there. I mulled it over in my mind and justified my actions by reminding myself it was not me or my children who were at risk from it. I could not judge or blame the man for wanting it despatched and no longer a threat to his family. I don't doubt I would want the same.

Further down the road we came across a somewhat crude and small sign pointing down a track into the tangled forest. The sign indicated there were Mayan ruins about one and a half miles away and so we turned off and headed towards them. Shortly before we got to them we came across a small grass hut on stilts with a long-haired hippy sitting outside it. We stopped and chatted to him for a while. He seemed to be a complete hermit, an American who had been given his hut by the local people. He told us he had been living in the jungle for about eight months and that for the first couple of months he had lived in a hammock with a rudimentary camp. The local Indians had been convinced he would be taken by a jaguar or the spirits so they had made the elevated hut for him. He was an artist and acted as a guide to those who wished to see the ruins. In his spare time he made 'genuine' Indian carvings and artifacts for gullible tourists, and spent the rest of his time hunting snakes and drinking the locally made alcohol. As we talked I began to wonder which particular police force he might be hiding from.

When we got to the ruins we found they were still largely enveloped in the marauding jungle. The excavators and archeologists had had only just started clearing the site. We examined what could be seen of the old Mayan structures and decided not to bathe in the muddy pool that was there, despite the intense heat of the day. Dirty as we were from the dusty road, it was obvious we would have emerged from the water filthier than when we went in. Regaining the road we arrived in Belize City just after mid-day, driving to the central square, parking and walking to a nearby tourist office to pick up a map of the city.

Whilst Belize was a capital city it had more the feel of a small colonial town about it. The streets were crowded and narrow, and as usual dirty, dusty and pitted with pot holes. Cars and bicycles jostled for space whilst trying not to hit pedestrians who walked everywhere but on the pavements. Many of the cars were British, Land Rovers being particularly prevalent. There was a colonial feel to the place, for me a step back in time to my days in

India. The police seemed to have been trained and clothed by the British police, and when we asked any of them for directions they were friendly, helpful and polite, as were the locals we spoke to in our time in the city. English seemed to be the lingua franca. We found a large police station where we did the paperwork for our vehicle pass, being told we would have to return the next day to collect it. As it was the middle of the day, the heat was intense and so we drove to the sea to swim. The water cooled us but we were disappointed to find it was dirty and murky, not the turquoise crystal clear waters we were expecting. We learned later that the clear clean waters were to be found further out around the islands lying offshore. We knew from our guidebook that there was a British Council office in the city and so, finding the address on the map, we walked to it and went into its library where we read our first English newspapers since leaving home. It was wonderful to catch up on international news, both of the UK and of the world, giving us a perspective on global events that had been so noticeably absent in the xenophobic and introspective media in the United States.

As evening was closing in we set off to find somewhere to camp for the night and drove to the south of the city. The area there could not have been described as salubrious, nor safe from the look of some of the shanty dwelling people there. We decided it would be wise to move on so returned across the city to the northern shore and settled down for the night ten feet from the water's edge on a clean, sandy beach. It was adorned with palm trees and fronted by large attractive houses that we concluded probably belonged to

Government officials. It could have been a film set for a Pacific Island epic movie needing only a romance infused couple rolling in the breaking surf on a white beach to complete the scene. This rather idealistic image was a bit tarnished when mosquitos swarmed down from their perches in the trees to welcome us and dine with us, or rather on us as we ate our boiled eggs and banana supper by our camp fire.

We woke at dawn, the 27th October, almost exactly six months from the day of our departure from the UK. It was Sam's birthday so we celebrated it with a breakfast of fresh grapefruit, bananas, boiled eggs and coffee, a meal that was the gastronomic equal of a full English at Claridge's. As the sun rose and we judged the city had woken to its new day, we put out our camp fire and cleared evidence of it, leaving the beach clean. In the city centre we stopped at the police station to collect our $5 insurance document and the vehicle inspection papers, issued without Adolf having been inspected or even looked at. Leaving Adolf parked we walked to the offices of the local newspaper, The Reporter, and asked a journalist there if the paper would like to write a story about us and our trip, a little human interest item to fill an empty column. He said they would and so we were interviewed and photographed before we made our way back to the British Council to read more newspapers in its library. It seemed odd to be sitting in the quiet room so far from home, surrounded by such familiar titles as *The Times, The illustrated London News, Women's Journal and Harper's and Queen.* We chatted to some fellow British travelers also catching up on the news. One had come up from Cape Horn on a bicycle. Leaving the library we walked to the market at the harbour. Fresh fish, vegetables and fresh turtle abounded. The giant turtles were kept alive to guarantee their freshness. To stop them running away, if turtle perambulation can be described as running, the sellers simply turned the poor creatures onto their backs, leaving them out in the heat of the direct sun. Whilst a very simple solution to your stock walking off, I found its cruelty shocking.

As I was standing looking at the desperate animals, their legs waving forlornly in the air in supplication, I chatted to an American traveller. Originally just passing through like us, he had ended up staying and for the last few months had taken up 'farming', his euphemism for growing marijuana. He told me he had about an acre of it, together with other vegetables he was also producing. I hoped for his sake he had his crop well hidden and that it would not be discovered. Marijuana, and the growing of it, was illegal and we had been told being caught with it brought an automatic sentence of 15 years in prison. Indeed, we had also been told the authorities were asking for the death penalty to be the mandatory solution to the growing drug problem in the country. England had finally abolished the death penalty in 1969 but the British Hondurans had not thought to be as humanitarian about the welfare of their criminals and in fact seemed quite enthusiastic about stringing up a regular supply of criminals guilty of the more heinous crimes as a deterrent to others. We had been reading reports in the local papers of pleas for clemency for a murderer who was due for execution at about the time we had arrived in the city. Being a British colony, we were told the final court of appeal for the terminally condemned in British Honduras was the Privy Council in England and the Council's decision was awaited as the condemned man no doubt sweated in the humidity of his cell. I felt the young American was playing a dangerous game with long term bed and breakfasting implications, one that was hardly worth the return from a meagre acre. No doubt he saw the risks in a different light and like so many before, assumed he would not be caught.

Leaving the market we returned to the British Council to read more news of home and the world at large, and then late in the afternoon walked to the Bellevue Hotel to have a couple of celebratory beers to mark Sam's birthday once more before going back to our seashore camp. Our plan was to leave for the Guatemalan border in the morning. As we sat peacefully chatting, half a dozen or so British soldiers came into the bar. They bought themselves drinks and came over and sat with us. The quiet beers soon metamorphosed into rowdy rums, cheap and extremely rough locally made stuff. The soldiers suggested we should join them in their local 'joint' where the drinks were cheaper, so we went out with them. The joint turned out to be up a dingy flight of stairs in a building down near the harbour. Through a discoloured and peeling old door at the top of the stairs we went into a large, dark and shabby room with tables and chairs arranged around a central dance floor. A juke box in the corner blasted out loud music and a number of scantily clad women were wandering around amongst the customers, all of them male. As the soldiers went in ahead of us some of the women made a bee line for them, and with the first flickering light of realisation it dawned on me we were in a brothel.

The soldiers were not yet ready for the attentions of the ladies and, looking at them, I realised a chap would have to be rendered comatose by alcohol first before engaging any of their services. This was clearly what the squaddies intended as they headed for a room at the back in search of a good portion of judgement dulling anaesthetic to help them face the task ahead. The rear room had a plain bar in it and more tables and chairs. A couple of older men were sitting at a table playing dominoes. There only appeared to be one drink on offer which was a rum that was poured into old used bottles from a barrel in a room behind the plain unadorned bar. A bottle of this home made jet fuel and four bottles of Coca Cola came to £1. Bottles and glasses were lined up and the soldiers poured with gusto.

The concoction tasted like nothing I had ever had before and made the tequila we had had in Chetumal seem like liquid honey. The affect of the drink was pretty instant, leading me to conclude later it must have been very near 100% proof, as near to pure alcohol as can be achieved in an illicit barrel over a fire in the jungle. I was aware I was moving around, perhaps even talking, but to this day I cannot remember why the fight broke out. Perhaps the locals in the dance room had come in looking for trouble. Perhaps one of the squaddies had upset someone. All I knew was suddenly the air was thick with flying bottles, chairs and fists, and Sam and I were in the thick of it. It was all the cowboy movies I had ever seen as a child rolled into one, my first real bar room brawl, and from the bruises I discovered over the next few days, I must have joined in with gusto. In the dim light I was aware someone was in front of me. Unaware who it was but not overly interested in receiving more lumps, in the time honoured tradition of doing unto others before they do it to you, I grabbed the man around the throat and in his crutch, lifted him horizontally above my head and threw him across the room. Popeye used to throw Bluto the same way after snacking on a quick can of spinach. Perhaps that was where I learned the trick, burying it in my subconscious for all those years. The man landed on the table where the two old men were still playing their dominoes, unfazed by the surrounding battle. He slid across it and onto the floor, scattering dominoes to the winds, disappearing over its far edge onto the floor. He stood up holding up one of his hands to stare at his little finger, now at right angles to its hand, and obviously just a little dislocated. His name was Taff and he was one of the soldiers with whom we had come to the bar, one of our new best friends. A slight case of mistaken identity.

Leaving the melee, Taff and I went down the stairs and out of the building to examine the damage to his hand under a street lamp. I apologised profusely for the redesign but he seemed to think it a normal by product of an average fun evening out. We agreed the finger's horizontal plane was somewhat beyond our skills to put right so I said I would take him back to Camp to get it fixed, if he could tell me the way. We set off in Adolf with Taff punctuating his mumbled directions with warnings to 'Mind the swamp'. Since he was slumped half conscious against the passenger door, his chin bouncing on his chest, I assumed he was hallucinating with this obsessive fixation on swamps so I ignored him and concentrated hard on trying to keep us on at least one of the three roads I could see swimming in our headlights. It was only later I learnt that the road to camp ran through deep, gelatinous swamps into which a vehicle could sink. The Army garrison had a special vehicle with huge fat tyres, adapted for the swamps. It was designed to extract any of their vehicles that went into the clinging morass. There were thirteen narrow bridges on the road and I managed to get Adolf through all of them which, considering I saw thirty nine of them was a minor miracle.

Arriving at the camp gates Taff announced us to the guard who waved us through on seeing the state of Taff's hand. As we passed he called out he would get someone to meet us at the medical building. Taff directed me to it and I parked and got out to help him through the door. We went into what was clearly an examination room and leant against the walls as an aid to remaining upright. After a short wait, the door opened and an enormous RSM entered, immaculately uniformed in razor creased trousers and jacket. Taff pushed himself off the wall and saluted the behemoth with his damaged hand, its little finger pointing at the ceiling.

"Good evening, Sir" Taff said in a loud voice, the Sir being pronounce 'Sah'.

"What's the problem?" the RSM asked.

"Problem with the hand, Sah" said Taff, holding out his mangled hand, its little finger now pointing at the wall.

The RSM walked over to him and, holding Taff's wrist and hand in one giant paw, grabbed the dislocated finger and pulled it hard. Taff held it up to see it was now back to normal, if somewhat swollen. He saluted again.

"Thank you, Sah" he said, all fingers now correctly on parade and pointing at his head.

As Taff and the RSM discussed Taff's state of inebriation, I turned my attention to a bucket that was on the floor. It was covered by a silver coloured lid. Intrigued as to why a bucket should need covering, I lifted the lid. Curled up inside, and filling the bucket, was an enormous snake, its body as thick as my forearm, its head and tail lying on top of the heap of its coils. It seemed to be fast asleep so, plunging my hand in I grabbed its tail and pulled it out to hold it up for the other two to see. It came out in one curled and very heavy piece, retaining the shape of the bucket. An eye opened and glared at me fixedly. I had always been told snakes were cold, heartless and emotionless. This one seemed pretty pissed off to me. There was an air of belligerence, indeed malevolence in its cold stare.

The nail-hard RSM and Taff immediately backed up to the wall, a look of terror in their eyes. I walked towards them with the snake still held high for them to see, the one thing they clearly did not want to do. I had no idea they were ophidiophobes and was fascinated to see how two grown men, one clearly trained to kill me with his little finger, could be so easily subjugated. Their heartfelt entreaties to "Fuck off with that thing" finally filtered through the alcohol and I returned the now stirring snake to its bucket, into which it seemed remarkably reluctant to be shoved. It was rather like trying to push limp spaghetti up a drainpipe. As fast as I pushed bits of it in, other bits emerged. It didn't seem to want to stay in its cramped quarters so a judicious foot on the lid was needed until it seemed to nod off again. It transpired it was a boa constrictor, apparently about eight feet long, and being gently chloroformed. Obviously it had not been in there long enough for the drug to take full effect. The fresh air once it was out of the bucket must have revived its senses, but not enough for it to think quickly, hence its inactivity as I carried it around the room.

The RSM had clearly had enough of us and dismissed us as he headed off for bed or a nerve calming whisky. Taff and I got back into Adolf and I drove us back into Belize to the bar. Sam was fast asleep on the harbour wall, inches from rolling over into the water below. We left him and went and had another drink before coming back and collecting him, pouring him into the back of Adolf where he lapsed back into his coma. I drove us all back to the Army Camp where I left Taff to negotiate his way back through the gates. With Sam fast asleep in the back I drove us to a rough track in the jungle near the airport to park up for what was left of the night.

The dawn cacophony of wildlife calls was not a welcome alarm for us. I awoke deeply envious of the snake and its chloroformed state of oblivion, a state of Nirvana I wished I could sink into for a few hours. We drove into Belize and went to the offices of the newspaper *The Reporter* to see whether they had published an article about us after the interview we had given them. They had not so we drove out of the City to the Army Camp and were met at the gate by Taff who took us through the security at the entrance and into the main camp. The camp covered a large area with roads and paths running through it past wooden huts and buildings. The sleeping quarters stood in militarily precise rows, reminding me of images of prisoner of war huts in the last war. Taff took us to his barracks and settled us into two empty bunks in the large dormitory. Still suffering somewhat from the night's activities, we all went out to the camp's swimming pool where we spent the rest of the afternoon, cooling in the water, reading and trying to recover as the sun beat down on us. At one point we wandered over to a sports pitch to watch a game of rugby. In the early evening we were taken to the canteen for an evening meal, which we ate with some of the men who had been involved in the previous evening's escapades.

It was amazing to sit down and have a full meal, our first for weeks. I had forgotten what a plate filled with food looked like and relished every forkful. The lads said we could stay in camp for a few days, although I had no idea whether they had cleared this further up the chain. Taff was a mechanic responsible for looking after the Army's vehicles and said he would carry out a full service on Adolf. He said this was one of the advantages of working for the largest company in Britain, GB Ltd.

As we sat and chatted over our meal, it became clear the squaddies intended going back into Belize for a repeat performance of the night before. It seemed their coital aspirations had been interrupted by the fight and they felt they had unfinished fun to attend to. I was in awe of their constitutions. Whatever it was we had been served to drink in 'their joint', it had the toxicity of arsenic and I was beginning to wonder if I had done any permanent damage to my brain or liver. I declined to join them and retreated to my top bunk in the barracks as they headed off joyfully for another evening of horizontal frivolity with the belles of Belize. For the next two days Sam and Taff crawled over Adolf. Two new tyres, brake linings, new dynamo, spares, an oil change and our oil reserves in the jerry cans replenished all served to revitalise a tired Adolf. We were also taken on excursions to the Quartermaster's stores for more malarial tablets, water purifiers and a 26 inch machete. We were like little boys in a toy shop, let loose among the shelves with no annoyingly restricting budget.

One morning I caught the Camp Army bus into Belize to cash a cheque at a bank. I noticed with amusement that the driver, a locally employed British Honduran, stopped a number of times on the way to pick up locals going into the city to do their shopping. His unofficial taxi service was a classic example of a little bit of opportunistic free enterprise although I suppose it could have been repeated acts of kindness but that would have been out of character in those regions. In the evenings we watched films. *The Ballad of Cable Hogue,* Sam Peckinpah's story of a hobo stranded in the desert who discovers a water spring and builds a stagecoach stop by it had us laughing in the aisles.

At the end of our third day in Camp, with Adolf rejuvenated from her days in the beauty parlour, Taff took us over the the Camp's offices where we met Major Hellis, who smilingly agreed with us that we had stretched our luck to the limits and didn't argue with our farewells and promise to leave in the morning. In fact we had two reasons that influenced our need to leave, the first being that the owners of the two bunks we had been given to sleep in were due back from ten days leave. More importantly, our seven day visas had one day left so we needed to be out of the country. We wandered over to the NAAFI bar for a couple of beers and then went to bed at a reasonable hour. In the morning we enjoyed another British Army breakfast, at which we were joined by the two returning soldiers whose bus had driven through the night from their leave up in Mexico. At one point in the night the bus driver had had to slam on the brakes as he spotted a man asleep in the middle of the road, fortunately picked up in the bus' headlights. Central America at night continued to live up to its reputation.

We said our goodbyes to Taff, Steve, Screwy, Alan, Frank, Rob and the many others who had been so kind to us. The Devon and Dorset Regiment had been gracious hosts. We gave them four hundred cigarettes we had bought in the NAAFI and they gave us two boxes of 'Compo' rations. Each box contained nutritionally balanced food designed to feed ten men for a day, or one man for ten days. To us they were a supermarket, capable of lasting us a couple of months with our reduced intake. Tins of stews, vegetables, beans, rice puddings, fruit cake, loo paper, matches. Someone in Whitehall had thought of it all, the loo paper being a touchingly sensitive inclusion. Thoughtfully there were ten sheets, not one, which would undoubtedly be a source of great relief and comfort to a troop of men out on exercise.

Leaving Camp we headed south and then west for the Guatemalan border. About ten miles from it we came into a small town called El Cayo where we found a garage that agreed to put on our new tyres and to buy the old ones. Whilst on our standards the haggard tyres were well past their best, for the British Hondurans they seemed to have tens of thousands of miles of use left on them, and then in a later reincarnation as sandals for dozens of pairs of feet. Leaving El Cayo we arrived at the border and passed through the British Honduran post without difficulty. The Guatemalans were a different matter, starting with the fact they wanted to be paid an after hours charge for our late crossing. After a prolonged argument they agreed to halve it and then produced endless forms that had to be filled in. A seal was put on the steering wheel although we failed to understand why, and then yet more forms were produced. Eventually we seemed to have given them enough information about ourselves. They stamped our Passports and we drove off, keeping going for about an hour until we spotted a disused quarry to pull into for the night.

At dawn we were on our way again, heading for Santa Elena, a small town on the shore of a lake called Lago Peten Itza. There was a small island at the end of a causeway, the Island of Flores, and we drove out to it. The town was tiny, constrained by the limits of the island and taking up all of it, and it didn't take us long to drive around and through it. A few narrow streets meandered between the old buildings and small, colourful red-roofed houses. We enquired at a cafe about the directions to the Mayan ruins at Tikal. We were told they were about forty miles away in a National Park north of the town. The narrow road to it ran through thick jungle and arrived at a small police hut by the road just before the ruins. The policeman wanted to see all our papers, our visas, our car permit. He leafed through them without showing any indication as to whether he could understand what he was reading and then, handing them back, waved us on. We drove across a long cleared strip in the jungle, a crude runway built in 1951 to ease access to the site and its exploration. Previously the ruins could only be reached by several days' trekking through the jungle with mules to carry provisions. Better restored and significantly bigger than the site at Palenque, the ruins were vast. Tikal's existence was never truly forgotten with references to it in 17th century writings, but it was in 1848 when Modesto Méndez, Commissioner of Petén, and Ambrosio Tut, the Governor, visited the site that international interest in it started. Archeologists started to clear and map the site in the 1880's.

    The ruins were magnificent, soaring above us like stairways to the stars. Perhaps that was what the Maya intended, to be nearer the cosmos and their gods. The largest temple, Temple number 4, was two hundred and twelve feet high, making the eighty feet of the Temple at Palenque seem more than modest, more of a bonsai pyramid. All the temples were made from locally sourced limestone. From the top of Temple number 1, a mere one hundred and fifty four feet high, we could see its taller sibling towering above the jungle, the Playa

Mayor in front of it. The climb up to Temple 1 was much steeper than the pyramid at Palenque and the steps more worn. Helpfully a loose chain ran from the top to the bottom, lying down the middle of the staircase. I had thought the Mexican version we had climbed was steep but this felt vertical, a cliff face in comparison and a vertigo sufferer's worst nightmare.

Like Palenque, the shrine at the top had three chambers, except here they were positioned one behind the other rather than side by side. The view from the top was spectacular, looking down on top of the jungle canopy that stretched to the horizon. Tikal's flat-topped temples stood proud of the thick forest, tips of the icebergs that had been enveloped by the trees and vegetation. Each temple had staircases running up all four sides and large roof-combs that further enhanced their height and dominance of the surrounding land. A local guide we chatted to told us that at one point, ten thousand Mayans had lived at Tikal between 600 BC and 900 AD, with nine twin-pyramid complexes, each with accompanying buildings. After 950 AD the site was deserted and all but empty except for squatters living in the buildings and the small thatched huts they built in the ceremonial squares. The city was possibly abandoned because of over-population, and a failure to farm sufficient crops to feed the inhabitants. We wandered around part of the site, entering buildings honeycombed with windowless rooms leading into each other and into the depths and heart of the structures. The rooms all smelt dank and damp and it was too dark to go far in as the light fell away quickly and we had no torches.

After a couple of hours we left the site and made our way back along the slender dirt road to Flores. We had in fact been on rough dirt roads since leaving Belize City and were covered in dust that had caked onto us like thespian panstick. Whilst no doubt an irritation to many travelers, the dirt roads with their uneven surfaces gave us an opportunity to do some clothes washing in our own little washing machine. We had a large circular plastic box with a tight fitting lid that served many purposes, including being a fruit ripener. When we needed a laundry we put our dirty clothes in it with some soap flakes and water, sealed the lid and then put the box in the spare wheel on Adolf's bonnet. As we drove over the rough ground, the box was vigorously shaken and we could see the soap bubbles developing inside. After a couple of hours all we had to do was empty the dirty water and rinse the soap out of the clothes, usually in a clean stream or a river.

Arriving back at Flores we drove out onto the island again and stopped by the lake, close to the water's edge. A can of bully-beef from the compo rations was more than adequate for an al fresco lunch before setting off for the road south to Guatemala City, over three hundred miles away. As we passed the tin of food back and forth between us, we gazed out over the still blue water of the lake that was being criss-crossed by birds flying about, busy with their daily chores. The road from the border to Flores had been quite bad but further south it soon deteriorated to very bad, at times with the jungle encroaching onto it on either side, once again scratching Adolf's sides. Half way through the afternoon we could see the skies ahead blackening, promising a huge deluge that we knew would turn the road into a quagmire. We drove into the rain as it sheeted down in monsoon quantities, cooling the overheated air. Stopping Adolf in the middle of the muddy track, we got out, stripped off our clothes, retrieved the soap from the communal washbag and had a glorious shower in the rain in the deserted forest. Apart from the drumming rain on Adolf's canvas and our heads, all was quiet in the jungle, even the black howler monkeys sheltering and closing their mouths to keep the rain out.

Refreshed and still wet, we climbed back in and carried on, our progress getting slower and slower as we slid and slipped around the road, fording floods and negotiating huge mud filled potholes and ruts. At about nine o'clock in the evening and in the pitch dark we came to the shore of Lake Izabel where the River Dulce fed out of its north eastern most corner. There was no bridge but there were signs indicating a ferry might be there. We turned the engine off and got out, not sure if the ferry would be running this late. We could hear its frantic puffing getting closer so assumed it was on its way back. When it arrived it pushed up against the muddy bank and we drove on. Since we were the only vehicle there, it immediately set off for the return journey but not before we had been asked to turn on our headlights so the crew could see the landing stage on the far bank. The ferry had no lights of its own and clearly relied on navigation by guesswork.

The river was quite wide and our headlights could not reach the other side so we turned on a Adolf's spotlight. Powerful and effective it threw out a pencil beam of searingly bright white light that shone for a few hundred yards. It was attached to the inside of the windscreen by a simple vacuum mechanism and was maneuverable from inside the cab so we could direct it like a searchlight to pick out objects ahead. When we had bought it in England we were not aware it could become a weapon of revenge. Our experience of Mexican truck drivers at night was that they seemed to be engaged in some form of competition to see who could attach the most and largest headlamps to the front of their trucks. Their candelabra hung like a suction of limpets and mussels on a rock face, and of course all had to be turned on as soon as the sun dropped below the horizon. No Mexican truck was equipped with the facility to dip lights, so we were able to spot these mobile towns coming along the road from miles away. Blinded, we would flash our lights at them to try to get them to tone it down. This usually resulted in them remembering a few they had not turned on and upping the ante with a bit more illumination. Our only chance of survival was a roll of the dice to guess where the road went and hope we were right.

One night a particularly over-festooned truck finally tried our patience too far as its driver gave us the full treatment. As we approached each other and he was within reaching distance of our spotlight, I turned it on from the passenger seat and picked out his face in his cab. It must have been like being poked in the eye with a sharp stick. The rapier beam must have instantly detached the truck driver's retinas from the back of his eyeballs. We could see into the fast approaching cab, bathed in glorious white light, with him hurtling towards us, ducking around in his cab to try to avoid the light, his head bobbing about like an apple in a water barrel at a fete. I moved the spotlight to follow his startled face, feeling like a wartime spotlight operator picking out night bombers over London. His truck began to weave around the road as he flapped a hand to get rid of the ferocious beam of light, any hint of where the road ahead completely lost to him. As we passed each other, inches apart in the narrow road, we could see the back of his truck aglow with red brake lights. Laughing maniacally we agreed he would have to sit by the road for half an hour to let the boiling vitreous and aqueous fluids in his eyes cool down and to get his sight back. Either way we felt victory was on our side and we had made our point, albeit with a game of wattage roulette that we had better not repeat if we wanted a chance at a long and fruitful life.

The antediluvian ferry wheezed up to the far shore's landing stage and we disembarked onto another dirt road, thankfully one in much better condition than the appalling track we had spent the last three hours on and which did not need four wheel drive to negotiate. About five kilometers from where our maps indicated we might be greeted by tarmac we pulled into a small quarry by the track and made camp for the night, which once again entailed no more than putting on the handbrake and dropping the mosquito net.

Getting up at dawn we reached the tarmac road within about fifteen minutes of setting off from our camp. It was a relief to be on a smooth surface for a while. To celebrate we decided to try to get some coconuts out of one of the trees by the road. Given our inability to climb the trees, the most obvious option was to give a tree a little shake by pushing it with Adolf's front bumper. This successfully dislodged and brought down on us a shower of detritus and irritated insects, but no coconuts so we abandoned our foraging and succumbed to buying three from some young kids. We drove on, stopping by a stream to change our front tyres for the new ones we had been given by the Army. Unfortunately one was flat so further down the road we stopped at a garage to get it fixed. It turned out it had a faulty valve and the man at the garage said he could mend it. With the correct machinery this would take a few minutes in England but he didn't have any of that, just large tyre leavers and time. We all threw ourselves into the task of getting the large tyre off the wheel by hand. Once off, he fixed the valve with wire, assuring us his Heath Robinson repair would hold, and then we put the tyre back on the wheel, inflated it and put it on Adolf. The whole process took over an hour and cost a few pesos. True to his word, the valve held for the rest of the trip. The ingenuity of the poor to resurrect the mechanical deceased is little short of miraculous, another of our many healing Bethesda moments on the trip.

Reaching Guatemala City in the mid afternoon, we had some difficulty working out how they arranged their street numbering. Like all cities it had a mixture of new and old buildings that we passed in our search for the British Embassy. We had given its address as a poste restante for anyone wanting to write to us, but when we finally found it we discovered there were no letters for us. We stopped at a small cafe and bought some freshly squeezed orange juice and a small sandwich filled with a local cheese. We asked the Canadian cafe owner for directions to the El Salvador border and after eating our little meal, set off in the general direction his flailing arm had indicated. One of the advantages of thrashing around a network of city roads completely lost is one gets to see a lot of its architecture. By the simple expedient of using our compass we kept Adolf's nose pointing south, eventually finding the road we needed, by which time we considered ourselves experts on the city's road network. Our habitual impromptu camp that night was another garage forecourt.

Our sleep was shattered twice in the night by the arrival of what appeared to be the entire Guatemalan police force, for once not paying us a visit but rather the garage owner. Lights blazing and flashing, their vehicles swept onto the forecourt and the occupants leapt out and started shouting whilst hammering on the front door of the garage. The sleepy owner appeared and was interrogated. We assumed the Guatemalan Police Manual states that interrogations should be carried out at a minimum of one hundred and fifty decibels. Sleeping on the ground at the end of the runway at San Francisco with jet engines in our ears was a quieter experience, especially as the disgruntled and uncooperative garage owner was trying to out-shout the police. It was hard to make out what it was all about but clearly they weren't inviting him to buy a ticket to the Policeman's Ball. After about twenty minutes the police climbed back into their cars, turned on their flashing lights and left. We slowly drifted off to sleep again, despite the freezing temperatures. Guatemala City is about five thousand feet above sea level, and we had not been as cold since our nights camping in Canada. We cannot have been fully asleep for long before the flashing lights reappeared on the forecourt and the police started attacking the garage door again. This time the recalcitrant garage owner refused to get out of bed and eventually the police gave up and left, showing great self-restraint by not shooting out the front door.

We set off in the cold pre-dawn, at times driving through thick low cloud. When we reached the border it was still closed, any Customs officer with any sense still deep under the bedcovers whilst wrapped around a wife, mistress or girlfriend. When they had finally extricated themselves from that warm, soft state of bliss, they proved to be courteous and efficient and we passed through without any delays into Hades, a dystopian chaos thinly disguised as the El Salvador Customs and Immigration post. Cars and trucks littered the open area in front of the building that housed the border post, like stones thrown randomly and haphazardly onto a beach. The interior of the building was dark and dingy and filled to overflowing with people who were all pushing, shoving and shouting for attention. The Immigration officials had already lost patience and were yelling back. As I fought my way to the front to get our Passports stamped and other documents cleared I wondered how long it would be before one of the big fat revolvers I could see on official belts would be fired into the crowd.

With sharp elbows and some assertive Imperialism in dealing with Johnny Foreigner, I got through the madding crowd to the counter and handed our Passports and car papers over to the bad tempered and frazzled official sitting hunkered behind a vintage manual typewriter. Leaning on the counter I looked down on his sweating bald head as he opened Sam's Passport on the typewriter to prepare typing in the details he needed. Passports in the 1970's were still the old dark blue, hard backed versions, distinctively British and mourned by we anti-Federalists when they were replaced by the anodyne uniformity of the red, European-looking version we all now use. The first page gave the holder's name and the Passport number. The next two pages listed distinguishing features, date of birth and occupation of the holder and displayed a photograph of the individual, but no name and no Passport number. It was these two pages that he opened as he set about typing in Sam's details. As he clearly struggled to work out Sam's name from the data in front of him, I reached down to turn the Passport back to the opening page, but he snatched it away in a fit of arrogance and piqued vanity, telling me he could do it and didn't need my interfering help.

With my elbows on the high counter, I watched as he stared at the pages in front of him, chewing the corner of his food encrusted moustache, dripping beads of sweat off the end of his nose. Where was the name? He was clearly puzzled and confused but too machismo to ask for help. It obviously dawned on him that people have three names, so I watched as the moment of inspiration hit him. Flexing his fingers he carefully typed in Sam's name as 'Brown Brown Nil' - the colour of his hair and eyes, and his list of distinguishing marks, there being none. We had been on the road long enough for me to know self-important officialdom that takes itself seriously does not like to be laughed at, so I looked away, and listened to the clatter of the typewriter's keys as he worked his way through our paperwork. I have no idea what I went in as, probably the same as I too had brown hair, brown eyes and no distinguishing marks. It didn't seem to occur to him as odd that we were both identically christened by unimaginative parents. I took the proffered Passports, now officially stamped, and pushed back through the struggling throng and into the fresh air.

Our next ordeal was Customs. The Customs officers were all dressed in green, ill-fitting Action Man type fatigues with plastic domed helmets that could be penetrated by an incoming pea from a pea shooter, let alone shrapnel or a bullet. They strutted about pompously, shouting at the milling people. Whistles blew and arms waved. The Customs post was in the middle of a market that had sprung up around it as the local entrepreneurs took advantage of the ebb and flow of humanity through the border. The traders and their customers all added to the chaos but Adolf's bumper was not something they were going to argue with as we inexorably pushed our way through the crowd and vehicles. The Customs officials looked into the back of Adolf and seemed unable to understand why we had no suitcases. They asked us where they were and when we replied we had none, they scratched their plastic helmets and discussed the problem. It never seemed to occur to them to ask us to lift the foam mattress, and we didn't volunteer to do so, even when they started asking us to empty out what little of our possessions they could see in the back. We argued that they could see it all as they peered into the back and eventually, after more heated discussions they finally gave up and waved us through. Our belongings spread out on the floor and exposed to the less than trustworthy, light fingered market goers was not an attractive proposition.

Gratefully leaving the mayhem of the border behind, we set off for El Salvador's capital city, San Salvador. After our disturbed night, early start and border post activities, we were hungry and decided to look for somewhere to stop for a light brunch. Our maps showed a lake ahead, Lake Coatapeque. Large and off the main road it looked as though it could be a quiet spot that might have a shoreline on which we could build a fire. The lake was beautiful, nestling in the caldera of an extinct volcano, possibly linked to the nearby Volcán de Izalco in the Parque Nacional Cerro Verde. The shoreline of the almost circular lake had been appropriated by the rich of El Salvador who had built large and expensive looking houses around the water's edge, each with its own private beach. We assumed few of them would want a couple of vagrants building fires and camping on their treasured bit of sandy shore, and so turned back from the shore and slowly drove round the lake. On its northernmost point we came across the imposing gates of the *Automobile Club de El Salvador*. Undaunted by their grandeur we drove through and up to the extremely smart colonial style Clubhouse where we announced ourselves to the concierge as members of the *Royal Automobile Club de Gran Bretaña*, on a goodwill visit and there to avail ourselves of the Clubs' reciprocal arrangements.

Despite our scruffy appearance and filthy vehicle he seemed impressed and ushered us in through the doors with our packed lunch under our arms. We walked through the hushed and cool building, our flip flops squeaking on the immaculate marble floor, coming out onto a terrace from which we crossed the manicured lawn that stretched graciously down to the lakeside. There was a wooden jetty that reached out into the lake with a bench at the end of it. Settling down on it we opened another tin of bully beef from our Army compo rations and ate it with a couple of bread rolls we had bought at the border market. As we ate our impromptu picnic in the peace and quiet, with only the gently lapping water beneath our feet to break the silence, we were able to enjoy the spectacular view across the lake to the sides of the caldera. It was not hard to understand why the rich and powerful had requisitioned the place for themselves, a haven away from the great unwashed riffraff like us.

Our meal finished we reluctantly turned our backs on our idyllic al fresco dining spot and drove on south east, through San Salvador the capital and on towards the border. Passing through Cojutepeque we came across a large local market and stopped to try to buy leather sandals to replace our in extremis rubber flip flops that we had bought in Washington. There were none there that were strong enough for the rigours our footwear faced in the months ahead so we left, driving on east through San Miguel, reaching the border at Santa Clara at about seven o'clock in the evening. The border officials said they wanted an 'after hours' payment to let us through, so we pulled over and parked for the night in front of the border post. Normal hours with no late exit penalty started at seven thirty in the morning but after some unseemly begging when we woke, the officials relented and let us through early. We drove over to the Honduran Immigration post to discover they didn't get out of bed until quarter past eight, rendering the out of hours payment on the El Salvador side useless and a scam, presumably dreamt up by the officials to supplement their salaries. We would have been irritated to have paid to spend the night in the international vacuum between the two borders.

The Hondurans had devised their own scam. A 'weekend' entry fee was their chosen sting and this time we paid as it was a Saturday and we had no desire to sit there for two days. I decided not to ask them how much of the fee actually reached Central Government's coffers. The question seemed redundant, the more obvious destination for the money being the local bar owner's coffers or into the local bordello madame's capacious bra. The southernmost side of Honduras narrows down like a peninsular between El Salvador to the west and Nicaragua to the east, the distance between the two borders being about ninety miles. We asked the border officials what time the eastern border into Nicaragua closed and they told us at mid-day and that it would then reopen on Monday morning. We prayed the Hondurans would not want to search Adolf since we had no real desire to be stuck at that border either, nor in the country for the rest of the weekend. Our prayers were answered as we were waved through Customs and we set off for what we calculated would be a two and a half hour drive with three hours in which to complete it.

Driving at speed through Central and South America was a hazardous game as the roads belonged to the potholes, the animals, both domesticated and wild, and the locals, both domesticated and wild and invariably drunk on a Sunday. The drunks were an additional hazard on roads that were lethal without them. Weaving around as they tacked their way home for the habitual weekly beating by a disgruntled wife, they provided a slalom course where the marker poles moved. The combination of drunk pedestrians and drunk drivers produced a living game of pinball. I assumed the beatings we occasionally witnessed on our travels being dished out on the roadside to some of the semi-comatose men were meted out by the wives in the knowledge their husbands were so drunk they would never remember in the morning how their bruises and contusions had been acquired. Perhaps the befuddled men assumed they had been in a fight. We weaved between all these static and mobile obstacles, dodging disgruntled pigs, aggressive car chasing dogs, vacuous chickens and the occasional meandering cow. All of these we repeatedly negotiated safely but it was inevitable that our luck should run out, to speak nothing of the luck of one of the moving obstacles.

The unfortunate victim happened to be a cow coming towards us about ten miles from the border. Slow of mind and heavy of capacious udder it was trotting along the road some distance behind the herd in front of it, all of them being driven along the road by a couple of farmers on horseback. We slowly threaded our way through the herd, the passing cows brushing along Adolf's side, the occasional horn clanging against the spare fuel and oil jerry cans. Full udders slapped on the inside of legs and from behind one or two came the slap of liquid dung splashing on the road. Emerging the other side, Sam accelerated hard away from the herd. The border was close but we were running out of time. The huge oncoming cow was on the other side of the road, the mounted farmer just behind it. As we came level with it, the animal veered to its right, straight into Adolf's path. Adolf caught it behind and under the left shoulder and our windscreen was filled with flying cow and broken glass. The cow then sailed past the driver's window upside down before crashing to the road to lie ominously still and silent, either badly winded or dead. It didn't seem a good time to us to stop and discuss bovine husbandry with what we assumed could be a slightly tetchy, machete wielding Honduran. Suppressing any gentlemanly instincts we might have, we accelerated away and kept on for the border as the farmer wheeled his horse around in the road.

Arriving at the border we nonchalantly walked into the Border Post without glancing at Adolf, only being aware that the driver's door was a little difficult to open. With our stamped Passports we returned and could see the whole front right wing had been crumpled in, but fortunately not badly enough to interfere with the wheel. Clearly the brunt of the impact had been taken by the front bumper, a sturdy piece of steel, and whilst we had no front side light and no indicator light on the driver's side, we were grateful the cow had not gone headfirst into the radiator. The unfortunate animal had literally had the stuffing knocked out of it as it had shat all along the driver's side of the vehicle. Sam and I agreed the delicate scent of cow manure was more pleasant than the slightly more acerbically astringent qualities of exploded cat, a scent still a clear memory.

Smelling like a farmyard, we drove over to the Nicaraguan Border Post and spent the next hour watching a diminutive Customs official searching Adolf. Assiduous in his task, he even swept the dust off the floor into little piles that he then sifted through. We assumed he must be looking for signs of marijuana ash or other drug use, and had to stifle smiles when he stabbed his finger on a pin that was hidden in one of the small heaps of dust. With two thirds of the floor boxes at the back still to examine he must have become daunted by the task, or just bored of it, because he suddenly stopped, put seals on the unopened boxes and sauntered off, leaving us to repack and make our way to the Border Post to get our Passports stamped.

Managua lay just over a hundred miles ahead of us on the south eastern shore of Lake Managua. The road to it took us past extinct and active volcanoes, evidence of the fault lines running beneath the country where the Cocos Plate meets the Caribbean Plate. Some of the active volcanoes puffed smoke into the sky, reminding us of the underlying threat to the stability of the country as the continental plates deep beneath jostled and elbowed each other for position and supremacy. Whilst Managua lay ahead of us, there was no particular reason for us to stop in it. Our intended destination was a hamlet on the south coast called San Juan del Sur that we had heard about on the travellers' bush telegraph. Descriptions of a peaceful and idyllic beach in a secluded bay made a visit irresistibly more attractive than a night in the city. When we arrived at the Costa Rican border we realised we had somehow missed the turning. Easy enough to do in a continent with few if any road signs and where roads on the map were often in reality no more than dirt tracks heading off into jungle. The track we needed was about fifteen miles behind us so, turning back we drove north again in the dark until we came across a place in the densely packed trees to pull into for the night.

Back on the road at dawn, the daylight helped us find the track to San Juan that corresponded with our map. We took the track and drove to the little village, arriving at the sea front with a small harbour to our left. The only way was right so we followed the track which soon deteriorated and narrowed, eventually opening onto the beautiful sandy beach that northward travelling contemporaries had told us about. They had not lied, perhaps only in so much as their description did not do it justice. The beach curved around a small bay with a headland to our right, and dotted around on it were a small number of vehicles. From the state of them, covered in dirt and travel worn, they all clearly belonged to fellow nomads. We parked Adolf near the water's edge and strolled over to chat to an eclectic group of wanderers from around the world. Meeting this loose federation of Americans, French, English and Canadians was stimulating. Nationality created no barriers as we all seemed to belong to one Wandering Nation with common shared interests, objectives and experiences, forging mutually supportive relationships that were revisited time and again as we re-met acquaintances in the months ahead. We spent the day housekeeping and tending to Adolf's needs with a minor service. When the urge took us, or the heat became oppressive, we bathed in the clear sea water of the bay.

As we busied ourselves with our tasks and chatted to the other residents of the beach, one of the French girls sunbathed topless on the sand. For our enlightened and liberated generation, this was not a matter of consequence and no one paid her any attention. This could not be said of the local man from San Juan who walked down onto the beach from the hamlet, on his way to wherever he was going over the hill at the other end of the bay. As he passed the very pretty and shapely girl dozing on her back in the sun, his eyes opened like soup plates and his head swiveled on his shoulders, like an owl surveying the world around it. A hundred feet past her, with his now head turned through a hundred and eighty degrees, he clearly forgot or completely lost interest in his original errand. He turned and retraced his steps slowly to walk back past the girl, transfixed by her slender and near naked form on the beach, his head rotating one hundred and eighty degrees the other way. Clearly the girls of San Juan del Sur were not in the habit of showing him their naked breasts, nor indeed any part of their unclothed bodies. I assumed his frequent or infrequent emissions were generally achieved in the pitch dark. Completing his second pass, he hurried off towards the village in what appeared to be a state of some excitement. From the expression on his face it seemed obvious to me his next emission was about to happen. It was probably going to come as something of a surprise to the hapless recipient, who was probably at that moment busy over a stove and preoccupied with her housework.

As the hours passed and we worked on Adolf, vehicles left the beach one by one, each heading off into their own unknown. By the mid afternoon only a French couple, Dorianne and Patrick and a quiet and quite odd French-Canadian called Andre were left with us in the bay. Dorianne and Patrick were travelling in a VW camper van that they had bought in Panama. They were on their way to California but intended over-wintering in Mexico. Andre was hitch-hiking south and had rented a small room in a house in the village. In return for a hot shower in his room, we agreed to take him to San Jose, the capital of Costa Rica. Our conditions were that first he should have no drugs on him and second that we would drop him a mile short of the Nicaraguan border and he would have to walk through under his own steam. We told him we would pick him up again a mile past the Cost Rican border.

With dusk falling we lit a fire on the beach with dried driftwood. As it blazed and we sat by its dancing light, two camper vans drove onto the beach and parked near us, one driven by a Swiss couple, Alain and Tildy, and the other by a Belgian couple. Like us, all four were headed south, Alain and Tildy to the Andes in Peru where they ran and managed a ranch as part of the Swiss Government's aid programme for developing countries. The aim of the project was to show and teach local farmers how to run a model farm or ranch. Alain was a vet and was breeding disease free cattle and sheep that would form the foundation of future expanded and widely dispersed herds and flocks. He was teaching modern animal husbandry that was hoped would be sustainable after his eventual departure. High altitude farming brought its own particular challenges. Within half an hour of sitting by our camp fire and chatting to us they had invited us to visit and stay with them at the ranch in Peru where they said they would show us their work.

As it was still warm, we decided to go for a swim. The sun was well below the horizon but still throwing up just enough light to see by as we ran into the water, accompanied by a dog that had appeared on the beach from the direction of the village. Splashing through the shallow water towards the swimmable depths, we realised cascades of light were pouring off us. The dog, which was leaping about amongst us in a frenzy of excitement, looked as though it was auditioning for the lead part in The Hound of the Baskervilles. I had seen a phosphorescent light before on Hilton Head Island but not as spectacular as the one we were creating with our cavorting and I was transfixed by it. We became children for a while, a magical step back through the door of adulthood into an untroubled world where we enjoyed a simple pleasure, laid on free by nature. We ran about in the dark, splashing and throwing flashing water around, watching cascades of twinkling light pour off our outstretched arms, kicking white flames into the air in front of us to light our way. It was exhilarating, and since it happened to be November the 5th, I knew it would forever be the most spectacular firework display I would ever see. The tumbling and dancing waterfalls of light burnt into my memory and only dementia will be able to steal the vivid imagery away. All good things come to an end and eventually we tired of our illuminated frolicking and returned to sit by the fire. Patrick played his guitar for us and I lay back in the cooling sand to stare up into a star-filled sky, consumed with the wonder of the beauty of the natural world in all its unexpected forms.

Sam and I were up at dawn and rekindled the fire which had been slightly dampened by some light rain in the early hours of the morning. We made coffee for ourselves and for our slowly stirring companions, had breakfast, said our farewells and set off for the border, which we crossed without any delays. On the Costa Rican side we discovered hot showers in the border post. Unaccustomed to such sophistication we luxuriated in them before starting the six hour drive to the capital, San José. Our plan was to contact my girlfriend's cousin, Robert Jagger, who lived in the city with Lupita, his Costa Rican wife. The long drive to the city was remarkable only for a narrow miss with another meandering cow that continued its peregrinations, oblivious of how close it had come to a premature death.

Everything we had read about Costa Rica repeatedly told us it was the most advanced and developed of the Central American countries, with a ninety eight percent literacy rate. The well maintained tarmac roads and flourishing farms were evidence of a more prosperous country than those we had travelled through since leaving the United States. The pot-hole free tarmac roads were a welcome change, not only for our bruised bottoms, but also for poor Adolf whose engine was now resting on her front axle, like an exhausted boxer bending over to rest his battered body with his elbows on his knees. She was in need of a bit of spa treatment, some orthopaedic work on her front suspension leaves and some plastic surgery to repair the cow damage that now disfigured her. The front springs were completely flat and needed to be replaced or re-tempered, an urgent task for us to undertake in San José before we took to South American roads, which we anticipated would be in even worse condition than we had so far experienced, and obviously far longer. Stopping at a garage, I used the owner's phone to contact Robert and let him know we would get to San José that evening. When we reached the middle of the city we dropped off Andre, our hitcher from San Juan del Sur, and went in search of Banco Lyon. Spotting a space by the roadside in a narrow street, we pulled into it to park, and I set off on foot to find the bank. My interest in it was based on the fact it was owned by the father of a schoolfriend, Peter Lyon. Having spent a number of my formative years with Peter, I took it for granted he might one day inherit a bank and, like him, did not think it unusual. With the benefit of hindsight, it seems an extraordinary legacy from which to benefit.

I eventually found the bank but it was closed and so I returned to find Sam and Adolf at the traffic lights at the end of the street. Sam was being harangued by an apoplectic blonde woman and there was a large, new and expensive looking Mercedes impaled on Adolf's front bumper. Its flank was dented and opened as though by a can opener. A Land Rover bumper is a fearsome weapon in traffic. The woman was clearly very wealthy, festooned in jewelry and immaculately dressed, in stark contrast to us in our torn shorts and scruffy shirts. She was very obviously cosseted and used to getting her own way, finding tantrums efficacious in achieving this. As she continued shouting Sam told me he had been told to move on by a traffic policeman. Getting to the red lights at the end of the street he had stopped and the Mercedes, driven by the woman, had drawn up next to him. When the lights turned green, and as Sam moved forwards, she accelerated and turned straight across his path in front of him. As the self-appointed mistress of the road she obviously expected cow-shit encrusted, exploded cat scented proletariat like Adolf and Sam to make way for her. The collision was unavoidable but in a structured and hierarchical society like Costa Rica's, wealth, privilege and status hold sway and she naturally expected us to carry the blame for the accident. As Sam and I discussed the predicament, she continued shouting at us that Sam should have got out of her way. The haughty are not gifted with humility.

The traffic was building up impatiently behind us, cars hooting, drivers shouting insults and protesting at being held up. A traffic policeman arrived and assessed the situation, quickly telling us the accident was not our fault and all would be sorted out. At that moment the woman's husband arrived, visibly blanching when he saw the damage to his beloved car, or perhaps more at the obvious expense of repairing the desecration to its side. He announced he was a lawyer and became extremely aggressive, issuing dire threats about suing us, the legal process to be garnished with a sprinkling of a couple of hours on a rack, a helping of thumb screws and topped off with general bankruptcy if we didn't settle the repair bill. In his particular court we were already guilty and the evidence was irrelevant. In a land where the rich rule, the policeman's focus became job preservation and he turned on us, saying we had to go to the police station.

We weren't quite under arrest, but that was inconsequential as we had little choice, so we got in our respective vehicles and followed him through the traffic, the bruised Mercedes on our heels. At the station the odds of a happy ending became slimmer as we were told that, as we were driving a foreign car with foreign plates, it would have to be impounded. The woman and her husband looked smugly satisfied.

At this point I asked if we could make a phone call, explaining we were expected by friends and we did not want them to think us rude for being late. Perhaps suspicious of our intentions, the police said they would like to speak to Robert themselves, so the station chief rang the number I had for Robert and Lupita, which seemed to have been answered by Lupita. He quickly explained the situation to her and, whilst glancing at the angry, pompous couple, had the decency and honesty to say we had been extremely calm and polite. Having finished his explanation he asked if we were known to Lupita and Robert and then listened to whatever was being said in reply. As he did so his expression changed. First a little blush appeared in his cheek, and then a frown and glance at the Costa Rican couple before he put the phone down. Lupita later explained to us that she had told him we were friends of her father, an ex Government Minister and still high up in Government, and also friends of her uncle, the President of the Costa Rican Central Bank. She also told us the woman was one of the wealthiest in the country. In a country that adheres to a strict hierarchy of power and influence, connections and who you know and are take precedence over money. The friend of the powerful is king and clearly a Government Minister trumped a lawyer.

With his newfound insight into our place in San Jose's social pecking order, the policeman told us we were free to go and could take Adolf with us, but if it was not too much trouble, could we leave a number plate which we could collect in the morning from the Court after filling out some forms. The volte face in our respective fortunes subdued the irate woman, puncturing her overinflated pomposity. Her husband immediately started haranguing her for being a useless driver. We left them to the apportionment of blame between themselves, assuming she would be withdrawing conjugal relations and favours for a few days, or until the rigours of celibacy became too much for him to bear and he ameliorated his attitude towards her. We climbed back into Adolf, pulled out into the stream of traffic and found our way to the suburb of Los Yoses where Robert and Lupita lived. Robert worked for The American Banknote Company as their Latin American representative and seemed to know everyone and anyone of importance south of the US-Mexican border. Handsome and elegant, when he had first arrived in San José a couple of years earlier, the rumour mill immediately spread news of his landing in local society. A woman at a party was heard to describe him as 'a seven flavoured ice-cream'. Robert quietly reveled in his reputation.

For the next sixteen days we got to know San José and its stratified society, governed and superficially repressed by Catholic mores. Status and image were paramount. For the sake of her honour we could not be seen alone in a vehicle with an unmarried girl from the top echelons of society. And yet the men who were complicit in making these artificial rules had well organised and discreet brothels they could visit. Sex for pleasure was bought. With your wife it was to have children. One of the bars we were taken to by a friend of Robert's was a less than well organised and indiscreet brothel. The prostitutes who worked in it took the men they picked up to nearby and extremely cheap hotels where they were charged $8 by the prostitute, which did not include the $1 cost of the room for its brief use. We were told a common scam was for the prostitute to leave the room on the pretext of going to the lavatory, at which point her pimp and friends would enter and pulverise the hapless punter, relieving him of his wallet, watch and any other valuables he might have. Given the circumstances of the mugging, the pimps were no doubt pretty confident very few men would report it to the police or their wives. A perfect crime. How the bruises were explained at home is hard to comprehend.

  The door of the bar was on the corner of a dimly lit street in a less than salubrious part of the city. The area was seedy and reminded me of the streets that I wandered near the police cells in Vera Cruz on the night we landed. A curtain hung over the open doorway. Pushing through it we found ourselves in a darkened room with a loud juke box, tables and chairs and a dance area where three or four couples were shuffling about in a desultory semblance of dancing. A small bar room opened off this dance area and we went in and sat on high stools at the bar, ordering our drinks as we settled into our seats. I swiveled my seat around, put my elbows on the bar behind me and surveyed the room. Out of about forty people in the room, only about ten were men. I had been sitting there for less than a minute when a young and very attractive girl walked straight up to me, stepped in close between my knees and put a hand firmly on each inner thigh. With such forthright marketing, it would have taken a Trappist monk to misread her intentions. With my crutch in a pincer grasp and my body pressed against the bar, there was no escape from the ensuing conversation as she came to the unsubtle point about her rates for the variety of services she was offering. This took some time since there seemed to be an infinite number, variety and ingenuity of them, some clearly requiring a degree of flexibility and double-jointedness. She seemed unimpressed by my declinature of all of them, moved her hands higher, pressed in closer and revised some of her rates, clearly prepared to haggle.

My only option seemed to be to claim incontinence as I slid off the stool and headed for the Gents the other side of the dance floor, which was now filled with more girls, milling about in their search for business. To get to the lavatories I had to pass through them and suddenly found a hand firmly in my crutch. Keeping moving I found my genitals became the object of a game of 'Pass the Parcel' as I was successively fondled, in a rather grasping, squeezingly assertive way, by each girl I passed. Their offers of a 'Good time for $8' were whispered repeatedly in my ear. Reaching the succour of the lavatories I pushed through the curtain to find it too was full of girls and some women of more senior rank no longer in the first flush of youth, somewhat more care worn and used with the look of second hand tyres. The propositioning in the lavatory was of a marginally less subtle nature than in the bar and on my journey across the dance floor. I found it hard to concentrate on my micturitions with a girl leaning on either shoulder, each saying "I'll hold that for you". There appeared to be no charge for 'holding.' I presumed the girls viewed it as advertising, a loss leader in their business model. Having completed my hand assisted journey back to my bar stool, we finished our drinks and left the bar for the relative safety of the dark streets. As we walked I mused on the other world I had glimpsed, a seedier life where desperation preyed on sexual need to produce a market in which self-respect became an inevitable casualty, collateral damage of the commodity on offer and the unbridled desire for it.

We had been in San José for a couple of days when we were invited to a party. We realised we were something of an oddity, a bit exotic for the superficially conservative society there, and offers and invitations had flowed during our stay. At the party we met a man who owned a large factory. He asked about our trip and was interested in Adolf. We told him about our problem with her flattened front springs and that we had been advised there was a garage in Panama where we could get them fixed. He very kindly offered us the use of his workshops and a couple of his mechanics so the next day, Adolf went off to the springs clinic and beauty parlour. The mechanics worked a miracle on her exhausted spring leaves, re-tempering them back to their old jaunty angle so the engine rode perkily clear above the front axle. The crumpled front wing and wheel arch were beaten out and repainted. She looked rejuvenated, jauntily self confident once more.

Early one morning we drove out of Los Yoses and went with Robert and Lupita to Irazu, the active volcano that broods menacingly in the wings and forty seven uncomfortably close kilometers to the east of the city. 10,300 feet high, it had last erupted in 1963. We parked near the top and walked across the dark, ash strewn surface, our feet sinking into the ground as though on soft sand. We stood on the edge of the main crater and peered into its depths. A fetid looking lake filled with pea green water lay far below us. There were in fact two craters and the one we were looking into was called Diego de la Haya. A thin, lone waterfall cascaded down the crater into the still water of the lake, creating the only sound in the thin air. The whole area was a moonscape of desolation, an eerily beautiful but barren land. The air was cool and we were told frosts were not uncommon on the top of the volcano. Birds and a small selection of adapted mammals could also be found on the slopes, including coyotes and long-tailed weasels.

While Sam was overseeing the work on Adolf, I went to Puntarenas, a port on the Pacific coast. We had heard there was a cargo ship there, the Saltillo, that was going to sail to Colombia and my mission was to find out if we could get on it with Adolf, saving us the drive down through Panama. When we rang the shipping agents they told us the Saltillo was due to dock the next day so I jumped on the train in the afternoon for the four hour journey through the rain forests to the coast. The train stopped at random places en route, sometimes at the door of simple huts by the rail line that were clearly home to some of the passengers. Arriving at Puntarenas after sunset, I walked down the single pier and discovered the Saltillo was moored out in the bay but would be docking early in the morning. I walked into the town, which was built on a peninsular jutting out into the Gulf of Nicoya, and found a room in Hotel Los Baños for under 50 cents. The room was large and square and had four prison style beds in it, each with a wafer thin mattress, so slim they looked as though they could be slid under the door. A head high partition ran down one side of the room with a gap for a door that led to the toilet and shower. The toilet stank and the shower was a pipe hanging down from the ceiling. The walls and ceiling of the room were festooned in cobwebs and as I chose a bed I saw a huge rat running along the top of the partition. It stopped at the mid-way point to stare at me, surprised that there was an intruder in the room, and then continued its journey, disappearing into a hole in the wall where the partition and wall met. With a bar of wet soap in my hand, I pulled back the top sheet of the bed I had selected and brushed the soap over the bed to collect any resident fleas and bed lice. The rat reappeared and ran back the way it had come, shortly followed by another. It seemed to be rush hour on the rodent highway. As it was late, I settled down for the night without bothering with a meal, wondering how many other people would be in the room when I woke. As usual when away from civilisation, I slept with my money belt around my waist. It contained a small amount of money and, more importantly, my Passport. My rucksack joined me in the bed, my arm through one of the straps.

Waking early, I had a cold shower and used the sheet from my bed to dry myself. I got dressed, reaching under the bed for my shoes. Putting them on I saw they had been chewed by the rats in the night, giving them a crusted pie finish around the toes. I walked back down to the jetty from which I could see the Saltillo had in fact docked. The security gate was down but was straddled by a guardhouse with doors either side of the gate. Going in the town side door, I walked brazenly through the room and out of the dockside door, nodding to the perplexed guard and giving him a cheery wave. Leaving him scratching his head I strolled down to the ship, boarding it via the gangplank. I chatted to some of the crew who told me the Captain was ashore and would be back at about at about ten o'clock. It was seven o'clock so I sat down on the bare deck in the sunshine to wait. After three hours I was told he would not be back until the afternoon so I decided to go and look for him at the shipping agent's offices. Back at the guardhouse I was apprehended and searched by the guard who had obviously been ruminating on my earlier cavalier entry. Finding nothing of interest, value or suspicion in my rucksack, he allowed me to go to find my way through the back streets of the town to the agents. The agent told me there was no chance of us getting aboard, particularly as two other travellers with a VW had been refused passage a couple of weeks before. Accepting this I wandered off for the station but, on the way, realised I had forgotten to show the agent our letter of reference from the M V Gela, so I went back and asked if the letter, and the fact we had already sailed on a cargo ship would make any difference. He felt it might but that I would have to speak to the head agent who would be back in the office at two o'clock that afternoon. With another three hours to kill, the hard steel deck of the ship was not an attractive proposition so I went to a cafe in a small square and worked my way through three cups of coffee as I waited. While I was sitting at a small table outside the cafe, a seagull shat on me, making me grateful cows didn't fly.

Back at the agents at two o'clock, I met the head of the operation. A pompous, self important man, he was dressed from head to foot in white, looking like a a shipping agent making a bad attempt to look like David Niven. Oblivious of how ridiculous he looked, he haughtily told me there was no chance of us getting on the Saltillo, irrespective of how many cargo ships we had been on or how many references we had. He was obviously not a man given to debate, confining himself to monologues. Frustrated, I had no option but to head back to San José, just managing to catch the solitary afternoon train and thus avoiding another night in the zoo that was the Hotel de las Ratas. Arriving back in San José, I caught a bus at the train station to Los Yoses and then walked back to the house.

It was time for us to leave and head south once more. Saying our farewells to all who had been so kind, hospitable and generous to us, we set off for the Panamanian border some one hundred and ninety miles away. Before getting there, we had one small obstacle to overcome. Cerro de la Muerte, Death Mountain, is 3,451 metres high and in the days when cars were not commonplace in Costa Rica was a soaring challenge on the three to four day journey on foot for those who needed to cross it. Temperatures at night drop below freezing, and in the thin air the sun's rays burn skin. For many of the poverty stricken people crossing it, ill preparation made it the last journey they ever made. To compound the climatic challenges, the lethal road over Death Mountain was an additional hazard to be faced. In later years it has been listed as number four in the world's most dangerous roads, and with good reason. Running from San Isidro de El General to Cartago, the road wound its way up and through the Tapantí National Park, in places rising to 2,438 metres. Later on in the drive our altimeter showed we were above 3,048 metres, high up in the clouds. Tapantí Park was the wettest part of Costa Rica, averaging between two hundred and fifty and three hundred inches of rainfall in a year.

The Park is filled with streams and waterfalls and the rain forest vegetation is thick and lush, as was the heavy mist we encountered which was known to add to the excitement of the road. At times the mist enveloping the road was impenetrable, and yet it seemed to be completely ignored by the lunatic truck drivers using the dirt road. Precipitous drops, a narrow track not really wide enough for two vehicles, and at one point a thin ridge where the vertiginous mountainsides fell away both sides of us all bore witness to the mountain's name. To add to the fun we had to be constantly alert for what might come around the next blind bend. Meeting trucks coming the other way was interesting, particularly if it was us who were on the precipice side of the road. At one stage as I drove Adolf slowly past one of the trucks, creeping forwards less than an inch apart, I looked out of the driver's window and could see Adolf's wheels on the edge of the track with no room to spare. Below was a drop of over a thousand feet to the valley floor below. Sam and I each used yet another of our nine lives on that road that day. At no stage was the drive less than exhilarating. At times it was a hairsbreadth from death. The combination of the dark at the end of the day and the swirling clouds eventually drove us off the road onto a side track where we settled down for the night. Commercial television crews now make programmes about roads like that and many others we drove on, ramping up the tension with sweating celebrities at the wheel and dramatic music to accompany their fear, all under the safe umbrella of a protective production team. For us at times they became commonplace.

An early start in the morning got us to the Panamanian border by nine o'clock the next day. Since the Customs officials on the Panamanian side were focussed on searching a large coach and its passengers, we were ignored and sailed through without delay. Our destination for the day was a beach at a place called Santa Clara. We had heard about it from the French couple on the Nicaraguan beach who said it was a quiet and isolated spot. We reached it at dusk, finding a long and deserted beach with its white sand fringed with a stand of pine trees that provided welcome shade from the heat of the sun in the middle of the day. We parked Adolf under the trees and very quickly started chatting to a young American couple from the Canal Zone who were renting a flat in the nearby village for a few days. They kindly invited us back to the flat for an evening meal, after which we walked back to Adolf for the night. In the morning our destination was the Balboa port on the

Pacific side. To get to it we had to cross the Puente de las Americas, the huge bridge crossing the southern mouth of the Canal. We visited many shipping offices and almost all were willing to ship Adolf to Colombia but none would take us as passengers. The Italian line quoted us $207 for Adolf and $53 each for us if we wanted to go to Cartagena, $70 if we wanted to go to Buenaventura, but the ship did not sail for another three weeks. We decided to drive to Cristobal, the port in Colon on the Atlantic coast and at the other end of the Canal, hoping to find an earlier sailing. Before leaving we bought Peruvian, Bolivian and Colombian currency on the black market.

Arriving in Colon in mid afternoon, we found the street where all the shipping agents had their offices and as we parked heard shouts from the other side of the street. Parked opposite us was another right hand drive Land Rover. It had 'Arctic-Antarctic Expedition 1972-73' written on its door and it disgorged six English people, three men and three women, all our age and all English. They were from Bristol University and had been on the road for five months, having shipped their vehicle from England to to New York. They said they had often heard about us on the way south but this was the first time we had met. Like us, they had been supported in a small way by one or two sponsors, one of which was Tampax. The company had thoughtfully donated twenty boxes, each containing two hundred of their useful little products. Somewhat unreasonably and discriminatorily they had declined to help Sam and me, pointing out the obvious flaw in our approach to them when explaining they couldn't see why or when we might need their handy gadgets and that no, they had not in fact been designed to deal with and stem the flow of a bad case of dysentery.

Joining forces with the Bristolians we found a fare of $200 for Adolf on a cargo ship and flights to Medellin for $35 each. The ship did not sail for five or six days so we led the others back to the beach at Santa Clara where we spent the next couple of days swimming, cooking over an open fire, working on the Land Rovers and lazing about. In preparation for committing Adolf to the rigours of the sea voyage south, Sam and I had bought a couple of rolls of chicken wire. Taking the canvas roof off, we covered the frame with the wire and then put the canvas back on. Our logic was that if an opportunist thief cut through the canvas, they would still not be able to get their hand into the vehicle. It is impossible to make a vehicle, or a house for that matter, impregnable against a determined thief but we felt this simple prophylactic would deter or delay the casual opportunists who no doubt infested the docks and ships, as we had seen on board the M.V. Gela in Le Havre and Vera Cruz.

One afternoon a group of young people who belonged to an evangelical sect called The Children of God came onto the beach. Their philosophy seemed to be that God would provide for them, which we all interpreted as them assuming they would be provided for by whoever they could sponge off. We felt they were a group of feckless chancers disguised as religious nuts, drifting about chanting their wares and beliefs. The chill of the cold shoulder we gave them penetrated even their thick carapaces of insensitivity and they moved off to another part of the large beach, no doubt looking for someone else who would share their food and shelter with them. On the first evening, as we all sat chatting around the camp fire under the trees on the edge of the beach, a couple of officers from the National Guard appeared on the beach. They asked us what we were doing, looking around our camp with alert eyes. It was pretty obvious they were after a bit of a bribe or protection money as there was no law saying we could not be there or camp there. They said they were collecting for entry to a Fiesta, although there was no evidence of any tickets in their hands, so tickets for the Policeman's Ball was the only item on their agenda. It is a useful lesson in life to know which battles to pick and, contrary to our usual stance of not paying bribes, our modest donation ensured we were left alone and not moved on from our rather idyllic seafront campsite, nor harassed whilst there.

After two days at the beach, we all set off for Panama in our short convoy of two Land Rovers, hoping to finalise the shipping arrangements and our flights south. Nothing was straightforward in Latin America and so our travel preparations for our short migration to Colombia ran true to form. It was Monday and the shipping agent confirmed the sailing date was Wednesday and they could take both vehicles. It was lunchtime and he said he would do the paperwork in the afternoon if we would come back, so we went off and booked eight seats on a Copa Airlines flight to Medellin. In the afternoon the agent said the ship would not sail until Thursday so the eight seats had to be cancelled and rebooked. By now, the shipping agent had had enough of the day and went home, telling us he would be back on Wednesday, Tuesday being one of the country's seemingly weekly holidays. There was nothing for us to do other than go into Panama Old City for a meal and a few beers at a bar. The area we were in was seedy and clearly a red light district. As we stood outside a bar discussing whether it was the one we wanted to use, a man came up to me and offered me $1.25 if I would have sex with him. I struggled to understand the 25 cents. Why not a round number like $1 or $2? Was the 25 cents a little tip, a pourboire for the quality, or perhaps quantity of the service he felt I might offer. Nor was he clear whether I was to be the postman or the letterbox in the assignation, which I felt would have been a useful bit of information in his marketing. He seemed disappointed when I declined his offer.

We entered the bar and by the end of the evening there were about fifteen fellow travellers around the table with us, talking and swapping stories. Some we had already met further north on our journey, including two Germans we had spent time with on the beach in Mazatlan in Mexico. This was a pattern that would repeat itself throughout South America. We would all bump into each other in towns and cities, sometimes by prior arrangements made weeks or months before. Panama Old City was like a hub airport, a collection and distribution point for young adventurers heading north and south. Apart from the group at our table there were at least three other tables of similarly eclectic groups of Americans, Africans, Europeans and some Asians. A United Nations of youth with a common cause, at peace and in harmony with each other in the grand endeavour of enjoying life and the common adventure we were all on, our individual nationalities an irrelevance. As we sat with the others, I admired my new sandals under the table. Sam and I had each bought strong leather sandals in a small cobbler shop in one of the back streets and had asked the owner whether he would attach shaped pieces of car tyre on the soles for us. He agreed to do this so we went to a garage and collected a used tyre. Using a hacksaw, we spent a considerable time cutting out four rough shapes that fitted the bottom of the sandals, which the cobbler then proceeded to nail and glue to the bottom of them, sculpting the edges of protruding rubber for an exact fit. They looked good for 40,000 miles and I felt confident I would not be slipping when out in the wet. The ingenuity of the impoverished around the world astounded me then, and still does to this day.

Leaving the bar, we drove out to a place called Las Cumbres where we knew there was a small lake. We had agreed to meet the Bristolian sextet there. One of them, Julian, had spent the evening with us, his companions having gone off to have dinner somewhere, so he came with us for a crowded night's sleep in the back of Adolf. Our peace was interrupted during the night by a couple of aggressive policeman, perhaps irritated by hangovers and intent on finding out what we were doing there. They seemed placated by the innocence of our explanation and drifted off to find someone else to annoy. When we woke in the morning, Julian's friends were there, obviously arriving some time in the night and after our confrontation with the police. After breakfast we drove back into the city and completed all the arrangements for shipping the vehicles. Once that had been done we were able to confirm our flights with some certainty. We did not need to drop the vehicles off at the Port until later in the afternoon so, needing some accommodation for the night, we set off to find beds in the city since sleeping on the streets was not likely to be the most sensible option. The Pension Familia was prepared to let us sleep on their roof for $1.25 each but would not offer a group discount for eight of us, so we went to a convent we had heard about where they said we could sleep on their floor for nothing. We unloaded the kit we would need for the few days we would be without the vehicles. Sam and John, one of the English group, took the Land Rovers to the Port for loading and we met them later in a bar and spent the evening there, again with other travellers and beer for company.

Supper was in a Chinese restaurant where I had Chow Mein con Carne, an amalgam of ingredients, a fusion of cultures that defied description. So did the huge cockroaches that climbed the walls and scurried around our feet in the restaurant, some at least three inches long. I had never seen cockroaches that large before, a testament to the body building properties of Chow Mein con Carne. I assumed if they could survive the restaurant's fare, I would be fine. Returning to the convent we slept a slightly uncomfortable night before catching the pre-dawn bus to the airport where we checked in our rucksacks and had a coffee before boarding an antediluvian Vickers Viscount. The last time I had flown in a Viscount was in 1957 when my family returned to England from India. The ceiling lining above my head was hanging down and the seats were collapsing and dirty. The plane's state of decrepitude made me feel flights on it were probably an aerial form of Russian Roulette. The likelihood of it crashing at some point felt like an inevitability. The trick was not to be on it when it did - the roulette bit. Staring out of the window as we taxied to the runway, I drew comfort from the Rolls Royce logo on the engine cowling, pleased to know I would be hitting the ground in style if we went down. We heaved up into the sky like an exhausted walrus after a couple of hectic weeks of the breeding season. I gazed down onto Panama and then the desolation of the Darien Gap. The next chapter of the odyssey lay in the great unknown of the South American continent. I could only guess at the adventures and risks ahead, and wonder.

Excitement doesn't come much better than in the opaque shadows of the great unknown.

Climbing Temple 1 at Tikal, Flores - Guatemala

A GIRL CALLED ADOLF

CHAPTER 10

South America - 1972-73

The journey south

Medellin to Lima

"Forget not that the earth delights to feel your bare feet and the wind longs to play with your hair."

Khalil Gibran

"Security is mostly superstition. Life is either daring adventure, or nothing."

Helen Keller

Of all the countries that lay ahead of us, and indeed behind us, we knew the biggest risks probably lay in Colombia. One of three countries that emerged from the collapse of Gran Colombia in 1830, it's reputation for danger was well known amongst travellers faced with the prospect of passing through it. The possibility of stabbings, muggings and mysterious disappearance were all fates that faced us. When I finally returned to England I bumped into one of two young Englishmen we met whilst there and he told me they were attacked in Bogota and his companion was stabbed, somewhat curtailing their own adventure.

The Presidential election had just taken place in the United States and Richard Nixon confounded logic by winning a second term with a landslide victory against Senator John McGovern, doing so despite the building storm of the Watergate break-in. Minority groups were volubly upset by his victory and an undercurrent of unrest simmered. Unrest also lay ahead of us further south as President Allende of Chile struggled to control a wave of strikes by forming a new People's Front Government. Often following a communist creed, Allende had formulated a policy of nationalisation, limiting farm sizes and spending money the country didn't have. I am sure Tony Blair and Gordon Brown modeled their years in power on Allende's blueprint of fiscal mis-management. Shop shelves remained empty as supplies of goods ran short and the lack of basic provisions helped to raise tensions. Allende's troops and police quelled demonstration with the enthusiastic physical robustness available to all despots. However, before we contemplated Chile or any other country, we had to negotiate Colombia, a country that still remembered well 'La Violencia', a period of bloody internal conflict in the 1940s and early 1950s. In many places the country was lawless.

The Marxist Revolutionary Armed Forces of Colombia, commonly known by the acronym FARC, was established in 1964 after Colombia's two main political parties finally agreed to share power, bringing to an end more than a decade of political violence. FARC, and another, smaller group of insurgents known as the National Liberation Army, or ELN, quickly became well established in the country. FARC was organised on military lines, commanded by a hierarchy of 'officers' with a senior military secretariat in overall control. The movement gathered popularity among the disaffected and was primarily established in the remote countryside, operating from hidden camps, but it also had an urban presence. FARC funded itself through controlling a large part of the Colombian drug production and trade, but also used protection, kidnapping and ransom and a good sprinkling of violent thuggery to broaden its business model and diversify its income stream. These Marxist revolutionary groups could be found in many parts of Latin America. The Shining Path in Peru, the radicalised students who formed the Montoneros in Argentina and the Tupamaros of Uruguay were all dangerous and in a constant relentless conflict with the authorities and it was easy to get caught in the crossfire in some way. Central America also had its own home grown versions with the Sandinistas in Nicaragua and the Zapatistas in Mexico. Despite the decades of conflict these disparate groups have engaged in, only Fidel Castro in Cuba and the

Sandinistas achieved their aims and formed permanent Governments. We knew we would have to be careful in Colombia, and indeed throughout South America as this was where the big boys played real games with potentially unpleasant outcomes, some of them permanent in an inconveniently terminal sort of way.

To our surprise, our geriatric plane did not land in the middle of the swamps of the Darien Gap but made it as far as the tarmac of Medellin Airport where the pilot dumped it on the runway like an overflowing rubbish bag being thrown out of the back door onto the ground. There was a collective exhalation of long held breath by the passengers and, just a little more alarmingly, by the crew. To look through the open door into the cockpit and see the Captain cross himself on landing is not encouraging. I didn't look back from the Terminal to see if he got out and kissed the ground, being more concerned about dealing with the Immigration officials in the airport. From the traveller's grapevine we knew a group of drug laden hippies had been caught at Medellin airport a couple of weeks before, as a result of which the authorities had clamped down aggressively on all visitors. Those with long hair or beards were being turned away and refused entry. All eight of us had made an attempt to smarten ourselves up, the three girls even taking to wearing dresses. Sam and I had beards as we had long ago given up shaving in cold water, and our clothes were distinctly more beaten up than Julian, John and Richard's who seemed to have a better developed fashion sense.

When we got to the Immigration desk, the six sartorially elegant English from Bristol sailed through without any difficulty but as soon as the Immigration and Customs officers saw Sam and me, their demeanor changed. Whilst we did not have long hair, we had beards and in their view we certainly fitted the profile of undesirables in other ways. Things were not looking too good. They demanded to know how much money we had. Always reluctant to reveal that to anyone, we pleaded poverty but showed them Adolf's papers and what money we had on us, proving we had a vehicle and would be able to get out of the country. Part of our problem was most of our money was still in sealed plastic bags under the footplate in the passenger well in Adolf, so even if we told them how much we had, there was no way we could prove it. The distinctly unfriendly officials made us sit down on a bench as they had protracted discussions amongst themselves, shaking their heads and looking over at us. We heard the word hippy mentioned a couple of times. The situation was moving from not looking too good to looking very bad.

We called Julian back and got him to show them his money, making him an involuntary guarantor for us. It was a bit late to come clean that we had more cash available to us than we had at first admitted. Eventually mollified, they agreed to let us into the country and we walked through the terminal to catch a ramshackle bus into the city where the bus driver dropped us off at the main coach station.

Our vehicles were being shipped to the port town of Buenaventura which was four hundred and seventy five kilometres south of us. The easiest way of getting there was to travel by bus to Cali where we would have to find a way to the port. We had a choice of buses to Cali from Medellin. The first bus left at mid-day, costing 48 pesos each and getting to Cali at ten o'clock that evening. For 60 pesos, which was just under $3, we could catch the bus that left at eight o'clock that evening, arriving at six o'clock in the morning. This seemed a very cheap way for us to spend the night rather than having to book into some hostel or Pension either in Cali or Medellin, so we elected for the night bus.

We took up residence at a couple of tables by the window in a cafe near the bus station, dumped our gear on the floor in the corner and took it in turns to look after it as those free of this duty wandered around the town to fill time and get some exercise. On my solitary wanderings I went into a workshop where men were hand beating large copper bowls, each about four feet in diameter. The radio in the cafe was playing Colombian music being broadcast by a local radio station. Listening to it I realised where Simon and Garfunkel had got their inspiration for some of their songs. In particular, the rhythms of '*Cecilia*', written in 1970 for their album '*Bridge over Troubled Water*' seemed to me to be straight out of Colombia. Perhaps it was just a coincidence but given Paul Simon's later ability to borrow music from other parts of the world I think he may well have been influenced by Latin America, its beat and the almost mystical Pan Pipes and the accompanying simplicity of the guitar of '*El Condor Pasa*'. Even now, after all these years, hearing the song takes me straight back into the high plains of the Andes where the haunting simplicity of the pipes are the perfect companion to the isolation of the high plains and passes of the awesome mountain range and of the condors that drift effortlessly above it.

At about seven thirty we boarded the 'Pullman Special' coach to Cali. The seats were rather cramped and were covered in a shiny faux leather, heavily disguised as plastic. When I reclined my seat it turned into a slide and I slipped down under the seat in front of me. If I was to stay in my seat, sleeping upright was going to be the only option. At midnight, four hours into the journey, the coach stopped and there was a general rush for a small cafe for those who wanted to get a drink or food, and the lavatories for those who wanted to offload drinks taken on board in Cali. It was a relief to stretch our cramped legs and walk around. When we boarded again I decided to lie in the aisle between the seats. Despite anticipating being pulverised as there was no discernible evidence of any suspension, I decided I would be more comfortable than in my glissé seat. The roads were atrocious. Pot holes and rain filled ruts created by heavy trucks plying their trade between the cities jarred the bus relentlessly. Mountain climbs with hairpin bends, none of which seemed to slow the driver, threw the complaining bus around. Wedging myself between the seats in the narrow aisle I felt like the dried beans inside a maraca in the hands of a demented child. I was beginning to wonder whether I would manage to get to sleep, when I felt something nibbling my feet. Looking up I saw one of the men sitting in the rear seats was leaning forward and tickling my feet. He was laughing and clearly thought it hysterically funny that I should lie on the floor. I couldn't work out why he felt the need to assault my extremities, and slid further down the aisle to get away from him and the possibility this was a Colombian foot fetishist's foreplay, the precursor to some form of blissful sexual union on the bucking back seats.

The next stop was at three o'clock when the driver and his assistant had a meal at a cafe in a small town. We again used the lavatories and walked around while the two man crew ate their food. Shortly before dawn, just after I had finally managed to fall asleep, I woke to the realisation there was a firm pressure and weight on my crutch. Looking up, I saw a girl, who was sitting in an aisle seat next to me, had put her bare foot on my genitals and was pressing down as if flooring the break pedal in a runaway car. At any other time I would have thought it funny to say she had her foot on the crutch, but the humour in this play on words was rather secondary to the extreme discomfort of her unasked for foot massage. I caught her eye in the gloom and she gave me a huge grin, pushing harder. I slid further down the bus and the blood supply to important parts of my anatomy was restored. I have no idea what her intentions were but think she was using me to stop sliding off her slippery seat as it surely cannot possibly have been the heterosexual equivalent of the foot man's advances earlier in the night.

The bus wheezed into Cali at six thirty in the morning and we all adjourned to a cafe to discuss how we were going to retrieve the vehicles. It was soon decided that Sam and I, and Julian and John from the other group, would catch the eleven o'clock bus that morning for the four hour, eighty mile journey to Buenaventura, leaving the others to go to a camp site just outside Cali. It was

Friday morning and we did not think we would be back until Monday at the earliest.

The bus to Buenaventura was definitely not a Pullman. Ancient, exhausted, dirty and with a windscreen that had so many cracks it resembled a spider's web, extra seats had been put in the front to accommodate more passengers, who sat on them in a line next to the driver. It soon became apparent there seemed to be a problem with the back axle. As we slid and careered over the muddy tracks that were little more than logging trails in the thick rain forests, the driver would occasionally stop and go to the back to inspect under the bus. I had no idea what he thought he was going to see, apart from the fact the wheels were still there. Looking at him I doubted there was any hope or expectation of his being able to do anything constructive about any problem he found. On any hill we came to, the nonagenarian bus would slow and struggle as the driver changed down through the gears. At a certain point, when the driver ran out of gears to descend to having reached gear basement, the young boy assisting him would jump out with a log and wedge it behind one of the front wheels to stop the bus slipping back down the road. The driver would engage first gear, rev the engine until it was howling in protest and then whip his foot off the clutch. We would lurch and leap off again, like a gazelle springing into a run to escape a predator. The young boy would grab his log and run alongside to catch the door and jump back on board.

When the bus pulled into the small bus station in Buenaventura, we stepped off, relieved to be safe. My relief was short lived. As I stepped down and my foot touched the ground, my crutch with its accompanying sitting tenants landed squarely in a young girl's welcoming hand. I wasn't sure whether this was more alarming than the rabid dog that was fitting and thrashing about on the ground next to us, rectally prolapsed and frothing at the mouth. Shockingly young, the girl made a number of exotic offers at bargain basement prices as I stood on the tip of my toes to try to lift myself out of her firm grip. She finally accepted, somewhat reluctantly, that I was unlikely to fall for her well hidden charms and let go, leaving me to hurry to catch up with the others. Like so many ports, Buenaventura was seedy, rough and not a place in which it was possible to feel safe. We walked through dirty streets and found the Grace Line office on the waterfront. A short, dapper and busy man took our Bills of Lading and rushed around collecting and shedding papers, stamping them and filling in forms, then disappearing off to other buildings. He clearly enjoyed being in charge and we were quite happy to let him get on with it.

While the agent was going about the business of retrieving the vehicles for us we wandered over to a hotel, the Gran Hotel, where we asked if we could have a room for four. They refused without explaining if that was on the basis that they thought us perverted, or because their rooms were too small. They recommended we try the Hotel Pacifico nearby and when we enquired there, they seemed quite happy for us to squash into one room, eager enough to take our money, indifferent to our comforts. Room 16 on one of the upper floors had two small beds in it and not much else. We pushed the beds together, reckoning we could lie across them like packed sardines. Back at the Grace Lines offices our efficient man told us his day had ended and he would finish off in the morning. The ship was due to dock at seven o'clock that evening and it seemed there was every chance we would get the vehicles back the next day.

We went to a bar for a drink. The Inca Bar was a typical drinking joint as can be found in any port, a place for the rough and tough to drink and pick up women who charged for their time and services. We each had a beer and then bought some bottles and took them back to our room in the hotel. It was hot and humid, and moving around created a patina of sweat that made clothes damp and stick to you. I decided I would like a shower. There was one shower on our floor, a cubicle with its door opening directly onto the main corridor. I undressed in our room, put a small towel around my waist and went out into the corridor to find the shower was occupied. As I stood waiting for it to come free, I realised a large number of young girls were wandering around, some in short, flimsy nightdresses. As they passed me, giggling and laughing, some lifted the hem of my towel and then ran off. Standing there in the thoroughfare, semi dressed girls popping in and out of rooms like figures in a weather clock, the dim flickering light of flames from the bonfire of realisation told me we had booked ourselves into a brothel.

Two of the girls occupied the room next to ours and they came out and asked if I wanted to use the shower in their room. Since we wanted to go out for a meal, this seemed a sensible option to save time so I accepted.

Their room was the same size as ours, simply furnished with two single beds, a small chest of drawers and a slim cupboard against a wall. The only thing differentiating the girls' room from ours was theirs had a small shower room off it, a Buenaventuran version of 'en suite'. There was no door to the shower room, and it had jugs and buckets full of water all over it. They were on the floor, on the window sill and teetering on the cistern behind the lavatory. The shower was a pipe coming out of the ceiling and turning on the single tap, I stepped in under the stream of cooling water. As I was washing, I turned to see the two girls were sitting on one of the beds watching, legs crossed and chins on hands with their elbows on their knees, their faces wreathed in smiles. It was a little late to be modest so I carried on with soaping my hair when, without warning, the water stopped flowing. This was the signal for the girls to jump up and rush into the shower room where they picked up the jugs and buckets and poured the water over me. The need for them was now quite clear as obviously the water system was less than reliable.

My shower finished, I dried myself off in front of my audience, thanked them for the hospitality and room service and escaped back to the sanctuary of our room to change for dinner. The sun had set and we wandered around the town, eventually selecting a dingy joint in the red light district. It was not difficult to be in the red light district in Buenaventura as it seemed the whole town was lit red, there being no other colour or form of existence available to the inhabitants or visiting merchant seamen. There didn't seem to be any other sort of district. Sitting down at a chipped and dirty table in the cafe, we each chose a bowl of a meaty soup, a plate of rice and a beer or two. The food was cold and the beer warm but this wasn't the sort of place in which you complained if you preferred to leave the joint without a knife sticking out of your ribs so we ate and drank our way through the unidentifiable meal as we chatted, and then settled the small bill and left. When we returned to the hotel my shower attendants were on their way out to work, dressed and heavily made up for the night's exertions and trade, presumably much of it up against some street wall or in deserted shop doorways. They greeted us as long lost friends with smiles and waves. We hurried upstairs, chaperoning each other through the girls hurrying out to their offices in the bars and streets.

In the morning the well organised man from the shipping agents turned up and we went with him down to the docks. He advised us we had to pay some Customs dues that would release the vehicles that day, otherwise it would be five or six days before we saw them. Whilst not normally given to paying bribes, we decided it was cheaper to do so than pay for another week in the Hotel Pacifico, running the gauntlet of its coven of girls. More papers needed to be drawn up and collected and we followed the agent about the dock acquiring forms like a vacuum cleaner sucking up confetti after a wedding. Each piece of paper seemed to need at least one stamp on it, some having to have another to confirm the first stamp. I decided if ever I got stuck in Buenaventura I would open a business selling ink pads to the agents at the docks. Finally we went to the two vehicles which had been unloaded and were sitting on the quayside. Adolf had been broken into, the rope securing the canvass at the back having been cut. As far as we could see nothing had been stolen. The other Land Rover had collected a couple of dents but we all felt we had got away with it lightly, although Julian and John decided to put in a claim to Grace Lines for the damage. We left them to the painfully bureaucratic process and, with the sound of stamping forms ringing in our ears, went back to the Hotel to clear out our bags. Since we had not come down with botulism we returned to the cafe we had used the night before for another bowl of meaty soup. Our seat in the window gave us a grandstand view of a matinee performance of some street justice being administered as a policeman enthusiastically beat up an unfortunate transgressor of some petty crime, rendering him senseless on the pavement. People walked past them without taking any notice.

What is normal to each of us is a moveable feast, dependent on nuances of culture and quirks of geography. In the middle of London a single policeman belabouring a helpless individual would be unacceptable, but in a rough port on the coast of Colombia it didn't warrant a second glance. It did remind me of some policemen we had seen in Los Angeles when we were driving through the city. They had arrested a man who was clearly very drunk, so much so he was defenceless. He also seemed to be well past his prime in age and physique, hardly a threat to a child let alone a group of steroid enhanced police. They had made him 'assume the position' up against their van, hands on its side and feet spread wide. I saw one of the police then hit him in the crutch. The poor man dropped to the floor by the van and they picked him up and threw him into the back, slamming the doors before driving him off. Civilisation is a thin veneer, quickly stripped away by power, stress, fear and anger. We watched the show outside the cafe as we ate, sticking to our rule of not getting involved. We were a long way from home, and a long way from help. A two man crusade to inculcate what we felt were better values in people who would have no idea what we were proselytizing about was always going to be a waste of time, fraught with potentially unpleasant consequences for us.

By mid afternoon the bureaucracy had been completed and we were free to leave for the journey back to Cali. Setting off in convoy, we stopped after dark at a small cafe selling its fare by the road. Dim light fell across the road from its windows and open door. Parking side by side in front of the small building, we went in and sat at a rickety table. Flies flew in slow formation around the room, like drones looking for a target, dodging the two naked bulbs hanging on dusty wires from the ceiling. A couple of tables were occupied by men who gazed at us without expression. We ordered a meal and the cook produced his signature dish, a semi cooked chicken that had been quartered and served with rice. My portion consisted of the chicken's arse and some intestines as the anorexic bird had not been cleaned out properly when killed, with many of its tubes and unattractive bits still inside it, a novel form of stuffing. It reminded me of our meals when we were picking grapes in California, except there the intestines had been in a tin rather than in a chicken carcass. Being grateful for small mercies, I was pleased to see they had plucked the unfortunate bird before cooking it. Things can always be worse in life, no matter how dire the situation. Our meal finished, we settled down in the Land Rovers for the night. We decided to leave them outside the restaurant, aware we were under the vigilant gaze of a fast asleep night watchman who was stretched out on the ground. Clearly drunk when we arrived, he had been weaving around outside bouncing off obstacles, and now seemed to have given up the unequal struggle of staying upright.

The hung-over guard woke us early in the morning, for no reason we could divine. Since it spurred us into buying breakfast coffees in the restaurant, perhaps it was his idea of marketing for the owner to ameliorate his slightly reduced effectiveness the night before and thus save his job. As we set off on the road again, the first rays of dawn were lightening the eastern the sky with nature's palette of morning pastels. We had arranged to meet the others in Cali at the cafe we had used before leaving for Buenaventura, their instructions being to be there at mid-day each day until the day we arrived. Since it was not going to take that long to get to the city we decided to find a place where we could bathe. A river was tumbling over rocks next to the track in the forest and we found a convenient path down to its edge. We lit a fire and put a kettle of water on it to make coffee after we had washed. The spot we chose seemed to be the local ford as every now and again Colombians waded across, some with horses. We lay in the river, letting it wash over us, ducking our heads in it's cooling water. The tinkling sounds of the water mingled with the bird and monkey calls in the verdant forest around us. We drank our coffees as we stood around letting the warm air dry us off. Putting out the fire we left our washing place and as we came down from the mountain range into a large flat valley, we stopped in a small place called Dagua so Julian could buy some buns. He was clearly unused to a diet of coffee and was hungry. About five miles outside Cali we came upon a police checkpoint. Unknown to us at that moment, these police stops were to become ubiquitous throughout the South American countries ahead of us. Often in extremely remote spots, they seemed to provide the police manning them an entrepreneurial opportunity for some extra income or provisions. The rule of the road was 'he who has the gun makes the rules'. This checkpoint was no exception.

The checkpoint was a very small brick built room by the side of the road. From it a chain hung across the road to a metal post on the other side. There were two policemen in the room and as we drove up, they emerged into the daylight. Dressed in jungle green fatigues, each had a sub-machine gun on his shoulder, each gun with a grubby finger firmly on the trigger. They demanded our Passports and when we gave them to them, it quickly became apparent they must be illiterate. The Colombian entry stamp was square, but so was the British Honduran version. I watched as one of the policemen flicked through mine until he came to the British Honduran stamp with its out of date visa. He studied it for a while and then, satisfied my Passport was in order and I was not an unofficial visitor, he moved on to the next document. Having been through all four Passports, he handed them back to us, at which point we expected the chain to be lowered and to be waved on our way. While his colleague had been checking the paperwork, the other policeman had moved around to the back of Adolf, whose back canvas was rolled up. He was peering in and said to us he would like to 'buy' some things from us as a souvenir of our trip, after which we could go on. The chain was still firmly across the road, blocking our path. I lifted our mattress and extracted from under it a white busboy jacket I had been given when we had worked in the restaurant at the Los Angeles County Fair. I held it up for him to see, but he seemed a little disappointed at the state of it. Our storage arrangements had left it looking like a crumpled handkerchief that had been much used by a man with a very bad cold, emphasised by the dried food splattered all over it. At this point he spotted Julian's British Army combat jacket, identical to the one I had which was also stored under our mattress. This excited his interest and he pointed at it saying that was what he wanted. He offered forty pesos, the equivalent of $1.50. Considering he could have had it for nothing at the point of a barrel up the nostril, I was impressed, but Julian mentioned that it had cost him over $50 and he couldn't part with it as he needed it for his travelling. Whilst disappointed, the man eventually backed down, still looking into the vehicles to see if there was anything else he might want, but it appeared there was nothing that appealed to him so eventually he waved us through. This form of harassment and opportunist extortion is both universal and timeless and I still experience it to this day in Africa. The remoter the place the more assertive and sometimes aggressive the official in the absence of any witnesses.

We arrived at the chosen café at ten o'clock in the morning. As we settled down, the waitress came up to us and handed us a note the others had left with her. It said they had met the Honorary British Consul who had arranged for them to stay at the British School in Cali, the Colegio Colombo Británico. We found our way to it where the four others told us they had been cared for and indeed feted by the teachers and the pupils. The school offered us the use of some showers, after which the Consul arrived. Tall, elegant, mustachioed and pipe smoking, Arthur Lawrence was kindness personified. He had arrived by ship from England in 1927, landing at Buenaventura as an employee of the Bank of London and South America, and had never left. Having spent some of my formative years in India, I knew a true colonial when I saw one. Their lives and demeanour are often an exaggeration of what they remember 'society' to have been back home. They often become a pastiche of a memory they still hold, a relic of a time and a world that has passed them by and moved on. They have little understanding or knowledge of the new order until they return on leave or to retire. Disillusionment and a sense of no longer belonging are a common result of returning, as is the realisation they would have been better to have stayed in their adopted home, the only world they are comfortable with.

Not only kind but generous, Mr Lawrence took all eight of us to the sumptuous County Club where he plied us with drinks and a large meal. After lunch we swam in the club pool, no doubt polluting it as ingrained dirt from the road sloughed off our bodies into the water. There was a small hiatus to my afternoon of relaxation when I dived in and pulled out a young girl who I had noticed was out of her depth and going down for the third time, unnoticed by the dozing life guard. Her frightened parents wrapped her in a towel and hurried off with her.

Leaving the Club late in the afternoon, we followed our Honorary Consul back to his rather palatial house where he gave us all dinner and where we met his sons, Michael and Peter. They seemed unsurprised to have transient itinerants at the dinner table so perhaps the Consul's altruism to us was habitual and extended to all British travellers he came across. We drove back to the school for the night replete and contented, if somewhat uncomfortable in a post Christmas Day lunch sort of way after the unaccustomed quantity of food we had eaten.

Shortly after we got up early in the morning, the children started to arrive for their day at school and immediately accosted us with questions about England, our trip, our lives. Intelligent and inquisitive, they were fascinated by and about everything we were doing. After a while Julian and I left the others facing the inquisition and went into Cali to change money on the black market. The well connected Honorary Consul, who seemed to know everyone of importance or useful in the city, had given us the name of someone who would give us a good rate. François Dolmeneque lived up to his reputation with the best exchange rate we had found. As we left he asked us not to be waving money or travellers cheques about as we left him as what we were doing was illegal, which was rather stating the obvious.

After changing the money, we went to a couple of shops for some provisions and replacement items that had been stolen from Julian's vehicle at the docks, such as knives and forks. The rest of the day was spent having drinks and meals with people we had met in Cali and then spending the night again at the school before Sam and I set off early the following morning having said our farewells to our hosts and also to the English group. Taking on about thirty gallons of fuel and fourteen gallons of fresh water, we headed south on the road to the Ecuadorean border. About sixty five miles south of Cali we turned off the road and headed for Silvia. We had heard there was a busy market there on Tuesdays and since it was Tuesday it seemed too good an opportunity to miss our first South American market. Silvia was quite high and as we climbed up to its 2750 feet altitude the air temperature dropped.

The town was packed with people. South American Indians in colourful clothes, blue and red blankets wrapped around their shoulders against the cold, brimmed hats on their heads. Quechua Indian women walked through the town spinning wool from hand held spinners as they walked. With a handful of raw wool in one hand and the spinner in the other, they fed the wool through their rolling fingers to join the thread on the spinner. Giving it a sharp twist they would drop it to the floor like a yo-yo, turning the wool into a thread. Sheep and pigs were everywhere, all blissfully unaware of their grizzly fate. Some emerged from local busses with their owners. Women sat on the ground, their produce spread out colourfully on blankets before them. Fruit, vegetables, household goods, pots and pans. It was all there. Some stalls were selling food, and they had bare wooden trestle tables with bench seats where customers could eat communally. We sat at one and ate black pudding, a loose mixture of blood and rice, and then had a cup of coffee each. Having eaten at roadside cafes and stalls on the way down through Central America, our stomachs seemed safely immune to the microscopic and toxic wildlife that no doubt inhabited, indeed infested what we were eating.

After finishing our feast we drove back to Piedamo on the main road and took the road south to Popayán where we headed for the central square, the ubiquitous heart of all South American towns. When arranging to meet other travellers, all we had to do was give the name of a town or a village and an approximate date and say we would meet up in the central square. The first to arrive would wait a day or so either side of the agreed date and if the others did not turn up, would move on, or carry on waiting if they wanted. It was a very simple and effective system for socialising on the road and for co-ordinating everyone's fluid and flexible diaries diaries. The meetings were always fun and satisfied the very basic human need to meet a friendly face who understands the shared experience. Just north of Popayán we had been passed by a Canadian on a motorbike who shouted at us he would meet us in the usual place in the town ahead. When we got to Popayán we joined him sitting outside a cafe where we all had a cup of coffee as we chatted. Richard was on a three month sabbatical and was on a road trip on his bike down to Cape Horn and then back again to Toronto. He showed us the kidney belt he wore under his clothes to prevent his kidneys becoming dislodged from the intense battering all our bodies took on the appalling roads we drove and rode on.

Finishing our coffee we left Richard and drove out of the town, at the edge of which the tarmac ended and we hit the dusty, potholed and rutted dirt road. The road climbed and fell through forest covered mountains, each corner a hairpin where meeting a truck coming the other way often brought us nearer the edge of the road and existence than any sensible driver would want. Driving the often single track rough roads was tiring, not only from the physical exertion of negotiating Adolf through, over and into the peaks and troughs of the track, but from being constantly alert to the very real possibility of meeting an out of control truck or vehicle coming down the hill or around the next blind bend. On the hairpin sections we first began to experience the native dogs and their apparent hate of vehicles. They would chase us down the road, barking and trying to bite the tyres. If we were going down hill, at a certain point they would disappear over the edge. After we had been around the next hairpin, they would appear again at our ear level on the bank having gone straight down it to cut us off. The chase would then start again. If we were going uphill, they would reverse the process and keep meeting us in the road after each bend. This would carry on until they must have felt we were outside their territory when they would return home and lie in wait for the next intruder.

We learned to play them at their own game. Seeing one lying in the road ahead, whichever of us was driving would lean out of the window and bark at it. The response was always instantaneous as the semi-rabid beast would run alongside barking and jumping up. We would then steer Adolf closer and closer to the edge of the road. The enraged slavering dog, fixated on us, would not notice it was being pushed sideways. When the road disappeared from under its feet it too would disappear unexpectedly over the side, its eyes suddenly widening in alarm. They never seemed to suffer any harm as they were always there waiting for us on the next lower section of the road where hostilities would be engaged once more. Sometimes a gentle nudge in a dog's flank with the driver's door would speed the disappearing trick.

Early in the evening we stopped outside a cafe in a tiny village called La Union. The cafe offered us an extremely cheap meal which we ate before crawling into Adolf where she was parked outside the front door. We felt it was generally safer to stop by a shop, cafe, garage or house than out in the emptiness of the forests, although that was not always possible. The night was disturbed a couple of times, once by someone trying to open Adolf's bonnet and once by a hand coming in under the canvas side and feeling around in the dark for something to steal. Thwarted each time, in the bonnet's case by reason of the fact it was padlocked, whoever the intruder was left us in peace for the rest of the night. A breakfast coffee back in the cafe provided our jump leads for the start of the new day and then we were on our way south towards Pasto. The road was narrow, dusty and once again tortuous and slow.

Pasto gave us the opportunity to take on more petrol. Never knowing when we might find it, we took every opportunity to keep our fuel levels constantly topped up, following our belief that in the middle of nowhere security could be found in a full tank. In one very remote village in the Andes we found someone selling petrol, advertising the fact with a large sign outside their ramshackle home, which was no more than a hut. Taking us into his one roomed home, he pointed to a corner of the room where there were two large oil drums with loose lids on top of them. Lifting one of the lids we saw it was filled with petrol, which accounted for the fumes in the room. Filling a bucket a number of times and pouring the fuel into our petrol tanks via a large funnel, he sold his fuel by the bucket rather than by the litre. Wisely we saw no signs of a fire or cooking equipment in the hut so we assumed his catering was conducted elsewhere in the village. I wondered whether his neighbours realised the size of the potential explosion they lived next to.

The road improved after the town and as we pulled up a hill out of it we passed a battered, green and patently geriatric Volkswagen camper van with a sticker saying 'Alemania' on the back. Feeling we were far enough away from the hut called Armageddon to be safe, we stopped at the top of the hill to make a fire for some coffee, beckoning the VW camper to pull in behind us. Two young Germans got out to say hello. Bernhard and Adolf had been on the road two weeks longer than us. Their camper van was originally owned by the Berlin police and they had lost count of the number of times the odometer had been around the clock. The vehicle was about ten years old and looked in need of a great deal of affection and attentive care to keep it going. Similar to us in so many ways, we warmed to them immediately and arranged to meet up with them in a town called Ibarra about seventy miles south of the Ecuadorian border. We had already told Richard the Canadian motorcyclist we would see him there for a beer. Finishing our coffees we set off and quickly realised we had a puncture. As we stopped to change the wheel, Bernhard and Adolf sailed by, laughing at our irritating hiatus. Their helpfulness as they drove off down the road covering us in dust was remembered and became the cause of practical jokes on them throughout the rest of the trip, all of which were reciprocated. Bernhard and Adolf were to become good and close friends, a friendship that outlasted our odysseys and for me exists to this day.

When we got to the border, the Aduana were enjoying their siesta and were not to be disturbed. They eventually emerged, sleepy eyed, stretching and yawning and stamping our papers lethargically, letting us through without any difficulties. As we drove into Ecuador we picked up a couple of American hitch-hikers called Jenny and Larry and took them with us for the eighty or so miles to Ibarra. The road deteriorated once more, covering us and the inside of Adolf in dust. Parts of the road were old and still cobbled as many roads in Ecuador had been. Once again we were climbing and dropping, maneuvering around hairpin bends, all contriving to slow our progress. We reached Ibarra just after dark and headed for the central square. Jenny and Larry went off to book a hotel room and we sat and waited until Bernard and Adolf drove in, shortly followed by Richard. Before settling down for the night with both vehicles parked in a dimly lit back street, we all went to a cafe for a very cheap meal, the species of meat of which was a complete mystery to me.

The morning saw us on the road south again. We stopped about ten miles down the road to build a fire on which we cooked a group breakfast. As we did we were surrounded by local Indians, many of them with children to whom we gave small gifts of empty tins, some of our old much-folded maps and some spare scarves. They were thrilled with them, running around in excitement, their bare calloused feet kicking up pebbles and dust. Throughout South America I was constantly amazed at how the Quechua Indians were able to walk on their naked feet, which were always so cracked and dry and looked so painful. They not only walked on the dirt and gravel tracks and roads, with or without car tyre sandals, they dug the fields and covered many miles on them through the Andes in the cold and wet. As we drove on, the scenery around became arid and bare as we left the rain forests behind. The road was still a mass of contorted bends and at a small town called Otavalo we dropped off the American hitchhikers Jenny and Larry. Otavalo was under the shadow of Imbabura, an inactive volcano forming a link in a chain of volcanoes. It had not erupted for about fourteen thousand years but its past activity had created fertile land on its slopes and surrounding planes, all of which were heavily cultivated with sugarcane, maize and beans. Animals grazed the grasses of the high meadows. As with so much South American culture, myths and stories were linked to the volcano, which was believed to be a womanising god who protected the land, throwing huge rocks at enemies.

The road after Otavalo disappeared under a landslide of mud and rock. We climbed up onto the fall to see if we could get Adolf over it. A bulldozer was busy clearing a path through it so we sat and waited for it to break through to the other side. A further landslip meant a hurried exit in reverse for a Land Rover that was being mountaineered over the pile of rocks by its impatient driver. He engaged common sense and also chose to wait for the road to be cleared. Arriving in Quito we drove around its narrow streets and spent time walking in the Old City. The Hotel Intercontinental refused me entry when I walked up to them in my shorts, torn shirt and sandals. Robert Jagger had said he might be there on business but I found out he was not by sending in the concierge to ask for me while I stood on the steps. There were no letters waiting for us at the Central Post Office, our Ecuadorean poste restante, and so we set off again for Latacunga, sixty miles to the south, passing Cotopaxi on the way. At 5,897 metres it is the second highest mountain in Ecuador. It has a classic symmetrical cone topped with snow and it stood out in the plains looking down on us in awesome, imperious splendour. It was a beautiful and breathtaking sight and its affect on me was perhaps best described in a poem by W J Turner:-

> '.... and never a word I'd say
> Chimborazo, Cotopaxi
> Had taken my speech away.'

The only thing to do was to stand in silence and gaze at its beauty, as any words would only devalue the spectacle, surely one of the wonders of the world. Cotopaxi was still active and had erupted many times in the previous two hundred and fifty years. The Andean people revered it as the place where the gods lived, and as a rain maker that ensured the surrounding lands were fertile. Despite being almost on the Equator, Cotopaxi had a glacier on it, which perhaps presented the greatest risk to the people inhabiting the surrounding districts and lands in the event of an eruption. If the pyroclastic flow and any accompanying lahar didn't destroy everything we could see, the devastation from the melt water from the glacier would be immense, deluging the plains and obliterating Latacunga. As we moved on we realised we were driving up onto the altiplano which our altimeter told us was at about 3,400 metres. Whenever we were up in the high Andes I was reminded of Dartmoor, except on a grand scale. Hundreds of miles of rolling, undulating grasslands in every direction, with snow capped mountains providing a backing canvas in the far distance. Llama and vicuña were often to be seen dotting the landscape, and condors effortlessly drifted high above us, their enormous wings outstretched to catch and ride the thermals. The air was thin and we were slowly acclimatizing to being at altitude in the northern Andean ranges. Any physical exercise or exertion was an effort. Walking left us breathless and with slightly aching heads, slowing everything we did.

Committing the beauty of Cotopaxi to memory, we headed south once more, passing through the small towns of Ambato and then Riobamba, after which the road effectively disappeared, leaving us a dirt track to follow as we climbed up and down valleys with vertiginous slopes and aggressive dogs to play with. More dust and dirt swirled into Adolf and our hair felt as though it had been coiffed with cement. At about 3,600 metres we were in thick mist, and then the rain came. It turned the track into a Cresta Run that we slid and tobogganed on, trying to avoid sliding over the edge of the narrow track into the valleys below, testing our four wheel driving skills to their limits. Again the extreme narrowness of the road made getting past trucks and busses coming the other way an adrenaline filled adventure, at times with part of our offside tyres almost over the edge. Whichever of us was driving would hang our head out of the driver's window to be able to see the wheels to keep them on the road. Shortly after a small village called Azogues one of our back tyres blew out under the unequal struggle. The explosion was startling, particularly to me at the wheel and as we were travelling at some speed. We pulled over to inspect the damage and complete a rapid wheel change. With our philosophy of back ups we had two spare wheels and were well practiced at changing them.

Reaching a reasonable sized town called Cuenca late in the afternoon we found a garage where we asked if they could mend the tyre. They could not, but we spotted a place selling fuel and decided to top up our tanks. It was not like a normal garage in that we had to squeeze Adolf into a small courtyard large enough for one car. As had become commonplace, we were surrounded by about fifty curious onlookers who crowded into the courtyard with us. Whenever we stopped anywhere we immediately attracted huge attention, and this fuel stop was no exception. While Sam put in the petrol I walked around and stood at Adolf's back, chatting to the onlookers whilst making sure no thieving hands busied themselves among our possessions. As we left the town we spotted a large, whole pig lying in a fire on the other side of the road. A Quechua woman was squatting next to it pushing fruitlessly at its great bulk to make it roll over in the flames. We stopped and walked over to help her, heaving it onto its back to its tipping point, when gravity took over and rolled it onto its other side. She started disemboweling it and while she did, she cut strips of burnt skin off and handed us pieces, indicating we should eat our pourboire for having helped her. Ash encrusted crackling was something of a novelty, but the hair had been singed and burnt off so we chewed at it enthusiastically like porcine chewing gum. It's unique selling point was it was fresh.

Night was falling and so we set off again, still in heavy mist. About twenty miles south of Cuenca, in the middle of remote and thick forest and on little more than a muddy track, we came across an adobe hut by the side of the narrow trail. It had a primitive covered porch that ran the length of the front. There was a space in front of the porch that was just long enough to take Adolf so we pulled into it, close to the hut and leaving room on the track for any vehicle to pass, although we thought it unlikely there would be anyone out in the dark at that hour. As we pulled in, the occupants disgorged from the hut like ants evacuating a nest. The couple who lived there had ten sons, who seemed to be aged between twenty and one. Just to break the pattern, they also had two daughters sprinkled in the ragout of boys, perhaps civilising them slightly. The whole family lined up and stood on the porch looking at us. We asked if they minded if we parked in front of them for the night and they delightedly said they would welcome it, urging us to join them on the porch. The father disappeared into the hut and came out with a bottle of a clear liquid that could have been water but for a slightly oily residue on the side of the bottle as it splashed around in his waving hand.

Aguardiente is normally the name for brandy but in this case it was a home made brew of unidentifiable origin and about 100% proof in alcoholic content. With a flavour close to distilled kerosene, it was lethal, on the mind and the liver. Very soon everyone was drunk. In the psychedelic haze I was in, even the one year old who shuffled around on the floor banging into legs and broken down chairs was weaving an inebriated path. The family asked us to sing for them, which we did, and they responded with a rendition that would have put the Von Trapps in the shade, singing and dancing in the flickering candlelight on the creaking wooden porch. We opened Adolf's bonnet and rigged up our small interior light for them, giving them their first experience of electricity at their home as it shone its thin light onto the porch from its perch on our radio aerial. Eventually we all retired to our respective beds, the Indian family into the small hut and Sam and I to Adolf, feeling sure we each had more room to spread ourselves out in the back than the family did. Sleep came quickly followed by a night of surreal dreams fueled by the cocktail of jet fuel and pure alcohol we had been given.

The dawn light brought with it the sounds of the family stirring for the day's work. We got up and washed and then the mother gave us a delicious cup of coffee and some home made bread and goat's cheese for breakfast. So often, those with the least give the most. We said our grateful farewells as the older boys and father shouldered farming tools and disappeared into the forest behind the hut. We took to the slippery muddy track again and drove all day for the Peruvian border. The going was slow and difficult, the track often still only one vehicle wide and with drops of over a thousand feet into the valley below. After about one hundred miles we reached Loja where we found a '*Vulcanizadora*' capable of repairing the big hole in our punctured tyre. The border at Macara was a further one hundred difficult miles away so, with our mended tyre back on board we set off. As darkness fell, we stopped in a small town to ask directions at a bar full of men drinking. Armed with their instructions we left the town and took the small dirt road they had told us to take. After a while the road narrowed and the heavy forest vegetation crowded in on us on either side. Suddenly we came upon a huge snake lying across the path in front of us looking like a large log in our headlights. Despite braking hard, it was too late and we drove over the poor creature. We didn't stop to go back and ask it, naturally assuming it might be a little irritated, but we were sure it was probably an anaconda.

Carrying on, we suddenly realised we were being followed. Bright lights began to shine behind us through the trees and it dawned on us we had perhaps been set up by the men in the bar, who had sent us down a deserted blind alley and were now chasing us but not to share a drink with us. We accelerated to the limit that was safe on the rough track, but still they continued to catch up, their vehicle lights becoming brighter as they inexorably neared us. When their arrival seemed inevitable, we stopped to face them, jumping out of Adolf to look back down the track, and were surprised by an oncoming roaring sound and then a large train passing close by us, a huge headlight lighting the forest ahead of it. We had not been aware that we had been driving along the track next to a railway line, hidden in the trees on our left.

We turned off the track into a small valley, driving up the dry river bed and stopping out of sight of the road to build a fire with the abundant dry wood we found there. Getting a bit carried away, we continued to build the fire until it was more of a 5th November celebratory bonfire than a camp fire, and then sat on the ground to watch the blue and yellow flames leap in the night air and lick their way along the lengths of the large logs stacked on the pyre. The light from the fire flickered on the steep river banks about us and played up into the leaves of the riverine trees.

We arrived at the border at about ten o'clock in the morning. It was a Sunday, the 5th December and the tattered remnants of 1972 were slowly sifting through our fingers. The Aduana Nacional official was completely drunk, slumped on his desk, fast asleep. We woke him and helped him up and to the desk with the stamps for our Carnet for Adolf. Before he would stamp it he demanded $2 which we objected to. Ten minutes of haggling ensued, at the end of which we gave him £1 sterling in return for which he gave us 13 Sucres in change, unaware he had been fleeced on the exchange rate. He reached for his stamp, stamped the desk a couple of times as he missed the document and then finally hit the bulls eye of our Carnet. Armed with it we drove to the border post down the road. There the border officials refused to let us through unless we paid $2 each for exit stamps on the back of our green entry papers. Another argument and session of haggling started but they were resolute. It was particularly irritating to find out our drunk official back down the road was supposed to have organised the stamps for us so we had to go back to him.

Our inebriated friend was no longer at his desk so we went into the town and found him in a bar with a fresh drink in his hand, more incoherent than before. Needing money for the stamps he refused a traveller's cheque and took us around the corner to a black market money changer who was probably his brother. The money changer offered me a ridiculous rate of 56 Sucres to £1. When I refused and demanded 62 Sucres, the official rate, he flew into an affronted rage. A very short man, he began hopping up and down, gesticulating like a frog in a blender. Frothing and shouting he became more aggressive. I didn't react and instead calmly continued to demand 62. His histrionics subsided and he started to haggle. We finally settled at 60 and did our transaction.

Armed with the freshly harvested crop of money, Sam and I bought our stamps off the drunk and then returned to the border where we were greeted like Prodigal sons. The border officials did a cursory search of Adolf and on doing so, found two police whistles we had with us. Their eyes lit up and they said they would like to 'buy' them, buy being a euphemism for 'take' in South American official-speak. We said we wanted 50 Sucres each for them which they reluctantly accepted. Having parted with the money they were delighted with their new badges of office. We could imagine them blowing them at anyone who displeased them at the border post. We were quite happy with our $2 worth of Sucres as we had sold them at a profit. Any amount of money, no matter how small, was far more useful to us than the whistles, which we had not used once since leaving England. Where we were going, no one was going to hear them if we blew them.

The Customs officers told us we would have to get our Immigration stamps in our Passports in a town called Sullana, about a hundred miles south west of us and from what we had heard of the road ahead, over three hours drive away. The officers told us the offices in Sullana were closed as it was Sunday but they would be open at eight o'clock in the morning. Rather than sit at the border all day, we set off. The road to Sullana ran across an arid desert, flanked on our east by mountain ranges. It was in appalling condition, dry and dusty with rutted tracks and potholes to negotiate. Every half an hour or so we came across road checks. These were usually marked throughout South America by a chain hanging across the track with a small wooden hut in which would sit a disconsolate and usually illiterate man nursing a large gun. Sometimes the police manning these check points wanted a 'toll' to be paid, and sometimes they wanted a present, quite often articles of our clothing. After the third check of the day we came upon a small town in the desert where a market was taking place so we stopped and bought a couple of bread rolls and some mangos. There was also a fuel pump in the town so we took on board some petrol at the princely sum of eight pence per gallon.

Looking about us it became apparent all the men in the town seemed to be blind drunk, staggering about or unconscious on the road. We were to learn that Sunday was 'drunk day,' the occasion when the men would obliterate their senses and perhaps the reality of their harsh lives on whatever they had brewed or distilled that week, often chicha. Chicha is brewed throughout the Andes, and has been for millennia. The Incas used it in their religious festivals, drinking huge quantities. Generally made from maize, but not exclusively so, it has the colour and appeal of thick horse urine. Maize is allowed to germinate and is then boiled and fermented. In some places, instead of letting the maize germinate it is chewed to a pulp, spat out and then allowed to ferment. In this case the finished product has the colour and appeal of condensed horse urine with notes of spittle and, on the assumption there is not one toothbrush in the Andes, overarching hints of rotting teeth and recent meals. The germinated variety had more allure to us, but there was no way of telling which was which when looking at a glass full of the stuff. I marveled at the resilience of South American kidneys that could filter the concoction in the quantities these hardy men took on board.

Sunday also seemed to be 'beat husband day'. As we left the town a Quechua Indian man, still wearing his hat, lay comatose against a bank by the road while his wife thrashed him remorselessly with a piece of wood. Now and again he would wave his arm, and lift his head to look around, but generally he lay there being tenderised, inured to the pain by the anaesthetic properties of copious chicha. Another man, equally senselessly drunk but somehow impossibly upright, swayed like a palm tree in a hurricane, gesticulating and shouting at his pulverised friend. Perhaps he was extolling the virtues of a bachelor life. As I watched the woman taking out a lifetime of frustration on the pulp that was her husband, I wondered if this scene was being re-enacted throughout the Continent. Did all the men wake on Monday mornings assuming they had been in a fight with each other, or run over by a truck yet again? Did their wives resume their position of servility and subservience as they patiently waited six more days for their next chance to vent their true feelings through the medium and anonymity of the weekly workout? The harshness of Andean subsistence living was alien to our pampered lives. These people would walk for two or three days to market, sell their wares, drink themselves to the lip of their graves, take a beating and then spend two days walking back home. This cycle of their lives was repeated whenever they had any produce to sell.

As we drove out of the town, we followed a local Indian bus. Possessions were piled on the roof, teetering left and right as the bus lurched over the rough road. Like so many South American buses, this one was based on the chassis of an exhausted bus from America, onto which an enlarged body had been fitted. The South Americans obviously felt constrained by the inner dimensions of a normal sized bus and so they extended the bodies so they jutted out at least two feet each side, completely hiding the wheels somewhere underneath. Buses were usually filled to bursting with people, pigs, sheep, goats and chickens. Strapped to the back of this bus was a pig, like a letter on a green baize notice board tucked in behind a criss cross of restraining ribbon. Its legs dangled in the air beneath it. It seemed remarkably resigned to its fate, fatalistically peering into the distance and perhaps welcoming the freedom of the outside rather than coping with the Black Hole of Calcutta that was the inside of the vehicle. We passed the bus when it slowed to negotiate a pot hole resembling a bomb crater, and headed off into the desert once more, soon passing through another checkpoint with its somnambulant guardian letting down the chain for us. When dusk fell we pulled off the track and parked behind a copse of trees where we knew we would be hidden from the road. Hordes of mosquitos descended on us and we dived under the shelter of the mosquito net, spraying the inside with noxious fumes from our DDT supply. Interestingly, having established the toxicity of DDT on humans, the United States banned the general use of it in about 1972, but still allowed it to be exported it to other countries until as late as 1985. We regularly checked our heads lest it had the same defoliating properties as Agent Orange, the spray of choice in the Vietnam war.

After collecting our immigration stamps in Sullana the next day, we skirted around the eastern side of the desert to Piura, and then the villages Olmos and Motupe before reaching Chiclayo. As we travelled south through the desert, on tarmac for a change, the landscape and vegetation changed. Initially we drove through scrub and anorexic trees that were struggling for life in the harsh, barren environment. This slowly changed to rock and sand with the trees disappearing and grasses becoming sparse. We reached San Pedro de Lloc by the coast at dusk, some two hundred and twenty five miles from Sullana. The good road had let us get some decent mileage behind us in the day so we pulled off into the desert sands for the night. The sky was clear of clouds and we had a one hundred and eighty degree light show to gaze up into. The beauty of deserts at night with no light pollution is breathtaking. To stare into infinity and the endless reaches of space, bejeweled with stars, is humbling and as we sat on the sand by our fire, I was overwhelmed with a sense of man's inadequacy. I reflected on my agnosticism for contradictions whilst searching for the answer to the genesis of the panoply of wonders above my head.

We carefully bypassed Trujillo in the morning, having no great desire to go into Peru's fourth largest city, and headed on down to Chimbote where we hoped to try some anchovies. The cold Humboldt current off the shores of Peru created perfect breeding conditions for the humble anchoveta to feed in vast shoals on the algae that welled up in the ocean. The Peruvians processed these little fish into fishmeal in such quantities that the country was the world's largest producer. The overfishing had brought the stocks to the point of collapse and we wanted to taste some fresh anchovies before they disappeared completely. On the outskirts of Chimbote we could see the evidence of the great earthquake that killed about 70,000 people on 31st May 1970. Measuring 7.9 on the Richter scale, the epicentre was a mere fifteen miles offshore. 800,000 people were left homeless and the tremors could be felt in Lima, four hundred miles to the south. Landslides of rock and mud travelling at two hundred miles an hour hurtled down the western slopes of the Navado Huascarán mountain.

South of Chimbote the landscape turned from rocky desert to sand. The road came down to the coast and we drove along it with enormous horseshoe sand dunes on our left, some encroaching across the road so that it disappeared under the sand. To our right we passed miles of beaches and scalloped bays. The land was deserted and we saw no other human life for hours as we moved south. At one point, we drove about half a mile across the sand to a bay, stopping by the water's edge where we stripped off and bathed in the ocean under a clear blue sky and a hot sun. Once again, as had happened in Marble Canyon in Death Valley, we had an intense feeling of isolation, of what it might be like to be the only people alive in the wilderness, dependent on our wits for our survival. It was a beautiful moment, feeling at one with nature and the wild world about us. Somehow we fitted into it. Thousands of red crabs ran about the beach like a low moving red mist, swirling about on the sand. They rushed in and out with the waves as the water came up and down the beach, in perfect unison and synchronised with the water's movement. I climbed a hill at one end of the bay and looked down on it, and then inland to the sand dunes that disappeared into the distance. Adolf became a toy sized vehicle in the vastness of the desert beneath me.

For the rest of the day we drove through the seemingly boundless sandy desert, passing through Huarmey, Barranca and Huacho, finally reaching the outskirts of Lima at the end of the day. We stopped at a luxurious development of large and new looking houses by the sea shore. The properties spread up the hill from the beach and seemed to be devoid of life. There were no shops that we could see and it looked very much as though the properties were weekend houses for the wealthy of Lima. We parked in the shelter of a hedge and a large sand dune and Sam retreated to bed with a stomach ache as I climbed the dune and stood alone at the top, an onshore breeze in may face as I looked down on the empty beach. To stand alone in the world seemed a fitting end to a day during most of which we had not seen another human being.

The first thing we noticed as we drove into Lima in the morning was that everyone ignored red traffic lights, perhaps thinking they were pretty street decorations put up in anticipation of Christmas. We had been warned, both by fellow travellers and by the guide books, that Lima was probably one of the worst places in the world for driving. Given our Mexican experiences, we had been intrigued by these dire warnings, wondering how anything could be worse. We quickly found out as we dodged speeding vehicles driven by colour blind maniacs who turned every junction with traffic lights into a bumper car ride at a fairground. We were looking for the British Embassy, and found our way through the maelstrom to Washington Square where it was based, getting there by seven o'clock, long before our Government's representatives had got out of bed. We went to a small cafe for a cup of coffee and as we sat drinking it, a young couple in the cafe asked us if we were English and travelling. When we said we were, they insisted on buying us a breakfast each. It was a wonderful act of generosity and altruism, all the more so for its sheer unexpectedness.

Fortified by the surprise meal, we spent the rest of the morning at the Embassy where we picked up some Peruvian maps. There were no letters waiting for us, but we were able to read some English newspapers, getting news for the first time for months. Being the end of the year, the newspapers conducted their usual roundup of trivia and news from the preceding year. A candidate for quote of the year was by Arthur Bremer who had shot Presidential candidate Governor George Wallace in Laurel, Maryland, not killing him but crippling him for the rest of his life. Bremer was quoted as saying, *"Today I am one trillionth part of history,"* which made me wonder at his motives for the shooting. Self-aggrandizement seemed to me to be the most likely reason, which was later confirmed in his autobiography, An Assassin's Diary. His story was to inspire the Hollywood movie, Taxi Driver, and apparently also John Hinckley to try to assassinate President Reagan. The tendrils of influence on the troubled mind seem to have no time limit.

The newspapers also told us the civilian President of Honduras, Ramon Cruz, had just been overthrown by General Oswaldo Lopez who had led a bloody coup in 1963 that overthrew the then incumbent President, Ramón Villeda. Knowing we would be driving back up through Honduras on our way north we wondered what changes we would find. It was the decision to go back to the United States that started us on the task of finding and visiting shipping agents in Lima to enquire about the cost of shipping Adolf to Panama from Lima. We had pretty much decided we would probably return to the United States rather than try and get on a cargo ship to Australia, our original plan. Given the probability of returning north, our choice was between driving or a cargo ship. We were quoted about $400 for Adolf and $300 each for us by one or two shipping agents and quickly came to the conclusion that, at 8 pence a gallon and a meal every other day at best, it was going to be a lot cheaper for us to drive back to Colombia than to use a cargo ship. It might also be more fun. We had some way to go before having to decide so, with our business completed we decided to leave the city, driving into the night for a couple of hours before stopping for the night down a track just south of Chincha Alta.

The majestic Andes and the rolling expanse of the altiplano awaited us.

Sunday morning at the market and waiting for the weekly beating.

Public transport, South American style - typical of the buses we rode on.

A GIRL CALLED ADOLF

CHAPTER 11

South America - 1972-73

Christmas

'Defeat is not the worst of failures. Not to have tried is the true failure'
George Edward Woodberry

'Change your thoughts and you change your world'
Norman Vincent Peale

Having left Lima behind, our next objective was to drive up into the Andes to find Hacienda San Juan where Alain and Tildy, the Swiss couple we had met on the beach in Nicaragua were working. The ranch was about nineteen kilometres outside a small town called Ayaviri, in an area called Chuquibambilla. Setting off before first light, we drove south all day and into the night as far as Camana, four hundred miles from Chincha Alta, returning to hugging the beautiful, completely deserted and wonderfully litter free coast. Once more the road was regularly obliterated by the remorseless march of sand dunes across it as they tried to return home to the sea. At Camana we turned east and headed inland, climbing up into the Andean foothills until exhaustion got the better of us at about ten o'clock when we pulled off the road for the night. I was feeling somewhat unwell and wondered whether it had anything to do with the ceviche I had eaten earlier in the day.

We were well used to eating off the streets, not shy of buying food from street vendors and road side cafes. Our logic was this was one way of building up our immunity to the life we were leading and the environments we found ourselves in. We had stopped purifying our water many months before shortly after landing in Mexico, and regularly did battle with flies as we competed for food. Some food vendors walked around towns with heated trolleys on which would be cooking an unidentifiable mass of meat, sometimes showing remarkable canine origins. Feral dogs roamed everywhere in packs throughout the continent and we could see no reason why the indigenous population would shun them as a food source as they were both free and fresh. Wrapped in warm tortillas that had probably been rolled out on some woman's grubby bare thigh, they would successfully beat off hunger pangs and seemed a sensible source of protein. Guinea pigs were also eaten and most poor families would have a small herd of them running around the floor of the house or hut. Whenever we entered a small house with them in I was careful not to tread on one.

The large woman selling ceviche from a palm covered stall by the road took 'grubby' to new depths, even for a Quechua Indian. A tall once-white hat on her greasy hair, fat hands deeply ingrained with dirt and finger nails so full of dirt we could plant potatoes under them, she was a compost heap on legs. She wiped her hands on the top layer of her filthy skirts, which I felt would just make them dirtier, and then put pieces of the fish on cracked enamel plates. Garnished with bits of onion and the marinading liquid, the fish had a somewhat oleaginous, phlegmy texture. Flakes of the translucent flesh slipped down our throats like oysters. I handed over a couple of notes to pay for the food and they disappeared down the canyon of her cleavage from which she then extracted my change. The cleavage was the purse of choice for all poor South American women and notes became blackened and wafer thin from the body oils and filth they absorbed. It was sometimes impossible to make out a note's denomination but the locals seemed able to work it out and we had not had one refused.

Arriving in Arequipa early the next morning, I realised I definitely had a problem of the alimentary variety. On the Bristol scale I reckoned it probably registered critical to imminent. The town seemed strangely quiet with no one in the wide streets that were lined with old, large, and imposing houses and buildings.

With beads of sweat glistening on my forehead and vision blurred with concentration, I banged on a set of huge, carved wooden doors that on any other occasion I would have stood back from and admired. One of the doors swung open and a young boy stood looking at me curiously, my ashen leprous face obviously somewhat startling him. Muttering 'Baños por favor' and 'Estoy desesperado', I shuffled past him as best as legs joined at the knees allowed, and found myself interrupting morning assembly at a small school. The tall front doors opened onto an open courtyard in the middle of the building. All the children were lined up in rows under the blue sky, with a line of teachers in front of them. They looked bemused at the intrusion but were clearly unwilling to come too close, perhaps also telepathically understanding wretched need when they saw it. I asked for the baños once more and a few of the teachers waved their hands in the direction of the back corner of the courtyard, keen to avoid being in the path of the biblical deluge they somehow knew threatened to engulf them from the tsunami in their midst. A couple of the children were delegated to take me.

    The anxious looking pair led me through the closely packed children, who parted like the Red Sea before Moses to allow the unclean one through. They took me to another and much smaller open space that led off the courtyard where a couple of cubicles with saloon swing half doors lay waiting. Behind the doors were French style, hole in the ground toilets which I used with the fortissimo brio of a full symphony orchestra. It must have sounded as though the entire wind section was playing next to Niagara Falls. I was in awe of how much a body cavity can hold. They must have heard it in Lima. I was aware assembly no longer seemed to be happening. There was utter silence from the adjacent courtyard and I assumed they had all run for cover. Under the door I could see a row of small feet and legs as some of the pupils stood facing the cubicle. After a period of continuous volcanic activity I washed using a small pail of water, pulled up my shorts and emerged to be faced by the row of children, each of whom was holding a jug full of water. One by one they entered the ruins of the toilet and threw the water in to try and bring the little room back to a state of use. It looked as though a vengeful farmer had let fly, disgorging the contents of a full muck spreader, and I noticed they threw the water at the walls as well as the floor.

Turning, I saw that assembly was not over. The courtyard was still full of horrified looking children and teachers. I smiled thinly as I made my way back through them, saying thank you as I went whilst wondering whether the building would have to be condemned. The front door could not come soon enough and I slipped through it and back out into the anonymity of the street, uneasy at the feeling of nagging doubt that the little school incident was the end of my problem. Indeed it was not, and for the rest of the day my strides were short and my stops frequent as a problem that was to last for seven weeks took its firm hold.

As Sam strolled and I shuffled and minced through the town, our eyes began to stream with tears and our throats burned. We were by the University and we were told by other weeping passers by that the students had released some chemicals into the sewage system as a practical joke, one that had apparently got a bit out of hand. I wanted so much to believe this, but did wonder if what was in the sewage system and causing carnage was the result of my earlier efforts at the school, potentially a more toxic release than anything the students could come up with in their laboratories.

Arequipa was called the 'White City,' possibly because of the pearly white volcanic rock sillar that had been used to build many of the old churches and buildings. The city sits at the foot of El Misti, a perfectly shaped six thousand metre high volcano, and near the higher mountain, Chachani. The city was founded in the 1540s by the Spanish and was extensively damaged in 1600 by El Misti's eruption. It was rebuilt and became a major trading and cultural centre. The buildings in the city were beautiful and elegant, particularly in the Plaza des Armas with its huge Cathedral on one side and colonnades and arcades on the other three. The San Camilo Market near the Plaza housed stalls selling craft objects and artisan designed leatherwork and carvings, all of which seemed to be on offer at outrageous prices. With our anorexic wallets firmly in our pockets, we left the city to carry on up into the high mountains.

El Misti was now shrouded in mist and so we could only see its lower slopes, which we soon left behind as we slowly climbed in the thinning air, reaching an altitude of 4,693 metres above sea level as we went over the Alto de Toroya Pass. We were now back up in the altiplano. Bleak and barren with only the occasional groups of vicuña and llama to interrupt the barren landscape, the grassy plains rolled out before and around us, with the usual snow capped peaks in the distance adding to the sense of immense scale. Rounding a corner of the narrow dirt road, we came upon two llama mating in the middle of the road. I had never seen llama having an tender moment before, so was not sure if their chosen method was normal or whether the female was a reluctant participant. She was lying down on the ground with the struggling male on top of her, and they were in no hurry to finish, even though I assume they had never occupied their connubial bed with a Land Rover as an audience before. Our path was blocked as they refused to move, or perhaps were in such a state of ecstasy they were immobilised, so we had no option but to turn the engine off and watch the show until the final curtain when the two love birds got up and sauntered off stage.

We were now above the snow line and parts of the road were covered with drifting snow. We passed a lake called Lago Sallinas in which hundreds of flamingos were standing. We stopped to look at them and immediately they started walking away from us. A couple of solitary condors floated above our heads on the mountain updrafts. Black clouds rolled in over the mountains and a huge storm broke over us in the afternoon, turning the dirt road into a river. As dusk fell we rolled into a small place called Juayacil having spent the whole day at over 4,000 metres. We each had a slight headache and were short of breath as we had not had time to acclimatise to the altitude. We bought an extremely cheap meal in a cafe in the town and then spent a very cold night on a garage forecourt. Our sleeping bags were buried in Adolf and, tired from the long day's travel, we had decided to leave them there for the night, making do instead by sleeping fully clothed and wearing our boots and thick socks. Our attire turned out to be a poor substitute that guaranteed a night of simulating trying to sleep in a butcher's cold store. The sleeping bag idleness moment was something of a mistake as the temperature had plummeted in the thin mountain air.

Our first task in the dawn was to extract our cold weather clothes from Adolf and to put some of them on to try to get some heat into ourselves. As we did, we lit a fire to make some hot coffee, more to clutch the steaming mugs in our hands than to drink the hot caffeine. With our hands finally functioning and altitude thickening blood returned to our fingers, we set off again along the dirt road, passing through a police check point with its usual chain necklace, before arriving in the small town of Ayaviri about an hour later. With a small cathedral and a central square, Ayaviri was a typical Andean town, largely self-sufficient in its isolated remoteness. With large distances and bad roads between the high altitude towns, each created its own micro-economy and infrastructure. A church or cathedral always dominated a central square, and there were weekly markets, women walking through the town spinning wool, drunk men just spinning and always the feral dogs. Collectivos came and went, dodging people and their livestock. Collectivos were a form of taxi system between the remote towns and villages. Always decrepit, perpetually overfilled they could be a large open backed truck, a pick up truck or an apology for a car. The destinations they visited were usually painted on the front of their bonnet, listed as a series of towns and villages. They would drive up and down the same route each day, picking up and dropping off passengers. Would be customers stood by the side of the road and waited, there being no particular timetable. This was often in the middle of nowhere and people would walk many miles from their mud huts to get to the road, often carrying large loads of goods for market. As I was to discover, using collectivos was usually a leap of faith, a glimpse of the next life if there is one as the vehicles hurtled over the dirt roads, brakeless and with the driver often unsighted from the outside world as he lurked behind the multitude of cracks in the windscreen, the dust and filth from the rough roads coating the vehicles, as it did us in Adolf.

We drove through the dusty town and took the track north, heading for Chuquibambilla about nineteen kilometres away where we found Hacienda San Juan, standing isolated in the high grass plains. The farm was a large and old adobe building with a number of outbuildings. Alain and Tildy gave us a warm welcome, despite having no idea we were going to appear that day, nor indeed whether we would ever turn up. It was the 16th December and a month had passed since we had all shared a night on the Nicaraguan beach. There were about seven Swiss nationals working on the farm, which comprised about six thousand acres, some four hundred of which were set aside for arable produce. The rest was given over to cattle and sheep. We quickly settled into the farmhouse, eyeing the luxurious looking beds Tildy said we should use that would have been considered lumpy old rubbish heaps in our other lives in England. Dumping some bags in our room we headed back into

Ayaviri with Alain to visit a couple of shops and the hospital.

As a vet, Alain explained he was occasionally called by the local doctor to help in certain medical procedures, the most memorable being when he had to go in and perform a Caesarean on a woman because the doctor had never done one. Black magic was a dark art carried out by the local witch doctor in the town, who's most memorable cure was to rid a man of interminable headaches with the aid of a skinful of home made alcohol for both of them, followed by a six inch nail and a hammer for the patient. Apparently when he nailed the patient's head to the floor the headaches stopped, proving the witch doctor was right. The witch doctor was confident the man would not be taking his headaches into the afterlife with him, and we were confident no one in Ayaviri would ever complain of migraines in the foreseeable future. When we returned from the town we went on to a neighbouring farm for lunch. San Francisco was owned by Ben Amin who was completely drunk, as were all his Quechua farmhands and staff. Food and alcohol flowed, most of which I avoided as I continued to struggle with the ceviche moments my system was trying to master. At the end of lunch Ben Amin decided he would like to break a young horse.

Ben Amin was short, stocky, muscular and clearly made of kevlar. The unfortunate beast was dragged to the ranch house, a rope halter tight around its muzzle. Ben Amin took the end of the rope in one hand and leapt onto the horse's bare back with the agility of a gymnast. Outraged by this unaccustomed indignity, the horse erupted in a frenzy of equine gymnastics as it tried to rid itself of the considerable weight of Ben Amin. Without the comfort of a saddle or the aid of stirrups he somehow stuck to its bucking and rearing back like a limpet to a rock. Perhaps he was just too drunk to be dislodged but I think he had been born to the saddle and had lived his life in one. As the rope tightened around the horse's muzzle, he pulled the terrified animal's head to one side and the two of them pirouetted, pranced, leapt and lurched in wide circles in the dust before us. Blood started to seep from the rope burns on the animal's face, its hooves flailed and its back arched, and yet the youngster could not rid of itself of this naturally gifted rider. Eventually, and in a definable moment, its spirit seemed to break suddenly. It stood still, flanks heaving, sweating and hanging its head to the ground. After a few moments in which he seemed to be confirming and enforcing his dominant authority over the exhausted animal, Ben Amin swung a leg over its neck and dropped to the ground, weaving his way back to the ranch's verandah for another drink as the horse was led away to recover. Our introduction to a more robust way of life and indifferent attitude to animal husbandry was over. It was as brutal as it was callously effective. We could see that Alain did not approve of the treatment meted out to the poor horse, but deference to the local culture prevented him from saying anything.

For the next four days we busied ourselves on the farm. There was a rather masculine looking stallion called Pepe strutting his stuff in a large field and Tildy decided she would like to ride him. Unfortunately Pepe had not had a saddle on his back for about five months.

Pepe had few plans that included a saddle on his back for the following five months either. Pepe was a bit of a free spirit. Alain and I went into the field and, corralling him in a corner, caught him and put a halter on his head which Alain asked me to hold onto tightly while he put on the saddle. Pepe and I stood head to head, our eyes inches apart as the saddle was thrown over his back. He widened his eyes and snorted nasal dew all over my face. Alain reached under his belly for the girth, threaded it and pulled it tight, painfully pinching Pepe's skin under his stomach in the process. The irritated horse reared up onto his back legs. Since I had a good grip of the rope attached to the halter, I went up with him, still head to head but now about nine feet off the ground. My face got another shower from his flared nostrils. I managed to tuck my knees up to my chest to avoid his thrashing front legs and hooves as they flailed beneath me. The descent was as fast as the take off as we crashed back down but fortunately I managed to keep hold of him as he pranced around, tossing me around like a conker on the end of a piece of string.

We managed to calm what to me seemed to be a completely wild horse and Tildy mounted up and set off across the plains for her ride. She was clearly an accomplished horsewoman as Pepe succumbed to her more subtle and feminine style of horse management. Alain, obviously impressed at my horse handling skills, asked me to help him inject a horse that he was treating. The mare was a lovely grey and had some form of infection, because of which she was confined to a stable in one of the outbuildings. When we entered the building I could hear her whinny in alarm. As we got to her stable door, she backed into the far corner where she stood glaring and snorting over her shoulder whilst presenting us with the business end of her rear quarters that were equipped with what seemed to me a formidable array and choice of weaponry. She was obviously fully aware of what was about to happen.

Alain handed me a halter and asked me to go over to her to put it on, kindly opening the stable door for me and ushering me in. He equally thoughtfully shut the lower half of the door behind me so he could lean on it and watch the fun. After some general trotting around and chasing in the confined space of the stable, I caught the frightened horse and got the halter on, once again taking up my now familiar place at the animal's head whilst holding the rope. There was quite a lot more nostril emptying in my face and I was beginning to feel as though I had been in a car wash. From the safety of his position the other side of the stable door, Alain told me to grab the mare's upper lip in my left hand and to push my thumb and index finger up her nose as far as I could, and then to squeeze as hard as I could. As I did this the mare quietened and stood perfectly still, whilst rolling her eye which was about six inches from mine. It struck me as amazing just how big and how angry a horse's eye can get when it feels it is being abused. Little red blood vessels meandered over the yellowed whites of her eyeballs in which I could see my face reflected. When she had calmed, Alain came in, gave her the injection in her neck and then retreated out of the stable, shutting the door behind him and telling me I could now let go.

To me this was death wish fulfillment, equivalent to putting down a hand grenade with its ring out. Up there with letting go of a slightly piqued black mamba I had been poking in the eye with a sharp stick, letting go of that horse was madness. I gauged the distance between me and the door and realised it was going to be a close call. The anaesthetic and calming affects of twitching the mare seemed to be wearing off and she was becoming restless. I let go and, in the way of all comic magazine heroes, with one mighty bound was out of the stable and slamming the door behind me with the horse inches behind. I completed my equine encounters on the ranch with a ride on Pepe a couple of days later. He graciously took me exactly wherever he wanted to go in the wilderness of the altiplano, completely ignoring any instructions I gave him with my pummeling heels or my steering with the reins. Fortunately, when he became bored of his peregrinations, he headed for home, somehow knowing where it was, as it was out of sight over the horizon and I hadn't a clue. My focus had been on staying on board rather than where our meanderings had taken us in relation to the ranch.

With the cupboard temporarily bare and in need of an evening meal, we ventured out for a bit of duck hunting. One of the birds we shot inconveniently fell into a small lake. Unwilling to leave it to waste I took my boots, socks and trousers off and waded out into the freezing, waste deep water to retrieve it. One morning Alain and I were up before dawn and went deer hunting. There were no trees, shrubs or bushes in the altiplano, just rolling grasslands, so the fact we didn't see a deer may have had something to do with the fact they had probably seen us first. Lying in the grass behind a rocky outcrop on a small hill, a colourful little humming bird appeared and hovered just in front of me, seemingly inspecting me to see if I had nectar potential. It was a stunning moment, one of those chance wildlife encounters that leave one breathless at the beauty of nature.

The cow Alain asked me to help him artificially inseminate was also left quite breathless at the uninvited assault on her hindquarters and the darker corners of her uterus. With her head held in a metal crush, the unfortunate animal was trapped as she awaited her non-consensual sexual encounter. My job was to stand in the crush next to her and to grab and squeeze hard the flesh in the crook at the top of her back leg and her belly. Squeezing animal parts seemed to be an essential part of Swiss veterinary practice. Alain told me this was to stop her kicking him, unaware or uncaring that whilst her leg seemed incapable of flying backwards thanks to my firm grip, it was perfectly capable of going forwards. The deeply affronted beast took repeated kicks at my legs and delicate parts. Alain's foreplay consisted of pulling on a plastic glove that went from his hand to his armpit and then shoving his whole arm into the cow. From where I was standing it was difficult to tell which particular orifice Alain had chosen to climb into. The cow took another kick at me and bellowed at the impertinence of the invasion of her privacy. Wearing the cow like a huge wrist watch on his right arm, Alain proceeded to insert and slowly feed in a long plastic tube with his left hand. When he was happy it was in place, he injected semen from a phial into the exposed end of the tube that was miraculously untainted by the cow shit the enraged animal had been throwing at him. The tube was of course long given the cow's important reproductive bits were half a metre away from daylight, so Alain put the tube to his lips and blew the little chaps in the tube deep into the cow where they could rush about and hunt for eggs.

    The insemination was part of the breeding program the Swiss Government was funding to help improve the quality of the cattle in the region. The cows in the barn cursed the Swiss Government and gripped their knees together every time Alain appeared in the doorway with a lascivious leer on his face. Unfortunately the product of one of Alain's earlier conjugal visits with one of the cows had unexpectedly and suddenly died so we loaded the calf's carcass into the back of a pick-up and took it back to the ranch where Alain and I carried out a post mortem. We hauled the calf up by its back legs to hang from a bar outside the back door of the ranch, its head hanging a foot off the ground. Slitting open its belly, we pulled its intestines out into a wheelbarrow. I glanced at the yards of slippery tubes and speculated how many cans of Kal Kan Stew for dogs lay coiled next to me. We delved about in the organs, opening the heart and lungs, and generally rummaged around in the body cavity until Alain concluded the calf had died of heart failure, perhaps brought on by the altitude.

    A similar investigation of a pig that had died was memorable for the delicate scent of the inside of a pig. Whilst the calf had not been pleasant, it was Parisian perfume in comparison to the pig. We gave its severed head to a Quechua woman who went a few yards off from us and sat with it in her lap, scraping the coarse hair off its face with a knife before carrying it off to cook it. Alain and I also caught a large lamb from the ranch's flock of sheep for our supper. Its fleece was tainted where one part was a dark brown colour. Because he was trying to purify the flock, Alain wanted it culled so it could not breed and pass on the blemish. We drove out to the flock in a pick up, finding it a couple of miles across the open grasslands. The birth-marked lamb seemed to know instinctively we were there for it. It rushed into the depths of the large milling flock, desperately trying to hide its telltale birthmark in the melee. I had not realised quite how difficult it is to run through a bunch of fast moving sheep. It was rather like running the hundred metre hurdles when the hurdles are moving about and tangling with your legs. We finally caught the poor animal and took it back to the farm where we put it in a shed for the night. In the morning I held it still while Alain killed it with a humane killer. We butchered it immediately and cooked it that evening over an open fire in the yard. It was quite delicious, although as I tucked into its succulent flesh, I tried to put out of my mind my bumpy ride in the back of the pick-up the evening before as we drove across the plains with the lamb trapped in my arms, sitting in my lap on death row and looking up at me imploringly.

Over breakfast the next day Alain said he wanted to go and see a peasant living on the land farmed by the Swiss enterprise. Apparently the man's daughter was somewhat simple and was once again pregnant, thanks to the attentions of her father who seemed to be on a mission not to improve or diversify his family's genetic mix. We drove out across the empty altiplano until we came to a small, single roomed mud dwelling with a doorway in it so small anyone entering would have to bend double to pass through. The hut was roofed with grass and turf, was absolutely tiny and stood alone in the wilderness. The pregnant girl was there, probably aged in her late teens, tending a bubbling pot hanging over an open fire. There was no evidence of her first child and I assumed it was asleep in the hut. About half a mile away across the fields we could see her incestuous father as he tilled the soil. Alain called and waved at him but he refused to come over to us, obviously well aware why we were there and perhaps even ashamed of what he had done. There was no sign of a mother, so clearly the two of them eked out an existence in their minuscule shelter. There was nothing more for us to do but leave, knowing this was probably not the last time the girl would bear her father's child, which again would probably be the result of a drunken Sunday afternoon's return to the hut. In the afternoon we took a papyrus boat across the plains to a river so one of the Swiss workers could paddle it back to test it out. Sam, Alain and I then walked to the cows to watch them being milked before setting off for a flamingo festooned lake where we sat for a while watching the beautiful birds as they waded in the water, heads down in it feeding. The walk back from the lake to the farm entailed another trouser-less wading of a stream.

  Four days after arriving, Alain announced he was driving to the coast to collect a shipment of sheep for the ranch that were landing from a cargo ship so I got a lift from him to Juliaca, a town about sixty miles south of Ayaviri. Sam and I had decided it would be fun to see if we had any letters waiting for us at our next poste restante, the main post office in La Paz in Bolivia and I volunteered to go, eager for a little adventure alone. Alain dropped me off in the town and I walked through it and out on the road south to Puno. After walking along the dusty road for about twenty minutes a truck stopped and I jumped up into it. As we rounded a corner on a hill above Puno I caught my first view of Lake Titicaca. It was a beautiful, rich, deep blue, and it was enormous, with the now familiar backdrop of snow capped mountains behind it in the far distance. Islands were dotted about in the water and we occasionally passed reed boats beached on the lake's shores. Some were out on the water with men fishing from them or maneuvering them around. The truck finished its journey at Puno so I jumped down and walked through the town, picking up a lift from three Canadians in an old VW van that looked as though it had been attacked by men with hammers. They took me about twelve miles down the road to a small village on the lake shore called Chucuito, explaining that the van was in the state it was because they had rolled it over on one of the appalling roads we were all travelling on. They also told me of a new Bolivian ruling stating that all visitors had to have visas before entry into the country but I decided to carry on south for the border and to take my chances when I got there.

Half an hour along the road the other side of the village I got a lift from a couple of Peruvians in a small pick-up. The driver was a pastiche of a Mexican bandit, with a drooping Zapata moustache that hung luxuriantly down each side of his mouth. From what I could see, it also climbed half way up his thickly forested nostrils. He drove as only a maniac could, a bi-polar sufferer in a manic phase with his right foot flat on the floor and the vehicle always in the middle of the dirt road. If he saw another vehicle coming towards us he drove straight at it, forcing it to swerve off the road. Each time they did this he and his companion laughed hysterically, their game of chicken obviously a source of delight to them. Since they were patently breathing and alive, I assumed they had yet to lose a game. It was a bit late to wonder if we were going to break the run of luck that day. We ourselves were bouncing around in the cab as the truck ploughed into potholes and deep ruts. It soon became obvious both the driver and passenger were high on drugs of some sort and possessed of a burning death wish. Slipping and sliding on the loose dirt we finally pulled into a town called Ilave where they stopped and headed for a bar and I headed for the road out of town.

It was mid afternoon and I decided I would see if I could get one more lift before nightfall. I had two options for crossing the border into Bolivia. Yunguyo was on a small peninsular that jutted out into Lake Titicaca and crossing there would involve trying to get a boat across the lake after negotiating the border. The alternative was a more southerly crossing at Desaguardero. I had no preference for either but it soon became clear that driving was over for the day as there seemed to be no cars or trucks on the move. Since a hitched lift was unlikely to be on the agenda, I found a very cheap bus going to Yunguyo, passing through Juli and Pomata on the way. The bus was small, and very cramped as it was full. As with so many South American buses it was carrying twice the number of people it was designed for. The front seat had been taken out and replaced by a simple bench on which about ten people sat, one of whom was the driver. As the bus drove up to me and I stepped out in the road to stop it, it was impossible to tell which of the faces close to the cracked windscreen belonged to the driver. I hoped it wasn't the one with his eyes closed and forehead and nose pressed against the glass, drunk or fast asleep.

The bus stopped and as I got onto it, the driver and his assistant got out and taped the battery back into the engine compartment where it seemed to have become separated from the rusted shelf it was supposed to be sitting on. Yunguyo was about fifty miles away and the journey was made interminable by repeated stops to put water in the over-heating radiator, or to keep tightening up the nuts on one of the wheels. The thread on the nuts must have been stripped or damaged and without constant retightening, the wheel was going to come off. The passengers all took these stops in their stoic strides as they sat chewing on their anaesthetizing coca leaves. The ride was the more memorable for the views across the lake as we drove along its shoreline, and for the interesting rock formations we passed.

The journey was also unforgettable for the sheer discomfort of sitting in seats with leg room designed for those who live in the altiplano. The Quechua Indian population all tend to be about five foot tall, with barrel chests that give them a voluminous lung capacity in the rarified air. I had to assume a foetal position in my seat with my knees high and pressed against the seat in front of me, my feet dangling in mid air. We stopped briefly in

Juli, which was also know as Pequeña Roma, or Little Rome. It acquired its nickname because it is surrounded by seven large round shouldered and terraced hills. In earlier centuries the Jesuits had chosen Juli as a missionary training centre and their influence in the region was reflected in the churches they built in the town. The next town before Yunguyo was Pomata, notable for a large pink granite church, Santiago Apóstol which was built in 1763. For me the town was the more memorable for the sight of a Quechua woman walking along the street who suddenly stopped and squatted down in the middle of the road, her skirts now hiding her feet as they came down to the dusty ground. She stayed on her haunches for a few moments and then stood up, continuing on her way spinning wool as she went. In the middle of the street was a puddle leaching down into the dirt.

We reached Yunguyo some time after five o'clock as dusk was falling. I extracted myself from the womb of my seat, dragging my rucksack behind me like a placenta, and clambered off the bus bent almost double. Once on the side of the road I slowly straightened my cramped legs and back, which seemed to have taken on the form of a corkscrew. The border was about two kilometres outside the town so I set off for it on foot, only to find the Aduana closed and deserted. I was stuck in Yunguyo for the night and so I walked back into the small town in the dusk to try to find somewhere to spend the night, prepared for a sheltered doorway if necessary. Stopping people and going into a couple of cafes to ask if they knew of a pension, it quickly became clear the 'white man' was not welcome as I was met with hostility and indifference. This was not the first time I had come across this reaction to visitors in South America. When Sam and I drove through towns or villages, if we were on a dirt or gravel road we slowed down to reduce the dust cloud we created. Occasionally we would be following an American car that would not reduce its speed, covering everything and everyone in dust as it barreled through at speed, the offending drivers oblivious of the shaking fists and aggressive looks they left in their dust coated wake. We concluded that for these often uneducated people, all white men were Americans, or 'Gringos,' and all were universally detested for their sheer insensitivity.

There only seemed to be one place to stay, the Hotel Amazonas in the main plaza, a very basic hostel where they wanted 40 soles for a bed for the night, and 20 soles for a meal. I tried to haggle the price down but they remained resolute, confident the only other option open to me was the doorway plan. The bedroom was more of a dormitory with a number of beds in it, but the room and my bed were relatively clean, which was as surprising as it was appealing. I booked my bed and went to the dining area to eat, chatting to one or two locals during the meal. Unlike others I had met in the town, they were happy to engage with me, particularly when I explained I was British and not American. As we talked I could hear what sounded suspiciously like a chicken being executed in the yard at the back of the hostel, but one that was fighting back and making the executioner's job rather difficult. A final squawk followed by silence hinted the chicken had lost. I asked the hotel owner if he knew about the recent and new Bolivian visa requirements. He told me I could get the visas in Yunguyo from eight o'clock in the morning. Wondering if he was correct, I went to my bedroom where a couple of other men were preparing for their night's sleep. One of them was washing his money in the sink under its only tap, a cold one. Whilst South American paper currency was generally absolutely filthy, I could not see what he thought he was going to achieve by washing it, other than perhaps to destroy the notes once and for all.

I climbed somewhat wearily into the bed and was instantly reminded of school and the beds I had endured there for so many years. The mattress was stuffed with a course fibre, much like that which might come from a coconut. Sharp strands protruded through the fabric, pricking my skin when I moved. The mattress was so old a deep trough had developed in the middle of it, giving me the feeling of lying in a sarcophagus or coffin. I was particularly cramped as I had most of the contents of my small rucksack in the bed with me and under my body to prevent anything being stolen in the night. As always, my Passport was in its leather wallet on the belt around my waist. The sides of the furrow in the mattress were quite defined and steep and so the only realistic way of sleeping was wedged in it on my back. This was also the enforced position for the other occupants of the room who quickly slackened their lower jaws and got going with the snoring. It was like sleeping in the engine shed of a busy railway terminus. Occasional outbursts of flatulence broke the syncopated rhythm of their sibilations. When I wasn't listening to my sleeping companions I was being serenaded by drunken Peruvians in the street outside. It was as though the few bars in the town had synchronised their throwing out times at half hourly intervals throughout the night, so regular were the various tuneless arias and duets.

In the morning I discovered the hostel owner was quite right. I was indeed able to get my Bolivian visa in the village. I passed through the Peruvian Customs without any great difficulties, although I was expecting a hard time over my currency declaration, or rather, lack of it. In an effort to reduce the Black Market in foreign currency, the Government had imposed currency controls and when entering Peru we had to declare how much money we had on us. Of course, we lied but that was not the point. Reality bit home on exiting the country as the exit control wanted a declaration of how much was left. For the difference they wanted bank receipts showing how much had been cashed at the official rate for the time in the country. Sam and I had bought all our Peruvian currency on the Black Market in some dark alleyway of a town in Panama at a rate some fifty percent higher than the official rate In Peru, so obviously had not felt a great need to go into a bank. I had spent a few minutes in Puno looking for one with the idea of changing a small denomination traveller's cheque to show willing, but I could not find a bank open so gave up and carried on with my journey.

It was now time to face the music and I decided a bit of brazen blagging was my only option. Preparing the field of play seemed important and so I removed the currency declaration from my Passport before going into the Immigration offices. The Immigration officer cheerfully stamped my Passport and waved me through so I set off on foot for the border. About a mile down the road I came to a police control point and then a further half mile on the Customs post where the officer on duty asked for my Passport and for my currency declaration. I pointed to my exit stamp and told him I had shown the declaration to the Immigration officer who had cleared it and stamped my Passport. The official scratched his head, showering me in a fine mist of dandruff and sawdust, and eventually gave up the struggle of trying to work out what he was supposed to do. He gave my Passport another stamp and I set off again for Bolivia.

The Immigration post for Bolivia was in a small village called Copacabana which was about ten miles down the road. I walked to the village in the glorious sunshine with the blue waters of Lake Titicaca on my left, and was not passed by one car or truck the whole morning. Che Guevara and his iconic image, beret on his head and gazing into the distance, were for me a part of Bolivia's recent history and as I walked I imagined into existence his footsteps on similar rough roads, perhaps even this very one. His presence walked by my side as we took in the emptiness and harsh beauty of the landscape together. In 1965, with the revolution and political iconoclasm in Cuba complete, the new order entrenched, the population subjugated, Che left the country to export Fidel Castro's particular brand of communism. In 1966, with a small and inadequate guerrilla force, he tried to incite Bolivians to rebel and overthrow the Government, but without success. The CIA recruited Félix Rodriguez, a Cuban exile, to take a trained team to capture Che in Bolivia. He was captured in La Higuera, where he was caught whilst trying to persuade impoverished tin-miners to join his revolutionary army. It was Rodriguez, operating under his codename of Félix Ramos and posing as a Bolivian Army officer, who ordered his summary execution after interrogating him in October 1967. Rodriguez's orders were to take Guevara alive but he ignored them, personally telling him he was to be executed and telling the soldiers not to shoot him in the face so the wounds would appear to have been inflicted in battle. Guevara's last words to the soldier who shot him were reputed to have been "*Know this now, you are killing a man.*" In an act of final indignity, the Bolivian Army moved and hid his body, refusing to say whether they had buried him or cremated him, but they cut off his hands and preserved them in formaldehyde before sending them to Buenos Aires for fingerprinting to prove he had been killed.

Che received the same compassion and end he had meted out to so many in Cuba, so perhaps our sins do return to judge us. For the families of his victims, there was justice at last in his fitting end, a ruthless coda to his violent life. A symbol worldwide for the oppressed and the underclasses in their rebellion against the ruling class, his brutal ruthlessness was routinely glossed over. As I walked, I wondered whether he had been 'shopped' to the CIA in Bolivia by Castro himself, who must have looked at Che's popularity and power base in Cuba with some concern for his own welfare and position. Despite only knowing Che from his handsome face on the front of so many T shirts, the populist symbol of the coming generation kicking against the traces of establishment, I was fascinated by his life and the contradictions it held. The unforgiving savagery of the man was in stark contrast to his almost deified legend. It was a sobering thought to me as I walked the long dirt road to Copacabana to know I was in the land where he had died.

In as much as his life was an extreme symbol of the revolution against the old order the young of the late 1960's and early 1970's had taken part in, perhaps Che's death was a parenthetic close to that time, the herald of the beginning of the end of our own insurrection. Most of that generation that I belonged to came to conform with the little bijoux accessories of a mature, grown up life such as spouses, children and mortgages. As I walked I reflected on the adage that anyone under the age of twenty one who is not a socialist has no heart, and anyone over the age of twenty one who is still a socialist has no brain. And yet Che was intelligent, educated and from a privileged background so how and why did he not shake off the belief systems of the young? I was distracted by the landscape and his ethereal footfalls next to me until my thoughts faded as my attention turned to some grazing vicuña in the distance.

I had the blue sky, the sun, the road and the world entirely to myself, apart from at one point in the track where I spotted a farmer ploughing his field. As he walked behind his plough, his wife walked in front of it, straining against the harness that tethered her to it as she pulled it through the heavy soil. Poverty has many manifestations, and somehow this scene seemed to encapsulate the concept of subsistence at the limit, the appalling harshness of absolute impoverishment as nothing else I had ever seen had done. And yet the indomitable spirit of this couple, their fierce will to live, to scratch a living and a life out of the land was strangely uplifting, and to me quite inspirational. By our actions we acquire and give life lessons, often oblivious of the impact we have on others. Standing on the track quietly watching the couple stoically work their land I knew the image would always stay with me, a paean to the human spirit's ferocious will to survive and its ability to overcome overwhelming odds.

Further down the dusty road a large dog in the distance started barking and then began running at me at full speed. It was definitely not popping over to say a friendly hello and for a pat on the head. With nowhere to hide I was quickly reminded rabies was an ever present danger in Latin America and being bitten by a heavily salivating dog was not the outcome I was looking for in my walk. I picked up some rocks from the road and stood perfectly still, waiting for the dog as it continued its raucous charge. When it got to about five metres from me I suddenly shouted loudly and ran straight at it, hurling rocks at it as I did. Counter intuitive but effective as the dog skidded to a halt in a spray of pebbles and dust, then turned and ran, yelping and squealing. It watched me from a distance in the fields, glowering and occasionally barking at me as I carried on with my peregrinations.

The small village of Copacabana was on a lovely bay on the lake, the land behind rising to encircling hills. When I arrived at the village I quickly found the Immigration office where I had my Passport stamped before going to the bus station. It was clear there was little if any traffic on the road for this border crossing so I decided to catch a local bus for the one hundred mile, five hour journey to La Paz. There was a bus leaving just after mid-day for which the driver wanted the princely sum of $1, so I booked a seat and then killed some time by wandering around the narrow streets. The ubiquitous central square was dominated by a large and gaudy church, or basilica. Built in a Moorish style, it contained a gilt main altar which was surrounded by 17th and 18th century oil paintings. More hung on the walls in the sanctuary, some seeming to peer around large statues of saints that had been thoughtlessly plonked in front of them. In the midst of poverty sat untold wealth owned by the Catholic Church. As I walked around the cool interior I wondered how much could be done for the Indians living out their subsistence lives on the plains in the environs of the village if all the riches I was looking at could be put to more practical use. An acquisitive Church has amassed vast wealth worldwide, much of it at times donated by congregations that had little to give. Were misguided missionaries sent out to convert souls that were in truth looked on by Rome as cash cows to be milked for the Vatican's coffers?

So often religion exported from the developed world has formed an uneasy partnership with the beliefs of local people. Somehow the preached upon often seem to find a way of homogonising the ancient gods their ancestors had feared and worshiped with the more recent version of a celestial potentate the fervent evangalising missionaries brought with them. Those proselytizing zealots brought with them a God who to my knowledge no one has ever seen, expecting unquestioning faith and belief from the heathens in that invisible, alien being. From the time of the Crusades, missionaries and dogmatists have condemned the indigenous people, pagans harangued for their belief in idolatrous gods, often punishing or killing them for their worship. Why should the God the missionaries brought with them be any more believable than that or those of the indigenous natives? The irony, indeed hypocrisy of this illogical stance must surely have been lost on the evangelisers. I wonder if illiterate congregations choose the god of the moment, the one they feel most appropriate to their situation at the time of their need. They would not be the first to back more than one horse in the race of life.

Emerging from the basilica into the glorious sunshine I made my way to the Plaza Sucre where the bus to La Paz was waiting. Bags, cases and boxes were already piled precariously on its roof. In comparison to the previous day's bus this seemed to be positively luxurious. It was already nearly full so I took a spare aisle seat, which I discovered was a recliner, able to fall back a whole inch. Fairly soon all the seats were taken, and still the passengers came on. Arguments broke out as people waved tickets and demanded their allocated seats. The driver and his young assistant came on and started putting stools in the aisle. An irate passenger started yelling at me, indicating that I was in his seat and my reserved seat was one of the stools so we swapped places and I settled down for four to five hours of hell. The passengers seemed to have an aversion to fresh air as all the windows were closed. The heat in the bus moved from uncomfortable to stifling. In the seat just behind me was a large policeman wrapped in his tight fitting green uniform, which encased him like glaucous cling-film. He wore dark glasses, chewed gum noisily and sweated under his ill-fitting and slightly askew wig.

Once the overladen vehicle left the village I realised why it was known as the 'Sand Express'. Dust and sand blew up through the holes and splits in the floor such that at one stage I could only just make out the driver in his seat at the front. We were all soon covered in a yellowish film of dust, red eyes peering out of our masked faces. Looking around at the others I was reminded of photographs I had seen of hill tribe people in Papua New Guinea who cover themselves in white clay in preparation for ceremonies or canabalistic feast. The bus lurched and backfired along the track, repeatedly throwing us against each other like snooker balls. We passed a bus that had left Copacabana earlier than us, its head start gone to waste as it had broken down. All the passengers were out of it and were pushing it down the road, to where I could not fathom as there was no indication from my map that there was any habitation ahead. We arrived at the shores of Lake Titicaca where we all had to disembark and climb into two small, rusty motorboats that set off for the far side while the bus was driven onto a motorised floating platform. When the platform reached the far shore some of the passengers held it tightly into the bank to stop it drifting off as the bus drove off it onto dry land. We all climbed back on and set off again, leaving Lake Titicaca behind us after the village of Huarina, from where we drove out across the emptiness of the altiplano.

La Paz held a number of highest in the world records, including the highest seat of Government and highest commercial airport. The official capital of Bolivia is Sucre where the judiciary are centred but in 1898 the Government moved to La Paz. The site of the functioning capital of Bolivia was chosen by the Spanish in the 16th century when they were in the country on their quest for silver. Built in a huge canyon created by the Choqueyapu River, the city is some 400 metres below the lip above, sheltered from the freezing winds on the altiplano above. As we stopped at the rim I looked down through the dirt encrusted, cracked windows onto the city below, its suburbs climbing the slopes like soap bubbles up the side of a washing up bowl. It was a breathtaking sight, as was the 4000 metre altitude that starved my lungs of oxygen and left me feeling slightly light headed. Having paused to catch its breath like a high diver readying for the plunge, the geriatric bus lurched over the edge and we descended into the crater. We arrived at the centre in the Casco Viejo District, stopping in a plaza the guide book had said was one of the most dangerous parts of the city. For a continent where risk was a by-word for we nomadic free spirits, in a country where 'Revolution' was deemed the national pastime and where a lamp post used to hang a past President had its own army guard, the adjectival 'most dangerous' was not necessarily what I was hoping for as a description of my place of disembarkation.

The plaza and surrounding streets were packed with people and I took a few moments to work out whether they were there to celebrate something or to throw stones at the Government. It was the 21st December, Christmas was in sight and people were smiling or just going about their business so I concluded the crowds had come into the city from the surrounding suburbs and regions for the holiday festivals and festivities. It was late afternoon and the first priority was to find somewhere cheap to spend the night. The bus shelter would be free but the chance of being alive in the morning, or if alive still in possession of my meagre belongings, was slim. I started to wander the streets and dark side alleys, entering dozens of Pensions, hostels and little hotels, all of which were extremely unwelcoming and hostile, aggressively turning me away, dismissively saying they had no rooms. Again I felt that being 'white' and therefore probably American was a distinct disadvantage. I had resigned myself to the bus shelter option with its accompanying night of fun with the less savoury elements of the city's disenfranchised criminal class when finally the owner of the 'Gran Hotel' said he had a room for me. In truth, it resembled a prison cell but this time there was only one bed in the room. This had much to do with the fact you could hardly squeeze a pair of legs in between the bed and the wall, let alone anything else. The windowless oubliette came with a key and a chance of some security for the night so I took it and then went out again to stroll around the streets. There was a large market in a nearby plaza that was festooned with Christmas lights and decorations. There were so many people in it I was reminded of Trafalgar Square in London on New Year's eve. I found a dingy cafe near the square to have a cheap meal before going for a walk in the streets and then returning to my room for a night's sleep.

In the morning I walked to the British Embassy in Avenida Arce. I sat on a wall waiting for it to open and was entertained by a Bolivian Army band. It was entertaining because each band member seemed to be playing a different tune. The dictionary definition of cacophony is '*a harsh, discordant mixture of sounds*', derived from the Greek 'kakos' for bad and 'phõnẽ' for sound. If ever there was an appropriate word for a situation, cacophony was the one. The gig was made funnier by the sheer enthusiasm of each band member, each playing their chosen instrument as loudly as possible, to their own rhythm and beat, oblivious of the flapping arms of the man conducting them. Despite my tortured ears, I was rather sad to leave the merry little band when the Embassy finally opened. I quickly discovered the staff were in the habit of forwarding all poste restante mail to the Correo National, the central post office in Avenida Mariscal Santa Cruz, a mere one and a half miles away. Before setting off I asked to see the letters waiting to be sent there and found a letter for Sam in amongst the dozens in the box.

  Putting Sam's letter safely in my rucksack, I set off for the walk across the city through the busy streets. At the Post Office I was told there were no letters, with the hostile indifference I was becoming accustomed to in the country. I refused to believe this and found a girl who I persuaded to show me where the letters awaiting collection were kept. She took me to two large, grubby cardboard boxes on a shelf behind the counter that were filled with envelopes. Going through them both twice, I found two more for Sam which I retrieved. Given the inefficiency of the system, I looked on three letters found as a huge success. With the letters safely stowed in my backpack and my mission complete, I set off on the long trek out of the city.

The Immigration office was in Rio Seco outside La Paz, about six miles away. Half way up the canyon I managed to get a short lift from a couple in a large and ancient American car weighed down by chrome. They dropped me off at the top of the hill where I stood for a while on the canyon rim for another wonderful view of the city below me. After walking on for a couple of hours I reached the Control post where I had my Passport stamped and was told I would have to wait until late in the afternoon for a bus to the border. After asking every bus and car driver for a lift I finally found a one who was going to Desaguadero, the southerly border crossing I had not used on my way into the country. I jumped on and found the rusting vehicle so full of people and their possessions that for the first hour on the atrocious roads I had to stand before finding a space on the floor to sit. Again, there was so much dust floating in it that at times I could not see the far end of the bus. When we got to any incline, the young helper jumped out and ran next to the bus with a log for the wheel chocking maneuver I had first seen when going to Buenaventura to collect Adolf off the cargo ship from Panama. About ten miles from the border we stopped at Guaqui so the driver could take out the carburetor and strip it down, emptying the sludge that had accumulated in it. Repairs completed we set off again, reaching Desaguadero by sunset. I passed through Bolivian Immigration without any difficulty but then discovered the Peruvians had shut up and gone home so I set about finding somewhere to spend the night.

To say the choice of places to shelter was limited would be an understatement. Desaguadero was a small border town where little happened apart from travellers passing through to and from Peru. I found an alojamiento, or 'lodging,' and agreed a rate of about $1 for a bed for the night. I had slept in some pretty rough places on the trip but none quite plumbed the depths this alojamiento bottom fed in. The room was filthy, as were the three iron beds that were in it. There was no electricity so I could not make out whether there were any visible bedbugs, and since there was no soap in the wash basin I could not do the wet soap trick for collecting bugs and fleas off the sheet. I assumed there was a sheet. The side walls of the room were made from panels from plywood packing cases, the window had two of its four panes of glass missing and the door into the room did not shut. The door opened onto a creaking balcony that ran along the outside of the building, reached by a set of rickety wooden stairs from the enclosed yard below. There were a number of bedrooms leading off the balcony and they all appeared to be in the same decrepit state. The finishing touch to my room was the smell, whose genesis I could not fathom since it hovered somewhere between sewers, extra virgin urine and matured mould. Looking up at the whole structure from the yard I was amazed the place stood up as it looked on the point of collapse. I went for a walk around the town and bought a meal for $1, sitting at a table next to the Immigration officer who was friendly and said he would see me in the morning.

To minimise the time I spent in the bug-infested bed, I was up and away by five o'clock in the morning. The other beds in the room were occupied with snoring men, they having come in some time after I had gone to bed. It was too early for Immigration to be open so I sat at a stall in a market in the main plaza and had a cup of coffee. Coffee in the Andean villages usually consisted of a cup of hot water into which you poured a liquid coffee essence that sat on each table. The usual brand was Camp Coffee Essence and the more you poured the stronger the coffee became. It was usually mixed with chicory and always tasted disgusting, but its nerve jangling flavour was the most efficient wake up call Sam and I had come across. When the Immigration office opened I got my Passport stamped, made my untruthful financial declaration and set off on foot for Puno, a mere ninety miles away. After seven miles walking by the lake in the blazing sunshine I reached the next village. Zepita was a tiny place with a small square overlooked by a small police station. The next town on the road ahead was Pomata, some twenty miles away. It was by now very hot and I decided it would be more sensible to sit it out in Zepita and wait for a lift, even if it took a few days, rather than walk in the heat and run out of water. Zepita was on the shores of the lake where I could go and gather water but I could see from my map that after the village, the road ran away from the lakeshore and I would no longer have access to it. The sun and heat were brutal and the risk of dehydration high. No one had yet worked out that you could put free water in plastic bottles and sell it world wide and make a fortune. Puddles, streams, rivers and lakes were our water sources in times of need. I decided if no cars passed I would make the walk in the cool of the night so I sat down in the dust and stared back at the empty road from Desaguadero.

It was about ten o'clock when I sat down and at four thirty that afternoon I was still there when the third car to pass through the village that day stopped to give me a lift. The other two cars that had gone through had not been inclined to stop for me. I did not feel the time I had there was wasted as it gave me an opportunity to watch Andean village life in real time, and to receive unexpected gestures of kindness that reaffirmed my view that so often it is those who have the least who give the most. After I had been there a few hours, a policeman walked over from the police station and gave me four bananas. Before him a woman had offered me 5 soles. Whilst worth about 10 cents, for her it probably represented the cost of a meal for her family. The obvious inference to be drawn from this munificence and humbling generosity was that I looked like a destitute refugee. I had not showered or bathed since leaving the ranch to go to La Paz and was a sandy colour from the dust off the roads and in the vehicles I had been travelling in. My clothes were stiff from it and, whilst I had not seen a mirror for many days, I could imagine my eyes were red and bloodshot as they peered out of the panstick mask that coated my face. My hair and beard felt like doormats in a busy farmyard.

At about four thirty, as the sun dipped to the horizon and the temperature began to fall fast, I was on the point of walking over to the police station to ask if I could spend the night in one of their cells when a small pick-up came into the village. The driver agreed to take me to Juli, about forty miles down the road. I jumped into the open back and squatted down behind the cab to shelter from the cold wind. We passed a couple of vehicles coming the other way and I noticed the driver of the pick-up had the peculiar habit of looking over his shoulder after the other car had passed, peering back through the filthy back window just behind his head. Each time he did this we veered across into the middle of the road. The last time this happened there was a another car just behind the first, its driver's eyes wide like headlights when he saw our bonnet heading straight for him. I braced myself for the inevitable but our driver slalomed around the little problem. As we slid sideways down the road I watched the other car pass us with an inch to spare, and I ticked off in my diary of life another life used up, perhaps even two. I have no idea whether I have more lives than a cat, but at that moment was pretty sure I had overdrawn my allocation. We reached Juli as the sun disappeared leaving a fire-lit sky in its trail. I climbed out of the back of the pick-up, thanked the driver and found an alojamiento that was marginally cleaner than the one in Desaguardero but this time with five beds in the room. It was cold so I rolled my sleeping bag out on the bed and slept in that, hoping the built in ground sheet the Army had so thoughtfully sewn into the bottom would be impenetrable to bed-bugs.

I caught my first lift at five thirty the next morning. It was Christmas Eve, a Sunday and the large open backed truck was heading for the market in Ilave, acting like a giant taxi as it picked up Indians on the road, each laden with produce. It was dark and bitterly cold as we all stood in the back but we made the town without incident, which was a novelty. My fellow passengers seemed to be fascinated by my sandals, the indefatigable leather ones with the Goodyear soles. Whilst many

Indians wore sandals made out of tyres, if they wore anything at all on their feet, none we had seen in South America had leather uppers and this group were no exception. Even though mine were beaten up, abused and in need of a re-tread, as far as the others in the truck were concerned they carried the Lobb's of St James' imprimatur, leaving me feeling quite the Beau Brummell and dandy of the group.

When we got to Ilave I walked through the town and got another lift from another small pick-up. There were four people sitting in a cab built for two. The driver gestured for me to get in, to be the fifth. Strange as this seemed, it was the preferred option. I calculated the back of the pick-up measured about three metres by two metres. I counted thirty four Indians in it, with their belongings. It was so overladen the top of the vehicle's wheels were hidden inside the wheel arches. My four companions in the cab were a cheerful bunch, happy to chat as we bowled along the road. We slid around on the dirt and gravel, almost bouncing the small party of thirty four in the back out of the vehicle whenever we hit a pot hole.

I was dropped off in a village called Acora where I managed to get yet another lift from three young men in an old white estate car. I climbed in the back and as we set off, I looked into the luggage area behind and threw my backpack over the seat. It landed on a canvas sack, which leapt up and started running around grunting and squealing. The pig inside it obviously objected to being woken up by being hit by a rucksack. Its presence answered one question that had troubled me as I had climbed in, and that was the origin of the appalling smell in the car, an odour the three occupants seemed to be oblivious of. The terrified animal seemed to have released a tsunami of porcine slurry that might have added much to the nitrogen cycle in some vegetable patch, but added little to the fragrance in the car. When I first got in I thought the three occupants had been farting to their hearts' content. Indeed, I wished they had and that they would continue as it might have toned the smell down a bit in the way of all pomanders. I got out of the car at Puno, conscious I was almost certainly an object of delicious attraction to the town flies.

My next lift took me to Juliaca which meant I was about seventy miles from San Juan, the ranch. The sky was cloudless again and it was mid-morning so once more the heat was intense. I walked out of Puno for about a mile and once more, because of the burning sun, I sat down by the empty road and pulled my jacket over my head to make a sun shade as I waited for a vehicle heading north. At two thirty in the afternoon a collectivo came along. From the destinations written on its bonnet I could see it was going to Ayaviri. I negotiated an acceptable price for the journey to the farm and climbed in to join two Brazilian men and two American women, one of whom appeared to be sucking on a bitter aloes. Perhaps she felt four of us squashed into the back was slightly excessive. For my part, in comparison to what I had become used to, it was positively palatial with room for us all to spread ourselves about. We set off, the unhinged bonnet bouncing up and down, the cracked windscreen creaking, the complaining suspension groaning and grating beneath us and the irritated American woman grunting her displeasure next to me.

About twenty miles short of Ayaviri we stopped in a village to negotiate a Christmas festival where the inhabitants had dressed in fiendish masks and costumes and were parading and dancing in the street. When the crowd had passed us the car pleaded for the Last Rites and came to a stop in a state of extremis. The engine was ominously silent and I also noticed oil was leaking profusely out of the seal in the middle of one of the back wheels, weeping like a stressed elephant's temporal gland. The Brazilians remained remarkably cheerful for the next hour or so as the driver and I plunged headfirst into the engine. We took the back wheel off to try and reposition what was left of the seal. I replaced the wheel, gambling that with just over twenty miles to go the car would reach the farm before the wheel overheated and seized completely. The grumpy American woman became increasingly morose and now appeared to have swapped the aloes for an irritated scorpion as something on which to chew. The driver and I ignored her and finally got the heap started, the engine purring like a tin can with a handful of pebbles in it being shaken. We all jumped in and set off before the engine stopped again. We dropped the others off in Ayaviri so they could find somewhere to stay for the night and then carried on for the final twelve miles or so to the ranch.

When we found it, night had fallen and it was pitch dark, as was the ranch. I walked down to it from the road and across the yard, letting myself into the deserted house. There was a note on the kitchen table from the others saying they had taken off to the high mountains for Christmas. There was no heating so I lit the open fire in the main living area, using dried cow dung for fuel as usual. While that started to warm the immediate area around it I went and had a cold shower to try to remove five days of travel from my hair and body. There was a tiny bit of food in the kitchen which I ate, after which I settled down in front of the fire to start reading 'The Godfather.' When the fire could no longer warm me I retreated to my bed fully clothed to try to get warm under the bedclothes.

Christmas Day arrived in the morning in the silent house. I was engrossed in my book and read it all day in the silent house, uncertain when and if the others would return. After having been on the road living on my wits for five days, I was glad of a day off in front of the fire. In the middle of the day an extremely drunk and incoherent Quechua Indian appeared with a plate of food for me. He spoke no Spanish and I did not speak Quechua so it was hard to strike up a relationship in the two minutes he was there. I wondered if he had been coming in every day with the same plate of food in case I was back. My Andean rechauffe dish seemed to be like lamb, but equally there were many llamas around, so I had no idea what it was. I wasn't too worried about its ingredients as it was very welcome. As dark fell the others finally returned from their stay up above the snow line. There were sixteen for supper, so a group of us co-operated in the kitchen to make a stew that was for me a banquet. Wine and beer flowed and it was well past midnight when the last one standing fell into bed.

Santa sailed over the ranch that night without a stop. No one minded as he was superfluous to the fun.

A GIRL CALLED ADOLF

CHAPTER 12

South America - 1972-73

A New Year and Machu Picchu to Buenos Aires

"It's not what you look at that matters, it's what you see."

Henry David Thoreau

"Keep your face always toward the sunshine - and shadows will fall behind you."

Walt Whitman

On the 27th December Sam and I walked out from the farm to the road to try to hitch our way to Cuzco, the launching point for the mysterious, nigh mythical Inca city, Machu Picchu. Not one vehicle passed, amplifying the isolation of the ranch, so the next day we went into Ayaviri and caught the 'San Cristobal' bus. Picking up passengers on the way, most just standing by the road in the middle of the barren altiplano, it soon became extremely overcrowded. Sam and I were jammed in the back seat with a drunken Indian between us. He had a bulging and rather smelly shawl draped around his shoulders. His bus ticket was stuck to his lower lip, where it hung limply for the whole journey of sixty miles to Sicuani. To this day, when I enter a public car park and reach through the window to take a ticket from the machine, I hang it off my lower lip as I drive around looking for a parking space, and as I do I think of that young Indian all those years ago. I wonder whether he is still alive and reflect on how different our lives and life experiences have been.

Half way to Cuzco he decided to show me the produce he was taking to market. Swinging the shawl off his back he dropped it in my lap and opened it to reveal half a sheep. Clearly the half of bleeding carcass he was showing me was quite dead, and I assumed the rest of it was too, wherever he had left it. We admired and caressed the front end of the dead sheep together, swatting the swarm of persistent flies that repeatedly descended on it for a banquet. His affection for the dead half animal on my lap bordered on the uxorious and I wondered whether his relationship with it when it was gamboling in the fields had been entirely platonic.

Just after a small village called Combapata the bus driver pulled out to overtake an old truck that was gasping its way along the dirt road. On those occasions I had been able to see through the crush of bodies in the bus and see our driver turn his steering wheel, it seemed he had to turn it a full half circle either way before the bus responded. It was very much like the delay in a yacht's response to a turn on the tiller, so we had been tacking merrily from side to side on the road since we left Ayaviri. As we drew level with the truck, our driver gybed straight into its side, throwing four extremely drunk musicians standing in the aisle onto the passengers seated around them, their instruments hitting some of their fellow travellers in the head. A huge argument ensued between the two drivers and between the mildly bruised but affronted passengers and the innocent musicians,. The cacophony was embellished with contributions from everyone else. Unfortunately for the truck driver, one of our companions on the bus was a policeman. With his shirt buttons straining against the unequal struggle of holding back his bulging stomach, he ordered both vehicles back to Combapata. When we got to the village square we all disembarked and watched as he took copious notes, harangued and blamed the innocent truck driver for the accident, presumably meting out some punishment, and then got back on board so we could continue our meandering journey, leaving the truck driver to deal with the arbitrary injustice of South American policing. A guilty bus driver would have delayed the policeman from getting home, or perhaps he was just the bus driver's cousin, so his one man kangaroo court added a portion of self interest with its justice. He who makes the rules in life controls the game. It helps to have a gun on your hip of course.

The bus wheezed into Cuzco late in the afternoon and we wandered through the unspoiled old town until we found a small alojamiento in a narrow back street. The Alojamiento Purcadores had a room available with a couple of bunk beds, little evidence of wild life roaming the sheets and a door that locked. Compared to the alojamientos I had used when hitching to La Paz, the Cuzco offering was Claridges, a good base for our time in the town. It was the 29th December and we planned on heading for Machu Picchu on the 2nd January when the train service to the iconic Inca city would recommence after the New Year holiday. For the next three days we explored the streets of Cuzco, marveling at the skill of the Incas with their perfect stonework, which for me reached its apogee in Calle Hatunramiyoc, the *'Calle de piedra de los doce angulos'*, close to the Plaza de Armas. It was a narrow cobbled street that first climbed from the main square and before dropping down towards the Plaza San Bas area of the town. One side of the street was an Inca wall built with tight fitting and big stones, one of which was massive and with twelve angles in it. The joints in the stonework were so tight a cigarette paper could not fit between adjacent blocks, a phenomenon that was to be repeated wherever we saw the legacy of those long dead stonemasons.

Cuzco was founded in about 1100 and later taken over by the Spanish who built their dwellings on top of the Inca walls and foundations. We visited markets where we haggled and bargained for clothes, something we noticed American tourists did not do as they unquestioningly paid the asking price for everything. Taking a leaf out of the Quechua marketing handbook, I bought an alpaca wool sweater in one market for 135 soles which Sam sold later that morning to an American woman for 970 soles. The mists of time have faded the memory of whether I bought the sweater for myself. One morning we climbed up to Sacsayhuaman, the ancient Inca ceremonial grounds on a hill above the town. The central square in the ruins, Chuquipampa, was bounded on one side by three huge Inca-built ramparts, nearly four hundred metres in length, with linteled doorways and some stones larger than those found at Stonehenge. Again, the stones fitted perfectly and no mortar was used in the construction. On the other side of the central square was an angled rock face smoothed by ice. There were three wide shallow troughs down it that made slides, the Rodadero, assumed to have been used by Inca children and as channels for beer to flow down during ceremonies.

With the New Year imminent, fellow travellers we had met on the road started to arrive in the town until there were twenty or more of us, all keeping to the loose arrangement we had variously made that we would all gather in Cuzco for the start of 1973. Our evenings were spent in bars, drinking local beer with a multi-national group of nomads whilst swapping stories of our respective journeys and mishaps. Australians, Canadians, English, Germans; once again at one of our intermittent gatherings it seemed every corner of the earth was represented. On New Year's Eve Sam and I rose before dawn and dragged one of the German's out of his bed to come with us to Pisac, about thirty kilometres north east of Cuzco. To get there we hitched a ride in the back of a truck that was working as a collectivo, taking dozens of Indians with their produce to the weekly Sunday market in Pisac. The village was tiny and built close by the Rio Vilcanota on the floor of a steep sided valley. As we rounded a corner on the narrow track high above the valley, the little village appeared far beneath us. The old Inca terraces stretched up the other side of the valley, reaching their zenith at the Inca fortress that dominated the skyline. After spending some time in the market in the village, the three of us climbed up the terraces to the top of the hill. Each terrace wall was two to three metres tall and the flat terraces themselves about four metres deep. There were many of them but the view from the remarkably well preserved fortress at the top down into the valley floor was spectacular, making the effort of the climb worthwhile. Leaving the others I carried on up to the top of the mountain and then walked along a narrow ridge to take in the scenery. The way down the back side of the mountain took me around its shoulder and through a five metre tunnel carved through the rock. Picking up the others we returned down to the village, arriving back in the market four hours after starting the climb and in time to pick up a collectivo back to Cuzco.

The New Year was seen in by a large group of us up in the ruins of Sacsayhuaman. We built a very large camp fire in the central square and sat around it trying to keep warm in the cold night air as we drank the many bottles of beer we had brought up with us. It was an eclectic party of youth from around the world. Someone played a guitar, others sang songs and some of us slid down the old Inca slides on the rock face. Some time in the early hours I lay down on the ground by the fire and fell asleep in its warmth, mainly because my feet were in it, something I discovered when I woke in the early dawn soaked by a heavy dew and with my trouser legs scorched by the embers. It was a novel place to start a new year. The last month seemed to have been a busy one on the world stage. With no international news available to us, we generally had absolutely no idea what was going on, but we had heard from others that two more American astronauts had landed on the moon, presumably to give a parking ticket to the illegally parked Lunar Roving Vehicle taken to the moon by the previous mission, Apollo 16. Harry Truman, the ex-President of the United States died and on Christmas Day the capital of Nicaragua, Managua, had been leveled by a huge earthquake with two-thirds of the buildings there destroyed. It was sobering to think we had driven through the city just weeks before.

On the 2nd January Sam and I caught the Indian train to Machu Picchu, shunning the significantly more expensive and less interesting tourist train with all its comforts and speed. We joined the mad rush for seats on the train and settled onto the unforgivingly uncomfortable wooden benches for the slow journey. The train was full of Indians returning to the many small settlements in the remote areas east of Cuzco. Young children sat on piles of produce that had been bought at the markets in the town and adults and children sat on the floor in the aisle of the aged carriage. A family sat crammed on the bench opposite me, our knees touching. One of them, a small boy about five years old, stared balefully and expressionlessly at me as he sucked and chewed on an albino-white chicken's foot. Whilst there were a number of live chickens in the carriage, clasped under restraining armpits, the owner of the foot being masticated in front of me was no longer attached to it, implying a somewhat sticky end for the poor creature. The boy's sibling was breast feeding, a common sight throughout South America, sometimes with children as old as four.

The train pulled out of the station and switch-backed backwards and forwards up the hill out of the town before heading north through Huarocondo to the Urubamba River near Ollantaytambo in the Sacred Valley. The river raged in spate next to us as we followed the valley floor, at times with the high mountains pressing in on us on either side. We would emerge from these misty, steep sided gorges into the wide spaces of the expansive valley, passing small isolated farmhouses in the rolling fields and grasslands and through tiny villages. The river next to us meandered back and forth, at times running peacefully and silently with hardly a ripple on its surface and at other times a boiling rage of rapids leaping over fallen rocks.

The train stopped regularly to put down and take on passengers. At each stop food and drink sellers stood by the open windows of the carriages offering up trays of food or chicha beer. We bought one or two small snacks, selecting the least filthy looking ones. As I was eating one a look of panic came on the mother opposite me. She detached the baby from her breast and, with one hand under its chest and stomach, pushed it face down out of the open window, its face into the wind and backside pointing back at Cuzco, at which it proceeded to defecate, copiously. For some reason the woman held a piece of rolled up cloth against the child's erupting backside. Whilst this simple act of desperation saved the side of the train and me sitting next to the window from a coating, its unintended consequence was to push a tsunami of the stuff up over the squawking infant's back. The child chewing the chicken's foot next to his mother continued to stare at me unblinkingly, taking the baby's novel if somewhat involuntary toiletry habits in his stride. This seemed to me to be a good time to go out on the open steps of the train, which had no doors into the carriages, and from there to climb up onto the roof where I sat alone with the wind and smoke from the steam engine in my face. At one point the train slowed to negotiate a small and recent landslide that had covered the track in mud and water. I climbed down and sat on the outside steps and watched the track and part of the carriage's wheels disappear into the mud as we slowly and resolutely negotiated a hazard that in England would have brought the entire rail system to a halt.

About two kilometres short of Machu Picchu, we alighted at a tiny place called Aguas Calientes where the track had a few grass huts next to it, forming a miniature hamlet. We tried to cross the river to look for the start of a trail we had heard would take us up the mountains and into the ruins via Wiñay Wayna, another Inca ruin close to and above Machu Picchu itself. Despite searching we could not find the trail and there was no one to ask about it so instead we came back onto the track and walked to Machu Picchu station through dripping tunnels carved through the rock of the mountains that soared up on our right. At Machu Picchu station we crossed over the river and climbed up to the ruins, a climb of on hour. We alternately followed the multi-hairpin dirt road to the top, over which bright blue mini-busses ferried tourists from the station to the ruins, and an indistinct narrow path straight up through the vegetation on the mountainside. Close by the entrance to the ruins was an old, wood-built alojamiento with a large covered verandah in front of it. We sat on the verandah and had a cup of coffee whilst surveying the ground around for a place to spend the night. Across the track in front of the alojamiento, the ground dropped steeply about two metres to a flat piece of grass by the edge of the plunge to the valley floor. It seemed to be an ideal camp site so Sam and I, and three Germans friends who had been on the train with us, rolled our sleeping bags out and settled in for the night under the stars. Being Teutonic and organised, Otto, Gunter and Heinz had a tent. Sam and I had the open sky.

Rising at five o'clock in the morning we were waiting at the gate to the ruins when the grumpy gate attendant turned up for work. It was still pitch dark but he let us in and we quickly made our way across the ruins to Huayna Picchu, which means 'Young Mountain' in Quechua. Logically, Machu Picchu means 'Old Mountain'. Huayna Picchu peak rises three hundred and sixty metres above the ruins and forms the iconic almost conical backdrop to the site, with the ruins laid out before it like wares on the ground in an Indian market. We had looked at the peak when we arrived in the afternoon and felt it might be possible to scale its precipitous flank and so decided to climb it in the morning to see the dawn arrive from its summit. To get to it we had to climb over a smaller one hundred metre hill and then walk out across a narrow ridge to its base. There was no discernible path, no handrails and no protective barriers and so we began clambering up the face, much of the time underneath the vegetation that grew on it. Near the top we came across old Inca steps and paths that had been cut into the almost sheer rock face. Each step on the Inca staircase was no more than about three inches wide and the steps were nigh vertical, like a ladder propped up against the rock. After about forty minutes of climbing we came out on the top of the mountain. Looking down we were unable to take in any view as we were shrouded in thick cloud. We settled down to wait for the weather to lift, sheltering in a cave at the top when it started to rain.

At about half past eight, the cloud suddenly broke beneath us, opening like a camera aperture. As the updraft of air pushed through the hole in the clouds the ruins were revealed to us, as were the mountains behind and around us. We could see up to the Sun Gate at the eastern end of the site. It was spectacular and the sight of the grandeur before us left us speechless. Behind us we could look straight down to the Urubamba River that ran far below and almost directly beneath us. I rested on a rock and gazed down on the relic of man's ingenuity, his ability to overcome the seemingly impossible to create the miraculous. Where did the Incas get the inspiration and the vision to dream into existence that monument to aspiration? The five of us sat in complete silence, absorbing the sight below us, each struggling to take it all in as the wind blew our hair and whistled in our ears.

Finally sated we climbed back down to the ruins and spent the day wandering through them, picking small, wild strawberries as we went. They were remarkably sweet and were growing on some of the terraces. For the first few hours we had the ruins largely to ourselves, with no more than about twenty other people there as the tourist train did not disgorge its passengers in the valley below until mid-morning. Whilst the ruins were said to have been 'discovered' by Hiram Bingham in 1911, in truth they had never been lost as there were some Indian families who lived about the place and farmed some of the terraces when good old Hiram was taken there by others who knew of its existence. He was in fact looking for the real 'Lost City', Vilcabamba, and to his death believed he had found it at Machu Picchu. The Inca deserted Machu Picchu in 1532 when the Spanish conquistadors arrived, escaping to Vilcabamba deeper in the heavily forested mountains. Machu Picchu was capable of supporting about one thousand people and it seems from remains found in graves there that most of the inhabitants were women, the 'Chosen Women of the Sun' who perhaps looked after the temples and tended to the priests' needs.

By mid-day large groups of people had arrived and the ruins filled with their chatter and noise. With the utter peace of the deserted ruins broken, we escaped and walked up the hill to the sentry post on the way to Wiñay Wayna. From there we had another spectacular view of the city in its eyrie setting high in the mountains. From the sentry post we walked back down into the ruins and out on the path at the back of them to the Inca bridge. Behind the city the Inca had built a 'back entrance, a narrow path on the plunging cliff face, but some way along the trail, about ten minutes from the city, they had left a five metre section unmade so the narrow path on the cliff face stopped and then started again. Across the gap they would put logs that could be withdrawn in times of danger, a form of horizontal drawbridge. Simple and ingenious, as so much of what they did seemed to be.

On our way back to the ruins it started to rain and by the time we reached the steps of the alojamiento the rain had turned to a monsoon like deluge, soaking us. Three centimetres fell in the next hour and the rain persisted until it was time for us to settle down for the night, in our now soaked sleeping bags. Sam and I rigged up a crude shelter with some canvas sheeting we found, hitching it to the bank beneath which we were to lie and then all crammed into the sheltered space it provided. Lying in my sleeping bag I felt as though I was wrapped in a wet sponge, the more so when the rain began to torrent on us again in the night as it brushed aside our futile attempts at protection from the elements. Sometime in the early hours we gave up the unequal struggle, gathered up our few possessions and retreated to the alojamiento's verandah where we sat out the rest of the night listening to the rain drumming on the tin roof.

Before first light, we set off down the mountain, eschewing the long track used by the vehicles and instead going straight down the meagre path through the vegetation. The side of the mountain was a five hundred metre mud slide, as was the path, and on some sections we involuntarily tobogganed down it, miraculously avoiding careering into trees and over cliff edges. From the bottom of the mountain we walked back down the track to the shacks and grass huts at Aguas Calientes where we bought our first meal for two days, a plate of eggs and rice each. The whole area has changed now and what used to be the stop at Machu Picchu is now a concrete monstrosity that has adopted the name Aguas Calientes. We waited for the ancient Indian train which puffed and steamed in at eight thirty ready for its run back to Cuzco. We had been told it was the last operating steam train in Peru. It was already completely full and so I spent much of the seven hour journey sitting on the open steps with my legs dangling over the side. One of our slightly less sensitive German travelling companions wanted a photograph of an Indian woman and her child. His chosen model was asleep on one of the benches in the carriage we were in, a child aged about two on her lap suckling at her exposed breast. The child also seemed to be asleep, even though it had her breast in her mouth. The German took his photograph from about a metre, and when the flash went off, the child jumped with fright and bit the breast languishing in its mouth. Not surprisingly this woke the mother up, quite quickly. I'm not sure whether happy would have been an appropriate word for her reaction as she re-homed her savaged breast. It again reminded me of the fragile relationship between travellers and tourists and indigenous people. A high price is sometimes paid for the foreign money the tourists bring with them, and it is easy to see why travellers are not respected, and indeed sometimes hated. After negotiating more damaged track covered in mud, we finally pulled into Cuzco in the afternoon and walked back to our room. Our few possessions were still in there and untouched, which was both a surprise and a relief. After an evening in a bar with many friends we retired to bed to prepare for another early morning start.

Dawn found us on the train to Puno and back at the ranch at Chuquibambilla in the afternoon, just in time for me to go with Alain to tend to a cow with a bit of hyper-inflation. The poor animal was blowing up alarmingly with retained gasses and Alain had to release the pressure. I hoped the rapidly expanding beast felt the indignities it was put through to alleviate its problem were worth it. I empathised with the cow since I was still quite troubled by the little alimentary issue that had struck me in Arequipa. It had kept me persistently on the hop for three weeks, and no doubt the school in Arequipa still quarantined. I had lost considerable weight on top of the slimming affect of our significantly reduced diet and now Sam had also succumbed. We had begun to wonder if we had hepatitis but there was little we could do about it as we were a long way from any medical help we could trust. Alain seemed remarkably reluctant to don his arm-length rubber glove and rummage around in our lower intestines for clues about the genesis of our illness.

With the cow gratifyingly deflated, if somewhat violated, we returned to the ranch in time to meet a group of ten Indians who had come in to the house with their musical instruments for an impromptu gig. They sat down in the kitchen and played to us for about an hour and a half. When they arrived one of them was extremely drunk. By the time they left, all of them were as they seemed to take their entertainment fee in the form of two cases of beer that Alain produced for them. Interestingly, no matter how much they drank their music was unaffected. There was a raw beauty in their playing, the haunting sound of the Pan Pipes that had wafted about the stalls at the market in Cuzco once more enveloping us, intermingled with the rhythm of a guitar and their singing. As they played I was fascinated by how the music seemed to transport each of them, where to I knew not but wherever it was, from their seraphic expressions it seemed to bring each of them peace and tranquility, an escape from the harshness and extreme poverty of their existence and the paucity of any pleasure in their lives.

On the 8th January we said our farewells to Alain and Tildy and set off south through Ayaviri, Juliaca and Puno where I was able to introduce Sam to the beautifully coloured waters of Lake Titicaca. I had forgotten how bad the road after Puno was, potholed as though it had been carpet bombed. We reached the border at Desaguadero just before it closed and went through both sets of customs effortlessly, stopping for the night in a field ten kilometres down the road. The night was disturbed by a vociferous drunk stumbling home, singing at the top of his tuneless voice. Torrential rain added a percussion section on our roof. When we woke in the morning we found Adolf had sunk into the mud, needing locked differentials and low box to get her out. The previously dry road was now a muddy skid pan and we slid and slipped our way along it.

Some way down the road we came across a wide river that was in full spate. It was clearly normally a fordable river as the road went into it and emerged the other side. We had no idea how long it would take for the torrent to subside so we decided it was time for a little risk-taking and adventure, despite the fact there didn't seem to be another human being or vehicle for hundreds of miles as we had not seen one car or truck that morning. The other missing piece of information was how deep the river was but we were never ones to let a bit of detail get in the way of merrymaking. We locked the differentials again, screwed the draining plug into the clutch housing and cleared up anything of importance on the floor at our feet. I engaged first gear in low box and set off slowly down the bank into the raging river. I was conscious we had no snorkel for our air intake or exhaust and that stopping or stalling were not options I had the luxury of taking. The water level quickly came up to the door handles and poured over the bonnet as the force of the water immediately started to push us down stream. As our back end started to slip away towards the distant sea, I turned the front wheels in the direction of the far bank and slowly we crept through the water, crabbing diagonally across until we reached the other side and pulled up out of the water. We opened the doors and let the water that was up to our knees cascade out. Sanity and common sense would have said we should have sat it out for a day or so until it was safe to cross, but it didn't seem to us that common sense and sanity added much to the fun that could be had, the adrenaline kick of a risk taken and survived. We opened the bonnet to inspect the engine and to empty water out of the air filter, from which we could see we had had only had a few seconds left before the air intake would have flooded and the engine drowned. A close shave indeed.

Driving down into La Paz we found a cheap pay car park that had a guard on duty and put Adolf in it, a useful base for us in the centre of the city. We walked to Plaza Murillo and saw the lamp post from which the body of President Gualberto Villarroel was hung after he had been killed in 1946. He had been wounded by rebels when they stormed the Presidential Palace at the climax of a week of bloody fighting. Despite being badly wounded, he was still alive when the revolutionaries threw him over a balcony to the street below, but quite dead when he hit the pavement, the sudden stop seemingly the last straw for his battered body. As with Mussolini just over a year before, Villarroel's body was strung up in a final act of public humiliation, but he was accorded the dignity of a lamp post rather than an Esso petrol station which was Mussolini's last hang out.

For the next two days we wandered around the city, visiting markets and sights that usually commemorated one of Bolivia's seemingly monthly revolutions. Walking around the witches' market, 'El Mercado de las Brujas' on Calle Jimenez and Linares, was fascinating. The stalls and one roomed little shops ran along the side of the cobbled street and we wandered up and down examining the seeds, herbs and artifacts that were for sale. Potions in bottles, bird feathers, frogs, toads and insects and medicinal plants were all laid out on small tables. Oddest of all were the dried foetuses, mostly of llamas but I also saw sheep and other animals. I had the strange and somewhat disturbing sense that it might even be possible to buy a human foetus if you knew the right witch, and she knew you. Fortune telling by soothsayers, medicinal diagnosis and administration of herbal remedies and spells for every situation were all on sale. We were told that new houses were built with a spell buried in one corner. When fields were ploughed and crops sown, spells for Pachamama, the god Mother Earth, were created to be buried in the corner of the fields to pray for a good crop at harvest and to bring good health, prosperity and happiness to the farmer and his family. The witches sat by their stalls in their colourful if somewhat filthy dresses and bowler hats, waving away any tourist who had the temerity to try to take a photograph, fearful the cameras would take away the power of their spells. Many of the witches had inherited their stalls from their mothers and grandmothers who had taught them their sorcery skills.

We visited the Central Post Office a couple of times and, despite the insistence of the officials that there were no letters for us, by rummaging through hundreds of uncollected envelopes thrown into cardboard boxes, we found a number addressed to us. Letters were something of a lifeline for us, an umbilical cord to the real lives we had left behind. Some we received had been written weeks or even months before we opened them and we knew ours were evidence to our families that we had still been alive when we had posted them. None of the communication facilities that are available in the twenty first century existed, and which are such an essential part of our lives today, existed when we travelled and so to all intents and purposes, for our families and friends we had disappeared off the face of the earth. The instant connection we all have now through email and mobile phones was unimaginable in the early 1970's, as laughable concept as a female Prime Minister of Britain or an African American President of the United States. News of our continued existence was always long out of date by the time it reached home. Despite our free-spirited wanderings we were always keen to learn of news from home and so our determined search in the bowels of the Post Office was born out of our desire to be connected.

Visits to the Immigration office were needed to get papers and Passports stamped. Since Sam and I had already been a couple of times by the time our German friends Bernhard and Adolf rolled into town, we offered to go with them to show them where the offices were situated. We jumped into their VW camper van and when we got to the office, parked at an angle against the pavement outside. When we emerged having completed the paperwork, we found a short, officious and obnoxious traffic policeman apoplectically hopping from foot to foot by the vehicle. His sense of traffic feng shui had clearly been grossly affronted and he was insisting the car should have been parked at a right angle to the pavement and not at forty five degrees. We were making the line of vehicles look untidy and this required some paperwork at the traffic police headquarters the other side of the city. He told us we would have to go with him to it and, despite some groveling to his self-inflated pomposity, he insisted there was no option. Accepting the inevitable, the four of us climbed in, Adolf and Bernhard in the front seats and Sam and I in the only two spaces in the back where one could sit. The traffic officer climbed in and found there was nowhere to sit so had to stand, bent double and swaying and lurching as we set off. We started to ask him why he was in the vehicle and whether it was because he wanted to buy it. This irritated him, his gravitas clearly insulted, and our attention was brought somewhat unsubtly to his gun, bouncing merrily on his hip as we travelled the uneven road.

We followed the barked directions the little man gave and were driving down a fairly wide main road in the heart of the city when, without a word passing between us, Bernhard turned the wheel and we plunged down a steep hill in a street that was at right angles to the main road. The policeman went berserk, shouting at us but unable to pull out his gun as he had both hands pressed against the ceiling above his bent and aching back as he tried to stay upright. At the bottom of the hill Bernhard turned right and then turned right again up a road that climbed the steep hill back up to the main road, thus going around the block. Still no word had been said between us when Bernhard suddenly started to jerk his foot on the accelerator so the van began to lurch as though struggling to climb the steep slope.

"Get out, get out, push" Bernhard shouted, still drumming the accelerator.

I pulled back the sliding side door and Sam and I jumped out and pretended to push the van, shouting and beckoning at the policeman to come out and help. He climbed down but Sam and I were by the door so there was nowhere for him to push. We each waved an arm to the back and told him to go and push there. With the van still lurching along, he went round, put both hands against the back and with head down started pushing. Sam and I jumped back in, I slammed the door shut and we roared off up the hill, leaving the policeman trying not to fall flat on his face and then standing in the street waving his fist and gun at us. He was a long walk from the police station we had been heading for. The telepathic communication between us for this unrehearsed jape was surreal and we laughed almost uncontrollably as we put as much distance between us and the no doubt incandescently irate imperious little official, who was now stranded in the middle of the city.

That evening we met about seven fellow travellers in a bar for a quiet drink. By two thirty in the morning, there were so many empty beer bottles on the table we were having to put them on the floor beneath our seats. We and other customers were standing on chairs and tables singing. The waiters were bringing out more bottles in buckets and some of them had given up the unequal struggle, rolled out some mats and gone to sleep on the floor leaving their colleagues to deal with the friendly mayhem. It was perhaps not a wise thing to over-celebrate when in the middle of a few weeks of the mysterious illness I had been struggling with and the next morning I felt sufficiently damaged to swear that I was giving up alcohol for life, and if not completely, then certainly in any excess. After spending the morning divided between recovering from the night's impromptu celebration of absolutely nothing and towing a broken down van belonging to nine Australians to a garage, we left La Paz for the long road to Buenos Aires. Adolf and Bernhard followed us in their VW van as we had decided to shadow them down south to help them through the difficult roads ahead. Their van was beginning to show its age and was not coping with the beating and abuse it was getting on the dreadful South American roads.

We drove up the steep hills out of the city and at El Alto, the town on the rim of the canyon, we came upon a barrier across the road with a police station next to it. Parking Adolf in the middle of the road in the blazing sun, I walked into the station where I was told we had to pay a toll for the road ahead. Adolf was parked on a road made of tarmac and about a metre the other side of the barrier the tarmac finished and the dirt road started. Slightly affronted by this I said we would not pay as it was not a metaled road. As I argued with the officials, trucks that had ground up the steep hill were banking up behind Adolf, the drivers hooting their deafening horns in irritation as their clutches strained to help their feeble brakes. The station was beginning to fill with irate truck drivers whose path was blocked by and the cacophony of horns and shouts outside was growing so large the policemen eventually gave up and told me to get going to clear the road. Despite the public opprobrium, being a recusant had its benefits.

Our next objective was to go to Cochabamba to visit its legendary market, La Cancha, one of the largest in Bolivia. We drove south on reasonable roads through Ayo Ayo, Sica Sica to Caracollo where we spent the night in a dark side street in the middle of the town. As usual we had to pass through police check points on the way. On some days we went through six or seven. At one isolated stop the lone policeman asked to have a look inside Adolf under the slim pretext of looking for contraband or drugs. He quickly spotted my old American Army jacket that had been my shelter from the sun, rain and cold winds, my pillow at night and that had become like a second skin. Pointing at it he asked me how much I wanted for it. I said I didn't want to sell it, so he swung his rifle off his shoulder, held the barrel under my nostrils and asked me again for how much I wanted. As we stared at each other and I wondered how I could manipulate the situation to keep the jacket, a car came around the corner in the road and the policeman quickly dropped the gun from my face and stepped back. I got back into Adolf and we set off. I marveled at the serendipity of there being another vehicle on the road at that moment, given that we could sometimes drive all day and not see another car or truck.

Taking the Cochabamba road we pulled ahead of Adolf and Bernhard as we drove across the flat altiplano, coming to a police stop and check point with a chain across the road. The lone policeman in charge of the check point asked us for a toll payment to pass through. We explained we had no money. Pointing to the VW's distant dust trail on the road behind, we said our friends following did and would pay for us, so the man let us through, much to our amazement. We drove on and climbed into the hills where, from a high vantage point more than a mile away, we pulled over and sat on the ground to watch the check point through our binoculars. The plains stretched out beneath us into the far distance in shades of brown and gold, arid and dry, a beautiful sight of awesome wilderness and grandeur with the bonus of a condor floating on the updraft from the mountain we were sitting on. We could see Adolf and Bernhard's dust trail as they slowly approached the policeman and watched as they got out to discuss the toll with him. When he started pointing in our direction the argument clearly started. Arms were waved, heads shaken, but even from that distance we could tell from his body language the policeman was resolute. They had to pay for us as he obviously refused to let down the chain until they had. By the time they reached us we had brewed cups of coffee for each of us over which we gave them our toll payment.

As we drank our coffee another VW van drew up next to us and an American got out, so we poured him a cup as well. Orlyn Reilly was a physicist who had worked for NASA. He lived in Cochabamba, and had done so for ten years. He had set up Bolivia's first tyre retreading plant in the town. He invited us to his plant to use the hot showers and to park our vehicles behind the locked factory gates, so we went with him to the town and did just that. As the next day was a Saturday and little was going to happen over the weekend we decided to go with Orlyn into the jungle to do some fishing. About one hundred kilometres from Cochabamba we left the main road and drove into the thick jungle for about twenty kilometres, crossing streams and rivers until we stopped and camped by a barren river that gave up not one fish. It mattered not to me that the fishing was unproductive as the setting and its isolation were beautiful. Steep sided mountains soared above us, covered in dense rain forest that dripped water on us. After an unproductive couple of days we returned to the town, once again fording the many streams and small rivers and passing a couple of Indian cemeteries on our way.

The market at Cochabamba, Bolivia's third largest city, was indeed huge, stretching all around us in the streets and plazas and seemingly taking over the whole town. Teeming with people and full of life, colours and scents enveloped us. A drunk lay fast asleep in the middle of the road as buses and trucks drove around him. We came upon a man who's party piece was shoving eight three inch nails up each nostril, and then inserting a six inch nail into each as well, driving the longer nails in with a hammer. The longer nails surely delved into the cavity of his skull, making porridge of the lower reaches of his brain. Somehow he lived so perhaps his skull was completely empty like a bare attic. We were the only non-Indians there and something of an object of interest. As we wandered around the narrow lanes and between the stalls and vendors, I was walking behind Bernhard when an Indian woman in a tall hat barged past me and bumped straight into him. As she then passed him I could see she had slashed his back pocket with a razor blade in an attempt to get at what she thought was his wallet. It was in fact his small address book and because she had cut too high, she had not been able to pull it out. There was a deep slash in its cover but it was reassuring to know it had saved him from what would have been an unpleasant and deep cut across his backside. We all knew about this method of theft in South America but this was the first time I had seen it happen in front of me. We had driven to the market from Orlyn's yard in the VW van and had parked. Before wandering around the market once more we were sitting in the van chatting when we noticed a small disembodied hand come up in front of the windscreen, grab hold of one of the windscreen wipers and start to try to pull it off. It was common practice to have detachable car parts such as hub caps stolen, and then offered back for sale. Headlights could disappear in the same way if the thieves had invested in a screw driver. Siphoning petrol from cars sitting at red traffic lights or in traffic jams was another little money spinner.

While we were in town Adolf and Bernhard had a crack in the front axle of the VW welded and with the work done we left Cochabamba, aware that south of the city the roads were in appalling condition, not helped by the large amount of rain that had been falling over the previous few days. The roads were indeed atrocious and many had been washed away. At one point it had completely disappeared so we retraced our path for about a kilometre and then drove down the bank into the riverbed that ran next to the road, Bernhard and Adolf following in their indefatigably indomitable van. They became stuck a few times and so we towed them through the more difficult parts until we found a point in the river bank the other side of the washed out section of the road where we were able to pull them out and back onto the road. We lost count of the number of flooded rivers we crossed that day. Driving into one village there were two enormous mud filled ruts blocking our path, obviously caused by the wheels of large trucks. Villagers were gathered on the bank above the road, watching like perched vultures for the next unfortunates to come along the road. The VW was ahead of us and sank to its underside in the morass, so this time we extracted it backwards before going through ourselves, towing it behind.

When we reached Potosi we decided to spend a little time resting from the rigours of the roads and wandered about the city. At 3,977 metres, it was the highest city of its size in the world and there was indeed a noticeable lack of oxygen there. Because we had spent so much time at altitude we were not too affected by the thin air but I was glad I had not just flown into it with no time to acclimatise. The city was founded by the Spaniards in 1545, who considered it to be the richest city in the world. They exploited the local mineral wealth in the indigenous mine workings in the mountain, Cerro Rico, extracting vast amounts of silver. When the silver began to run out, the town went into decline but was somewhat resuscitated by the discovery of tin in the twentieth century. Leaving Potosi we splashed, slipped, skidded and waded our way across rivers, occasionally dragging the VW behind, until we reached the Argentinian border at Villazon where we crossed without too much difficulty, although the Argentinians took about two hours to complete our paperwork. Adolf was emitting a sexy throaty roar as her exhaust pipe had cracked under the unrelenting abuse.

The road on the Argentinian side was no better except we now had to cross a relentless succession of fords, or '*Vados,*' where the flooded fields poured across wide dips in the road, turning them into rivers in torrent. It was clear the road had been purposely built with this succession of about fifty fords, spaced at regular intervals in order to alleviate the flooded fields in the heavy rains and to allow excess waters to flow away naturally with the fall in the land. The rain was still coming down steadily when we came to one of the fords that had a queue of cars sitting in the road. We drove up past them to find a particularly deep and fast flowing vados that was a river too far for the ordinary domestic cars and beyond their drivers' courage. While Bernhard and Adolf waited by the flood, we drove Adolf slowly into the water. The torrent once again poured over her bonnet which disappeared out of our sight, but she didn't falter and we made it to the other side. We then got out our tow cables, hitched them to the tow bar, backed Adolf down into the water and walked the free end across to the VW van which we then pulled across. The water was so deep the van floated off in the fast current so we had to pull it across quickly. As we emptied the water out of the van and unhooked the rope, some of the passengers waiting on the other side shouted out to us to be towed across as well so, for a small fee charged to each, we pulled most of them across. One car was a VW Beetle and, being extremely light and airtight, like the VW van it bobbed up like a small boat, bouncing around like a little yellow duck on the sea at the mercy of the waves. Without its wheels being on the road beneath, there was nothing to stop it flowing away. We could see the two terrified elderly passengers peering through the windscreen as the car disappeared off down stream. Again accelerating hard we pulled them across fast. Once on dry land again, it was obvious from their expressions they felt they had had a glimpse of the next life. Despite having taken our trousers off to wade backwards and forward across the river, we were completely soaked by the rain, and extremely cold as the process had taken about an hour. One car driver gave us the remains of a bottle of vodka as a thank you and a few sips helped to warm us. We repeated the process a couple of times further down the road, one of the crossings being equally deep, but were pleased to have earned enough for a couple of meals for the four of us.

Leaving the vados behind we began to descend from the Andean plains and as we did so, the air temperature started to climb. About forty kilometres south of Humahuaca we reached tarmac, the first we had seen for a long time. We could begin to see how much wealthier Argentina was than Bolivia. The comparison was quite stark with respectable cars on decent roads, more frequent villages and towns, houses of brick and tile rather than adobe and straw. Factories and shops hinted at widespread industry and commerce. Bolivia seemed to have been shades of brown and straw and often barren whereas northern Argentina was green and lush. At Metan we stopped to buy some milk and bread and spent the night in a free camp site that had a swimming pool and hot showers. The next day the sun blazed in a blue sky. While we worked on some essential maintenance on our beaten up vehicles, a small group of Argentinian girls offered us some food, cooking us steaks on a fire and giving them to us with salad and fruit for lunch. Our stomachs were completely unaccustomed to both the quality and the quantity of the food, and we lay back in the sun in a state of euphoria after the meal, which somewhat delayed our departure. We finally left in the late afternoon and headed for Tucuman where we had a meal in a German owned restaurant before then heading further south into the night.

The next large town on our route to Buenos Aires was Santiago del Estero and as we set off for it from the marshland in which we had spent the night we agreed to meet Bernhard and Adolf there. We still intended shadowing them all the way to the capital as we were concerned their old camper was in extremis. They went ahead of us as we tidied up our campsite and put out the fire. When we rolled into the town we spotted them ahead of us by the road in a heated discussion with a large group of heavily armed police. We pulled up behind their VW and got out to find out what the problem was. Distracted by what was going on we had forgotten that because of the heat Sam and I were driving in nothing more than a pair of boxer shorts and with bare feet, probably not the best attire in which to be negotiating with police. They quickly included us in the barked order that we should all four go to the police station with them for questioning. We had no idea what their issue with us was, and no explanation was offered. The police had an open Jeep but obviously not trusting us, put one of their number in the VW with Adolf and Bernhard and one in Adolf with us. Positioning their Jeep between us, they started our little convoy, in our case with a heavily armed policeman sitting on the box between our seats. The rest of the police sat jammed into the back of the Jeep, which looked like a hedgehog with rifles sticking up and out of it in a small forest of bristles. In the distance ahead I could see a petrol station. We had established the policeman between us spoke no English so I said to Sam I was going to pull into the garage after the two vehicles ahead had passed it to see what happened. I lifted my foot off the accelerator just enough to let the two vehicles pull ahead a little, opening a gap between us and the Jeep but not such that the policeman should become suspicious.

The VW and the Jeep sailed past the garage and as we came level to its second entrance I turned Adolf into it without any warning, exposing the weakness in the policemen's plan. Our passenger went berserk, shouting and threatening us with his gun. Of course, the police in the Jeep had a quandary. Should they stop to see what was happening and to rescue the man with us, or should they chase the VW. Either way, one of their colleagues was potentially in trouble. They chose to follow the VW whilst waving and pointing assorted armaments and artillery at us. As our man ranted and frothed, I ignored him and got out and started filling Adolf with petrol, still dressed only in boxer shorts. Eventually the others arrived with the VW and ordered us to put on some trousers and a shirt which, in the circumstances, was not an unreasonable request and one we complied with.

With Adolf replenished and sated, we set off again with dire threats in our ears not to try any more stunts. When we arrived at the police station in the centre of the town, we were marched into a large, rectangular and largely bare room. A fan hanging from the ceiling turned slowly in a desultory effort to move the hot air around. There was a table at one end and a policeman sat on a wooden chair behind it, a picture of the President of the country high up on the wall behind him. Down the wall on one side of the room, opposite the windows, were a couple of low benches and we were made to sit on them in a row, like swallows on a line. Lined up in front of the windows a large group of the armed police stood watching us with distaste, as though they were looking at exhibits in the reptile house of a zoo. Nothing much seemed to be happening, and we still had no idea why we were being detained. Unlike some of our other escapades, this one was a bit serious with an unpleasant outcome moving from a possibility to a probability.

I went up to the table and demanded to see the British Consul, banging the table with my fist in the appropriate and time honoured fashion of all arrogant imperialists born to privilege and unprepared to take any nonsense from Johnny Foreigner. One of the policemen came over and shoved his machine gun barrel into my chest and pushed me back across the room into my seat, which we quietly agreed between us indicated we might just be in a bit of trouble. We were well aware of Argentina's '*Los Desaparecidos*', the missing who simply disappeared and were never seen again, their fate unknown. The Montoneros, a left wing urban guerrilla movement that despised democracy, came together in about 1970 and was committed to violence. The terrorist group was extremely active and had exploded a bomb in July 1972 in the Plaza de San Isidro in Buenos Aires and so it seemed logical the authorities would be nervous and on high alert. As we sat awaiting our fate under the listless flies that patrolled the ceiling, we speculated that because of our beards and scruffy appearance the police thought we might be activists in the movement. The sun filtered through the room's windows that seemed yellowed by nicotine and I gazed through them at the trees outside, their leaves moving gently in a light breeze. I envied the birds their freedom as they flitted between the branches.

After we had been in the room for about an hour the policemen told us we had to go with them to the Central Police Station. They had casually ignored our often repeated requests for an explanation and for our respective Consuls, evidence of their complete disregard for international conventions. We were bundled out of the building, surrounded by a group of the police, all armed with machine guns. They made us sit on benches in the back a police Jeep. Once the spare places had been filled with more police we set off across town. I was sitting at the back against the back door and next to the Jeep's spare wheel. There was a small open window at my back that let in a welcome draft that vaguely cooled the humid Jeep. I noticed the nuts holding the spare wheel onto the inside of the door seemed a bit loose so as we went across town I undid them one by one and threw them discretely over my shoulder out of the window. It is important in life to go down fighting to the end.

When we arrived at the next station they made us climb out and then marched us through the central arch of a colonnaded front, through large heavy doors. They took us through the big building, across a wide courtyard to a small dark room at the back that overlooked another courtyard, but one that was small and dirty and enclosed within high walls. It was the sort of place one would expect to find had blood splattered bullet holes in the end wall. None of the police had spoken on the journey over so we had no idea what they had in mind, but our imaginations were beginning to assume whatever it was might be quite vigorous and probably painful, if not terminal. With us lined up against a wall in the room they pulled down large ledgers and thumbed through them, checking the names on our Passports against the information in the books, which turned out to be records of people with criminal convictions. From their conversations we knew they had not found anything about us, which was hardly a surprise and which we took to be a bit of a positive. In the range of possible outcomes it moved us from the terminal towards the vigorous and painful option open to them, which we felt would be something of a result, given the alternative.

There was a plain table in the middle of the room and one of the policeman put a large box onto it as we watched in awed fascination. When he opened it we saw to our relief it was a fingerprinting kit. We had half expected wires and terminals, one end of which might be attached to sensitive and rather private parts of our anatomy that only Matron normally saw, the other end being connected to the National Grid via a wall socket. For the next half an hour they fingerprinted us and took our photographs, serial numbers above our heads in true criminal style. As each of us had our fingerprints taken we wiped our blackened fingers over every surface we could find. I was last and when they had taken mine, I asked one of the policemen if there was a cloth I could wipe my hands on. He said no so I wiped them on his rather smart white shirt. The room went very quiet as I stood in front of him waiting for his reaction which, to his eternal credit in the face of the idiocy of youth, was to reach over to a shelf to pick up a large bar of soap. He handed it to me without a word, pointing to a stand pipe in the courtyard. As I went out to it to wash my hands, I looked at the soap. It was a large, crudely made block that was translucent and the colour of weak tea, and I immediately thought of stories and photographs I had seen of the Nazis making soap from human body fat. It was a sobering thought. I washed my hands, as did the others, after which we were taken back through the station and driven back to our vehicles and told to go.

Santiago del Estero was founded in 1535 by the conquistadores and was one of the oldest cities in Argentina. Somewhat run down, with much of its history long gone, it did have some interesting museums but not interesting enough to make us want to stay, given our experience with the police and the time they had wasted. We left and took the road south to Córdoba about four hundred and thirty kilometres away, driving through yet another blizzard of butterflies that again made us stop a number of times to clear our front grill which became thick with them, making Adolf's engine overheat. We made it all the way to Córdoba and spent the night outside the city, leaving for Buenos Aires early in the morning. We were still seven hundred kilometres from the capital and we felt with a good day's driving on the now excellent Argentinian roads we could almost get there in the day, but this was not to be. Within a short distance the VW started making some ominous noises that sounded expensive and immedicable, bordering on the terminal. It eventually went on strike, shutting itself down in protest. We turned around and towed the van back to Córdoba in the hope of finding a VW dealer or garage, parking in a quiet residential street. It was siesta time and everything was shut so we brewed some coffee as we waited for the city to wake up. As we did so we started chatting to a man who was looking at the two vehicles. When we explained our problem he said he had a friend who had a garage who might help.

It was through that one small piece of luck that we came to spend the next three days in Victor's garage, mending our vehicles and being fed, alternately by him and his family and by Eduardo, the owner of a pizza restaurant where we bought a pizza each on our first evening. Bernhard and Adolf had to get a couple of parts made for their engine and we had to mend our silencer. While Sam did some work on the engine, I slid underneath Adolf on the dirt floor of the garage to take the silencer off. The back wheels were off and her axle rested on a hydraulic jack. As I lay on my back working at the nuts holding the silencer, one of the wheels of the jack suddenly sank into the earth floor and Adolf lurched sideways above me. One of the chassis beams was inches above my face. Time stopped as I lay still, and then slowly slid out from under the unstable weight hovering over me. As I put the wheel on to prevent damage if Adolf tipped over she lurched once more. If I had still been beneath her, it would only have been as a memory. Somehow I knew I had used another life in that moment and, given the number Sam and I had used up on the trip, I wondered how many we had left, how many chances we could continue to take.

Our well of good luck seemed to have no bottom. As we worked in the garage a doctor who regularly had his car serviced there came over to chat to us. Sam and I took the opportunity to talk to him about the chronic diarrhoea we had both been affected by for six weeks. Whilst we had never let it stop us doing anything we had both lost a great deal of weight and it was clearly debilitating. The doctor said he would see us in his consulting room that evening. We went to him at the end of the day and after he examined us, he declared us to be 'as strong as oxen.' He gave us some tablets for whatever he thought was causing our problem, and also some clear liquid in a couple of bottles for the severe stomach cramps we had been having. We had no idea what the bottles contained or what the tablets were but, reassured by the large number of framed qualifications on his wall and the fact he lectured in medicine at the University, we took the medicine over the next few days and the diarrhoea stopped. His altruism was another example of the kindness, friendliness and generosity of the Argentinians. Apart from the police in Santiago del Estero whose attitude to us was perhaps understandable and ultimately justified, any people we had met had gone out of their way to welcome us to their country and to show us great hospitality, even to the point one evening when Victor took us out to see the sights of the city and spent the whole time kerb-crawling and negotiating with a number of prostitutes. He was looking for a present for us, one he thankfully failed to deliver. I reflected on this seemingly innate benevolence and friendliness years later as our troops landed on the Falklands and battle with the Argentinian Army commenced in earnest. It seemed to me both sad and incongruous for us to be fighting and killing men I was sure were no different to the wonderful people we had been selflessly helped by when we were in their country. As ever in war, I felt the politicians who wanted to fight a war should be allowed to do so, amongst themselves and thus ridding us of them. A utopian if somewhat deluded wish.

With the vehicles serviced and repaired, we bade our generous hosts farewell and took to the road again, stopping for the night in Rosario where Bernhard managed to put out all the lights in a street by reversing the VW into an electricity pole. As it swayed back and forth shaking the suspended wires, sparks and flashes flew out of junction boxes and the street went dark. We decided it might be sensible to find another street for the night. We moved off as people came out of their houses to ask each other what was going on. The next morning we were no more than thirty kilometres outside Rosario when the VW engine stopped once more. We had about one hundred and sixty kilometres to go to Buenos Aires and so decided to tow the slumbering vehicle the whole way. To relieve the boredom of the tarmac road, and to get the leg of the journey over with, we did so at speeds of up to one hundred kilometres an hour. Whilst it was an exciting ride for Sam and me, we could only imagine what it was like for Bernhard and Adolf as they careered along the road close behind us, dodging Argentinian drivers coming the other way who insisted on overtaking irrespective of what was on the road ahead of them. Since Adolf was a right wheel drive vehicle, overtaking anything for us was always quite challenging in the Americas. Doing so pulling a camper van at speed was doubly so.

It was my turn at the wheel as we approached a large truck ahead of us. I asked Sam to look ahead to see if the road was clear and edged out when he said it was, accelerating hard to get past the long truck. I quickly glanced in my mirror to make sure the VW was following. I could see Adolf at the wheel of the VW and from the expression on his face it was clear he was questioning the wisdom of the decision to overtake. Sam suddenly shouted there was something coming, but we were committed. I instinctively knew if I braked the VW would probably career into the back of us, so unexpected was the problem, and given our commitment to the manoeuvre. I had no option but to swing the wheel the other way. Still accelerating we overtook the truck on the inside on the wide dirt track that ran along the side of the road. Spraying gravel and stones everywhere, yawing and sliding around in the dirt, I could see Adolf behind us fighting the wheel to keep the VW upright, his knuckles a blur as he swung the steering wheel one way and then the other. We emerged at the front of the truck to the confusion and amazement of the driver, who kept his hand on his horn until we finally disappeared from his view, laughing maniacally.

On the outskirts of Buenos Aires we pulled into the car park of a very smart hotel and took the VW engine out to fix the problem, the sixth time Bernhard and Adolf had taken it out since they had left Berlin. Irate and smartly dressed hotel staff appeared and blanched at the oil slick now spreading across their car park. Quite reasonably and understandably they ordered us off the premises so we put the engine in the VW and pushed it out into the street where repairs continued until the problem was solved. The starter motor had given up the unequal struggle so it was removed in a form of 'starterectomy', and we agreed the van would have to be push started from then on, making it important not to park it facing uphill anywhere.

Buenos Aires was an impressive city, particularly the Avenida 9 de Julio, the largest of the many tree lined boulevards. Carrying fourteen lanes, some separated by wide grass and tree lined strips, it is one of the widest avenues in the world. We parked the vehicles and walked for a few hours around the city, which was remarkably empty. The Argentinian Grand Prix was being run that day, Sunday the 28th January, and Buenos Aires was watching it, either at the race track or on their televisions. Parts of the city, particularly the financial district, reminded me of London. With its expensive shops, sophisticated restaurants and cafés and elegantly dressed residents, the city was as different to the crudeness and simplicity of the Andean plains, villages and towns we had passed through as day is to night. The girls walking about and in the cafes were all quite beautiful, European and Scandinavian blonde with lovely olive skins. We assumed the mixing genes of large numbers of European settlers with those of the indigenous Argentinians they had married had resulted in the stunning hybrid population we saw.

In the afternoon we drove out to the coast at Quilmes to swim in the sea but it and the muddy beach were both filthy. There seemed to be thousands of people there who, clearly not interested in motor racing, had crammed together for the afternoon. The place was teeming with mosquitoes so we drove into one of the streets nearby to cook a meal. As we parked we noticed we were next to beautifully manicured grounds with sports pitches, woodlands and impressive buildings. We had read about an English based school in our guidebook called St George's College and walking down to the gates to the campus discovered we had parked right next to it. We asked the guard on the gates if he would ask the

Headmaster if we could come in. He disappeared into the school's grounds and came back a short while later to tell us the Headmaster would like to speak to us. We drove in through the gates and up to the main building where Colin Graham, in an act of altruistic kindness and generosity, welcomed us and said we could camp in a corner of the grounds. For the next three days he, his lovely wife Joan and their daughter Kate gave us an idyllic base just outside the city where we swam in the school's open air pool and camped in safety. They entertained us with meals and when the six young British in the Land Rover we had been with in Panama and Colombia also turned up, allowed us all to enlarge our camp site of squatting vagrants in the grounds. One evening we roasted a whole lamb over an open fire. It was tied with wire to an iron cross in the shape of a St Andrew's cross which was stuck in the ground next to the fire at an angle so the lamb leant out over the fierce embers. I had cooked a lamb in a similar way with Alain at San Juan in the Andes and once more I felt it was probably the only way lamb should ever be cooked. It was absolutely delicious.

While we continued to drive into Buenos Aires each day, enquiring about ferries to Montevideo and Uruguay and seeing more city sights, Bernhard and Adolf enquired about tickets for flights back to Germany as their trip was soon to be over. It was fortunate it was since, without us accompanying them they were not going to get far in their VW. They seemed unreasonably, and somewhat ungratefully reluctant to be towed by us again after the truck overtaking incident. Perhaps their desire to get back home alive was greater than ours. We left the

College for the last time, saying our farewells to the Grahams, and turned north for Paraguay, once again shadowing Bernhard and Adolf who wanted to see Paraguay before they flew home. For Sam and me the long trek back to Los Angeles had begun. The combination of the lure for Sam of seeing Dorine again, the lack of available shipping to Australia and the wear and tear on us of our way of travelling made us yearn for some respite and so the decision had been made to return to California and the United States. Before doing that we wanted to go to Asunción in Paraguay and to see Rio de Janeiro. By our calculations we had a minimum of seventeen thousand kilometres to cover to get back to Los Angeles. As we headed north I had an intense feeling I was going home, taking that first step back, and my mind turned to my girlfriend waiting for me. I hoped. I could not have any clear understanding of what settling back into that old life would be like, or how hard that would be.

There was much to do and see before that was to be faced and ignorance of any difficulties ahead was bliss.

Early morning coffee in the mountains.

A bit more early morning coffee in the mountains.

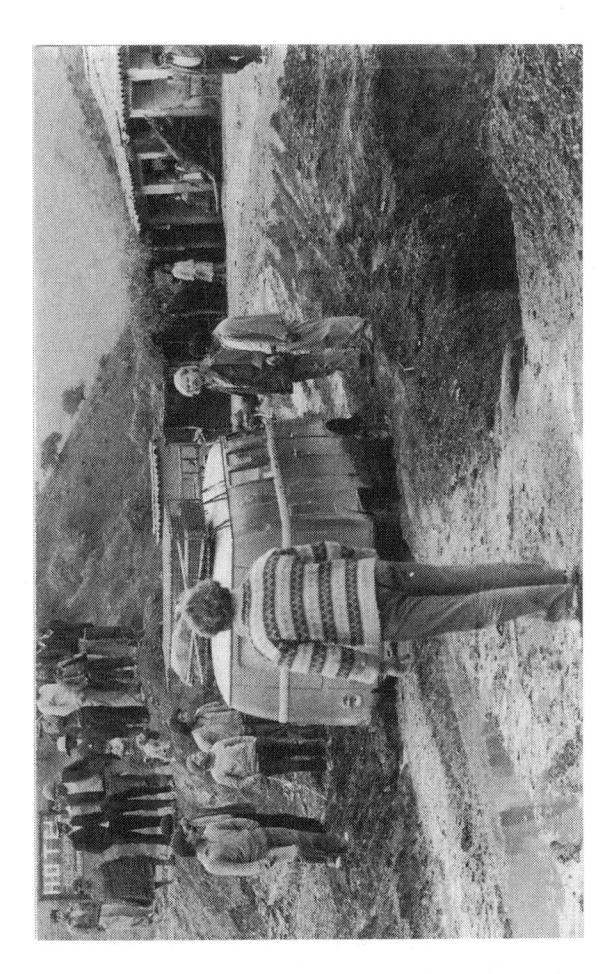

Rescuing Bernhard and Adolf's VW van in the Andes.

Haggling with a street vendor at the market in the Andes.

Five star dining, Andean style.

A GIRL CALLED ADOLF

CHAPTER 13

Buenos Aires to Medellin

The long road back - 1973

"And so you touch this limit, something happens and suddenly you can go a bit further. The danger sensation is exciting. The challenge is to find new dangers."

Ayrton Senna

"If you can keep your wits about you while all others are losing theirs, perhaps you just don't know what's going on."

With apologies to Rudyard Kipling

We left Buenos Aires on the 31st January realising we had been on the road for nine months. The land north of the city was a flat, featureless landscape with long, straight, sleep-inducing roads. Our time in South America was running out because of the limitations of our Carnet so we drove all day and long into the night, stopping at two thirty in the morning in a garage forecourt near Santa Fe, having covered about five hundred kilometres of our route towards Paraguay. The heat had been so intense during the day we had to stop Adolf under the shade of a tree for the two hottest hours as she started to overheat. One long hill we had to climb took three attempts. As we climbed it, the temperature gauge followed suit and two thirds of the way up the hill it hit the red so we quickly turned in the road and freewheeled back down, allowing the rushing air to waft over the radiator. At the bottom we stopped and grabbed our water bottles. Filling our mouths we sprayed and spat water onto the radiator to add to the heat exchange. Our second attempt at the hill produced the same result, with more water spraying when we came to rest. There was no option but to let the engine cool right down, so we parked off the road and opened the bonnet to allow the heat to disperse. We took the opportunity to eat a pineapple and a couple of oranges we had bought for our lunch, reserving another pineapple for our supper.

Having overcome the obstacle of the hill, we came into a small town and saw a bank where we decided to cash a traveller's cheque as we were slightly short of cash. We parked Adolf and Sam and I walked to the bank. As we did so, I noticed a tall, slightly balding man walking next to me and staring at me. Glancing across at him, he smiled lasciviously and flicked his tongue in and out of his mouth at me, like a lizard scenting the air. Ignoring him we turned into the bank where we changed our cheque and then distributed the cash between or shorts' pockets. We headed for the revolving doors and I went into them ahead of Sam. As I emerged onto the pavement in the sunlight, I looked up and saw the tongue licking man walking fast across the pavement straight at me, his arm and hand stretched out towards me. Without asking him what he wanted but assuming it was our money, I hit him very hard on his jaw, which lifted him off his feet and dumped him on the pavement on his back where he lay, now more like an upturned crab than an amorous lizard. Sam and I turned right and walked quickly to Adolf and left town quickly before the dazed man could complain to the authorities. South America was a dangerous place to be at times and this was one occasion when having a cozy chat about the man's intentions had not seemed a sensible option to me.

After a brief sleep we set off north again and covered another five hundred kilometres, pulling up at dusk in Resistencia near the Paraguayan border, where we found a fruit stall and bought some fruit to make a salad. Sitting on Adolf's bonnet in a street in the town, we started cutting up the fruit and throwing it in the plastic bowl that more usually acted as our washing machine. As had so often been the case since we had been in South America we attracted a large crowd of inquisitive people who gathered around us, asking us questions about what we were doing and where we had come from. In the crowd was a group of girls our age who asked us if we would like to go for a swim. We said we would so they led us to an enormous house nearby that turned out to be owned by an executive of the Argentinian national airline. He seemed to have turned his house into some form of private club, open to all his friends. There were pieces of bric-a-brac all over it, together with photographs of him with the likes of J. F. Kennedy and Claudia Cardinale. This was clearly a man used to moving in high society, which made us something of an anachronism and out of place in our tatty shorts and beards, so much so people there insisted on taking photographs of us. We wondered which frames our images might be put in and next to whom we might be placed, the antithesis of suave and elegant in the midst of high society. So many wanted to talk to us we never did get our swim but the girls took us to another house where we were allowed to use the hot showers, after which they took us to a nearby bar where they bought us beer in another act of Argentinian generosity.

The following day we reached the border and, passing through Argentinian Immigration and Customs, crossed the Paraguay River by ferry to arrive at a Paraguayan border post that was basking in the blazing sun under a clear blue sky. It was mid-day and it was hot and humid. The Immigration and Customs controls were in a large building with a concrete canopy in front of it, much as one finds at the entrance to a smart hotel. The canopy was not wide and the shade from the sun was inviting so we parked Adolf under the middle of it, with the VW immediately behind, and walked in to complete the paperwork. Our guide books made no mention of an entry fee or tax when going into the country so we were somewhat surprised to be asked to pay for the privilege of going into Paraguay. We refused to pay, saying we had all been robbed in Buenos Aires and the British Embassy there had given us just enough money to get to the border. We said we were going into Asunción to collect more money contained in a letter that had been sent for us to collect the house of a friend, one Victor MacDougall. We prayed they didn't try and trace the mythical Victor in some phonebook.

It was quite clear the officers didn't believe a word we said, so we repeated the story with some embellishments about severe beatings and being shot at in the robbery, adding some choice opinions about the meanness of the British Embassy for not giving us enough money, for putting us in danger of coming near to terminal starvation with no funds for food on the journey up from Argentina. It is an adage of life that once you have publicly spun a tissue of lies, you have little option but to stick to the story. The deeper into the story you go, the greater the fall from grace if you ultimately admit your dishonesty. From Profumo through Jonathan Aitken and Jeffrey Archer to Chris Huhne, there are many politicians and celebrities who must wish they had heeded this aphorism and started out with the truth, rather than allowing a court to wrest it from them. The officers were unimpressed by our imaginative fictional embellishments, and told us so, whilst also telling us we could not go through without paying. For our part we were convinced there was no such thing as an entry tax and the officials had merely made it up to disguise a bribe for themselves. Thus, as far as we were concerned, they too had gone too far into their fiction to admit it.

We had an impasse of fibs and fantasy that could only be broken by the first to blink, the first to confess and relent. We had been arguing for over an hour when the officials began to ask if they could buy things off us. They were quite keen on Sam's Mickey Mouse watch, one of the matched pair we had bought early on in our trip in the States, but were reluctant to pay the $15 he demanded for the $5 timepiece. We offered them dirty towels, used underwear and other detritus from our vehicles but these bargain basement sale items were not popular. By now a long queue of irritated travellers were being sautéed in the sun as they waited to get through the narrow passage under the canopy that was blocked by our two vehicles. Pressure was building on the officials to do something so finally, they emptied their pockets between them and paid our fees for us, an entry tax that did indeed exist, whilst also buying us an ice cream each. The four of us had the grace to admit to each other we felt just a little guilty as we returned to the vehicles licking our cool ice creams before driving into Paraguay and on to Asunción.

In the city we left Bernhard and Adolf, who also had friends to see, and made our way to an address we had been given by Sam's father before leaving England. Sam's father was an essential oil merchant who specialised in supplying the perfume trade. One of his biggest suppliers was Roberto Amigo who exported oils around the world, including Petitgrain oil. Petitgrain oil is a citrus based essence derived from boiling and distilling leaves and twigs of wild orange trees. It can be used in its own right and is said to have therapeutic qualities, calming and soothing. It is also regularly used as the base in many perfumes and blends particularly well with such fragrances as bergamot, sandalwood, lavender and rosewood. We found our way to Roberto's house where he welcomed us like Prodigal Sons, introducing us to his wife and two daughters before then sitting us down to set out his itinerary and plans for us, clearly hoping we were going to spend a month or more with the family. He handed us a bundle of letters that had been awaiting our arrival, a welcome sight as once again we had not heard from anyone for a couple of months. Roberto told us he was building a block of apartments as an investment where, whilst it was not yet complete, he would lend us one of the apartments for the duration of our stay. And so it came to be that we moved into a bare, undecorated top floor apartment with a couple of camp beds in it, running water and showers and fresh and clean sheets on the beds. He might just as well have put us into the penthouse suite of the Ritz in Piccadilly.

In the end we spent eight days in Asunción, during which time Roberto, his family and his business partner Samuel Arditi showered us in generosity and hospitality. We had most of our meals, including all our breakfasts, at the Amigo house, and were often taken to restaurants or to an extremely smart club on the Paraguay River where Roberto was a member. The heat and humidity in the city was intense and on some days we had as many as eight cold showers each. Within five minutes of coming out of the shower we would be soaked in sweat again.

By the time we arrived in Paraguay in February 1973, the country had been ruled by General Alfredo Stroessner for twenty five years. He declared himself to the world to be the country's democratically elected dictator who habitually won between 90% and 98% of the popular vote. Elections were in full swing as we arrived and, unlike in 1958 when Stroessner appeared alone on the ballot, there were opposition candidates. It was common knowledge the opposition was severely harassed and the voting fraudulently rigged. The method of voting was for the voters to ask for the polling ticket of the candidate for whom they wanted to vote, somewhat compromising the anonymity of a vote. Stroessner ensured no polling tickets were printed for the opposition candidates. A further disincentive that dissuaded dissenting votes was the likelihood that anyone asking for an opposition candidate's ticket would receive a little visit from the military in the early hours. Nocturnal house calls often ended in a long swim in the Paraguay or Chaco Rivers, all of it at along the riverbed whilst wearing some extremely heavy neck jewelry from General Motors' car battery or engine block ranges.

It was rumoured the sixty one year old General was grooming one of his sons to succeed him. Young Freddie was addicted to cocaine. His brother Gustavo was an enthusiastic homosexual, which was something of a disadvantage in a country where machismo heterosexuality was the only acceptable sexual status and where homosexuality was significantly lower than bestiality or wife beating on the scale of inappropriate afflictions or depravities. He was universally despised.

The fiercely anti-communist and autocratic Stroessner was supported by the United States through strong economic and military connections and significant military aid, but he clearly eschewed any support in building a functional family. History was still alive in the minds of the fearful educated classes who were aware of the disastrous results of a previous episode of Presidential nepotism. When Carlos Antonio López died on the 10th September 1862, he was succeeded by his son, Francisco López who led the country into the disastrous Paraguayan War. Lasting five years, at the end of it Asunción was occupied by the Brazilian Army, an occupation that lasted until 1876. It is hard to think they had too much difficulty in this act of suppression since about two thirds of the country's population were massacred in the war. Thanks to the country's heavy reliance on Catholicism as the main religion, enforced abstinence from contraception has helped replenish the numbers to sustainable levels.

The city of Asunción was founded in 1537 and was laid out in a grid system, with tree lined avenues and small shady parks and squares for people to relax in. Lapacho trees grew everywhere but we were too early in the year to see their fecund pink blooms filling the city with colour. Colonial buildings with sturdy balconies mingled with the country's Guaraní culture. Many of the local population still spoke Guaraní rather than Spanish. Evidence of the work of the ubiquitous Jesuits could be seen in early settlements and many churches. The López Presidential Palace had the grandeur that befitted the haughty Stroessner's self importance while the Metropolitan Cathedral, almost bridal white, seemed a solidly reliable monument to the strength of the Catholic

Church in the country. The city is the longest continuously inhabited area in the River Plate basin and is sometimes referred to as 'Mother of Cities' since it was from Asunción that many expeditions set out to found other South American cities and settlements.

As the days in the city passed, we regularly met up with Bernhard and Adolf. On one occasion they took us to the German Club for a cup of coffee. They had been working hard to sell their VW camper van but unsurprisingly, given its battered condition, unsuccessfully. One afternoon they turned up at the flat we were using euphoric that they had not only sold it but for $450. It wasn't worth $10. A couple of days before completing the deal, a nut had fallen into one of the brake drums. The brakes were almost useless before the intrusion of the nut, let alone afterwards. The windscreen had recently developed a crack across it, but on the basis cracked windscreens in South America were an expectation and the lack of cracks an oddity, we didn't see this as a negative in the marketing process. The venerable old vehicle was on its death bed, the beating heart of its geriatric 34 horse power engine suffering atrial fibrillation. The kindest thing to have done would have been to anoint it with chrism and administer the Last Rites to it as a Viaticum to its last resting place in between Paraguay and Argentina, but the pragmatic need of funds for Bernhard and Adolf meant that sentiment was put aside and the poor car was dusted down for her trip to her last home.

We helped Bernhard and Adolf clear out those few possessions they could travel with and agreed to take them both down to the border the next day. They were quite eager to get out of the country before the policeman who had agreed to buy their vehicle found out just how decrepit and damaged his new camper van was. We hoped he would be able to come to terms with the fact all his camping in it would probably have to be done in his garden if he had one, otherwise in the street outside his house. Changing gear was always going to be a challenging experience for him. Bernhard and Adolf had taken out the gated guide for the gear leaver and so finding an appropriate gear was a lottery of luck. Our final farewell at the border was a sad moment as we had become close friends through our shared adventures. A peripatetic life inevitably brings with it a succession of partings and I had become very used to saying good-bye and not looking back, only forward to the next town, the next border and the next escapade.

Saying good bye to Bernhard and Adolf was more piquant than any other farewells we had experienced on the trip. Through our many conversations we had agreed the reason we were travelling the way we were was because we could. We had the freedom to do so. We had not had to go off to fight in a World War, and those who had were responsible for the liberty we enjoyed. Adolf's father had had three Nationalities. Born in Austria and quite contentedly living as a proud Austrian, after the Treaty of Saint Germain in 1919 he was forced to become Czechoslovakian, having to learn a new language and re-do his military service for his new enforced Nation because of the quirk of where he happened to live. The Anschluss in 1938 saw the installation of Hitler's puppet Arthur Seyss-Inquart as Chancellor and Adolf's father's new nationality as a German with another World War ahead of him to be endured. Adolf was born and grew up in Bavaria and perhaps his father moved there because of its fierce independence, a State whose population think of themselves as Bavarians first and Germans second.

My own father had served in the Army in the Second World War in the Baluch Regiment in India. As a lowly Major he was instructed one afternoon to prepare to leave immediately for an important task, without being told where or what it was to be. After a long flight he found himself in Tehran where he was thrown into the detail and arrangements of the Tehran Conference. Held between the 28th November and the 1st December 1943, the Conference was a meeting for the Allies to discuss strategy. Held in the Soviet Embassy in Tehran between Roosevelt, Churchill and Stalin, the Conference discussed a wide range of issues, including Iran's independence, Finland's right to negotiate its own terms with Russia, Poland's post war future and the general form of a post war settlement. While he was doing all this, my mother was a fire watcher in England, sitting the nights out in high towers looking out for fires from falling bombs. Neither we four nor any of the other young travellers we had met had had to experience the horrors of War. The separation, the killing, the deprivation and, even as the callow youths we were, we appreciated this and the choices we had in our lives that gave us the independence to see the world and to do as we pleased.

We left Asunción a couple of days after Bernhard and Adolf, heading east and crossing into Brazil at the eponymous Puerto Presidente Stroessner on the Rio

Paraná. The town of Puerto Presidente Stroessner was founded in 1957 when it was named Puerto Flor de Lis, but one of the benefits of omnipotence is the ability to name streets, towns or cities after yourself. Over the decades the town had become the central clearing house for anything stolen or counterfeited in illicit factories in the three neighbouring countries. Cars stolen in Brazil were brought over the border to be sold, their provenance of no concern to bargain hunters from Asunción and elsewhere in Paraguay or down in Argentina. Jewels that sellers purported to be semi-precious stones, or even emeralds that in reality probably originated from stained glass windows stolen from churches or more simply, sandpapered pieces from broken beer bottles. Caveat emptor was the mantra of any informed shopper in the city.

We crossed the borders without any difficulties, apart from being somewhat taken aback by the difference between the Spanish spoken by the majority of Latin America and the Portuguese spoken in Brazil. The Brazilian roads were in good condition and so we made fast time across the rolling fields, passing through quiet little farming villages and big countryside, some of which was covered in scrub. Every fifth car seemed to be a VW Beetle or VW van and we later discovered there was a huge VW factory where the vehicles were assembled, having been shipped over in kit form from Germany. It was sobering to think that at one stage the endless farmlands we were driving through had been rain forests, now cleared by settlers to add to the problem of deforestation. The excellent roads meant that in the two days after leaving Asunción we were able to cover about one thousand three hundred kilometres, finally stopping late at night near the burgeoning city of Sao Paulo.

As dusk fell on the second day, I was at the wheel as we merrily barreled down the road. Sam was brewing a coffee-on-the-move with our much used immersion heater. We were in that comfortable zone of complacency drivers and passengers settle into on a long run when, without warning, a cow trotted out in front of us in the dim twilight. Hitting it at that speed was going to be messy, for us and for the cow, but it was too late to brake so I veered sharply to avoid it. As we slalomed towards it, the beast spotted us and engaged reverse gear, its rear hooves losing some traction in the liquid shit it dumped in terror all over the road behind it. As the inside of the vehicle filled with flying cups, coffee granules, immersion heater and hot water, I tried to control Adolf's shimmying, convinced the cow was going to slip under our wheels. Fortunately we only clipped it lightly. I concede that 'lightly' is a subjective opinion and possibly not one shared by the cow, which hobbled back to the side of the road to regroup and plan its next excursion out into the traffic. Another close shave, for us and particularly for the cow.

We skirted around the western outskirts of Sao Paulo the next day, the fast growing city shimmering and gleaming in the bright sunlight, and drove into the labyrinthine streets of Rio de Janeiro late in the afternoon, making our way to Copacabana Beach via the Avenida Presidente Vargas. We swam in the warm sea and were toweling ourselves dry in the street by Adolf when a young Englishman came up to us and introduced himself. Robert Cook was visiting his parents, who were living in Rio where his father was working. He had been in the city for about ten days and he was interested in how we came to be there. As we talked to him, the Land Rover with the six Bristolian travellers in it rolled to a stop behind us. They were trying to catch a cargo ship back to Panama from Rio but were not having much luck as no ships from the city seemed to stop at Panama. After agreeing to meet up at a bar later in the evening, Sam and I went off to find the British School in Rua da Matriz to see if we could park in their grounds. Conveniently sited in the middle of the city it would have been the perfect place at which to base ourselves but they were somewhat reluctant to allow us in, instead helpfully directing us to a nearby Catholic Church. The priest was out so we went back and met up with the others, having supper on Copacabana beach. After supper Sam and I drove up into the mountains behind and towering over the city and parked in a National Park with stunning views of the city beneath us. The Corcovado, the Christ the Redeemer statue, floated in the dark before us, illuminated in a pale green, almost luminous light.

I was up alone at dawn and sat on the ground as I watched the huge red sun rise slowly out of the sea. The sky was dark red, becoming more pastel as the light increased. In the growing light I could see the twinkling city below reflected in the still waters of the large lagoon just behind Copacabana beach, Lagoa Rodrigo de Freitas. It was an unforgettable moment, and as I sat looking at it, huge iridescent butterflies warmed by the rising sun flapped around in the forest about me as they went about their busy butterfly business. After fixing a problem with

Adolf's electrics we drove back down into the city and went back to the Church where the parish priest said he would be delighted to let us stay there. He insisted on giving us two dire warnings.

"Under no circumstances should you spend a night up in the National Parks in the hills behind the city. They are extremely dangerous as they are close to the favelas, and people who camp up there get killed."

We chose to remain silent about our night in the Park close to the favelas as there seemed little profit to be gained from a confession and absolution for our transgression.

"Also" he said, "if anyone stops you and demands your money, give it to them. I bury the ones who say 'No'". So far, we had nothing to confess or hide on that subject but knowing Rio's reputation we knew that could change.

The church provided a wonderful base and relatively safe haven for us in the heart of the city. The gates to the courtyard opened out onto the side street and were locked at night, such that on one evening we arrived after they had been closed and had to climb over them, reminding us the security they offered was perhaps somewhat illusory. We bought a couple of bags of oats and mixed it with cold water and ate it uncooked for our meals. Despite the fact we were under a little pressure to leave South America by the beginning of April, we spent six days enjoying Rio, relishing the relaxation. I quickly came to the conclusion it was a city for lovers. Beautiful people strolled hand in hand on the wide pavements and stunning beaches of Copacabana and Ipanema. It was easy to understand the genesis of the lyrics to the 1960's song, 'The Girl From Ipanema'

> "Tall and tan and young and lovely
> The girl from Ipanema goes walking"

Made famous by recording artists like Frank Sinatra, the song is one of sadness that the girl walks by on her daily route to the beach or elsewhere in the city without ever looking at the singer sitting at the cafe. The girl it was written about, now called Helô Pinheiro, became something of a celebrity and a symbol of the beautiful youth of Rio.

We were too early for the Carnival, Mardi Gras, but there were bands and dance groups in the street practicing for it. Loud, noisy, colourful, they were a wonderful appetizer for what the Carnival would be like. We drove up to the Corcovado to look down on the city and across to Sugar Loaf Mountain. The mountain is one of a chain that runs through the city in a line. When looked at together they are said to look like a sleeping giant, with Sugar Loaf being his raised knee. The juxtaposition of the sophisticated city with its marinas, expensive shops and beautiful beaches and the horrors of the favelas, the slums that cling to the mountainside above the city was starkly apparent to us as we looked down from our vantage point. Late one afternoon we caught the cable car to the top of Sugar Loaf to watch the sun set behind the illuminated statue, once more seeing it float in the darkness, seemingly unsupported in the air after the sun had set behind the mountains. Whilst I was enthralled by the view, I remember thinking how much better Sugar Loaf would look without its cable car station on top, and the cables stretching out and tethering it to the city.

Rio was vibrant, hectic and often exuded an undercurrent of violence. Crossing any street was to dice with death as busses, taxis and cars seemed to target pedestrians and drive straight at them, playing an urban form of 'chicken' with potentially disastrous consequences. Sometimes we were on busses when this happened and it was quite clear what the drivers were doing when they spotted someone in the road and aimed the bus at them, seeing how close to them they could get without actually hitting them. They drove fast with the window next to them open and a piece of flat wood sticking forwards out of it to direct the rushing air onto them, a crude form of air conditioning. One afternoon we saw one unfortunate who had been hit by a bus that misjudged just how close it could go to him. His body lay unattended and uncared for, his feet sticking out forlornly and poignantly from under a plastic sheet as the driver and spectators examined the dent in the front wing of the bus. The callousness of their indifference to his fate underlined the low value in which life was held throughout South America. As I passed him, prostrated and twisted on the ground, I thought of his mother at the moment she first held his little naked, wet, newly born body. I thought of all the love, care and hope she invested in him over the years to bring him to this point, his life cut short, his potential never to be realised, her grandchildren never conceived. The love of a parent for a child is fathomless, imbued with hopes and wishes that are, or should be, altruistic, unconditional and focussed on delivering a rounded child safely into adulthood where it can take the reins of its life in its own hands and guide itself into the future. To lose a child before nature's natural conclusion is beyond cruel and must leave the bereaved parent asking what all that love was for.

The beaches in Rio were wide and hot, the sand so hot it was almost impossible to walk bare foot on it in the middle of the day. Beautiful people were strewn all over it, interspersed with some not so attractive shapes. Biting insects hid in the sand and nipped now and again. We body surfed in the waves on Copacabana, crashing onto its steeply shelving beach, exfoliating our skin on the rough sand. On a day when the sea was quite rough, we watched a large, very fat woman at the water's edge. Standing up to her calves in the water, plump hands resting on hips that jutted out like mantelpieces, she suddenly disappeared under a huge wave that reared up when it hit the steep shelf of the beach, engulfing her. I have seen wildebeest disappear under the water in a crocodile's jaws in the same way. After half a minute or so this particular wildebeest resurfaced fifty metres out to sea, spluttering and howling, head back with her mouth wide open like El Zacatón in Mexico, the world's deepest water-filled sink hole. The woman's family rushed into the water and swam out to tow her back, like tugs pulling in an oil rig that has broken from its moorings, beaching her on the sand for some chest and voluminous breast pressing, all to the sound of loud wailing on the beach. Given the size of her, I felt whaling was probably a more appropriate description of the rescue. I was reminded of Gregory Peck in the film Moby Dick, playing the obsessive Captain Ahab, trapped in the ropes on the flanks of his nemesis, the doomed white whale that took him to the deep where they died together in a terminal embrace.

Robert Cook and his parents showed us many kindnesses, feeding us the occasional meal and letting us shelter out of the burning sun at mid-day in their apartment near the beach. Robert was so badly sunburned on one day that for a couple of days he could not even stand the weight of a T shirt on his raw and peeled shoulders. The sun was brutal and whilst Sam and I could spend most of the day in it due to the exposure we had had to it, Robert made the mistake of thinking he could too. To show our gratitude to him for helping us while we were in the city, we suggested he might like to change his plans and fly back to England from Lima rather than Rio, hitching a ride to the west with us. And so it was that he was riding as our passenger when we left Rio for Sao Paulo and our return trip to Paraguay. My final act before leaving Rio was to shave my beard off. In truth, I tried to shave it off myself but no razor we possessed was up to the job and my attempts were excruciatingly painful so I found a barber shop on Copacabana beach that also offered wet shaves. My fertile mind nagged at me that I could be entrusting my life to a closet psychopath who was armed with a cutthroat razor. The warm towel wrapped around my face to soften the beard was comforting, but it was a leap of faith to tip my lathered face back and let a complete stranger scrape at my throat with such a lethal weapon. It went through my mind he could easily have been Sweeney Todd's Brazilian great nephew. I was only slightly reassured by the fact there was no meat pie shop next door.

We left Rio and headed south, pulling onto a petrol station forecourt at about midnight about seventy kilometres from Sao Paulo. We had discovered that most petrol stations in Brazil seemed to have a shower in their toilet and so we tried to use them for our overnight stops in order to have a cold shower in the morning before setting off for the day's drive. Leaving early in the morning we drove for twenty four hours, covering the one thousand kilometres to the Paraguayan border in one run, reaching the Iguazu Falls by seven o'clock in the morning. The Falls were at the meeting point of the borders of Brazil, Paraguay and Argentina and we accessed them from the Brazilian side through the town Foz do Iguazu. The Iguazu River drops over the Paraná plateau just over twenty kilometres above where the river meets the Rio Paraná. The longest of its two hundred and seventy five drops was eighty two metres, and the Falls were four times the width of Niagara. The multitude of individual falls seemed to form terraces as we walked in the mist and spray along the paths on the edge of the thundering water. There was a rickety walkway out over the falls that took us to the edge, from where we could look over into the broiling chasm below. Exotic and at times impossibly colourful wild birds flew about us and there were butterflies everywhere, at times buffeted by the updraft of air from the cataracts. The early morning sun created rainbows in the mist hovering over the Falls, and to enhance an already unforgettable experience we were the only three people there.

After a couple of hours at the Falls we crossed the border and headed for Asunción. We were on a long stretch of dirt road in the forest when I spotted a cow some way ahead standing across the road, seemingly fast asleep. It had a pair of large horns protruding out in front of its head. Emulating Rio's bus drivers I asked the other two how close they thought I could get to the unsuspecting animal's nose. With the tedium of long hours on the road, this seemed to be a good challenge to perk up the day. I lined up Adolf's right hand side with the front of the cow's nose and was delighted to win the game by clearing its damp nostrils with centimetres to spare. Unfortunately for the cow I forgot and miscalculated two things. First, the cow's rather fine set of horns, sticking out a smidgen more than a few centimetres in front of its head. Second, Adolf's rack of three Army jerry cans down her side. The sound of a cow's horn meeting a rack of jerry cans at speed has the vibrato timbre of a giant tuning fork that has been hit hard on a piano. The impact when the cans clipped the tip of the horn did not break it, and perhaps the cow would have wished they had as that might have reduced the vibrations in its poor head. Its brain must have been like a blancmange in a blender. Looking back we could see the poor beast staggering around the road, front legs flailing like a ballerina's temps de fleche, the sounds in its head surely rivaling the bells of Notre Dame Cathedral under full swing on Bastille Day, its eyeballs rattling like pebbles in a shaken can. We decided the poor animal probably took home an udder full of butter that evening, given the shaking it had received and the vibrations coursing through its body. We went on our way feeling just a little guilty.

Arriving back in Asunción we hardly felt we had been away. We moved back into the flat we had used, putting up an extra bed for Robert, and then collected some more letters that were waiting for us at Roberto's house. Yet again, Roberto and his business partner Samuel Arditi entertained and cared for us for the two and a half days we were in the city.

Roberto took us into the rain forests where we saw how Petitgrain was made in the forest factories. When we saw them we realised 'factory' was a euphemism and a gross over exaggeration. Sheltered under an open sided structure of wooden poles with a roof thatched with grass and leaves, the site was situated on the edge of an extensive grove of bitter orange trees. A large oil drum sat over a fire, with a pipe leading from it down into a small clear stream. The pipe ran under the water for about five metres before exiting and emptying into another large oil drum. About two hundred to three hundred kilograms of orange leaves were put into the drum over the fire and boiled. The hot vapour from the boiling water dripped down the pipe and was cooled within it in the water in the stream, turning back into liquid to be collected in the second drum. Roberto told us it took about one oil drum of leaves to produce one and a half to two litres of liquid oil. He said most 'factories' used wooden drums so the metal ones we had been looking at were considered quite modern. The scent of orange blossom in the air was heady as we walked down to another stream and swam in the warm water.

In the evening Roberto took the three of us out to a restaurant. It turned out the *Paraguai* was the most expensive restaurant in the city. As was quite usual, all the tables were outside. The food was delicious and we were entertained by Paraguayan musicians, dancers from various South American countries and a magician. At a table near us a young couple sat opposite each other as they dined. Sitting at the table between them was a woman dressed in black. Grey hair poked out from under a scarf and her face had the expression of someone chewing on an irritated scorpion. Her lined skin hung from her face like crumpled washing on the line and stray hairs on her chin waved gently in the breeze. She sat back in her chair, silent and unsmiling, her hands folded in her lap. We had grown used to seeing chaperones on our travels but it was still always a surprise when I compared the courtship rituals, rules and conventions of Latin America with the liberal life we as a generation took for granted in England. From the expression on the young man's face, it was clear there can be no more effective a bromide to quell the libido than a girl's grandmother, and no less distracting than it would be if her mother played a blow torch flame over his bare backside as he made love to her.

Saying farewell on the afternoon of the 24th February, we drove down to the River to catch the ferry. It turned out to be a wooden raft that we were told could take six vehicles. Some of the planks of wood on the raft were completely rotten and crumbling. We joined five other cars on it and a few feet after leaving the bank the contraption ran aground in the mud. The only solution was for a few of us to jump in the water and push the raft, which fortunately was enough help to clear it for its voyage across the river. As the raft had no engines, a small boat was tied up next to it and pushed it around and across the river. Crossing the border we drove into Clorinda in Argentina, looking for a garage where we could change Adolf's oil. Whilst there were one or two who could do it we felt they were too expensive and so drove on south through Formosa, reaching Resistencia at three thirty in the morning, once again parking on a garage forecourt. A couple of hours later we woke and the garage owner allowed us to do the oil change in his garage, which had an inspection pit. As we worked we talked to the mechanics and one or two inquisitive passers by who were attracted by Adolf. We discovered the road to Salta was just passable. Whilst the route went through vast uninhabited regions, and at times might be rough going, it had the attraction of being well north of Santiago del Estero where we felt the police might not be too pleased to see us again. Also we wanted to try and drive the shorter route to Lima through Chile rather than the longer way round up through Bolivia.

Setting off we came upon a group of men in the road who were waving us down. Uncharacteristically, we slowed and came to a halt a short distance from them. The general rule of travel in South and Central America was not to stop for anyone, irrespective of whether they looked broken down or injured. Such accidents or breakdowns were often fake, any unfortunate Samaritan falling for it being set upon by accomplices hidden in the bushes. In this case the group were all out in the open and seemed to be in festival mood and wanted to share some maté with us. We had drunk maté a number of times before, one person in Paraguay calling it *'Paraguayan Fanta'*. Ubiquitous in South America and particularly in the more southern regions, maté is a drink made from an infusion of dried herbs that are chopped and ground and placed in a gourd. To drink the tea a straw called a bombilla is used, acting both as a straw and a filter since the end that goes in the cup is bulbous and closed but with holes, allowing it to act as a sieve. The extremely friendly men in the car confirmed we should be able to make it through to Salta so finishing our drinks we set off for it, soon leaving the tarmac for a dirt road, which is when one of the back tyres exploded. We had noticed a large split in it so were not too surprised at its flatulent protest at more abuse.

Salta was about eight hundred kilometres from Resistencia and we reached it at about four thirty in the morning, having once again driven through the night. We had not reached a tarmac road until about an hour out of Salta. After a couple of hours sleep by the road we drove into Salta and tried to park in a small gap in the line of cars by the pavement in the Plaza 9 de Julio. Almost immediately we were greeted by a passing Englishman who lived in the town. Jeremy Grimson had seen the Union Jack on Adolf's tailgate and was intrigued to know what we were doing in the town, and indeed in the continent. Before he offered us the use of hot showers and a meal, he told us the convention in the town was for parked cars to leave their handbrakes off so incoming cars wishing to park could push them forwards or backwards with their bumpers. For the next two days he was a wonderful host, treating us to a couple of meals and letting us use his bathing facilities whenever we wanted. One morning we were having a coffee in a cafe and chatted to a Canadian girl who had lived in Chile for three years. She said she had recently left the country because life there had become intolerable. Industries were closing down and food, commodities and petrol were in extremely short supply, often impossible to obtain. She said the Communist regime had managed to destroy the country in two years and with an election due on the 4th March, huge riots and a revolt by the people were anticipated.

President Salvador Allende came into power in 1970 as leader of the Unidad Popular, a coalition Government. He assumed power after signing an official agreement with the Christian Democrats, but insightful observers felt this had merely been a ploy to obtain control. To this day I see similarities in our own flawed democracy. The difference between Party manifestos as elections approach, and the reality of any new Government's true agenda once it attains power, particularly if that power is based on a significant majority, is at times astonishing. New Labour's promise of a referendum on Europe, so carelessly and shamelessly brushed aside when the moment came to keep the covenant, is only one example of what I believe has been a series of majority led autocracies in the United Kingdom. And we are told by our arrogant political leaders that our democracy should be exported to the ignorant heathens and savages who only know dishonest leadership, despite their civilisations often being many millennia older than ours.

Once in control of the Government and the country, Allende started to implement a wide ranging program of nationalisation of large industries, including banking and copper mining. Land seizures for redistribution, which were started under the previous incumbent Eduardo Montalva, were accelerated and pushed through by the Minister of Agriculture. All estates of over eighty hectares were seized, a rebalancing act that took a mere two years to complete. Perhaps the Zimbabwean Government read South American history before starting out on their land seizures and redistribution. On a massive spending spree of the country's money, Allende quickly pushed up blue collar workers' wages by up to forty percent, and a further twenty percent the following year. He did this in conjunction with a policy of price controls, a toxic commercial cocktail with only one inevitable result. To enforce his controlled price regime his obsequious Administration brought in State controlled distribution networks. He provided free milk for the young, free education, nationalised health care and increased State welfare.

There was no doubt that for a short while the lot of the poorest in Chile improved significantly, but it did not take long for the ramifications of rampant socialist profligacy on the economy to be felt with dramatic shortages of food and essentials, the genesis of the violent unrest that lay ahead of us. The psychological impact on people of deprivation is dramatic, but it is known that this is exacerbated if those same people have first been shown an improvement in their impoverished lives before it is snatched away and they are returned to their previous state of penury. Their reaction is significantly more violent than it would be if they suffered loss without first having been shown improvement. Deny a child a sweet from the cupboard and it will be upset. Give that child a sweet and then take it away again and get ready to deal with an apoplectic tantrum. The impact of the nationalisation program on relationships with other Governments, particularly the United States, became strained. Racial tensions within the country increased dramatically as the oppressed turned on each other in internecine disputes. President Nixon was determined to back the overthrow of Allende through the CIA. He had spent substantial sums of US taxpayers' money in an ultimately futile attempt to prevent Allende gaining power in 1970.

In November we had heard of huge strikes in Chile, led initially by the truck drivers. The Government response was to seize many trucks and to have Government supporters and the Army drive them to keep deliveries and the infrastructure going. Riot police heavy-handedly dealt with strikers and protestors, which had led to further violence in retaliation, leaving the country teetering on the edge of civil war. The place was unpredictable and volatile, a powder keg with the fuse lit and with time running out, the potential for catastrophic violence always near the surface. It was against this backdrop that we were planning our entry into Chile. Whilst the wise choice would have been to turn north into Bolivia and then west into Peru to avoid Chile, the lure of crossing the Atacama desert was strong for Sam and me, if somewhat more muted in our guest passenger, Robert, who was looking somewhat pale at the prospect of what might lie ahead as he listened to our conversation with the Canadian girl. One of the issues to be faced in Chile was the requirement to change money at the official rate of $1 to 35 Escudos. Travellers were supposed to change

$10 a day at this rate, and evidence these quotidian transactions on exit from the country. We bought 350 Escudos for $1 on the black market in Salta, so eager were the money changers to get rid of the worthless Chilean currency, resigning ourselves to sorting out the currency declaration problem when we left Chile.

Leaving Salta we drove to San Antonio de los Cobres, about one hundred and fifty kilometres from the border at Huatiquina, a place so small it was not marked on the maps. In San Antonio we looked for somewhere to repair our herniated and ruptured tyre but no garage had the equipment so we set off for Huatiquina. Expecting to find a border post, we came across a solitary hut by the track, near which was a route sign with a Chilean road number on it. Clearly we had somehow crossed the border and were some way into Chile so we asked the hut owner where the Aduana was. He was busy butchering a cow strung up from a beam. Wiping his bloodied hands on his filthy trousers, he told us it was back in San Antonio. We had no option but to drive back, stopping to sleep in a side street in the town when we reached it late that night. In the morning we found the Customs office but they could only stamp our Carnet, Adolf's bond. They told us we would need to get our Passports stamped at the border so we set off again, driving through desert scrub and a barren, at times rocky landscape. We passed through Huatiquina again after which the scrub gave way to the endless expanse of sand and rock of the Atacama, a brutal desert where salt deposits covered everything, at times giving the impression of the land being dusted in snow under the bright sun. Che Guevara had crossed this same desert in his youth years before on the life changing journey that, combined with his experiences in Guatemala turned this right wing middle class professional into the Marxist firebrand he became.

The Atacama was stunningly beautiful in its harshness. In the utter wilderness and emptiness of the desert, with just a faint track to follow, we drove through the naked land where there was little sign of any life other than an occasional pile of bleached bones. We followed the compass to keep us heading west. At one point we passed a small lake, a complete anomaly in the arid waterless desert, its rim fringed with thick encrustations of salt. Flamingos standing in the water moved slowly away from us in the way of flamingos throughout the world, keeping a wary eye on us as they walked out of range of whatever it is they fear. We came upon the Chilean Immigration post at Toconao. It consisted of what resembled a cricket scorer's hut, a wooden shack with a door on one side. There was a man in it, dozing quietly in the silence. He stamped our Passports but made no attempt to complete a monetary declaration so we left him to his sleep and drove on. It was noon, with the sun high above us and not a tree in sight under which to shelter. We lost an hour at one stage when the dynamo burnt out and we had to replace it.

We passed through Calama where we filled our petrol tanks and bought some food, sufficient to sustain us for a while if we became stuck in the desert. Our shopping spree was also triggered by the fact that because of the rate of exchange we had got in Argentina, everything was costing ten percent of its true value. We had no desire to leave Chile with any of its currency as no one was particularly keen to buy devaluing Escudos. In the town we saw a phalanx of riot police coming down the road. Dressed and masked in their intimidating black protective clothing, shields on their arms and batons in their free hands, the reality of the tensions in Chile were there before us. Thankfully the police were not particularly interested in us, so we skirted around them through some side streets and left the town. Just after Calama we passed Chuquicamata, a huge open cast mine. There was a large police check point by the mine where they examined all our papers and then waved us through, once again without making any mention of a money declaration. Night fell and we drove on into the dark, picking out the track in the sand ahead of us in Adolf's lights. Just before Maria Elena we turned north and drove on through the night, passing through a number of police check points without stopping, no doubt waking the befuddled and dozing police as we did. None came after us so perhaps sleep was preferable to racing after us through the dark desert. At one check point we came up behind a queue of cars waiting to get through. In the headlights of the car at the front we could see the barrier was up so we drove down beside of the line of vehicles, through the barrier and on into the night, half expecting bullets to come flying through the back of the canvas top. Perhaps the police were so surprised at the insulting audacity of the manoeuvre they were transfixed until it was too late and we were gone.

At six o'clock in the morning, as dawn was breaking, we came upon a police control point that was barricaded and which we could not get around. Our papers were scrutinised and the back of one of the stubs in our Carnet was stamped, a meaningless gesture but not one we were eager to discuss with the police. The 60 Escudos they wanted for this was most definitely discussed and we trotted out our usual story of being robbed and abused and so they let us through. We reached Arica at eight o'clock. Arica was the border town, and we had driven over one and a half thousand kilometres from Salta with only the briefest stop. We had some Escudos left and so used them all buying spare engine oil, again at an extraordinary bargain price. Next was the border and time to face the music.

We drove down to the border post which was about ten kilometres north of the town and parked in front of the steps leading up to the building. The sky was a beautiful clear blue and the sun was already throwing out heat. Sam and I made Robert lie quietly on the mattress in the back of Adolf, covering him up to his neck with a sheet. We told him to lie still and not to move, and then went up into the post with our Carnet and Passports. Dealing with the Carnet first, the officers became confused as it had not been stamped correctly. We appeared to be in the country illegally, and they became extremely agitated. We told them we were in a hurry to get to Lima as we had a passenger who was very ill in the Land Rover and we had to get him to hospital for a big operation. This seemed to end their indecision so they rectified the error by giving us the stamp we needed, together with an exit stamp.

The Immigration officers were less understanding and accommodating when they told us we were deficient some '*formularios*', some forms. Additionally, because we had somehow by-passed the Argentinian border, we had no exit stamps in our Passports, which puzzled them. They were incandescent, shouting at us and asking how we had got into the country and how long we had really been in it. With a country so at unease with itself, a country so given to violence, aberrations are not tolerated and tempers short, with itchy trigger fingers always an opportunity for disastrous over-reaction. We repeated our sick passenger routine, with some terminal illness embellishments, which again presented them with a conundrum. To carry on delay could endanger a life, but then there was the issue of the missing formularios. What to do? They were obviously in a quandary, pulled apart by the opposing forces of the decisions before them. They insisted on seeing the patient so we took them out to Adolf and showed them Robert, lying perfectly still in the back under the sheet, eyes closed and now looking a genuine pasty white, no doubt revisiting the wisdom of his decision in Rio to accept the offer of a lift to Lima. Perhaps his memory of our conversation on Copacabana Beach, where we had outlined the fun he would have if he came with us brought to his mind our differing interpretations of the definition of 'fun'. Robert's prostrate acting skills, albeit assisted by terror, seemed to tip the balance, so the officers took Sam and me back into the border post and produced the forms we should have had in our exit documents. We filled them in which made smiles appear on the officers' faces, although smiles was a relative term. More accurately they stopped scowling and shouting, which we interpreted as euphoria. They were happy, and so were we as they stamped our Passports and waved us through. The confusion about the validity of our presence in the country and their obsession with their bureaucratic processes had made them completely forget to check our financial transactions, or lack of them. Since they had no real idea how long we had been in the country, trying to explain why we had not changed $10 a day, and exactly how many such changes we had missed would have been challenging. We counted our blessings, walked nonchalantly to Adolf and drove unhurriedly through the border barrier into the two hundred metres of No Man's Land between the two countries.

On reaching the barricade on the Peruvian side, all three of us got out of Adolf and waved cheerfully to the Chileans, who were watching us, clearly still puzzled. They responded by waving fists and guns, shouting obscenities at us as Robert's Lazarus moment revealed they had been duped. Now we only had the Peruvians to deal with, but first we had to stand still, respectful of a flag raising ceremony that must have been a daily event. Since there was no need for subterfuge or obfuscation, Sam stood by Adolf as I took Robert into the border post to complete the paperwork to enter Peru. Once again a financial declaration was needed and I stated that Sam and I had $60, showing him the notes that I took from the pocket of my exhausted shorts. The Immigration officer was unimpressed and responded by giving the two of us seven day visas. Normally I would have argued for longer but because we were in a hurry to leave South America before our Carnet ran out, I accepted his kind offer. I completed the Immigration papers for Sam and me, listing my occupation as 'Janitor'. When I finished our paperwork the Immigration officer turned to Robert.

He asked him how much money he had and Robert, in his innocence of South American ways, took out his wallet and pulled out all his money, which must have been a few hundred dollars. I was standing in between Robert and the official and intercepted the notes he was about to show the man. In full view of the watching officer I pulled off the majority of the large denomination notes, put them back in his wallet and told Robert to put it back in his pocket. I then counted out just under $100 and showed it to the officer who wrote the amount down on Robert's papers, seemingly oblivious of, or perhaps confused by, the sleight of hand carried out in front of his eyes. As always, the obvious is not always apparent if done boldly enough. Our eyes so often see what they expect to see rather than the truth, and hence I always remain cynical of one person's view or record of history. The officer stamped our passports and we walked out, free to enter Peru.

Lima was about one thousand four hundred kilometres north and we would be following the Pan American Highway that ran down the western coast and which for most of the way to Lima hugged the coast. We decided to drive to Lima in one long run, continuing the process of Sam and me driving in shifts. There was little except desert between us and the capital, and we needed to get Robert to the airport to catch a flight, so we set off along the stunningly beautiful Peruvian coastline with its huge sand dunes on our right that once again sometimes encroached on and completely covered the road. As night fell a heavy sea mist rolled inland making driving extremely difficult, particularly when the road disappeared under sand for long stretches. To add to the fun, the condition of the road deteriorated dramatically. At two o'clock in the morning we reached a small town called Palpa, a few kilometres after the coast hugging road turned inland. As we drove through the deserted and sleeping town, the ignition light came on indicating an electrical problem so we pulled up under a street light and took out the dynamo. We cleaned it and retested it but by four o'clock it was clear it had a big problem so we decided to stop in the town until it's inhabitants stirred and we could find a garage. We had been travelling non-stop for forty four hours so a couple of hours' sleep was welcome.

When the sounds of the town stirring for the day disturbed our sleep, we found a garage where a mechanic took the dynamo apart and decided it was only in need of some lubrication. When we put it back in, it worked so we set off for the four hundred kilometre run into Lima, which we reached late in the afternoon. We made our way to the British Embassy where there was a message for us from Father McHugh, a priest who had taught me at school when I was eight years old, and who was now running a Mission in Lima. The message gave his address on the Ancon road in Sol de Oro, a relatively poor area in central north Lima. We drove there and for the next three days used the Mission as our base as we sorted out a flight for Robert, looked for a spare dynamo for Adolf and resupplied ourselves with a few provisions. Our staple diet on the move had now been reduced to porridge oats, eaten uncooked in cold water and which fortunately I really enjoyed. Extremely cheap, filling and providing energy, it seemed to us to be a perfect survival solution. It had the added benefit of not being canary yellow and on a cob. Whilst it was some months since we had last had corn, the memory still lingered. Thanks to the Argentinian doctor, who we had rushed through beatification straight to sanctification, our alimentary systems were no longer in overdrive and had settled back to normality, so whilst we were not putting on any weight, we were no longer continuing to lose it.

One morning Father McHugh took us up into the '*pueblos jóvenes*', also called the *Barriadas* the shanty towns on the hills above Lima. He said the only reason we could go into them and come out alive was because we were with him. Like the favelas in Rio, or any shanty towns or slum dwellings in the world, the poverty was extreme. There was a tension in the air and it was obvious the place was probably largely self policing. The Barriadas seemed to have a hierarchical pecking order. The water supply was at the foot of the hills, so the wealthier slum dwellers possessed the shacks in that area. Their shacks were made of either wood or in the more luxurious ones, with breeze blocks. Corrugated iron roofing provided good shelter, and many of the huts had large dogs sitting on the roof, sometimes chained to a post. We were told they were there to stop people trying to break in through the roof.

As we moved slowly up the hill through the narrow passageways between the crude dwellings, their structure deteriorated. Wood and brick continued up the slope for a short distance and then the corrugated roofs disappeared to be replaced by old dismantled packing cases. The brick and wood walls became plywood until finally, right at the top of the slopes, the most underprivileged eked an existence of futile hell in tiny shelters of cardboard and plastic. Rubbish was strewn everywhere and the stench was at times overpowering as there was no sewage system other than the ground. Children ran barefoot in ragged clothes, their skins grimed with ingrained dirt. Stray chickens dodged the children's feet as they scratched the earth for food. It was here, in this abyss of despair, that the priests and nuns from the Mission did most of their work. At times that work must have seemed completely hopeless, and ultimately pointless. How does one make a difference against such overwhelming odds? It was impossible to comprehend the sense of entrapment the shanty town dwellers in the Barriadas must have felt, in many ways no different to that of someone serving a life sentence, or sitting out the hours on Death Row in a prison, existing suspended in a pointless life whilst waiting the freedom of spirit that perhaps can only be found in egalitarian death's soothing embrace.

    Robert bought a Varig ticket to England and the following evening we dropped him off at the airport for his flight to safety and sanity. With only two days of our seven day Peruvian visas left, and with the abiding pressure of our Carnet's imminent demise, we too left Lima for the one thousand three hundred kilometre drive to the Ecuadorian border. Retracing our southerly steps through Chimbote, Chiclayo, Lambayeque and Piura, we hugged the coast and made it to the border at Aguas Verdes, passing through at eight o'clock in the morning without being searched by either side. The only delay was from the inefficiency of the Ecuadorians. It reached new heights, or perhaps given the deleterious affect on the spirits of all those trying to get through their labyrinthine systems, plumbed new depths. Just after the Ecuadorian border we came across a police check point, a common and regular feature of Ecuadorian roads. On that one day we were stopped at check points seven times, but managed to race through about a dozen others where there was no chain across the road, passing the police huts before the occupants could get their feet off their desks and their hands on their guns. Driving down a long, straight stretch of road that was raised above the fields on either side, I was studying the crops in the field trying to make out if they were pineapples when I noticed a long and gentle bend coming up in the road ahead. As we went into the bend I also noticed we seemed to be going straight ahead. Glancing across at Sam, I realised he was perfectly happy in his slumbers, eyes firmly closed and fast asleep with his dreams, readying to launch Adolf off a two metre bank into the field below. I grabbed the wheel and turned us into the corner in a gentle slide, still touch and go as to whether we went over the edge. We stopped for a coffee to energise both our brains and to provide them with a bit of stimulant that would keep us awake. Yet another close call with the 'spare life' cupboard beginning to look a bit bare.

Heading north for Quito, we drove through thousands of acres of banana plantations, visual evidence of Ecuador's pre-eminence as the largest exporter of bananas in the world. Now and again we would pass enormous piles of discarded bananas, some of the piles higher than Adolf's roof. We stopped at one and rummaged through the mountain of fruit, picking out handfuls of perfectly presentable bananas, delighted at replenishing our larder which was now bare, even of porridge oats. After driving through the seemingly endless plantations that alternated with thick rain forest, we began to climb and found ourselves driving above the snow line. In between Ambato and Latacunga we stopped and bought a plate of hot food each from an Indian woman who was selling her food from a small cart. About the size of a tea trolley, it had a tray of burning coals underneath a hot plate on which the remains of an animal lay in shredded tatters, a commonly seen open air restaurant in South American towns and villages. About the size of a dog, we wondered if it had indeed been one of the thousands of stray dogs we saw roaming the streets wherever we went. While hitching back to Peru from La Paz I had sat in a square of a town and watched a pack of about twenty of them. Feral and filthy, they moved into the square and quickly picked up the scent of a bitch that was walking across the other side. She was clearly in season as the dogs rushed over to her, surrounded her and proceeded to gang rape the poor animal, ignoring its squeals and snarls of protestation under the weight of the savage and compassionless assault and violation.

Our chosen point of exit from Ecuador was Tulcan, two hundred and twenty kilometres north of Quito. We picked up an American hitchhiker who was also heading for the border as we left Quito. Chip had had all his money stolen and we agreed to help him with his trip north. It didn't occur to me until weeks later to wonder whether he too used the 'robbed of all money' ploy. Passing through Ibarra, we detoured to a race track we had heard about where the public could drive on the track. We found it at Yahuarcocha Lake just outside the town. The race track ran around the lake and the drive on it was wonderfully scenic. We assumed the many cattle wandering around on it would be removed if a race meeting was in progress. The road immediately north of Ibarra went through a series of bends and hairpins as we drove further up into the mountains. The road was at first cobbled before deteriorating into a dirt track, a relief from the juddering cobbles. It started to rain and the conditions became so bad we had to engage four wheel drive to stay on the road. At Tulcan we stopped in a street in the dark and went to sleep, the three of us crammed in the back of Adolf.

In the morning we dropped Chip short of the border and crossed to Ipiales in Colombia without any difficulties from either set of Aduana. Our plan was to drive to Popayán north of us. The road to Pasto was good, tarmac and well maintained but from Pasto it turned to a dirt road again, one that twisted and climbed yet again up into the mountains, slowing our progress. Some time after dark it became too dangerous to carry on given the narrow road and steep sided valleys, so we pulled into the rain forest and settled down for the night, to the deafening chorus of libidinous frogs broadcasting their sexual intentions.

We reached Cali just after mid-day the next day and found the six Bristolian British and their Land Rover parked in the grounds of the British School. They had been quoted a price of $350 to ship their Land Rover from Buenaventura to Panama on a ship that was sailing in two days time. It was a Sunday so there was nothing Sam and I could do until the morning apart from sit in a cafe with the others and drink coffee and chat. In the morning the woman at the shipping company told us she would not be able to let us know if Adolf could be fitted on board until mid-morning, which in South America could be translated as mid-week so Sam and I decided to drive to Buenaventura and make our enquiries there. Julian and John came down with us with their Land Rover. To our surprise we discovered the road to the port through the jungle had been upgraded to a tarmac road from the glorified logging trail it had been when we last went down it, so the journey took a mere two hours. At Buenaventura the Grace Line staff welcomed us back like prodigal sons, clearly remembering our last visit. They said they had space for Adolf and quoted us $347 so we completed the paperwork and took Adolf down to the quayside where we entrusted her to the dockers. We caught the five thirty afternoon *'Autobús Especial'* to Cali. It was a beaten up old bus that lumbered and heaved its uncomfortable way back to Cali. In the mountain sections where our speed slowed the driver had the peculiar habit of driving whilst leaning back in his seat, his hands behind his head. Perhaps that was the *'Especial'* part of the journey. When we reached Cali we found the Bristolians in the cafe by the bus station. They were booked onto the Pullman bus to Medellin that left at ten o'clock that evening but when we enquired we were told it was full so Sam, Julian, John and I had no option but to catch the *'Autobús Ordinario'* that left a couple of hours later. Ordinario had a special meaning of its own in South American bus travel vernacular, so we didn't anticipate much sleep.

There was much about the bus and the eleven hour trip to Medellin through the night that was not so 'ordinario'. For a start the driver was a frustrated Formula 1 racer, desperate to overtake anything in his path. Seeing red lights in the distance spurred him into a chase. When he finally caught up with the vehicle in front, he demonstrated his overtaking techniques, some of which bordered on the suicidal. He and his drunk assistant obviously had some scam going with extraneous passengers. We left the bus station with almost every seat taken, but on the way out of town stopped a number of times to take on board what appeared to be groups of friends or relatives. Each newcomer handed over cash that disappeared into the driver's pocket for a bit of illicit bonus. We thought this bit of free enterprise would end after we left Cali but in fact it continued throughout the night, all the way to Medellin. One of these stops was in a small town where the driver bought a coffee for himself, and we took the opportunity to do the same. There was another bus next to ours and it seemed to have a leaking radiator. The driver was fixing it with used coffee grounds from the cafe. He was spooning them into the top of the radiator and then washing them in with more water. The principle seemed to be the grounds would be carried by the flow of the water to the puncture in the radiator where they would congregate at the offending hole like migrating wildebeest at a river crossing, blocking the exit. Since the radiator looked like a colander we felt the Heath Robinson repairs were on the short end of temporary.

In the early hours of the morning John, who was sitting dozing next to the window with Julian in the aisle seat, suddenly felt something moving in his lap. Opening his eyes in the dim light, he saw a man standing in the aisle and leaning over with his hand in his clothes around his waist area. John grabbed the intruding wrist and the man quickly pulled back and hurried to the front of the crowded bus, pushing past others standing or sitting on the floor between the seats. He got off the bus the next time it stopped. John could see his jacket and shirt had both been cut, and in the morning had the satisfaction of finding a blood stained razor blade on the floor beneath his seat. The man had obviously cut himself on the razor when he had been grabbed by John, so we felt his attempt to steal anything that might be in John's pockets had been foiled with a healthy dose of equitable retribution.

    We arrived at Medellin at ten thirty in the morning, miraculously alive, and only five minutes after the others in their more expensive Pullman. It was somehow deeply satisfying to us that it had broken down on the journey. John, Julian and I went to find a travel agent where we booked flights on the plane to Panama that afternoon and then we all headed out to the airport where we boarded a plane that was both significantly larger and younger than the one we had flown in on our way south.   Our departure was delayed as a huge storm broke above us. During the delay some police boarded the plane and came up to a young and swarthy looking man sitting in the seat in front of me. They loudly told him he had to get off the plane and, when he refused, slapped him around and hauled him out of his seat, pushing him forcibly backwards out of the door. About twenty minutes later he reappeared and retook his seat, either exonerated or somewhat poorer as the result of a substantial bribe. The storm slowly cleared and we finally lifted off. I looked down on Medellin and the Colombian forests beneath me as we headed north, bidding South America a fond and silent farewell. It would be about thirty five years before I would step foot on its soil again, but its memories have never faded in that time. It left an indelible imprint on my mind with its music, colour, scents, immense landscapes and doughty people who lived lives no soft Europeans or Americans could. Their toughness and resilience was inspirational to me, and would ever remain so.

And now, I was on my way home, the last leg to that longed for reunion. It would be slightly longer than I anticipated.

A GIRL CALLED ADOLF

CHAPTER 14

Panama to Asheville

"I have seen more than I remember, and remember more than I have seen."
Benjamin Disraeli

"Dream as if you'll live forever. Live as if you'll die today"
James Dean

The plane's wheels touched down with a comfortingly firm thump as we landed at Panama's old airport. We slowly made our way into the Immigration office and Sam and I found ourselves at the back of the queue. The Bristolian six were let through without a second glance but once again for Sam and me it was a very different story. For some reason both the

Immigration and Customs officials seemed to take a dislike to us, which we felt was a bit unreasonable. Even the slapped about passenger had gone through on the nod. We were asked how much money we had, our answers getting the usual raised eyebrows of disbelief. The pompous official wanted to know whether Sam had been to Iran since there were some Arab country stamps in his Passport. Our proposed length of stay in the country was of particular interest. For some reason they seemed to disbelieve our stated intention of driving straight through and on north to the United States.

Once Immigration finished with us and given us short term visas, we were ushered over to Customs in the Customs hall. There were a number of long, low, knee height tables in the hall and we were made to empty out our rucksacks onto one of them. The Customs officer then started going through our meagre possessions, one by one, lifting each item and examining it carefully, looking inside the book we each had, opening bags and feeling clothes. My rucksack contained a bag of oranges we had bought from a man by the roadside in Colombia in exchange for a couple of old school rugby shirts we no longer wanted and the officer put these to one side, telling us they were "Prohibido". We argued the point with him, convinced they were going to end up in his fruit bowl at home, but he was adamant and became more irritated, which is when he found the joke. As he flicked the pages of my book he came across my bookmark. Four small, innocuous sheets of paper stapled together on which were printed a rude cartoon, given to me by a friend as we left England and which I had forgotten about and indeed thought nothing of. As he leafed through the small four pages, a premonition told me we were in trouble. Catholicism was rife in Central and South America and taken somewhat seriously. Our fundamentalist Customs officer was as fundamental and rabid as they come, or made himself appear so. He looked affronted when he saw the last of the four pages, especially as the very visual joke was not exactly heterosexual. He shouted at me,

"Pornografía! Esto es asqueroso!" - "this is disgusting!"

He had missed the point. It was meant to be. When he folded it and started to put it in his pocket, I assumed it was going the same way as the oranges, but this time confiscated so it could be shared with his colleagues for a private chuckle. I reached across and grabbed it from his hand and tore it into pieces.

"Si no puedo tenerlo, no se puede" I said firmly - "If I can't have it, nor can you".

The man went ballistic and shouted at us,

"Espera aquí, voy a llegar el jefe!" "Wait here, I am going for the Chief".

He turned on his heel and strode purposefully through the door to the offices behind. As the door slammed shut behind him, Sam and I grabbed our possessions off the table. We stuffed some of them roughly into our rucksacks, picked up the rest and sprinted through the Customs hall and out of the building, clutching our bags and loose clothes to our chests. The sleeve of an old shirt I was carrying flapped a farewell behind me as I ran. Serendipitously there was a bus about to leave for the Old City and we jumped in to find the Bristolians already on it. As we pulled away, Sam and I scanned the front of the building but no one emerged, and once more we appeared to have got away with it. I did wonder what the doubtlessly bemused 'El Jefe' said to the unfortunate Customs officer who had no doubt dragged him from his warm tortilla and coffee to show him an empty table devoid of perverted travellers awaiting sentence.

The bus took us into the Old City of Panama where we found a flat roof on top of a Pension to spend the night on the tiled floor under the stars for the princely sum of $1 a head. Beds on the roof would have been extra. That evening we all went to a Chinese restaurant for a very cheap meal. Towards the end of it I decided to use the toilet, which was at the back of the building next to the kitchens. There were very few lights but I could make out the whole place was alive with the largest cockroaches I had ever seen, some longer than my thumb. They were climbing the walls in the small and cramped unisex toilet and scurrying about on the floor of the kitchens, which I could see a few metres away through the doorless toilet. The Chinese cooks were busy with their woks and meat cleavers over open fires, the light from the flames dancing on their sweating faces. I assumed the copious rivulets of sweat I saw dripping off them generally ended up in the food as a slightly brackish jus.

Our meal finished we left the restaurant and Julian and I went down a dark side alley towards the sea front to catch a cooling sea breeze. We passed a policeman in the alley who was having a special tender moment up against the wall with his 'girlfriend'. Her bored face over his shoulder as she chewed her gum and scratched an itch on her nose was not that of someone in the heady paroxysms of ecstasy, more that of someone focussed on the financial benefits of the seedy transaction. The alley opened out onto a path by the sea, which was about five metres beneath us. From our vantage point we had a wonderful view of the city at night, its yellow lights reflected in the water. As we stood chatting and taking it all in, another policeman appeared, also with a girlfriend. When he suggested to us he didn't want us to hurt ourselves or fall in the water and that we could get an equally good view of the city and its lights from a nearby road, we took the hint and moved on, leaving him rearranging both his and the girl's clothing against the coital wall.

It took a couple of days for the ship to arrive from Colombia and for the vehicles to be unloaded and cleared for release. Adolf had been broken into again but once more nothing was missing, largely because anything of the slightest value or usefulness was securely locked away in the boxes on the floor in the back. We bade farewell to the Bristolians yet again and after looking for a couple of souvenirs for our families in England, left the Old City, crossed the Bridge of the Americas and headed for the border, stopping at a small place called Santa Clara for a swim in the sea. The journey to San Jose in Costa Rica was uneventful, apart from a long delay at the border due to the number of people waiting to cross. Robert and Lupita Jagger welcomed us back warmly and kindly housed and entertained us for the next four weeks. The length of the stay was unexpected and unplanned but resulted from Sam's continuing sinus problems that were causing him increasing breathing difficulties, and which at times were painful. We decided to find out if an operation in Costa Rica would be cheaper than in the United States. When it turned out that it would be, especially when the surgeon said he would do it at half price, we decided to get it done. Dr Niehaus had trained in the United States and seemed to be extremely capable. His skilled hand meant the operation was a success, if somewhat uncomfortable for Sam.

With the tests running up to the operation and a period of recuperation after it, we stayed in Costa Rica much longer than we had anticipated. It was not a hardship, thanks to Robert and Lupita's welcoming wider family. It also gave us time to do some repair work and plastic surgery on Adolf. We took off the silencer and had it re-welded. The crumpled front wing which, despite the work we had done on it in San Jose on our way south, still resembled General Manuel Noriega's face. Later to become President of Panama, General Noriega was known as 'Pineapple Face,' such was the state of his pitted skin. We also read books, wrote letters and visited a few sites of interest, with another visit to the volcano summit for a lungful of sulphur. One afternoon a Circus came to town so we went to see it. It was chaos. Trained pigeons flew out of their cages and refused to come back down and sit on stands or the performer's arm, preferring to roost on the hire wire. A chimpanzee got bored of its routine and climbed up to join the pigeons on the high wire where it cavorted and swung, screeching at its trainer below, driving the flustered birds higher up into the tent. Most of the performers did two or three acts so they were clearly short staffed, but somehow the chaos added to the fun and enjoyment.

    On the 11th April we left San Jose and drove up into Nicaragua, crossing the border and reaching Managua, the capital. It was in the late afternoon and we arrived in time to see the sun setting on a scene of utter devastation. Whilst we had heard about the earthquake on 23rd December, it was not until we saw it that we could truly comprehend the affect of it on the city, a city we had driven through just a few months before. Thousands of people had been killed with about a quarter of a million left homeless as three quarters of the city was shaken by the severe quake. Fires had broken out and the city was cut off from the world with no power, and no news coming out of it. Bodies had been entombed and because of the fear of disease becoming epidemic, whole blocks had been bulldozed and turned into mass graves. There seemed to be an opaque haze over the ruined city. The sun hung suspended in the sky above it, its light diffused and weak as it shone through the dust that still drifted in the air. Block after block had been bulldozed into gigantic heaps of rubble, each fenced off with high posts and strands of wire. Each individual block must have contained countless bodies. We passed a single story house which, on closer inspection we realised had originally been two stories. The clue was the back half of a car that was sticking out of the side of what was left of the building. Clearly it had been half in half out of the garage when the house had collapsed, cutting it in half as if by a guillotine. I wondered if the driver was still in it when the house collapsed, caught at the wheel at the moment of parking, much as the residents of Pompeii had been caught and frozen in time as statues.

We live each day with thousands of thoughts passing through our minds. Some stop in our consciousness, resting a while to be mulled over, to be worried about or smiled at. Others pass on, not important enough for examination, or perhaps just too awful for reflection. At night those thoughts become dreams, fantasies our brains use to make sense and order out of the maelstrom of our lives. What is it like to be sitting at the wheel parking the car, walking down the street, sitting in a chair, a sentient being, but a nano second later for those thoughts to end, instantly crushed by the end of life as conscious thought is replaced by eternal void? We are ever only one heartbeat away from eternity. There is only ever the now, and in those heaps of rubble and ruined homes in front of us lay all the hopes, dreams and plans that had distracted their owners from enjoying their individual present moments. We are conditioned to worry about the future and regret the past, but at that last moment, what is their value when there is only ever the now?

A large block of apartments was tilted to one side with huge open cracks down the side of the building. Armed military personnel patrolled the streets and seemed to have a tight control of the city, or what little remained of it. Seeing such awesome and awful destruction on such a grand scale brought into perspective the magnitude of the task that faces rescue services when faced with a humanitarian crisis such as the one Managua was presented with in December. Of course, dealing with the initial aftermath can only be the first tiny step on a long journey of rebuilding and trying to normalise life for those affected. Can there ever be any semblance of normality for those who have lost everything, including their family? The homeless, the frail, the orphans. All catapulted into a new life that can so often only be an existence, an hourly fight to survive for just one more hour, one more day. Surely there can never be any going back. Fearful of being voyeuristic, we slowly drove through the ruined city and slept that night at the Honduran border as we waited for it to open in the morning.

Crossing into Honduras, the officials fumigated Adolf with a spray that was probably both carcinogenic and a respiratory irritant. Cholera and other diseases are the progeny of disasters and the Hondurans were understandably keen to avoid their import from an infected area. With Adolf's windows and back open to clear out the fumes, we drove across the narrow neck of Honduras and crossed into El Salvador where the Customs officers decided to search us. For an hour they crawled all over Adolf while we unhelpfully sat on a bench and watched. One of the officers gleefully emerged with a brown paper wrapped box he found in one of the boxes and, calling over his colleagues, ceremoniously and expectantly opened it with a knife. His loss of face in front of his colleagues as he brought out a china bowl we had bought in Panama as a gift, rather than the anticipated few kilos of drugs, was worth the inconvenience we had been caused by the hour we spent sitting watching his antics. It brought to an end his interest in us as he waved us to go. We drove off and reached San Salvador late in the afternoon, driving to the elderly and very elegant sister of someone we had met in Costa Rica who had told us we would be well looked after if we visited her family when in El Salvador.

And indeed we were. Donña Salino was a wealthy lady who lived in San Benito, a well to do area in the city with expansive luxurious houses all sheltering behind high walls and locked gates, a clue to the political unrest in a troubled country. Her house was a large, luxurious, single story building set in its own grounds. Beautifully tended flower beds framed an immaculate lawn and dotted about were trees from which hung weaver bird nests. The floors of the house were pale marble tiles, cooling the rooms, and the huge plate glass windows in the drawing room made it feel as if the garden came into the house. There was no evidence of any husband but her twenty three year old son, Poncho, and her daughter, Luce, lived with her. Poncho came home just after we had arrived and showed us our rooms, on the way to them opening a huge cupboard in a corridor outside his bedroom. On the top rail were many suits, trousers and jackets and on the bottom rail hung about fifty beautifully tailored shirts, ironed and starched to perfection.

We stayed two nights with Donña Salino, spending a full day trying to find a tyre that would replace the decrepit spare sitting on Adolf's bonnet. San Salvador did not seem to have such a tyre, despite our exhaustive enquiries, so we bade the family farewell, thanking them for their kindness before setting off for the border with Guatemala. We reached Antigua in the evening and parked on a square of grass next to a cafe that provided us with a cheap meal for supper. Sitting high in the central highlands, Antigua is the old capital of Guatemala and has some beautiful old buildings built in a baroque style, heavily influenced by the Spanish. There are a number of ruined churches, their destruction having taken place in a huge earthquake in 1773 that also destroyed much of the town. As a result of the seismic volatility of the area, the capital was moved to a safer place, which became Guatemala city. From the town we took a side road off the main highway and went to Lake Atitlán, the deepest lake in Central America. Created by volcanic activity, it was huge and quite beautiful, with the conical volcano San Pedro on its western shore. A group of colourfully dressed Guatemalan Indian girls were walking along its shore, completing the idyllic scene and the tranquility of the moment. We drove into a plush hotel with a private beach on the lake and had time to get in one drink before being asked to leave, presumably on the premise we were a health hazard and clearly some form of toxic waste. It would have been unreasonable not to sympathise with their view.

From the Lake we drove the forty kilometres to Chichicastenango, Not only did the name seem impossibly exotic with its rhythmical cadences, we knew it had a huge local market that we wanted to see. Driving to it we climbed into the heavily forested hills, passing hundreds of Indians walking along the road towards the town, many bent double under huge bags of goods they were taking to the market to sell. The village rested on its perch on a mountain top, some two thousand metres above sea level. The reality of the experience was greater than the expectation. We parked Adolf in a small square and negotiated with a young boy to guard her for us. We held up two $1 bills, handing him one and telling him he would get the other if Adolf was not broken into nor interfered with while we were away. We strolled off and then watched him from the other side of the square as he fended off inquisitive nascent criminals and thieves with a large stick, desperate for the other half of his salary, a fortune for him and a very small insurance premium for us.

The Sunday market was indeed huge, running through the village like water running into and spreading out over a dried up wadi. The main streets, the little squares and the side streets were filled with produce sellers, the majority being colourfully dressed. Bowler and tall white hat wearing women sat on the ground with their wares spread out before them on old rugs. Colourful clothing seemed to be the hallmark of Guatemala. Richly coloured shirts with intricate designs sewn into them were everywhere and we each bought one for $3. Everywhere we looked and walked we saw fruit and vegetables, wooden carvings, masks like those worn by dancers in traditional and festive dances, flowers, pottery, herbs, some for medicinal remedies. Pigs snuffled in pens with vegetable debris thrown to them, and chickens strutted about with frowns and nervous glances as they watched out for the omnipresent sharp knife. The staples of life were all there and thousands were in the town to buy the essentials that sustained their simple lives. Two churches faced each other across the main square, each with a flight of steps up to it. Drunk Indian men cavorted on the steps, singing and shouting and letting off fireworks, perhaps in some form of preparation for Easter, or maybe to ward off evil spirits embodied in their wives. I sensed inevitable beatings and bruised flesh in the air as women glowered at them.

There were a number of open air eateries with pots of soup and unidentifiable brown slurry bubbling over open fires. Plates of tortillas and other food were laid out under a light dusting of opportunistic flies. We sat down on benches at a trestle table at one of the stalls and ordered chicken soup and bread. Thin and with the same DNA as used dishwater, it had the unique selling point of being hot, something we appreciated as the town's altitude and the overcast day meant it was cold. Sitting opposite me at the table, his hat askew on his head, was an old man who also had a bowl of soup, except he had obviously ordered the de-luxe version from the menu as his bowl had two whole chicken heads floating in it. As he swirled the liquid around, the beaks tapped the side of the enamel bowl and the red comb on the male head waved in the swell his spoon created. Grinning to show gums with alopecia, he picked up a head and chewed and sucked on it, its beak poking out at me from between his lips. Warmed by the soup we returned to Adolf and her Praetorian guard of one, paid him what we owed and left the village having spent about four hours there.

As a result of our unplanned four week stay in Costa Rica, we were now in a hurry to get back to California and Los Angeles. Sam was keen to see Dorine again and I had come to the conclusion that a year on the road was probably enough without adding an extra leg of uncertain length getting to Australia. It was pretty obvious Sam and Dorine were eager to make a go of their relationship as each seemed to have found their soul-mate in life. This left me with the choice of travelling on alone, which did not worry me, or going back home to my own soul-mate, a far more alluring and attractive proposition with the softness of femininity back in my life becoming an irresistible enticement. With our thoughts turning to home, and the exciting anticipation of that homecoming, we reached the Mexican border at eight o'clock in the evening at La Mesilla having driven up through Totonicapán and Huehuetenango. We crossed without difficulty, although the sleepy Mexicans took a long time to complete their paperwork, and then drove on some miles up the road in the dark, dodging drunken Mexican drivers weaving their way home, eventually pulling off onto the side of the road to sleep, and to avoid being delivered to a different and more permanent form of oblivion than the alcohol induced one the Mexicans were in.

The next morning we left early and drove the seven hundred and seventy kilometres to Oaxaca, driving all day to reach the city by nightfall and to ready ourselves for the last leg to Los Angeles. We had decided to do the long drive in one. The finishing line was in sight and we had a strange compulsion to cross it, as though somehow in the last few days we had tipped over an invisible limit either to our endurance, to sharing a bed, to the lack of civilisation but perhaps, most truthfully, to the lack of feminine touches in our lives. Perhaps we had tired of being the unwashed, grubby and tired traveller. Setting off at dawn on Monday 16th April, we drove non-stop for two thousand four hundred miles. It took us two and a half days, driving through two nights on the lethal Mexican roads where the nocturnal drivers and somnambulant pedestrians contrived to throw everything in their arsenal of drunken lunacy at us. Our only stops were to refuel and to check Adolf's levels. At times we even changed drivers without stopping, setting the manual cruise control and swapping over seats whilst on the move. What little food we ate was prepared by the passenger and shared, quite a bit of it ending up in our laps when on bad roads or avoiding Mexican obstacles such as cars coming at us on the wrong side of the road. Where possible the passenger lay on the mattress in the back to try to get some sleep when not on driving watch. Peeing out of the open back of a moving Land Rover became easier each time we did it, proving the adage practice makes perfect. It was not a skill I felt I would need again in my life.

It was an exhausting and yet exhilarating effort, a feat of endurance that had no particular logic to it other than the challenge and the need to finish the race. Cuautla, Mexico City, Morelia, Guadalajara, to the coast at Mazatlan, Culiacan, Los Moches, Hermosillo and finally the border at Nogales. Our drive through the northern remnants of our time in Central and South America read like the fast turning pages of a Rand McNally atlas. The United States Customs seemed delighted to see us, quickly and efficiently dealing with the paperwork and even wishing us a safe onward journey. This was an unaccustomed charm offensive from people who normally seemed to ration themselves to just the offensive. Perhaps our toxicity was such they just wanted us out of the border post as quickly as possible. We drove up through Tucson and Phoenix and then turned west, skirting to the south of Joshua Tree National Park, which at any other time we would probably have camped in for a week's exploration. Palm Springs welcomed the dawn with us and later the sun beat down on us as we entered the Gordian knot of the Los Angeles freeway system. Cars hooted at us, passengers and drivers waved and we waved back in the euphoria of survivors who have endured difficulty and danger. Every time I see long distance sailors returning from round the world races I am reminded of the spontaneous welcome we got from the Californians who passed us on Los Angeles' freeways that afternoon. We brushed our teeth as we drove, freshening up to meet civilisation.

Driving through Los Angeles we made our way to where Dorine was working and, picking her up, drove to her apartment in Santa Monica. With glasses of wine in hand we sat up late into the night to chat and catch up, our feeling of exhaustion being held at bay by her interest in the last six months of our trip. Because I had decided to fly back to England I needed to get work to earn the money for my airline ticket. Whilst I could have tried to get work in Los Angeles, I knew I would become the gooseberry in the room as Sam and Dorine renewed and refreshed their relationship, a role I had no desire to play. I decided a bit of gooseberry bush pruning was needed and so told them I would go to Asheville in North Carolina where I felt pretty sure I could rent a room and find illicit work. Knowing the Ford family there would be an advantage as I felt they would be well connected with people looking for someone to work on their gardens, paint their houses and do other casual jobs.

Before I left, Sam and I needed to clear out Adolf, which we spent a whole day doing. She turned out to be an amalgam of an Aladdin's cave of treasure and long lost but loved possessions, and an Augean Stable of detritus. We were amazed at how much junk we had in her. We agreed that Sam would sell her as she was not really suited to a town life and we felt keeping her would be like keeping a Springer Spaniel in an apartment in a city. In any event, we both needed the money. I had a strange sense of disloyalty to her, subconsciously anthropomorphising her by imbuing her with feelings. Adolf was a Land Rover, not a person, but she had saved us so many times that she had become the third person on the odyssey, more essential than either Sam or me. She had been our life support system, our lunar lander in an alien world and we had abused her appallingly. We had submerged her in swollen rivers, driven her down dried up or full river beds with the gravel and rocks scraping her underside, taken her to altitudes few vehicles could reach, driven her at speeds Land Rovers could only dream about in their breathless nightmares. And yet she had never really let us down. Her few menopausal tantrums, her occasional headaches, her rare hormonally induced protests were only ever brief and we owed her our lives, literally. We both felt extremely sad to bid our faithful friend farewell.

Some of my clothes I was able to stuff into my rucksack but there was a bit of overflow so I bought an extremely cheap suitcase for the rest. Thus it was that on the afternoon of Easter Sunday, four days after getting back to Los Angeles, I said fond and sad farewells to Sam and Dorine and caught the five o'clock afternoon Greyhound Bus for Asheville. I had a strangely uplifting sense of being back on the road again. I had grown so used to being on the move and to travelling that I found a strange comfort in the motion of the bus, of seeing new sights over yet another hill, of the mystery of the unknown just ahead around the next corner. The peripatetic life of the hobo is strangely addictive and I quite understand someone's inability to settle down in one place, no matter the comforts and security that might bring. By travelling non-stop for the next two days and nights, with four changes of bus at Greyhound termini, I reached Asheville at seven o'clock in the morning on Wednesday 25th April, a day after my birthday. The journey was tiring, boring and uncomfortable, only lifted for one sector when I travelled with a young man who spent his life moving relentlessly around the States in Greyhound busses or by hitching rides in trucks and cars. He stopped at towns on his endless and seemingly random journey to find pool halls where he played professional pool, challenging the locals to play for money and betting on himself. He seemed to me to be like a modern day gunslinger from the Wild West, the bad guy riding into town to outdraw the fastest gun in the saloon. As he and I chatted and dozed, we passed through Arkansas and Tennessee where I saw evidence of the damage caused by huge floods that had only recently subsided.

When I got off at Asheville I found that my suitcase was not on the bus with me, which was hardly surprising given the changes I had made. I was reassured by the nonchalant Greyhound staff that it would arrive within a couple of days, and was impressed by their optimism. Shouldering my rucksack, I walked into town. It was too early to start the hunt for a room to rent, and too early to phone the Fords so I went into a diner and had a light breakfast. The watch strap on my Mickey Mouse watch had broken so, finishing my coffee I walked down a street to find a replacement when I heard my name called out from the other side of the road. Larry Ford was standing on the pavement, an envelope in his hand and mouth wide open with an incredulous expression on his face. He was heading for a post box to post the letter before going to his office, so I crossed the street, shook his hand and walked with him to his office, explaining why I was in Asheville and what my plans were. Larry insisted I stay with the family in their new house and rang Ellen to tell her. She was equally welcoming, in that typical American way, and so it was I spent the next month with them and their three lunatic but lovable sons.

I did indeed fill my days with odd jobs, some odder than others. I caddied on a golf course for a group of Larry's important clients, and they tipped me handsomely, despite my ability to confuse a driver with a putter. I felled trees for a company clearing land, I painted houses and wooden decking, built a patio, cleared people's basements and worked on gardens where horticultural skill or knowledge was not essential. When I worked for matronly widows, they would pay me almost half hourly visits with coffee, tea, sandwiches, insisting I sit and rest and chat to them. Some invited friends for lunch to introduce 'the Englishman' and so they could listen to me speak. The English accent was something we had discovered people liked to hear all over the States. Check out girls would ask us to 'say something', anything, and would sit there with a rapturous expression on their faces as we talked to them about the nutritional value of a can of dog food.

One of my employers was Charlie McCullough. He was a doctor and had been one of the doctors assigned to look after and accompany President Nixon on Air Force One when he flew anywhere. He was a surgeon working in the hospital in Asheville and was careful not to do any manual work that might damage his hands as without them his career would be over. It seemed apt that I was working for Charlie at the time Nixon gave his memorable televised speech to the nation about the Watergate scandal, ultimately his denouement and shame. Getting back to the house after a day's work, I watched him deliver his smoke screen oration to the nation. To me his most memorable words in it were,

"We must maintain the integrity of the White House, and that integrity must be real, not transparent. There can be no whitewash at the White House"

All these years later I wonder if Richard Nixon was Lance Armstrong's role model as he pursued his own Everest of achievement, his own pinnacle of power. Perhaps both were driven by the same aphrodisiac, one that made Nixon look directly and unblinking into the camera to utter those fateful and hypocritical words as he lied and squirmed to maintain his hold on his country's supreme office. For some the end always justifies the means.

One weekend I went down to Hilton Head Island with Larry and Ellen and another friend, Ted, and spent a few days sailing Ted's boat around Calibogue Sound. I wrote to my girlfriend suggesting she come out to the States and join me so I could take her travelling for a while, but I heard back that she had returned to Greece with two friends and so would not be able to make it, so I wrote to say I would come home and see her whenever she got back.

In the first week of June I said farewell to the Fords and a large number of people who had been both kind and generous to me and caught a Greyhound Bus to Washington DC and then another out to Washington Dulles International Airport to catch a British Airways flight home to London Heathrow.

The odyssey was over.

A GIRL CALLED ADOLF

CHAPTER 15

Epilogue

'A template for life'

"A life without risk is not a life worth living"

David Fettes

The huge British Airways Boeing 747 lifted off the runway at Dulles International Airport in Washington and heaved itself up into the night sky. Its frame shuddered under the strain and power of the four mighty engines howling beneath wings that curved impossibly to the stars above. I had never been in anything so big in my life. Well, perhaps St Peter's in Rome but that didn't fly. In my window seat I looked down on the lights of the city as they slid beneath me, my forehead pressed against the vibrating window. Clouds scudded beneath us, and then the lights were gone as we climbed up into the thicker clouds. In the seat next to me was my mother who had come out for my last two weeks in Asheville. Settling back into my seat my mind tried to rationalise and take in the last thirteen months. More importantly, there was the future to be faced and I had absolutely no idea what I wanted to do in it, or with it. Should I worry?

    I had no conception of how difficult the next eighteen months were to be. Everything had changed, and I didn't realise that included me. For a start, I was about 28 lbs lighter than when I had set off. Suntanned, hair bleached blond by the harsh sun in the tropics and possessed with a freewheeling mind that believed anything was possible, I had become used to a life without constraints. The timetables and diaries mere mortals used to structure their time and their lives had become alien to me. I nevertheless realised I had to settle back into life, make a living, re-engage with society, find somewhere to live. I was not sure if I was excited by the prospect, or terrified of it. What I knew I was excited about was Nicola's eventual return from Greece, whenever that would be. I wondered if she felt the same. Was there a future for us? Was there someone else in her life now? Had I thrown the dice once too often? Would the biggest risk I had ever taken in my life, and ever would take, prove to have been a disaster? These questions would not be answered in one overnight transatlantic flight so I ate my meal and relaxed in the comforting movement of the plane as it brushed its wings through the invisible air that miraculously held its vast bulk in the sky.

Clearing Customs at Heathrow, a couple of friends were waiting for me in Arrivals. It was touching that they had made the journey out so early in the morning. Returning home tired, I showered and then sat with friends as they came and went through the day, chatting and catching up on their news. As I did so, I felt strangely disjointed, separated from lives that had not changed while I had been away. A few relationships had broken up to be replaced by new ones, but other than that, the same people still went down to the same pubs for the same conversations. And those conversations seemed so mundane and banal, the topics inconsequential. As the next weeks went by the feeling of detachment grew in me, a sense of separation and difficulty in connecting with life back in England. For me it seemed miraculous that I could go to a tap and turn on water that we could all drink with impunity, without fear of becoming ill. Whilst Sam and I had stopped sterilising our drinking water in the first few days after landing in Mexico, we were lucky to have had cast iron constitutions that had been able to withstand all the assaults on them, only finally succumbing to some noxious ceviche from a toxic roadside seller in Peru. To turn on a switch on the wall and to have electricity was amazing to me, a simple luxury the developed world took for granted. It seemed to me there was half a continent of people who could not do that, and yet in England, no one thought about it until it was unavailable, at which point they became irritated at the inconvenience, their lives brought to a disastrous halt. Not for them sitting out on the road to chat to neighbours in the evenings in the hope of passing car or truck lights that might fleetingly illuminate their faces. The magic of these benefits in the developed world has never left me. To this day I feel the same and am always grateful for what others consider to be a right. The little things that annoyed people or that they complained about seemed unimportant when juxtaposed with the vivid memory of a peasant woman pulling a plough through the hard soil simply to exist, one day at a time. I felt I was living in a form of social and time warp, in a world where everyone had mistaken the difference between need and want. I had seen 'need', and now I was surrounded by 'want' and it was unattractive.

There were unexpected outcomes no one could have warned me about. Large groups of people were difficult for me to be in or go into. I had become used to my own company and my own thoughts for great tracts of time. I now internalised thoughts that I used to express in conversation. I didn't have to think in Spanish anymore. I was constrained by time, by people's diaries and watches whereas I had been used to a life without any agenda, with no particular appointments, where time had no value and was our own to use and squander as we pleased. The strictures and mores of society and a structured life constrained me. The freedom of the open road beckoned me back with its siren call of the free spirit, answerable to no one. Yet somehow I felt that was not the right path for me, although it was one I could easily have taken. There were other things I wanted out of life other than being a hobo, a travelling bum, rootless and drifting, leaving no legacy other than yet another footprint on the sand of yet another desert, soon to be airbrushed away by the wind.

A year on the road such as the one Sam and I had lived through cannot help but change you. I learned much about myself in that time. When I left England I was convinced I was destined and earmarked to be the Managing Director of the world, Chairman designate of any and every corporation on the planet. I learned that was never going to happen. I learned I had limitations, mental and physical, and I learned to be comfortable with that, to be at peace with myself. To be at peace is not to be complacent as they are mutually exclusive, although for some they can be synonymous. Somehow acceptance of the few skills I had and the multitude I didn't have became a platform of confidence and self-belief, the springboard to believe anything was possible. That was, and remains, one of the many positive outcomes from all Sam and I had faced together, and overcome. How could I have known as we boarded the M.V. Gela in Le Havre that the following thirteen months would shape me for the rest of my life? It was just a jaunt, an adventure we were embarking on. And yet I learned everything we do influences us in subtle ways, moulds us in our relationships, our manners, our reaction to events.

A few days after I returned the phone went at home and, over a crackly line from Athens, Nicola gave me her flight details and her time of arrival at Gatwick the following day. In 1973 parking at Gatwick's single terminal was on a gravel strewn car park right opposite and outside the entrance to the building, a short walk to the doors. The flight was coming in mid-morning and, unable to sleep because of excitement, I left home early and drove to the airport, parking the car with about an hour to spare. I couldn't sit still at home. I had to be doing something to make the time go faster. I realised this was the one moment that had sustained me for the last year, the one thing I had longed for, dreamt about and almost rehearsed in my subconscious mind.

The terminal was busy, as airport arrival halls always are. People milled about me and I watched passengers coming out of the Customs hall that lay frustratingly hidden behind its screening doors. Some walked nonchalantly through, perhaps seasoned travellers who had been away a short time, no one at the airport to greet them. Others had anxious expressions as they searched for family or friends in the crowd. When they spotted whoever they were looking for their faces lit up. Some quietly walked to each other, a shake of the hand or kiss on the cheek and they would merge into the crowd as they disappeared. Others shrieked, abandoned their luggage trolleys and ran to a loved one, to become entwined in welcoming arms, a nose nestled in a neck to infuse the familiar scent of a lover, father, mother or child. Greetings are the same the world over and airports are a window on many human emotions. Tears, joy, excitement and anticipation suffuse the Arrivals hall. Close by in Departures, the antonymous spectrum of emotions reminds me of what I had come to realise as Sam and I journeyed. For every greeting, there is a farewell, to be followed by more greetings. Sadness, apprehension, worry and sometimes despair are on view for all to see at the parting. All of these I had felt thirteen months before when Nicola and I had said goodbye to each other. I understood, and now empathised with the throng waiting for that magical moment of recognition and reunion. We somehow drop our inhibitions at airports and live in a small enveloping bubble we mistakenly think makes us invisible. We often unashamedly say our farewells or dispense our greetings as though we are in the privacy of our own homes.

I stayed back from the crowd and stood by the doors into the Terminal, leaning against a pillar at the entrance. I spotted Nicola immediately she came through from Customs, but it was clear she could not see me in the crowd. She frowned slightly as she searched for me, the seeds of doubt and I hoped disappointment evident as she thought I may not have shown up. I saw her look at me and do a double take as she realised the skinny guy with sun bleached hair and the happy smile was her hot date for a cup of coffee in a cafe in Dorking on the way home, where we started our own journey of rediscovery, that first step at the doorway of the rest of our lives. It is easy to invest huge expectations in a reunion with a loved one, expectations derived from an increasingly active and rose-tinted memory. Our imagination thrives on separation, growing images and hopes exponentially as we role play what our return will be like, what we are going to say, how we are going to act and behave. All these dreams of course, for that is what they are, are moulded and shaped from our own perspective, our fantasies, and don't take into account what can be completely different thoughts in the minds of those left behind. The reality of rebuilding a relationship after separation is only truly understood by those who experience it. The trauma of being torn apart, even voluntarily, causes inevitable changes. The extreme experiences of one or both parties shapes and changes them and for those who have stayed behind and patiently waited, a complete stranger can be the person who returns. Those dreams and fantasies that have flowered in our minds are shattered. The completed jigsaw we thought our lives have become has been kicked off the table and now lies in pieces on the floor.

Because of that year away I am now acutely aware of how long-term hostages or prisoners of war and their families can struggle to rebuild their lives and relationships once they have been reunited. When that first honeymoon period of re-exploration and rediscovery is over and the new characters emerge like metamorphosing butterflies from vegetative pupae, reality must be faced and dealt with. Will the emerging creature be a toxic moth or a beautiful butterfly. Sometimes there can be no rediscovery as everything is new, nothing familiar left of the old relationship. The families of brain damaged people, stroke victims or dementia sufferers must surely have to undergo the same realignment in their relationship with their loved ones, but in their case the role becomes one of a duty bound carer. Can the new person be loved or do they become resented or hated?

For Nicola and me an extra pressure came from well meaning questioning from many quarters about when we might marry so, when we were offered the opportunity to go to Spain for a couple of weeks shortly after we were together again, we jumped at it and took off for the sun. It was a perfect opportunity to spend time together out of the harsh lights of the vicarious interest of others. As we returned from Spain, I somehow knew the only way to assuage the urge for the open road, to deal with the wanderlust that lay so shallowly beneath the surface, was to create challenges filled with risks to be faced and surmounted. That decision, that Damascene moment, laid the foundations for a new way, a template for our life together that was to shape so many decisions that awaited me and us, decisions that lurked unseen over the horizon of our future, as they do for us all.

I had been right to hope. The gamble had paid off. Having put every chip I owned on red and spun the wheel in the Casino of Life, it was a relief to see the little ball of outcome nestle down on the chosen colour. I could stop holding my breath. We had won through, and for that I remain eternally grateful and have a family about me that justifies that gratitude.